THE RELIGION OF HUMANITY

Copy of Raphael's 'Madonna di San Sisto', taken by Positivists
as a symbol of Humanity, LPS 5/4

THE RELIGION OF HUMANITY

The Impact of Comtean Positivism on Victorian Britain

T. R. WRIGHT

April 1986

$ 44.50 cloth

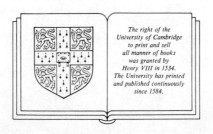

The right of the
University of Cambridge
to print and sell
all manner of books
was granted by
Henry VIII in 1534.
The University has printed
and published continuously
since 1584.

CAMBRIDGE UNIVERSITY PRESS

Cambridge
London   New York   New Rochelle
Melbourne   Sydney

Published by the Press Syndicate of the University of Cambridge
The Pitt Building, Trumpington Street, Cambridge CB2 1RP
32 East 57th Street, New York, NY 10022, USA
10 Stamford Road, Oakleigh, Melbourne 3166, Australia

First published 1986

Printed in Great Britain at the University Press, Cambridge

British Library cataloguing in publication data
Wright, T. R.
The religion of humanity: the impact of Comtean
Positivism on Victorian Britain.
1. Comte, Auguste–Influence 2. Positivism
3. Great Britain–Intellectual life–19th
century
I. Title
941.081   DA533

Library of Congress cataloguing in publication data
Wright, T. R. (Terence R.) 1951–
The religion of humanity.
Bibliography: p.
Includes index.
1. Philosophy, English–19th century. 2. Posi-
tivism–History. I. Title.
B1568.5.W75   1986   146′.4′0941   85–16615

ISBN 0 521 30671 X

GG

CONTENTS

v

Contents

ILLUSTRATIONS

ACKNOWLEDGEMENTS

Research for this book has taken me to libraries throughout Britain as well as France and the United States. I would like to thank the staff of all those libraries in the List of Abbreviations for their help and co-operation. I would also like to mention a number of other libraries not included in that list: the Bibliothèque Nationale in Paris, the Central Library, the University Library and the Library of the Literary and Philosophical Society of Newcastle upon Tyne, Durham University Library, including the Chapter Library and the Sharp Library, and finally the Firestone Library at Princeton University. I am particularly indebted to the trustees of the Procter Fellowship, which enabled me to travel to the United States, and to the Committee of the Research Fund at the University of Newcastle upon Tyne, which provided me with a series of grants to visit libraries elsewhere.

Among the many individuals who have helped me in my work I should mention first the supervisors of my D.Phil. thesis at Oxford on 'George Eliot and the Religion of Humanity', Mrs D. N. Bednarowska and the Revd Dr D. G. Rowell. Others who have given me valuable help and advice include Dr F. C. Baier, Dr William Baker, Dr Andrew Brown, M. Paulo de Berredo Carneiro, Mrs Marcella Carver, Professor Pierre Coustillas, Miss Lesley Gordon, Professor G. S. Haight, Miss Julia Harding, Mr E. D. H. Johnson, Dr U. C. Knoepflmacher, Dr Douglas Paschall, Dr Angela Raspin, Dr Bernard Richards, Dr D. B. Saunders, Mr Gordon Straughan, Professor R. K. R. Thornton and Professor Martha S. Vogeler. I have to thank Dr Ewan Klein and Dr Hermann Moisl for helping me to overcome my fear of the word-processor and Mrs Judith Hunter and Mrs Janet Wheeler for helping me to compile the bibliography on the central computer of the University of Newcastle upon Tyne.

Permission to quote previously unpublished manuscript material was kindly granted by Major Reginald Harrison; Mr Alexander Murray; Mr Jonathan Ouvry; Miss Joyce Quin; the trustees of the estate of the late Miss E. A. Dugdale; the Henry W. and Albert A. Berg Collection; New York Public Library; Astor, Lenox and Tilden Foundation; the Beinecke Rare Book and Manuscript Library at Yale

Acknowledgements

University; The Bodleian Library, Oxford; the British Library; the British Library of Political and Economic Science; the Brotherton Library at Leeds University; Cornell University Library; the trustees of the Thomas Hardy Memorial Collection, Dorset County Museum; the Co-operative Union Ltd for papers in the Holyoake Collection; the Harry Ransom Humanities Research Center, University of Texas; the Houghton Library at Harvard University; the Maison d'Auguste Comte, Paris; the Carl and Lily Pforzheimer Foundation, Inc., New York; the University Libraries of Birmingham, Hull, Liverpool and Strathclyde; the Libraries of Imperial and University College London; the Master and Fellows of Trinity College Cambridge and Balliol College Oxford; the National Library of Scotland; and Dr Williams' Library, London. I have taken the liberty of standardising spelling and punctuation and of correcting mistakes in French, when I have noticed them. I would also like to thank the British Library, the British Library of Political and Economic Science and the Bodleian Library for permission to reproduce photographs in their possession.

The editors of the following periodicals have kindly allowed me to reprint material which first appeared in their pages: *Durham University Journal*, *George Eliot–George Henry Lewes Newsletter*, *George Gissing Newsletter*, *Modern Language Review* and *Review of English Studies*.

My deepest thanks, however, are reserved for friends and relatives who have seen this book through the various stages of its production, in particular my parents and my wife, Gabriele, without whose constant help and encouragement it would never have been finished.

ABBREVIATIONS

BIBLIOGRAPHICAL REFERENCES

The bracketed references apply to the alphabetical bibliography at the end of the book. Most of the abbreviations are self-evident ('AC' for Auguste Comte, 'GE, *AB*' for George Eliot's *Adam Bede* and so on). Abbreviations of titles of books are expanded in the bibliography, where they can be found under their authors' names. Periodical abbreviations, which are listed separately, are always italicised. If figures alone appear in brackets the other details can be found in the previous reference.

MANUSCRIPT LOCATIONS

BC	Brotherton Collection, University of Leeds
Berg	Berg Collection, New York Public Library
BI	Bishopsgate Institute, London
BL	British Library, Add. MSS
BLUL	Brotherton Library, University of Leeds
Bod.L.	MS Eng. Lett., Bodleian Library, Oxford
Bod.M.	MS Eng. Misc., Bodleian Library, Oxford
BP	Papers of Edward Spencer Beesly, University College London
BPH	Papers of Otto Baier, Brynmor Jones Library, Hull University
CL	Comte Collection, Liverpool University Library
CUL	Cornell University Library
DCM	Dorset County Museum
DWL	Dr Williams' Library, London
Fraser	Fraser Collection, Liverpool University Library
GECB	'George Eliot's Commonplace Book', Yale
GS	Papers of Sir Patrick Geddes, T-GED, University of Strathclyde
HH	Papers of George Holyoake, Holyoake House, Manchester
HMP	Harriet Martineau Papers, Birmingham University Library
HP	Papers of Frederic Harrison, British Library of Political and Economic Science
HRC	Humanities Research Center, Austin, Texas
JP	Papers of Benjamin Jowett, Box C, 'Comte', Balliol College Library, Oxford
LPS	Papers of the London Positivist Society, British Library of Political and Economic Science
MAC	Maison d'Auguste Comte, Paris
MP	Papers of Sir Gilbert Murray, Bodleian Library, Oxford

Abbreviations

NLS	Papers of Sir Patrick Geddes, National Library of Scotland
Nuneaton	'George Eliot's Notebook', Nuneaton Public Library
Pforzheimer	MSS, Carl and Lily Pforzheimer Library, New York
QD	Malcolm Quin Diaries, in the possession of Joyce Quin
TCC	Add. MSS, Trinity College Cambridge
THP	Thomas Huxley Papers, Imperial College London
WPP	Walter Pater Papers, Houghton Library, Harvard
Yale	Beinecke Library, Yale University

PERIODICALS

AHR	*American Historical Review*
BC	*British Critic*
BEM	*Blackwood's Edinburgh Magazine*
BFR	*British and Foreign Review*
BJS	*British Journal of Sociology*
BP	*Birmingham Post*
BQR	*British Quarterly Review*
CH	*Church History*
CM	*Cornhill Magazine*
CMH	*Cambridge Modern History*
CR	*Contemporary Review*
DM	*Daily Mail*
DUJ	*Durham University Journal*
EB	*Encyclopaedia Britannica*, 9th Edition
Ec.R	*Eclectic Review*
ELH	*English Literary History*
ELT	*English Literature in Transition*
FHS	*French Historical Studies*
FM	*Fraser's Magazine*
FQR	*Foreign and Quarterly Review*
FR	*Fortnightly Review*
HJ	*Hibbert Journal*
HLQ	*Huntington Library Quarterly*
HS	*Historical Studies*
JBS	*Journal of British Studies*
JHI	*Journal of the History of Ideas*
JMH	*Journal of Modern History*
KR	*Kenyon Review*
LDP	*Liverpool Daily Post*
LG	*London Gazette*
LQR	*London Quarterly Review*
MG	*Manchester Guardian*
MLR	*Modern Language Review*

Abbreviations

MNL	Mill News Letter
NBR	North British Review
NC	Nineteenth Century
NCF	Nineteenth-Century Fiction
NQ	Notes and Queries
NQM	New Quarterly Magazine
NR	National Reformer
NRev.	National Review
OED	Oxford English Dictionary, [1933] 1961
PMG	Pall Mall Gazette
PMLA	Publications of the Modern Language Association
PP	Philosophie positive
PR	Positivist Review
PRSL	Proceedings of the Royal Society of London
PYB	Positivist Year Book
QR	Quarterly Review
RDM	Revue des deux mondes
RES	Review of English Studies
RMS	Renaissance and Modern Studies
RO	Revue occidentale
SAQ	South Atlantic Quarterly
Sec.R	Secular Review
SEL	Studies in English Literature
SHR	Southern Humanities Review
SLI	Studies in the Literary Imagination
Soc.P	Sociological Papers
Soc.R	Sociological Review
SP	Studies in Philology
SR	Saturday Review
TLS	Times Literary Supplement
TQ	University of Texas Quarterly
UTQ	University of Toronto Quarterly
VN	Victorian Newsletter
VPN	Victorian Periodicals Newsletter
VS	Victorian Studies
WG	Westminster Gazette
WI	Wellesley Index to Victorian Periodicals
WMC	Working Men's College Magazine
WR	Westminister Review
YES	Year's Work in English Studies

INTRODUCTION

'When some future historian of opinion deals with the speculations current at the present day', wrote Leslie Stephen in 1869, 'he will find few more remarkable phenomena than the development of the Comtist School' (*FM* LXXX (1869) 1). The main aim of this school was the propagation of the Religion of Humanity first expounded in the later writings of the extraordinary French thinker, Auguste Comte, who died in obscurity in Paris in 1857. This book considers the extent to which the Comtists succeeded in making an impact in Britain. It is in some ways a very limited study, given precise definition by the focus on Comte. But it is also a massive undertaking because nearly all the major British thinkers of the second half of the nineteenth century seem to have studied Comte, even if very few of them committed themselves to the Religion of Humanity. Comte's influence, it is the aim of this book to demonstrate, far outweighs his reputation. Not only through his acknowledged disciples but through an extraordinary range of philosophers, sociologists, historians, theologians, novelists, poets and men of letters, many of them concerned to disavow his influence and to ridicule his pretensions, he can be shown to have made a significant contribution to the less dogmatic but more pervasive humanism of the twentieth century.

The Religion of Humanity, with capital letters, refers to the specific set of ideas expounded by Comte. It is also conventional to refer to Positivism with a capital 'P' when discussing his thought as distinguished from the general positivist principle that all ideas incapable of empirical verification should be dismissed as meaningless. Humanism and the empirical tradition, of course, have deeper roots than Comte. He was not, even in his own reckoning, an original thinker but a systematiser of ideas which had been in circulation for some time about the world and the way we invest it with meaning. He saw himself as offering a systematic reconstruction of belief on the

1

basis of centuries of scientific and philosophical advance at the expense of theological faith. The 'Western Revolution', Comte's term for this long negative process which he believed to have eroded the fabric of Christendom, had left a spiritual vacuum which the Religion of Humanity was designed to fill. In so far as the official Church of Humanity barely survived his own century he can be seen to have failed. But a consideration of the general impact of his ideas encourages a less damning estimate of his achievement.

The path followed by Positivism in Britain fits a typical pattern:

One person procreates a thought, a second carries it to be baptised, a third begets children by it, a fourth visits it on its deathbed, and a fifth buries it.
(Freud 1976: VI 134)

The first chapter of this book records the procreation of the Religion of Humanity by Comte and Clotilde de Vaux through the spirit of the age, placing Comte briefly in his French context and passing quickly over his disastrous life to an analysis of his ideas. Careful attention is paid to his works, wherever possible in their English translation, both for their intrinsic interest and because they were so carefully studied by so many British writers. The second chapter considers Comte's first British followers, John Stuart Mill, George Henry Lewes, Harriet Martineau, George Holyoake and a number of lesser figures, some of whom, it has to be admitted, occupy the lunatic fringe of Victorian thinking. Mill and Lewes, however, brought Positivism an immediate philosophical status which it took some time to lose. It was Richard Congreve who carried Positivism to be baptised for it was he who founded the English Church of Humanity. Chapter three follows organised Positivism through its infamous schism of 1878 to the formation of a rival centre for the Religion of Humanity presided over by Frederic Harrison, Edward Beesly and John Bridges; it describes and attempts to classify a variety of committed Comtists.

The begetting of children is perhaps the most interesting part of the story and a major part of this book will accordingly be devoted to a study of what uncommitted people made of the Religion of Humanity. Chapter four provides a chart of this widespread discussion of Positivism in the press and in the universities. Men like John Morley, Leslie Stephen and Henry Sidgwick have long been known to have been sympathetic to the Religion of Humanity. What may cause a certain surprise, however, is the interest taken in it by John Ruskin, Matthew Arnold and Walter Pater, not to mention liberal theologians such as Mark Pattison, Benjamin Jowett and Brooke Westcott. Historians seemed to be particularly attracted to Positivism, especially at Cambridge, where a succession of Regius Professors presented Comte as a major contributor to the understanding of history. Only the scientists seem to have been almost unanimously hostile to the pretensions of Positivism, none more so than Thomas Huxley and Herbert Spencer.

Chapter five considers the prominence of Positivism in nineteenth-century fiction. It is my somewhat controversial contention that the novels of George Eliot and to a lesser extent Thomas Hardy and George Gissing, all of whom can be shown to have studied Comte closely, formed an important vehicle for the general diffusion of Positivist ideas. A number of other writers, including Mrs Humphry Ward, George Meredith, Henry James and H. G. Wells, took an interest in Comte and gave further publicity to his ideas, criticising, modifying and developing them in the creative process. Chapter six visits the Religion of Humanity on its deathbed, tracing the declining fortunes of the *Positivist Review*, following the progress of Positivism from London to the provinces, where it flickered into exotic liturgical life in Newcastle and Liverpool, and studying the revival of some of its leading concepts in the work of sympathetic academics such as Patrick Geddes and Gilbert Murray. The final chapter delivers the funeral oration, attempting to diagnose the causes of death and then reading the will, assessing the nature and extent of the Comtean legacy.

The Religion of Humanity was a systematic attempt to found a humanist religion which differed from other forms of religious humanism, whose lower cases reveal their humble informality, in claiming to have established the three essential elements of religion, a creed, a cult and a code of conduct, on a scientific basis without resort to unverifiable supernatural hypotheses. All Comte's beliefs, whether philosophical, historical, moral or religious, were based upon empirical evidence, at least in theory. Metaphysical questions about the existence of God or a future life, since they could not be proved or disproved, played no part in the Religion of Humanity. Comte did, however, preserve what he considered best in Christianity, arguing that Positivism fulfilled rather than destroyed previous religions.

The Religion of Humanity needs to be seen in the context of the wide-ranging contemporary attack on Christianity from the point of view of science, ethics and history, as well as the general *Secularization of the European Mind in the Nineteenth Century* (Chadwick 1975). Comte gave precise and systematic expression to what was a commonplace view among intellectuals that the old religion must give way to the new. Fundamentalist Christianity was seen to be contradicted by the discoveries of geology and zoology, the theory of evolution offering a direct challenge to any literal understanding of Genesis. Dogmatic Christianity, it was argued, entailed belief in an immoral God who delighted in eternal punishment, in the suffering of his opponents and in the sacrificial atonement of an innocent victim. The historicity of the New Testament was undermined by higher criticism, which rejected the miraculous and reduced the content of the gospels to the moral and the mythical. A modified liberal Christianity began to emerge from this three-pronged attack, accepting many of the scientific, moral and historic assumptions hitherto regarded as hostile to faith. The followers of Comte, however, who despised such compromising attempts to put new wine into old bottles, demanded a clean break from the existing churches.

Among those who rejected all forms of Christianity the Positivists were the most positive, the most definite and precise, in their religious reconstruction. Secularism, for example, was 'basically an agitation for a scheme of rights', in particular the right to free thought and speech (Royle 1974: 292) and most of its leaders were not just anti-Christian but anti-religion of any kind. There were parallel institutions to the Church of Humanity such as the Ethical Movement, which developed a recognisable religious ritual based on an idealist philosophical position. Many other forms of religious heterodoxy found a temporary home in London, all catering for a clientele which could no longer muster belief in traditional Christianity but could not survive without some form of faith. The Religion of Humanity, while no less temporary than these other movements, remains the best documented in terms of printed and manuscript sources, the most interesting in terms of the intellectual quality of its adherents and the most pervasive in terms of its influence on the mainstream of British thought.

The Positivists were never very numerous. It was estimated in 1869 that they could all be fitted into 'a small dining-room' (McCarthy 1899: 380) while the joke about their schism was that they had come to Church in one cab and left in two. Harrison was amazed at the red-carpet treatment he received in the United States, for at home he was only 'a crank who lectured a small lot of fanatics in a dingy hole' (W. S. Smith 1967: 102). The official list of the London Positivist Society ran to 93 members by 1891 while the number of subscribers to Congreve's sacerdotal fund rose to 137 by 1898 (McGee 1931: 185). These figures, it should be stressed, represent the high-water mark of Positivist adhesion. Yet their impact was out of all proportion to their numbers. No student, it was claimed, could 'pass through the 'sixties untouched by curiosity about the new philosophical system' (Herford 1931: 41) and from 1860 to 1880 it seemed impossible for any major 'literary or scientific figure who ventured into public controversy' not to 'defend his position in relation to Positivism' (*VS* VII (1964): 398). To John Seeley, newly elected as Regius Professor of Modern History at Cambridge in 1869 with clear instructions to combat this threat, 'the very air seemed full of Comtianism', which appeared 'irresistibly triumphant' (Rothblatt 1968: 153, 177). Ardent young clergymen also felt bound to take up the cudgels against Comte, who continued to occupy a large 'space in the minds of the young men of the eighties' (Pease 1963: 14) and to provoke general interest until the turn of the century.

The Religion of Humanity has not, however, had a good press. Historians of nineteenth-century thought too often dismiss it as the exotic aberration of a coterie of eccentrics, a minor post-revolutionary pseudo-religious cult. It is a paradox recognised by Sir Isaiah Berlin in the first of the Auguste Comte Memorial Lectures that the founder of Positivism, who can be seen to have affected the very categories of our thought, is open to ridicule on a number of issues:

> his grotesque pedantry, the incredible dullness of his writing, his vanity, his eccentricity, his solemnity, the pathos of his private life, his insane dogmatism, his authoritarianism, his philosophical fallacies, all that is bizarre and utopian in his character and writings. (Berlin 1954: 3–4)

Comte was an archetypal hedgehog, in Berlin's terms, attempting to fit the universe into a simple, all-embracing pattern (Berlin 1967: 39–40). It is scarcely surprising that he has proved so difficult for foxes, who are more prepared to take experience as it comes, to swallow. But he offered those with a similar need for a complete system of beliefs a fully articulated form of humanism. His personal eccentricities should not preclude a recognition of the powerful attraction he exerted upon a particular type of temperament.

There have, however, been few impartial treatments of the Religion of Humanity, perhaps because of the fierce reactions his ideas continue to provoke in those of a different temperament. The major historian of *European Positivism in the Nineteenth Century* writes with undisguised distaste of 'the grotesque pedantries of Comte's minutely detailed religious ritual' and 'the contrived character of the religion in general' (Simon 1964: 162), which managed to combine 'the worst and weakest aspects' of a whole range of ill-assorted contemporary ideas (Simon 1963: 46). Another historian of the movement, which he places firmly within the context of other *Secular Religions in France*, recognises that the 'elaborate and somewhat artificial systematization of the new religion can easily hide its essentials' (Charlton 1963: 88). The fullest published *History of Organized Positivism in England* discusses the details of the religion more sympathetically but reduces its significance, finally, to its 'promotion of conciliation' (McGee 1931: 234). Some of the political and social aspects of the movement have been discussed (R. Harrison 1959, 1965) and its aspirations to spiritual leadership placed in the context of academic radicalism (C. Kent 1978). None of these historians, however, have made full use of the abundant manuscript material available.

The huge amount of hitherto unpublished evidence on which it draws, its treatment of the Religion of Humanity as the culmination rather than the aberration of Comte's thought and the wide range of literary figures it discusses distinguishes this book from its predecessors. It concentrates very much on the individuals concerned in the movement, attempting to bring out as clearly as possible the character and temperament lying behind their religious conviction. The story of Comte's transformation of character under the influence of his love for Clotilde de Vaux has been told before but the inner struggles of many of his English disciples, so amply documented in their notebooks, letters and diaries, have not so far received the close sympathetic treatment they deserve.

The Religion of Humanity, then, can be regarded as a kind of experiment in religion, an attempt to see whether a totally humanistic creed could satisfy the hearts and minds of those who found Christianity, for whatever reason, inadequate. At the same time, it can be seen as a particular product of its time, a systematic philosophy which provides the historian of ideas with a measure, a piece of litmus paper by which to test Victorian religious chemistry, a thermometer with which to gauge the temperature of their dissatisfaction with Christianity and their desire for an alternative faith. Yet another appropriately scientific analogy might liken this study of Positivism to a cross-section made through the strata of Victorian opinion, revealing unsuspected relationships at a deep level between seemingly disparate religious thinkers. It is the fullness and range of opinion expressed about the Religion of Humanity which makes it such a fruitful point of entry into the Victorian mind. Positivism, as my post-mortem will argue, was very Victorian. But some of the questions it raises about religion, perhaps even some of its answers, remain of interest to humanity in any age.

THE BIRTH OF POSITIVISM: AUGUSTE COMTE

Life and context

'Comte did not discover the Religion of Humanity', one of his followers insisted, 'but only put into organic shape the floating aspirations of his century' (FH 1913: 267). He is rightly regarded as a representative figure, 'at once a symbol and producer of the intellectual climate' of his time (Willey 1973: 217). He made no secret of his intellectual debts, his major works including long tributes to his many precursors or 'spiritual fathers'. Born in 1798, he belonged at least in part to the eighteenth century, fulfilling many of the aims of the encyclopedists and maintaining their faith in the unity of the sciences. The very title, *Discours préliminaire*, which Comte was to use twice, advertised his debt to d'Alembert. Turgot provided the essence of his law of human progress, Montesquieu and Condorcet the basis of his political thought. His knowledge of science can largely be attributed to the École Polytechnique, the positive nature of whose teaching, he observed, was absolutely free of all theological and metaphysical 'mélange' (Gouhier 1933: I 123).

Comte can also be seen as a Romantic, with his emphasis on feeling and his idealisation of the Middle Ages. His affinities with German thought, which was particularly influential in France during the Second Empire, include Lessing and Kant, both of whom were translated by his fellow-Saint-Simonians, Eugène Rodrigues and Gustave d'Eichthal. He also discovered a positive spirit in Hegel (Littré 1863: 156–7). It would be wrong, finally, to omit his links with British empiricism, in particular with David Hume and Adam Smith, both of whom he recommended to his disciples. These thinkers all occupy prominent places in the Positivist Calendar, the eleventh month of which sets out in schematic form his view of the major contributors to western philosophy (see p. 34).

Most important of all the contexts within which the Religion of

Humanity should be understood, however, is the French Revolution and its aftermath. Comte's rituals, for example, grew from the revolutionary cults of Reason and the Supreme Being. As early as 1794 there were official festivals to celebrate Humanity and her benefactors. Comte, who was convinced that he would follow in the footsteps of La Révellière-Lépaux, grand pontiff of theophilanthropy, and preach in Notre Dame, regarded the church of St Geneviève, which had been renamed the Pantheon after the Revolution but also reconsecrated twice under different Napoleons, as the first Temple of Humanity. The French Revolution certainly looms large in his thought, the Positivist era beginning in AD 1789, year 1 of the Positivist Calendar.

The post-revolutionary thinker who has been said to have exercised the most powerful influence on Comte is Saint-Simon, whose service he entered as secretary in August 1817. He remained a disciple for two years and a colleague for four. Before meeting Saint-Simon Comte had already repudiated God and King and was seeking the regeneration of society through science but he had not systematised these ideas or talked specifically of a spiritual power, the rehabilitation of the Middle Ages, the three states or the classification of the sciences, all of which can be found in Saint-Simon's work prior to his association with Comte (Gouhier 1933: I 235–6). Saint-Simon too sought to reorganise society on the basis of science, looking to the science of history above all to predict a glorious future in which industrial progress would transform the natural world. His ideas, however, were propounded sketchily and unsystematically in letters, dialogues and accounts of visions. While admiring the fertility of his imagination, Comte soon came to feel that he was too inconsistent and changeable to rank highly as a philosopher.

The differences between the two emerged clearly when they wrote separate *avertissements* to Comte's 'Prospectus des travaux scientifiques pour réorganiser la société' in Saint-Simon's *Catéchisme des industriels* of 1822. Saint-Simon complained that Comte had treated only the scientific part of the system, omitting its sentimental and religious aspect while Comte insisted that his main purpose was to raise politics to a science of observation (Littré 1863: 15–25). Comte certainly recognised the stimulus he had received from Saint-Simon but was repelled by his late religious phase, which found expression in *New Christianity*, a sentimental celebration of the powers of love. The intellectual side of Saint-Simonism was still present in the *Exposition* of 1828–9, with its combination of natural law, neo-Catholic restoration and progressive philosophy of history. But the movement developed under Père Enfantin into a crusade for the political and sexual liberation of women, seeking the Female Messiah on the banks of the Nile. Understandably eager to dissociate himself from such unscientific behaviour, Comte explained in two public letters of 1832 that his liaison with Saint-Simon had ended as a consequence of these growing religious tendencies (AC, *CI* I 65–72; III 7–14). His disclaimer of all interest in establishing a new religion, especially a mere parody of Catholicism, however, reads ironically in the light of his later work, while his description of his former mentor as 'a depraved charlatan' (AC, *Pol* III xviii) seems more than a little ungrateful.

Comte's earliest work was published anonymously or under Saint-Simon's name. His early essays, some of which have been reprinted under the dramatic title, *The Crisis of Industrial Civilization*, were mainly political in emphasis. 'A Brief Appraisal of Modern History', first published in 1820, analyses the decline of the old social system established by medieval Catholicism and the rise of the new social system ushered in by scientific advance. His 1822 'Plan of the Scientific Operations Necessary for Reorganizing Society' was even more explicit in its attack on contemporary anarchy, especially the negative revolutionary principles of liberty, equality and the sovereignty of the people. A new science of society must be reconstructed, as he maintained in two essays of 1825 and 1826, 'Philosophical Considerations on the Sciences and Savants' and 'Considerations on the Spiritual Power'.

Having come to the conclusion that a complete overhauling of human knowledge was the essential preliminary to any social reorganisation, Comte announced a 'Cours de philosophie positive en soixante-douze séances', to begin in April 1826. Only three of these lectures were delivered, however, before the pressure of work combined with marital problems to bring on mental breakdown. After a spell in an asylum and a suicide attempt in the Seine, Comte recovered sufficiently by 1829 to renew the series, which formed the basis of his *Cours de philosophie positive*, published in Paris in six volumes from 1830 to 1842. In this astonishing survey of intellectual progress, Comte attempted to show how each of the sciences, first mathematics, then astronomy, physics, chemistry and biology, had become positive, that is, based on empirically verifiable laws. Finally, he claimed, social physics, the historical study of the collective development of societies, was now sufficiently advanced to join the other sciences.

The last few pages of the *Cours*, omitted from Harriet Martineau's condensed English translation of 1853, outline Comte's plan for future writing, to include a four-volume study of sociology and a treatise on education and morals (AC 1896: II 415–19). The four sociological volumes which comprise the *Système de politique positive* came out one a year from 1851 to 1854 and were seen by Comte to institute the Religion of Humanity. The first volume expounds the 'Introductory Principles' of the world (cosmology) and of life (biology). The second, 'Social Statics, or the General Theory of Human Order', explains Comte's concept of the family, the state and Humanity. The third presents an outline of human history under the title, 'Social Dynamics, or the General Theory of Human Progress', while the fourth expounds his 'Theory of the Future of Man', giving details of his utopia. The English translation of the *Système*, the respective volumes of which were the responsibility of Bridges, Harrison, Beesly and Congreve in turn, were published from 1875 to 1877.

In addition to his major works, Comte wrote a number of shorter books designed to convey the basic outlines of his system. *A Discourse on the Positive Spirit*, published in 1844, was the introduction to a series of public lectures on astronomy. Intended as an introduction to working-men of the intellectual and social teaching of the Positive Philosophy, it was translated by Beesly in 1903, with a helpful 'Explanation of Philosophical Terms' and 'Explanatory Notes'. *A General View of Positivism*, published in Paris in 1849 and translated by Bridges in 1865, was included in the first volume of the *Système*. Five chapters deal successively with the intellectual and social aspects of Positivism and its relation to the working classes, to women and to art before the conclusion outlines the liturgical details of the Religion of Humanity. *The Catechism of Positive Religion*, published in Paris in 1852 and translated by Congreve in 1858, represents yet another attempt to popularise Positivism, this time for women. A suitably submissive woman asks a confident priest to explain first the 'General Theory of Religion' and then various aspects of the worship, the doctrine and the regime. The *Appeal to Conservatives* of 1855, which was not translated until 1889, was designed for statesmen. All these summaries, in particular the *General View*, provide a good introduction to Positivism.

A warning should be given about Comte's style. Put bluntly, he is 'one of the most tiresomely long-winded bores of all times' (*TLS*, 23/8/74: 903). His most enthusiastic translators have acknowledged the incessant recapitulation, the wearisome repetition of epithets and the abstract and allusive language which were partly a result of his scorn for preparation or revision. The improvement often gained in translation is evident, for instance from a comparison between Beesly's polished version of *A Discourse on the Positive Spirit*, which cuts Comte's long sentences to manageable length, and the more literal version produced by W. M. W. Call. Lewes tried to persuade Comte to cut down 'the length of the sentences and the superfluity of words', suggesting that he go through his manuscripts striking out most of the adverbs along with all anticipation and recapitulation of ideas (AC, *CG* IV 240–1). Comte himself recognised the defects of style in the *Cours*, proudly announcing in the *Système* that he had limited all sentences to five lines and all paragraphs to seven sentences (AC, *Pol* IV xii–xiii). But something rather more drastic would have been required to make him a pleasure to read.

Comte retained in his works an optimism belied by the successive disappointments of his life. Tutor in mathematics and then entrance examiner at the École Polytechnique, he was passed over for a variety of chairs to which he thought himself entitled. Angered by lack of recognition, he wrote a bitter preface to the final volume of the *Cours* in which he attacked the officials of the École Polytechnique for not granting him the chair of mathematics. He won a legal case against his publisher for prefacing this introduction with an 'Editor's Opinion' but this only led to his losing his job as examiner. Mill organised a fund to cover his loss of revenue for 1844, half of which was provided by the ancient historian, George Grote. Failing to realise that this was only intended as a temporary expedient, Comte fell out with Mill and later with Lewes for not drumming up sufficient support. After the formation of the Positivist Society in March 1848, however, he was assured of a regular subsidy.

Most of Comte's practical ventures ended in ignominious failure. He tried on three occasions to establish the *Revue occidentale* before abandoning journalism to 'littérateurs'. He remained optimistic for some time about the adhesion of working-men to the Positivist movement. Addressing them in the *Discourse*, for example, he argued that the proletariat was the most disposed of all classes to accept Positivism on account of their common sense, their freedom from the taint of metaphysical and literary speculation, their appreciation of science and their lack of self-interest (AC, *Disc* 130–47). But he soon found them too impatient for political change properly to understand the historical point of view (AC, *Pol* I xxiv). The Positivist Society itself was soon torn by political and personal differences. All of its members had welcomed the uprising of February 1848 but Littré and some of his liberal colleagues disapproved of Comte's enthusiastic welcoming of Louis Napoleon's *coup d'état* in December 1851 and the society split in two, leaving Comte with less able but more submissive supporters. He lost all hope of the Positivists achieving much by themselves, advocating in the last few years of his life, before his death from cancer in 1857, a Religious Alliance with Catholicism, Protestantism, Judaism and Islam.

One of Comte's problems was his inability to co-operate. He tended to interpret sympathy as complete agreement and was frequently surprised at the 'desertion' of men who had never been his disciples. His reaction to criticism was paranoid and his letters accordingly littered with complaints of persecution and conspiracy. In France this took the form of complete silence, in Britain of overlooking his social aim or claiming that it was an addition to his original philosophy. He claimed that Littré's ostensibly political break was actually motivated by personal animosity which had been brewing for some time among 'tout l'Institut, la plupart des rouges, et mêmes les débris du saint-simonisme' under the satanic influence of his wife. The imminent struggle between the true and the false Positivists was to be fought under the banners of the two women in his life, Clotilde de Vaux, 'l'ange qui ne cessera jamais d'avoir trente ans', and his wife, 'le démon qui vient de commencer sa cinquante-unième année' (AC, *CI* I 84).

Comte called his marriage to Caroline Masson 'the only capital error of my whole life'. They separated four times altogether, first in 1826, after which she nursed him to recovery, and finally in 1842, after which she constantly threatened him with returning if he failed to provide her with financial support (AC, *Con* 511–16). Her dispute with the Positivists continued long after his death, culminating in 1870 when she challenged his will on the grounds of insanity. His relationship with Clotilde only lasted a year before her death in April

1846 at the age of thirty. Even in that short time, however, their relationship reveals some of the emotional problems which wrecked his marriage. Having begun by offering 'the affection of an older brother' (8), Comte was soon complaining of insomnia brought on by thinking about her. He grew ill and depressed, lamenting 'the grossness of my sex' (16) and suffering a nervous crisis similar to that which precipitated his earlier suicide attempt. He signed his letters, 'Your devoted husband', while Clotilde replied to her 'tender father' (68–9) and seems to have offered little encouragement to his emotional ardour.

Comte's love for Clotilde could only thrive after her death, when she became transfigured into his guardian angel and even the Goddess of Humanity, conscious idealisations of the real person he had known. The prefaces to his later work constantly acknowledge the moral regeneration effected by her 'angelic influence'. His private cult of her memory involved weekly visits to her grave and daily prayers, which consisted mainly of 'pictures and images . . . which served to recall the chief events in his year's intimacy with his beloved saint', combined with reading extracts from their correspondence (A. Crompton nd: 40). Morning prayer comprised forty minutes' 'Commemoration', kneeling before her altar and thanking her for the emotional regeneration she had helped bring about, followed by twenty minutes' 'Effusion', kneeling before her flowers and reciting some of his favourite formulas. Evening prayer was half as long and took place 'In bed, seated' and then 'lying down'. 'Prayers for midday' involved reading the whole of her final letter to him along with lengthy passages from Virgil, Dante and Petrarch (44–71).

All this, of course, brought ridicule and scorn but seems to have effected a marked improvement in Comte's nervous condition. Two British visitors he received in the 1850s were struck by his 'benevolence and purity'. One, who had been taught by the austere young mathematician, could hardly recognise the 'old gentleman in a dressing gown' who reminded him of St Francis (*NC* II (1877) 621–31; AC, *LH* 125–33). George Lewes, treasuring his own Madonna, wrote sympathetically, some would say sentimentally, of Comte's devotion to Clotilde:

the angel who had appeared to him in his solitude, opening the gates of heaven to his eager gaze, vanished again, and left him once more to his loneliness: but although her presence was no longer there, a trace of luminous glory left behind in the heart of the bereaved man, sufficed to make him bear his burden, and to dedicate his days to that great mission which her love had sanctified.

(Lewes 1853: 7)

Such was the change in Comte's emotional outlook brought about by his worship of Clotilde that he spoke of starting a second philosophical career as a result of her influence. He had always intended to make the Positive Philosophy the basis of a new religion, he insisted, but there was a difference of method between the *Cours* and the *Système*. The first retained 'the objective method' which allowed for no generalisations incapable of empirical verification while the second regarded 'the subjective method' as the only source of complete systematisation, introducing 'the higher logic' whose principle was 'the ascendency of the heart over the intellect' (AC, *Pol* I xii). The new religion, in other words, had been proved only upon his pulse. He had protested against the association of Positivism with dryness of heart before meeting Clotilde (Gouhier 1933: I 26) but there can be little doubt that the Religion of Humanity would not have taken the form it did without the emotional regeneration she helped to bring about.

In spite of Comte's acknowledged change of method, which upset many of his followers, most critics have agreed that there is a unity of purpose evident throughout his work. He intended from the beginning to reorganise society on the basis of science; what changed was his confidence that his system could be verified in time to effect that reorganisation. He therefore relaxed the requirements of verification and constructed a confessedly hypothetical but nevertheless complete religion. Its constituent elements, philosophy, history, sociology and ethics, were always part of the Positive Philosophy. They remained extraordinarily static, in fact, since Comte failed to keep up with developments in science after the completion of the *Cours*, refusing to read new books in the interest of what he called cerebral hygiene. The only new elements appeared in the worship. All of these areas will now be examined, particular attention being paid to any development to be found in the later works. What is remarkable, given the absurdity of Comte's life, is the power of his ideas, eccentric, utopian and badly presented though they were. His writing deserves careful attention for its own sake as well as for the fascination it was to exercise upon the minds of so many British thinkers.

1   Engraving after a portrait of Auguste Comte,
    by M. Léonard, LPS 5/3

2 Engraving after a portrait of Clotilde de Vaux,
by M. Léonard, LPS 5/3

The Positive Philosophy

Two main concerns of the Religion of Humanity may properly be called philosophical: the problems of knowledge and free will. Comte has been too easily dismissed as a scientific realist who followed eighteenth-century notions of popular good sense at the expense of all metaphysical enquiry into the nature of the reality of the external world conveyed to us by sense perception. Although he began with a straightforward trust in the accuracy with which sense-data report the existence of an objective reality and repeatedly insisted on the need to acknowledge the invariable laws of the universe, his abandonment of the 'objective method' for the 'subjective method' indicates a growing dissatisfaction with the realist position. He always denied the possibility of making meaningful statements about causes or essences, but utility finally replaced reality as the organising principle of his philosophy. This development, however, and his terminology require more detailed explanation.

Comte did not invent the word 'positive'. Derived from *ponere*, it had been in use from 1300 to describe anything explicitly 'laid down'. The sense of 'relating to fact' dates from the sixteenth century while its common use in opposition to 'metaphysical' stems from the eighteenth (*OED* VII 1152–3). Comte extended its meaning still further, the *Discourse* and the *General View* supplying six synonyms: real, useful, certain, precise, organic and relative (AC, *Disc* 65–70; AC, *Pol* I 44–5). The *Appeal* even added a seventh: sympathetic (AC, *Appeal* 46). By this stage the word had clearly expanded to include anything which formed a part of his system. Explaining 'The Intellectual Character of Positivism' in the first chapter of the *General View*, Comte found it easier to define negatively. It was neither atheism, which gave an absolute answer to the question of a first cause, nor materialism, the encroachment of the lower sciences on the domain of the higher. It was not fatalism, since it acknowledged the modifiability of the external order, nor optimism, since it recognised all the defects in nature (AC, *Pol* I 36–44). In his 'Final Estimate of the Positive Method' at the end of the *Cours*, he adopted the wise tactic of equating it with common sense (AC, *Phil* II 512).

Comte's initial assumption was that science revealed an external order of the world. The priest in the *Catechism* announces 'the existence of an order, which admits of no variation' as the fundamental dogma of the Religion of Humanity (AC, *Cat* 58). The idea of a capricious personal God finds no place in the positive religion because it subverts this basic principle. 'What becomes of the wonderful order we have traced,' asks the priest, 'if we introduce an infinite power?' (218). Theological belief is seen as a form of egoism, granting arbitrary power to an individual will. Recognition of the many defects in the actual constitution of the real world, on the contrary, prevented Positivists from forming their opinions in accordance with their desires. The scientific spirit differed from the theological and the metaphysical, Comte explained in the *Cours*, precisely because of its 'steady subordination of the imagination to observation' (AC, *Phil* II 68–9). Although he became increasingly aware of the impossibility of attaining exact objective truth, the principle of subordinating every hypothesis to the test of empirical observation remained at the heart of his system.

As early as 1817 Comte enunciated another central principle of his philosophy: 'Everything is relative' (AC, *Essays* 23). The belief that we can know nothing about things in themselves but only the relations of things is central to Positivism, which abandons the search for causes in favour of the elaboration of the laws of relation. Positivism, the priest insists, 'never explains *why* a thing is, it limits itself to the question, *how* it is' (AC, *Cat* 57). All human conceptions, according to a central Positivist law, pass through three stages: the theological, the metaphysical and the positive. From being explained as the result of supernatural wills or abstract essences phenomena are finally seen to be related to each other by fixed and invariable laws. The sciences are classified according to the speed at which this process takes place. Beginning with mathematics and ending with morals, they display increasing particularity, complexity, dependence, modifiability and connection with man.

A desire for system and synthesis lies at the heart of the Religion of Humanity. Comte's own obsession with unity is clear even in his early essays, which complain of the moral and social anarchy resulting from the 'absence of any preponderating system, capable of uniting all minds in a communion of ideas' (AC, *Crisis* 199–200). The *Cours* advocates a similar unanimity of outlook. Although the laws of the external order need not be reduced to one, they should be homogeneous. Men must have order, he warns, and if this need is not met by science they will return to theological and metaphysical explanations (AC, *Phil* I 14–17). The 'radical sense of the word *Religion*', the priest explains, lies in these fundamental aims of '*unity*' and '*synthesis*', which '*bind together*' man and the world (AC, *Cat* 46–51). The Religion of Humanity brings reason, feeling and action into harmony: this is 'The Positive Theory of Human Unity', the title of the opening chapter of the second volume of the *Système*.

Comte's desire for unity eventually overcame his principle of verification. He had never doubted the place of imagination in science, arguing as early as 1820 that a science only became positive when a hypothesis was propounded to combine its observed facts (AC, *Crisis* 93). The *Cours* too insisted that 'facts cannot be observed without the guidance of some theory'. Without this framework for research, science degenerated into the lowest form of empiricism, the barren accumulation of unrelated facts (AC, *Phil* I 3–4). Empiricism and mysticism were the opposite extremes, the Scylla and Charybdis between which the *Système* attempted to steer. In order to achieve the intellectual synthesis required for moral and social harmony Comte consciously relaxed the burden of proof, accepting a theory 'subjective' in origin 'when it sufficiently explains the essential phenomena, without waiting for the *objective* verification' (AC, *Pol* III 21). This represents a clear change in method. Whereas synthesis was introduced into the *Cours* in the interest of analysis, the 'Religious Logic' of the *Subjective Synthesis*, which 'no longer confines itself to the domain of verifiable hypotheses' (AC, *Subj* 34), reverses the emphasis. Logic is no longer to be defined as an instrument 'calculated to reveal to us the truths which human necessities require' but as the '*normal concert of feelings, images and signs to inspire us with conceptions which meet our moral, intellectual and physical wants*' (23). Utility becomes more important than reality (16).

Comte's letters confirm this change of emphasis from analysis to synthesis, from reality to utility (AC, *Letters* 117–18). Most of his writing, however, insists on the need to combine the objective and subjective methods. The priest explains, for example, that there is no objective unity, only 'a purely relative and human one; in one word, a subjective unity', which could help to mitigate the harshness of the world revealed by science (AC, *Cat* 160–1). '*Between Man and the World*', Comte writes in the *Subjective Synthesis*, '*we need Humanity*' (AC, *Subj* 30). His systematic regeneration of fetishism creates a

Positivist Trinity by adding the Great Fetich and the Great Milieu, symbolic of the Earth and of Destiny, to the Great Being at the centre of his religion. These are not real, of course, in any objective sense. As the priest explains,

The only essential difference between subjectivity in its later and its primitive shape is this. In its later shape we must be fully conscious of it, and openly avow it, no one ever confusing it with objectivity.

(AC, *Cat* 92–3)

The Religion of Humanity, in other words, offers a comforting fiction in the face of a hostile and meaningless universe.

Death is perhaps the most obvious way in which the objective world fails to satisfy man's subjective requirements and Positivism accordingly provides him with an 'ideal resurrection' through the power of the imagination, a 'subjective immortality' in which the dead live on in the memory of the living (AC, *Pol* I 210). Our best attributes are purified by death, Comte claims, for instance in the process of 'subjective assimilation' through which the attributes of the dead pass into the minds of the living (IV 90–3). The Positivist belief in subjective life is given formal and ritual expression in the sacraments and festivals celebrating those who are incorporated into Humanity.

Comte's elaborate subjective synthesis never denies the central tenet of his philosophy, that there is an objective reality which cannot be altered. It is the very grimness of the external world which necessitates religious comfort. A passage of the *Catechism* which George Eliot was fond of quoting describes life as 'a necessity admitting modifications', to which our response is 'destined to be a compound of resignation and action', submitting to the inevitable and altering what we can (AC, *Cat* 61). Under theological systems, Comte argued in his early essays, man had believed himself the centre of the universe able to exercise indefinite control over phenomena. He had now to learn the limits of his power. His own nature, for example, was unalterable in essentials, although individual instincts could be accelerated or retarded in their development. Similarly, in politics, there was a limit to what legislation could achieve. '*Scientific Provision*', he asserted, could '*avert or mitigate violent Revolution*' and aid progress. It could not alter the general course of events (AC, *Crisis* 136–48).

The most modifiable phenomena, according to Comte, were the

most complex, the most human, 'the phenomena of life and acts of the mind' (AC, *Phil* I 470). But even his cerebral theory insisted on 'the necessary invariableness of the human organism', the essential characteristics of which remained the same. It was not possible, for instance, to create or destroy faculties, only to modify them. Any vision of society, therefore, should not contradict 'the known laws of human nature' by supposing 'a very marked character of goodness or wickedness to exist in the majority of men' (II 113). Within these limits the main task for mankind was 'the continual improvement of its own nature' (AC, *Disc* 47). Morals, as the priest explains, are 'the supreme art' in two respects: they are the most important, and they afford the largest scope 'for wise action on our part' (AC, *Cat* 199).

Comte repeatedly denied that his system was deterministic. There was a difference, he insisted, between 'modifiable' and 'absolute fatality', and everyone in his system remained responsible for his conduct (AC, *Letters* 39). The *Cours* dismisses 'the supposed necessity of human actions' while attacking unrealistic optimism. The resignation demanded of the Positivist did not carry with it the heavenly rewards open to the Christian, only 'a permanent disposition to endure, steadily and without hope of compensation, all inevitable evils' (AC, *Phil* I 470; II 45). The most striking feature of man's predicament, the *Système* insists, was 'the necessity of struggling against difficulties of every kind' (AC, *Pol* I 23). The main merit of this struggle was that it was shared: men 'are involved in the same miseries, and therefore stand alike in need of mutual help' (339). There was not much to celebrate in the Positivist view of life as 'the constant struggle of Will against Necessity' (III 135–6).

If the Positive Philosophy was optimistic, as is often claimed, it offered a very restrained form of hope, calling for a realistic appraisal of man's harsh predicament combined with a determined effort to achieve whatever amelioration was possible. That so many Positivists, including Comte, suffered from anxiety and depression, given the bleak comfort afforded by their religion, is hardly surprising. If they were not already so by temperament, and this may well have led them to Comte in the first place, his philosophy was likely to push them in that direction.

History and sociology: the three stages

At the centre of Comte's religion was a product of historical and sociological observation, Humanity, the 'Great Being . . . constituted by the beings, past, future and present, which co-operate willingly in perfecting the order of the world' (AC, *Pol* IV 27). Individuals were its ministers, through their service of other 'composite beings' such as the Family, the Country and the West. The concept of Humanity was designed to meet men's religious needs and to replace God. When the woman complains in the first conversation of the *Catechism* that Positivism affords insufficient 'stimulus to the holy affections', the priest points to the idea of Humanity continually struggling against the necessities of the universe in the quest for perfection as 'a better object of contemplation than the capricious omnipotence of its theological precursor' (AC, *Cat* 62–4). He is careful to explain in the second conversation that Humanity does not include everybody who has ever lived but 'those only who are really capable of assimilation, in virtue of a real co-operation on their part in furthering the common good' (74).

Comte insisted on the reality of Humanity as revealed 'by close investigation of objective fact'; it was the notion of the individual apart from the race which was the abstraction (AC, *Pol* I 267–8). There are significant differences in the roles Humanity is called upon to play. At the end of the historical survey of the development of mankind in the third volume of the *Système*, for example, Humanity becomes almost Hegelian, achieving 'a full consciousness of her destination' (III 532). Notice too her acquisition of the feminine gender, particularly when treated as an object of sentimental attachment. She becomes providential in the *Appeal to Conservatives*, where 'all prior beliefs' are explained as 'spontaneous institutions thrown up in succession by the instinct of the Great Being to guide its incomparable preparation' (AC, *Appeal* 62). Objectively considered, however, she remained incapable of action except through the services of her individual ministers, achieving reality only in the consciousness of those individuals. She appealed to Positivists such as Littré as an object of devotion and love on which they could focus their humanitarian ideals and to which they could feel a sense of belonging (Littré 1863: 525).

The two feelings Comte regarded as essential ingredients of the Positivist faith were a sense of solidarity with Humanity in the present and continuity with her in the past and the future. Solidarity in the sense of dependence upon others was undeniable:

The man who dares to think himself independent of others, either in feelings, thoughts, or actions, cannot even put the blasphemous conception into words without immediate self-contradiction, since the very language he uses is not his own. (AC, *Pol* I 177)

Continuity too was central to Positivist education, in which individuals were made to repeat the history of the education of the race. The third volume of the *Système*, 'Social Dynamics, or the General Theory of Human Progress', begins with an assertion of the importance of historical study. Scientific history, however, is distinguished from previous annals, which merely described isolated facts in chronological order. The history which supplies the foundation for sociology is a study of the development of human society, proceeding from the general to the particular in illustration of the basic laws of human progress.

The historical analysis provided by the *Cours* is limited to western civilisation, 'the vanguard of the human race'. It is abstract rather than concrete, aiming to establish general laws which will explain 'general phenomena which everybody is familiar with', referring to names and dates only in order to elucidate these laws. It provides a working model, a series of 'landmarks' around which 'subsequent observations' may be placed (AC, *Phil* II 181–4). The treatment of history in the *Système* is, if anything, even less specific, 'verification and development' of its details being left to others (AC, *Pol* III xi).

The founding hypothesis of Comte's social dynamics was the law of the three states or stages in which the development observed in the other sciences, from the theological through the metaphysical to the positive stage, was applied to all human history. The theological stage began with fetichism, the attribution of will to inanimate objects, and developed through polytheism to monotheism, reaching its culmination in the Catholic feudal system of the Middle Ages. The spontaneous decomposition of Catholicism at the beginning of the metaphysical stage led to the outright rebellion of Protestantism, Deism and finally the French Revolution. But throughout this negative stage a positive process was also discernible in the sciences, which revealed one by one the working of invariable laws until it became possible to construct a complete synthesis of scientific knowledge and to reconstruct society on a positive basis.

A providential undertone can be detected beneath this analysis. Comte refers to the intellectual evolution of Humanity under the Greeks, the active contribution of the Romans and the affective evolution brought about by Catholicism. It is left to Positivism, of course, to provide the final harmony of thought, feeling and action. Although the three stages can be linked with rough chronological periods, a mixture of all three is discernible in any single period. The struggle between the positive and metaphysical spirit discernible in Aristotle and Plato resumed in the medieval disputes between nominalism and realism. Positivism itself drew much of its inspiration from 'that memorable season in human history which Protestantism is pleased to call the dark ages'. Catholicism, which had taken ten centuries to develop, was not designed to die out altogether but to find new life in the Religion of Humanity (AC, *Phil* II 294–303). Positivism could therefore be seen as a development of Catholicism:

> For those alone are worthy to be called successors, who continue or carry into effect the undertakings which former times have left unfinished; the title is utterly unmerited by blind followers of obsolete dogmas, which have long ceased to bear any relation to their original purpose, and which their own authors if now living would disavow. (AC, *Pol* I 281)

Modern Christianity, in other words, had failed to develop in accordance with the religious needs of the age.

Comte's treatment of Christianity is altogether radical. He has little time for Christ himself, 'one of the many adventurers who would at that time be constantly making efforts to inaugurate Monotheism; aspiring, like their Greek forerunners, to the honours of personal apotheosis'. Jesus had not been original in his moral teaching, according to Comte, and, if he really had known that he would rise again in three days, had not been called upon to make much of a sacrifice (III 346–9). The early drafts of the Positivist Calendar had in fact included Jesus but Comte resolved the debate on this question by ruling that his claim to rank with God forfeited his right to be considered a great man (F. J. Gould 1920: 85).

Comte, like Gibbon, considered the rise of Christianity to have been an inevitable product of the needs and conditions of the time. Greek philosophy had already outlined a coherent system which went beyond polytheism. The Romans had built an empire through military power but required an internal bond of unity to consolidate their conquests. The civic impulse, the mainstay of Roman morality, had weakened; idleness and wealth had bred mischief while religious observance had degenerated into hypocrisy and scepticism. The need for a universal morality was clearly felt and Christianity arose to provide it, the separation of the spiritual from the temporal power being exaggerated by its origin under a hostile regime and the doctrine of the incarnation further strengthening the independence of the priesthood by giving divine authority to the revelation with which it was entrusted. St Paul, who realised all this and in 'sublime self-abnegation' accepted a 'founder who had no real claim' (AC, *Cat* 394), is credited by Comte with being the 'real founder' of Catholicism (250). He alone 'grasped the doctrine as a whole', propounding a theory of nature and grace which anticipated Positivist teaching on egoism and altruism (AC, *Pol* III 346). The early Christians displayed 'the heroic perseverance of men who felt themselves charged with the moral future of the human race'. The early fathers receive less generous attention, as worthy individuals suffering from the pernicious influence of Greek metaphysics (349–50).

Although Christianity is presented as having performed a useful educational role in the development of the race, its doctrines come in for scathing attack. The *Cours* singles out the 'dogma of exclusive salvation' and the 'damnation of all heretics' for moral obloquy:

nothing is more confirmatory of the provisional destination of all religious doctrines than their gradually leading on to the conversion of an old principle of love into a final ground of insurmountable hatred.   (AC, *Phil* II 275–6)

The Christian concern with personal immortality, Comte argues, encourages an 'exorbitant selfishness, for ever occupied with its future lot' (288). The same moral objection to Christian obsession with individual salvation finds expression in the *General View*, in which theology, which 'fixed men's thoughts upon a visionary future', is contrasted with chivalry, which concentrated their energies on the world around them (AC, *Pol* I 205). The book ends with a fierce attack on monotheism, 'the sole effect' of whose doctrine 'is to degrade the affections by unlimited desires, and to weaken the character by servile terrors'. Comte, like Marx, objects to the way in which the poor are deprived of social improvements on the assurance of compensation in an imaginary future life. There is no possibility of a compromise between theology and Positivism, he insists; a choice must be made between them (320–1).

The *Catechism* begins with a similar rejection of Christianity, taking particular objection to 'a morality which proclaims that the benevolent sentiments are foreign to our nature', refers the origin of labour to 'a Divine curse' and 'puts forward women as the source of all evil' (AC, *Cat* 10). Positivism, in contrast, founds its hopes on benevolent human instincts, 'the inclinations which lead all creatures to a mutual union, instead of devoting themselves separately to their Creator' (251). The 'unparalleled selfishness' fostered by Christianity is the subject of further attacks in the *Système*, which launches a full-scale onslaught on the concept of God. The 'radical imperfection' of the world made it impossible for Comte to accept that there could be a God who was both omnipotent and morally perfect. The 'principle of omnipotence' was harmful in itself, since it encouraged unreal hopes and glorified the 'apotheosis of absolute egoism' (AC, *Pol* III 348–77).

Medieval Catholicism managed to contribute to human progress, Comte argued, in spite of its faulty doctrine. The priest in the *Catechism* expresses admiration and respect for his predecessors for finding 'such powerful resources in a faith which was radically defective' (AC, *Cat* 405) while the *Cours* describes the Catholic separation of the spiritual from the temporal power as 'the greatest advance ever made in the general theory of the social organism', introducing into society a moral power wholly independent of political rulers. For priests preached a morality that was universal, applying to nobles and plebeians alike. Under polytheism the masses had been doomed to stupidity but Catholicism prepared everyone to perform his social duty through such rites as confession (AC, *Phil* II 261–74). Catholic priests extended their moral influence by undermining theological conceptions, restricting the scope for further divine revelation and developing new doctrines, such as the real presence, to substantiate their own position (276–7). Other doctrines are seen in the *Système* to have encouraged the development of altruism. The doctrine of grace, for example, although describing human impulse in terms of divine inspiration, emphasised the need to control the egoistic instincts and was therefore 'indirectly favourable to the growth of the higher sympathies'. Even the love of God gave vent to these feelings 'and any kind of exercise is calculated to strengthen them'. The idea of God becoming man bestowed new dignity upon humanity while the worship of the saints contributed to the 'culture of the heart'. Even the damnation of unbelievers could be justified as a temporary measure for establishing the power of the priesthood (AC, *Pol* III 378–88).

Catholicism had been most influential, according to Comte, in the field of 'domestic morality', penetrating every relation and developing 'the sense of reciprocal duty'. While sanctioning paternal authority it raised the position of women by freeing them from the need to work and 'sanctifying the indissolubleness of marriage' (AC, *Phil* II 291). Catholicism also anticipated Positivism in the construction of ideal objects for worship, concentrating

in the Founder of their system all the perfection that they could imagine in human nature, thus constituting a universal and operative type, admirably adapted to the moral guidance of humanity . . . and they completed the lesson by the addition of that yet more ideal conception which offers as the feminine type the beautiful mystic reconciliation of purity with maternity. (290)

Polytheism might have developed the worship of women even more fully, but Catholic adoration of the Blessed Virgin had provided the Religion of Humanity with a model for Positivist prayer.

Comte particularly admired the development of chivalry under medieval Catholicism, bringing with it the emancipation of serfs as well as women, involving a 'true sense of the social dignity of labour' and inculcating in the strong a sense of responsibility for the weak (AC, *Pol* III 412–13). He also extolled the aesthetic impact of the Middle Ages, especially their cathedrals, 'those religious edifices which are the most perfect monumental expressions of the ideas and feelings of our moral nature' (AC, *Phil* II 297–8). He was a fervent admirer of Dante, Petrarch and, above all, Thomas à Kempis, whose *Imitation of Christ* was to become an integral part of Positivist liturgy:

Posterity will never cease to revere the crude but sublime outline of the systematic picture of human nature . . . In reading it, we may, by merely substituting Humanity for God, continually recognise the spontaneous presentiment of the normal harmony of our existence. (AC, *Pol* III 460)

Catholicism, however, had been left behind by the intellectual progress which it failed to incorporate after 1300 and, forced to become reactionary in order to survive, attempted to stifle some of the most important scientific discoveries. It could no longer function as a synthesis of knowledge although it had achieved its main mission, the education of men's feelings, and many of its most important features were retained, if slightly modified, by the Religion of Humanity.

History and sociology

The Western Revolution, the title given by Comte to the second, metaphysical, or negative stage in the development of mankind, also served a purpose, bringing about the downfall of Catholicism and fostering the rise of Positivism. It is described in two early essays as a transitional state, dissolving the old system by bringing the revolutionary principles of private judgement and liberty of conscience to bear upon the spiritual and temporal powers and ushering in the new in the form of scientific advance (AC, *Crisis* 87–8, 216–25). The *Cours* traces the progress of Protestantism, its variant forms, Lutheranism, Calvinism and Socinianism, marking the successive stages of the dissolution of the theological system and bringing political revolution to Holland, England, America and finally France (AC, *Phil* II 304–62).

Comte became increasingly more definite about the type of society which was to emerge in the final stage of human development. His early essays envisage scientists exercising the spiritual and industrialists the temporal power. His 'Considerations on the Spiritual Power' insists on the priority of spiritual association, based on common beliefs and feelings, over temporal association, based on common interests. Left unregulated, as the political economists desired, the industrial spirit led to the despotism of the wealthiest. It was therefore up to the spiritual power to provide the moral unity required in any society by enforcing the duties expected of each class (AC, *Crisis* 214–45). The liberal and fundamentally anarchic principles of political economy also come under attack in the *Cours* (AC, *Phil* II 61–4), which goes on to explain 'Social Statics, or Theory of the Spontaneous Order of Human Society'. The individual, Comte insists, belongs to the family which belongs to society. Domestic life is therefore a preparation for social life, whose fundamental principles of co-operation and obedience are enforced by the spiritual power.

The exact composition of the spiritual power is not spelt out in the *Cours*, which is also diffident in predicting the nature of temporal authority in the positive state. Any stipulation of details is seen as altogether premature. The distinction between private and public is abolished: work and wealth become social responsibilities, open to the moral supervision of public opinion. There is a hierarchy within the temporal power, with bankers at the top, followed by merchants, manufacturers and agriculturalists. Everyone finds the situation best adapted to his abilities, although professions would normally be hereditary. The spiritual power is the arbiter of all disputes, with a special responsibility to protect the weak. These conditions are confidently expected to produce a united, ordered and peaceful Europe, with France, of course, at its centre.

The *Système* presents a somewhat rosy view of the working classes as natural philosophers whose preference for the real and useful derives from common sense uncontaminated by metaphysical education. Their domestic ties are strong, since they are not so absorbed in personal interests, and they preserve a 'sincere and simple respect for superiors' combined with a powerful sense of solidarity. Even their drinking habits are admirable, such cultivation of the social instincts being infinitely preferable to 'the self-helping spirit which draws men to the savings-bank'. They are, however, unfit for political office and must abandon the demand for rights, including the vote. 'The workman must learn to look upon himself, morally, as a public servant', content to remain within his own class (AC, *Pol* I 151–7).

Public opinion plays an important part in Comte's utopia as the main guarantee of political morality. All Positivists are to live openly, submitting their actions to its judgement. Established by a sound educational system, it is maintained through social institutions such as salons and working-men's clubs, in which women, workers and philosophers combine together in the common interest. Comte's later works add little to these general suggestions but additional and often ridiculous detail. Concepts such as the gratuitousness of labour, designed to emphasise the importance of duty rather than reward as the motive for work (II 332), and the 'Utopia of the Virgin-Mother', a belief that artificial insemination would eventually replace sexual intercourse as the means of reproduction (IV 242), were to do nothing for his popularity.

Ethics, worship and art

Positivist ethics rested on the somewhat shaky foundations of contemporary physiology. Bichat's discovery of the laws of intermittence and habit, by demonstrating the possibility of transforming voluntary acts into involuntary tendencies, increasing or diminishing the faculties by exercise or disuse, provided a basis for the belief in human perfectibility (AC, *Phil* I 453–6). Gall and Spurzheim had also revealed the possibility of developing and channelling innate instincts.

Phrenology was only 'a scientific hypothesis', many of whose details remained to be tested by further investigation (468–80). But it contributed a great deal to Comte's own cerebral theory.

The most important part of this theory, which provided the basis for Positivist ethics and worship, was his analysis of the ten 'affective motors', the chief sources of action, which were divided into two main classes: the personal or egoistic and the social or altruistic. Arranged in order of increasing altruism there were firstly the five egoistic instincts: that of preservation, the sexual, the maternal, the destructive or military and the constructive or industrial. Next came two intermediate propensities: pride or love of power and vanity or love of approbation, both of which were essentially personal but were made at least partly social by their reliance on others for gratification. There were finally three altruistic propensities: attachment, veneration and benevolence or universal love. Love and respect for individuals were seen to lead to love of communities which culminated in the highest feeling known to man, love of Humanity (AC, *Pol* I 557–68). Five intellectual functions were used to channel these affective motors in order to produce three practical qualities: courage, prudence and perseverance, the whole system being reproduced as a diagram entitled 'Positive Classification of the Eighteen Internal Functions of the Brain, or Systematic View of the Soul' (see p. 33).

Positive morality, then, was a matter of 'compressing egoism' and 'developing altruism', disciplining the personal instincts and channelling them in useful directions. The instinct of self-preservation, for example, which was responsible for our bodily requirements, needed to be controlled by sobriety rather than starved by asceticism. The sexual instinct, which was too often 'stimulated unduly by the brain', could be disarmed and discredited by the fuller development of the altruistic instincts within the family (IV 246–52). Positivists were taught to develop basically egoistic faculties such as the maternal instinct into a higher kind of feeling.

The family, the first and smallest community to which everyone belonged, played a crucial role in the Positivist development of the sympathies. The love of a child for its parents was seen as 'the starting-point of our moral education', the origin of a sense of reverence for the past. Brotherly love helped to implant a sense of solidarity, parental love a concern for the future. Conjugal love, 'the most important of all', was indissoluble even by death (I 75–6). It was marriage which

31

afforded the most important prospect for the channelling of egoism into altruism. For the sexual instinct originated a tie which could develop a man's higher instincts until he was 'sufficiently pure . . . to dispense with this coarse stimulant' altogether. Widowhood became preferable to marriage for this very reason and remarriage was therefore ruled out altogether (AC, *Cat* 320–5). Comte never ceased to deplore the sexual instincts as the most disturbing of the egoistic propensities, 'the least capable of being usefully transformed', one of 'the chief imperfections of human existence' (AC, *Appeal* 75).

Women, it is clear, occupy a somewhat paradoxical position in the Religion of Humanity. The *Cours* describes them as mentally inferior but emotionally superior to men, their function being to educate men's feelings (AC, *Phil* II 135–6). The chapter in the *General View* on 'The Influence of Positivism upon Women' elaborates on their educational and religious role. They 'represent the affective element in our nature, as philosophers and people represent the intellectual and practical elements' (AC, *Pol* I 164). Their influence is to be felt through the family, of course, but also through *salons*. 'Modern sophisms about Women's rights', however, receive little sympathy (196). If women attempt to compete with men in the practical sphere, Comte warns, they will not only fail but suffer moral damage. Their education, he accepts, should be the same as men's in order to equip them for their educational task. The woman in the *Catechism*, who fears that 'her ignorance exposes her to the ill-concealed contempt of a son puffed up with pride of knowledge', is reassured that she will receive a thorough education enabling her properly to fulfil her role as wife and mother (AC, *Cat* 291–2).

Women also occupy a central position in Positivist worship. One of the aspects of medieval Catholicism which met with Comte's full approval was its adoration of the Virgin and this is developed even further in the Religion of Humanity, whose central symbol is a Goddess or Madonna. The *General View* also recounts from Comte's own experience how 'constant adoration of one whom Death has implanted more visibly and deeply on the memory, leads all high natures . . . to give themselves more unreservedly to the service of Humanity' (AC, *Pol* I 192). These elements from the history of mankind and from his own personal experience are developed in the Religion of Humanity into a complete system of worship whose object is the exercise and consequent strengthening of the altruistic instincts.

POSITIVE CLASSIFICATION
OF THE EIGHTEEN INTERNAL FUNCTIONS OF THE BRAIN,
OR
SYSTEMATIC VIEW OF THE SOUL.

PRINCIPLE.

Instincts of Preservation.......... { of the Individual, or *nutritive Instinct*.......... 1		
{ of the race, or.... { *sexual Instinct*.......... 2		
{ *maternal Instinct*.......... 3		
Instincts of Improvement.......... { by destruction, or *military Instinct*.......... 4		
{ by construction, or *industrial Instinct*.......... 5		
Temporal, or Pride, desire of power.......... 6		
Spiritual, or Vanity, desire of approbation.......... 7		
ATTACHMENT.......... 8		
VENERATION.......... 9		
BENEVOLENCE or Universal Love (sympathy), *humanity*.......... 10		

INTEREST .. — AMBITION ..

ATTACHMENT — VENERATION — BENEVOLENCE

7 PERSONAL — 3 SOCIAL, Gene-Special, and. — 10 APPETITIVE MOTORS. Propensities, when active; feelings, when passive.

AFFECTION, THINK TO ACT.

IMPULSION. (THE HEART.) — Decrease of energy, increase of dignity, from the back of the head to the front, from the lower part to the higher, from the sides to the middle.

MEANS.

CONCEPTION	Passive, or Contemplation, hence objective materials.	Concrete, or relative to Beings, essentially *synthetical*.	 11
		Abstract, or relative to Events, essentially *analytical*.	 12
	Active, or Meditation, hence subjective constructions.	Inductive, or by comparison, hence *Generalisation*.	 13
		Deductive, or by co-ordination, hence *Systematisation*.	 14
EXPRESSION......	Mimic, oral, written, hence *Communication*		 15

5 INTELLEC-TUAL FUNCTIONS.

TO THINK, TO ACT),

COUNSEL. (THE INTELLECT.) — Knowledge, or vision, for the sake of provision, with a view to provision.

RESULT.

ACTIVITY.. { Courage.......... 16		
{ Prudence.......... 17		
FIRMNESS, hence *Perseverance*.......... 18		

3 Practical Qualities.

(TO LOVE, ACT FROM

EXECUTION. (THE CHARACTER.)

SUMMARY OF THE CEREBRAL THEORY.

These eighteen organs together form the cerebral apparatus, which, on the one hand, stimulates the life of nutrition, on the other, co-ordinates the life of relation, by connecting its two kinds of external functions. Its speculative region is in direct communication with the nerves of sensation, its active region with the nerves of motion. Its affective region has no direct communication except with the viscera of organic life; it has no immediate correspondence with the external world, its only connection with which is through the other two regions. This part of the brain, the essential centre of the whole of our existence, is in constant activity. It is enabled to be so by the alternate rest of the two symmetrical parts of each of its organs. As for the rest of the brain, its periodical cessation of action is as complete as that of the senses and muscles. Thus, our harmony as living beings depends on the principal region of the brain, the affective; it is from this that the two others derive their impulse, and in obedience to this impulse, the two others direct the relations of the animal with the external agencies which influence it, whether such relations be active or passive.

(*Positivist Catechism*, p. 179.)

3   Positivist cerebral theory, Appendix to AC, *Cat*

33

POSITIVIST CALENDAR,

ADAPTED TO ALL YEARS EQUALLY; OR,

CONCRETE VIEW OF THE PREPARATORY PERIOD OF MAN'S HISTORY,

ESPECIALLY INTENDED FOR THE FINAL PERIOD OF TRANSITION THROUGH WHICH THE WESTERN REPUBLIC HAS TO PASS: THE REPUBLIC WHICH, SINCE CHARLEMAGNE, HAS BEEN FORMED BY THE FREE COHESION OF THE FIVE LEADING POPULATIONS, THE FRENCH, ITALIAN, SPANISH, BRITISH, AND GERMAN.

		FIRST MONTH. MOSES. THE INITIAL THEOCRACY.	SECOND MONTH. HOMER. ANCIENT POETRY.	THIRD MONTH. ARISTOTLE. ANCIENT PHILOSOPHY.	FOURTH MONTH. ARCHIMEDES. ANCIENT SCIENCE.	FIFTH MONTH. CÆSAR. MILITARY CIVILISATION.	SIXTH MONTH. ST. PAUL. CATHOLICISM.	SEVENTH MONTH. CHARLEMAGNE. FEUDAL CIVILISATION.
Monday	1	Prometheus ... *Cadmus.*	Hesiod.	Anaximander.	Theophrastus.	Miltiades.	St. Luke ... *St. James.*	Theodoric the Great.
Tuesday	2	Hercules ... *Theseus.*	Tyrtæus ... *Sappho.*	Anaximenes.	Herophilus.	Leonidas.	St. Cyprian	Pelayo.
Wednesday	3	Orpheus ... *Tiresias.*	Anacreon.	Heraclitus.	Erasistratus.	Aristides.	St. Athanasius.	Otho the Great ... *Henry the Fowler.*
Thursday	4	Ulysses.	Pindar.	Anaxagoras.	Celsus.	Cimon.	St. Jerome.	St. Henry.
Friday	5	Lycurgus.	Sophocles ... *Euripides.*	Democritus ... *Leucippus.*	Galen.	Xenophon.	St. Ambrose.	Villiers ... *La Valette.*
Saturday	6	Romulus.	Theocritus ... *Longus.*	Herodotus.	Avicenna ... *Averrhoes.*	Phocion ... *Epaminondas.*	St. Monica.	Don John of Austria. *John Sobieski.*
Sunday	7	NUMA.	ÆSCHYLUS.	THALES.	HIPPOCRATES	THEMISTOCLES.	ST. AUGUSTIN.	ALFRED.
	8	Belus ... *Semiramis.*	Scopas.	Solon.	Euclid.	Pericles.	Constantine.	Charles Martel.
	9	Sesostris.	Zeuxis.	Xenophanes.	Aristæus.	Philip.	Theodosius.	The Cid ... *Tancred.*
	10	Menu.	Ictinus.	Empedocles.	Theodosius of Bithynia.	Demosthenes.	St. Chrysostom ... *St. Basil.*	Richard I. ... *Saladin.*
	11	Cyrus.	Praxiteles.	Thucydides.	Hero ... *Ctesibius.*	Ptolemy Lagus.	St. Pulcheria ... *Marcian.*	Joan of Arc ... *Marina.*
	12	Zoroaster.	Lysippus.	Archytas ... *Philolaus.*	Pappus.	Philopœmen.	St. Genevieve of Paris.	Albuquerque ... *Sir W. Raleigh.*
	13	The Druids ... *Ossian.*	Apelles.	Apollonius of Tyana.	Diophantus.	Polybius.	St. Gregory the Great.	Bayard.
	14	BOUDDHA.	PHIDIAS.	PYTHAGORAS.	APOLLONIUS.	ALEXANDER.	HILDEBRAND.	GODFREY.
	15	Fo-Hi.	Æsop ... *Pilpay.*	Aristippus.	Eudoxus ... *Aratus.*	Junius Brutus.	St. Benedict ... *St. Antony.*	St. Leo the Great ... *Leo IV.*
	16	Lao-Tseu.	Plautus.	Antisthenes.	Pytheas ... *Nearchus.*	Camillus ... *Cincinnatus.*	St. Boniface ... *St. Austin.*	Gerbert ... *Peter Damian.*
	17	Meng-Tseu.	Terence ... *Menander.*	Zeno.	Aristarchus ... *Berosus.*	Fabricius ... *Regulus.*	St. Isidore of Seville ... *St. Bruno.*	Peter the Hermit.
	18	The Theocrats of Thibet.	Phædrus.	Cicero ... *Pliny the Younger.*	Eratosthenes ... *Sosigenes.*	Hannibal.	Lanfranc ... *St. Anselm.*	Suger ... *St. Eligius.*
	19	The Theocrats of Japan.	Juvenal.	Epictetus ... *Arrian.*	Ptolemy.	Paulus Æmilius.	Heloise ... *Beatrice.*	Alexander III. ... *Becket.*
	20	Manco-Capac ... *Tamehameha.*	Lucian.	Tacitus.	Albategnius ... *Nasir-Eddin.*	Marius ... *The Gracchi.*	The Arch'ts of Mid. Ages. *St. Benezet.*	St. Francis of Assisi. *St. Dominic.*
	21	CONFUCIUS.	ARISTOPHANES.	SOCRATES.	HIPPARCHUS.	SCIPIO.	ST. BERNARD.	INNOCENT III.
	22	Abraham ... *Joseph.*	Ennius.	Xenocrates.	Varro.	Augustus ... *Mæcenas.*	St. Francis Xavier. *Ignatius Loyola.*	St. Clotilde. [*cany.*
	23	Samuel.	Lucretius.	Philo of Alexandria.	Columella.	Vespasian ... *Titus.*	St. Ch. Borromeo. *Fredk. Borromeo.*	St. Bathilda. *St. Mathilda of Tus-*
	24	Solomon ... *David.*	Horace.	St. John the Evangelist.	Vitruvius.	Hadrian ... *Nerva.*	St. Theresa. *St. Catharine of Siena.*	St. Stephen of Hungary. *Mathias Cor-*
	25	Isaiah.	Tibullus.	St. Justin ... *St. Irenæus.*	Strabo.	Antoninus ... *Marcus Aurelius.*	St. Vinc't de Paul *The Abbé de l'Epée.*	St. Elizabeth of Hungary. [*vinus.*
	26	St. John the Baptist.	Ovid.	St. Clement of Alexandria.	Frontinus.	Papinian ... *Ulpian.*	Bourdaloue ... *Claude Fleury.*	Blanche of Castille.
	27	Haroun-al-Raschid.. *Abderrahman*	Lucan.	Origen ... *Tertullian.*	Plutarch.	Alexander Severus ... *Aetius.*	W. Penn ... *G. Fox.*	St. Ferdinand III ... *Alfonso X.*
	28	MAHOMET. [*III.*	VIRGIL.	PLATO.	PLINY THE ELDER.	TRAJAN.	BOSSUET.	ST. LOUIS.

		EIGHTH MONTH. DANTE. MODERN EPIC POETRY.	NINTH MONTH. GUTENBERG. MODERN INDUSTRY.	TENTH MONTH. SHAKESPEARE. THE MODERN DRAMA.	ELEVENTH MONTH. DESCARTES. MODERN PHILOSOPHY.	TWELFTH MONTH. FREDERIC II. MODERN POLICY.	THIRTEENTH MONTH. BICHAT. MODERN SCIENCE.
Monday	1	The Troubadours.	Marco Polo ... *Chardin.*	Lope de Vega ... *Montalvan.*	Albertus Magnus *John of Salisbury.*	Marie de Molina.	Copernicus ... *Tycho Brahé.*
Tuesday	2	Boccaccio ... *Chaucer.*	Jacques Cœur ... *Gresham.*	Moreto ... *Guillem de Castro.*	Roger Bacon ... *Raymond Lully.*	Cosmo de Medici the Elder.	Kepler ... *Halley.*
Wednesday	3	Rabelais ... *Swift.*	Vasco de Gama ... *Magellan.*	Rojas ... *Guevara.*	St. Bonaventura ... *Joachim.*	Philippe de Comines. *Guicciardini.*	Huyghens ... *Varignon.*
Thursday	4	Cervantes.	Napier ... *Briggs.*	Otway.	Ramus ... *The Cardinal of Cusa.*	Isabella of Castille.	James Bernouilli. *John Bernouilli.*
Friday	5	La Fontaine ... *Burns.*	Lacaille ... *Delambre.*	Lessing.	Montaigne ... *Erasmus.*	Charles V. ... *Sixtus V.*	Bradley ... *Römer.*
Saturday	6	De Foe ... *Goldsmith.*	Cook ... *Tasman.*	Goethe.	Campanella ... *Sir Thomas More.*	Henry IV.	Volta ... *Sauveur.*
Sunday	7	ARIOSTO.	COLUMBUS.	CALDERON.	ST. THOMAS AQUINAS.	LOUIS XI.	GALILEO.
	8	Leonardo da Vinci ... *Titian.*	Benvenuto Cellini.	Tirso.	Hobbes ... *Spinosa.*	L'Hôpital.	Vieta ... *Harriott.*
	9	Michael Angelo ... *Paul Veronese.*	Amontons ... *Wheatstone.*	Vondel.	Pascal ... *Giordano Bruno.*	Barneveldt.	Wallis ... *Fermat.*
	10	Holbein ... *Rembrandt.*	Harrison ... *Pierre Leroy.*	Racine.	Locke ... *Malebranche.*	Gustavus Adolphus.	Clairaut ... *Poinsot.*
	11	Poussin ... *Lesueur.*	Dollond ... *Graham.*	Voltaire.	Vauvenargues ... *Mme. de Lambert.*	De Witt.	Euler ... *Monge.*
	12	Velasquez ... *Murillo.*	Arkwright ... *Jacquard.*	Metastasio ... *Alfieri.*	Diderot ... *Duclos.*	Ruyter.	D'Alembert ... *Daniel Bernouilli.*
	13	Teniers ... *Rubens.*	Conté.	Schiller.	Cabanis ... *George Leroy.*	William III.	Lagrange ... *Joseph Fourier.*
	14	RAPHAEL.	VAUCANSON.	CORNEILLE.	LORD BACON.	WILLIAM THE SILENT.	NEWTON.
	15	Froissart ... *Joinville.*	Stevin ... *Torricelli.*	Alarcon.	Grotius ... *Cujas.*	Ximenes.	Bergmann ... *Scheele.*
	16	Camoens ... *Spenser.*	Mariotte ... *Boyle.*	Mme. de Motteville ... *Mme. Roland.*	Fontenelle ... *Maupertuis.*	Sully ... *Oxenstiern.*	Priestley ... *Davy.*
	17	The Spanish Romancers.	Papin ... *Worcester.*	Mme. de Sévigné ... *Lady Montagu.*	Vico ... *Herder.*	Mazarin ... *Walpole.*	Cavendish.
	18	Chateaubriand.	Black.	Lesage ... *Sterne.*	Fréret ... *Winckelmann.*	Colbert ... *Louis XIV.*	Guyton Morveau ... *Geoffroy.*
	19	Walter Scott ... *Cooper.*	Jouffroy ... *Fulton.*	Mme. de Staël ... *Miss Edgeworth.*	Montesquieu ... *D'Aguesseau.*	D'Aranda ... *Pombal.*	Berthollet.
	20	Manzoni.	Dalton ... *Thilorier.*	Fielding ... *Richardson.*	Buffon ... *Oken.*	Turgot ... *Campomanes.*	Berzelius ... *Ritter.*
	21	TASSO.	WATT.	MOLIERE.	LEIBNITZ.	RICHELIEU.	LAVOISIER.
	22	Petrarca. [*and Bunyan.*	Bernard de Palissy.	Pergolese ... *Palestrina.*	Robertson ... *Gibbon.*	Sidney ... *Lambert.*	Harvey ... *Ch. Bell.*
	23	Thomas à Kempis *Louis of Granada*	Guglielmini ... *Riquet.*	Sacchini ... *Grétry.*	Adam Smith ... *Dunoyer.*	Franklin ... *Hampden.*	Boerhaave ... *Stahl. Barthez.*
	24	Mme. de Lafayette. *Mme. de Staël.*	Duhamel (du Monceau) *Bourgelat.*	Gluck ... *Lully.*	Kant ... *Fichte.*	Washington ... *Kosciusko.*	Linnæus ... *Bernard de Jussieu.*
	25	Fénélon ... *St. Francis of Sales.*	Saussure ... *Bouguer.*	Beethoven ... *Handel.*	Condorcet ... *Ferguson.*	Jefferson ... *Madison.*	Haller ... *Vicq-d'Azyr.*
	26	Klopstock ... *Gessner.*	Coulomb ... *Borda.*	Rossini ... *Weber.*	Joseph de Maistre ... *Bonald.*	Bolivar ... *Toussaint-L'Ouverture.*	Lamarck ... *Blainville.*
	27	Byron. *Elisa Mercœur and Shelley.*	Carnot ... *Vauban.*	Bellini ... *Donizetti.*	Hegel ... *Sophie Germain.*	Francia.	Broussais ... *Morgagni.*
	28	MILTON.	MONTGOLFIER.	MOZART.	HUME.	CROMWELL.	GALL.

Complementary Day ... **Festival of all THE DEAD.**

Additional Day in Leap-years ... **Festival of HOLY WOMEN.**

Seventh Edition, Aug. 1855, in *Appel aux Conservateurs*, p. 115. Paris, Monday, 22 Charlemagne 67 (9th July 1855). *Positivist Catechism*, p. 259.

The provisional era begins January 1, 1789 (see *Pos. Pol.* iv., Eng. trans., p. 347).
The names in Italics are those of the persons who in Leap years take the place of their principals.

Positivist prayer, the 'solemn outpouring . . . of men's nobler feelings', is totally liberated from the self-interest inherent in Christian petitions (209). The 'Definitive Systematisation of the Positive System of Worship' describes the object of the 'Positive cultus' as 'the direct and persistent encouragement of our instincts of sympathy'. For the expression of 'emotions in idealised form' purifies them of 'their ordinary admixture of egoism' (IV 81). The purpose of 'The Worship as a Whole' is also explained in the third conversation of the *Catechism*, where the priest distinguishes between a Positivist, who 'prays in order to give expression to his best affections', and a believer in God, who petitions for benefits. He is careful to emphasise, however, that prayer is only a supplement to action: the Positivist thinks altruistic thoughts in order to improve his capacity to perform benevolent acts (AC, *Cat* 106–9).

Careful attention is paid in the *Système* to the technique of Positivist prayer, which has to be definite:

Prayer would be of little value unless the mind could clearly define its object. The worship of Woman satisfies this condition, and may thus be of greater efficacy than the worship of God.

Finding a woman to idealise, a counterpart to Clotilde, should not present a problem:

No one can be as unhappy as not to be able to find some woman worthy of his peculiar love, whether in the relation of wife or of mother; some one who in his solitary prayer may be present to him as a fixed object of devotion.

She need not be alive, since she could be resurrected in the imagination, but if a Positivist were really to be at a loss to find someone among his acquaintance then he could turn to history or even invent an 'ideal' for himself (AC, *Pol* I 209–11).

The *Catechism* presents Positivist worship as a form of art which places greater emphasis on moral than physical beauty. It has at its disposal all 'the accumulated stores of human art, the esthetic treasures of Humanity'. Worship, like art, must achieve a balance between realism and idealism, subordinating the ideal to the real in order to avoid mysticism. But the 'ideal must be an amelioration of the real, or it is inadequate for its moral purpose'. The worshipper should be conscious all along that he is creating a subjective ideal:

The Positivist shuts his eyes during his private prayers, the better to see the internal image; the believer in theology opened his, to enable him then to perceive outside an object which was an illusion.

But the priest warns the woman that meditation should work 'from without inwards', fixing precisely the place, the seat, the attitude, and lastly the dress of the object of worship (AC, *Cat* 89–111).

Comte made no secret of the extent to which Positivist worship was an extension of his own experience. The preface to the *Système* describes the way in which his adoration of Clotilde rekindled his love for his mother and led him to regard Sophie, his cleaning lady, as his subjective daughter, the three of them becoming his guardian angels. Worship of wife, mother and daughter, he explained, strengthened 'the three sympathetic instincts, attachment between equals, veneration for superiors, kindness to inferiors' (AC, *Pol* I xv–xix). Widows, as we have seen, make the best angels, since they are freed from all sexual association. Following the pattern of his own devotion to Clotilde, Comte recommended an hour's prayer on getting up, half an hour before going to bed, and a quarter of an hour at midday (IV 103). All this comprises the Positivist model of private worship while its public worship focusses upon woman as a symbolic figure, representative of Humanity herself. The banner Comte specified for use in religious services was to portray 'a woman of thirty years of age bearing her son in her arms' (I 312), the resemblance both to the Madonna and to Clotilde being obvious.

The Religion of Humanity places a huge responsibility upon the priesthood. Comte's early essays envisage the spiritual power being comprised of general scientists who were to have a thorough grounding in all the positive sciences (AC, *Crisis* 210). His 'Seventh Circular' sets a rigorous standard for entry to the priesthood, requiring a thesis and an interview on each of the seven sciences (AC, *Circulars* 65–6). A priest should be at least forty-two, must renounce all property, wealth and power, and must be married, since he can hardly dispense with the angelic influence of woman (AC, *Cat* 300–3). His chief function, of course, is educational. He has no power but that of public opinion.

Positive education is divided into two main periods, the spontaneous cultivation of the affective and aesthetic instincts at home from birth until puberty followed by systematic lectures on the sciences from puberty until adolescence. The first fourteen years are unsystematic, the first seven being completely under the mother's care, the second seven bringing regular studies of a 'purely aesthetic kind'. In the succeeding seven years each individual must 'systematically go through the objective ascent which it took Humanity so many centuries to accomplish when left to its own natural efforts' (283–8). The individual, in other words, repeats the evolution of the race. For his first seven years he is a fetichist, for the next seven a polytheist, avoiding only theological belief as a transitional phase between fetichism and Positivism.

Seven was a significant number for Comte. The nine Positivist sacraments, for example, are to take place at seven-year intervals. First, at birth, comes Presentation, the equivalent of baptism, when each individual is given two patron saints. At fourteen comes Initiation, when the child passes from the care of the mother to that of the priest. Through Admission, at twenty-one, each individual becomes a servant of Humanity before Destination, at twenty-eight, sanctions the choice of career. Marriage, ideally, is entered upon by men at thirty-five and by women at twenty-eight. Maturity comes at forty-two and Retirement twenty-one years later. Transformation is the last duty of the individual, when he names his successor, thus ensuring the continuity of his work. Finally, in the Sacrament of Incorporation, seven years after his death, 'a solemn judgement' is made by public opinion on his worthiness to be buried in the sacred wood surrounding the Temple of Humanity, symbolising his attainment of subjective immortality (128–36). How important these details were for Comte is difficult to establish. Some of the sacraments, as we shall see, became a regular part of Positivist practice, but the stipulated ages were taken only as a rough guide.

The Positivist Calendar is an important feature of the Religion of Humanity, extending the Catholic cultivation of saints to great men of all ages and encouraging both reverence and emulation. It is divided into lunar months, each named after one of the great contributors to human progress, with a different saint for every day (see p. 34). Comte initially suggested an equivalent of hell, preserving the wicked in perpetual infamy (AC, *Pol* I 82) but later abandoned the idea (IV 351). He recognised that his 'historical cultus' gave a disproportionate emphasis to modern times, but this was because there were no available representatives of earlier periods of human history. He remained open to new suggestions, accepting Shelley, Spenser, Bunyan and Burns on the recommendation of various British Positivists. Some of his inclusions and omissions appear strange and the whole idea came in for much ridicule and sarcasm, but it was an essential feature of the Religion of Humanity. For, in Comte's own sad words,

To live in others is, in the truest sense of the word, life ... To prolong our life indefinitely in the Past and Future, so as to make it more perfect in the Present, is abundant compensation for the illusions of our youth which have now passed away for ever.   (AC, *Pol* I 278)

The great men celebrated in their calendar afforded the Positivists real historical objects for their veneration.

The fact that poets feature so prominently among the Positivist saints is an indication of the centrality of art, and literature in particular, in Comte's system. His 1822 'Prospectus' had insisted upon the importance of art, which could provide 'a valid picture of the amelioration which the new system should bring about in the condition of mankind' and so help to achieve the requisite 'moral revolution' (AC, *Crisis* 156). He claimed that his mental crisis of 1838 increased still further his appreciation of the value of art (AC, *Con* 49). The *Cours* recognises both its propagandist function and its power to elevate and soothe the mind (AC, *Phil* II 397–8, 559–60). The chapter on 'The Relation of Positivism to Art' in the *General View* places particular emphasis on the importance of literature. Science could explain fact but art beautified it, cultivating our sense of perfection. So although the poet's 'mental and moral versatility' often made him an unreliable guide, he could assist the spiritual power by idealising and stimulating goodness and beauty. Art could not, of course, be valued for its own sake, 'held out as the aim and object of existence'. Its true purpose was 'to strengthen our sympathies'. For poetry, Comte claimed, 'does actually modify our moral nature', achieving 'moral improvement' by bringing feeling, thought and action into harmonious activity (AC, *Pol* I 221–41).

Comte planned great festivals of art to celebrate the sense of solidarity and continuity with Humanity. But, aware of his own incapacity to create the 'poetical pictures' he envisaged, he had to content himself with developing aesthetic principles and describing the sort of works he would like to have written (AC, *Subj* 3). His aesthetic theory is most clearly expressed in the *General View*, which insists on the subordination of the ideal to the real and recommends the construction of typical characters 'on the basis furnished by science'. Women and workers should write about personal or domestic life, philosophers about public life. Two sorts of writing are given special prominence: 'prophetic pictures of the regeneration of man', involving 'the systematic construction of Utopias', and historical works contrasting the present with the past (AC, *Pol* I 253–5).

Historical novels seem to have had a peculiar fascination for Comte, who was a great admirer of Manzoni and Scott. The *General View* goes into some detail on the role of art in 'representing the great historic types' which could help to familiarise students of history 'with poetic descriptions of the various social phases and of the men who played a leading part in them'. The Positivist poet would go even further in this direction than Corneille, Manzoni and Scott. He would so thoroughly identify himself with all past historical stages as 'to awaken our sympathies for them, and revive the traces which each individual may recognise of corresponding phases in his own history' (242–5). Comte's insistence on the importance of propagating Positivism and extending men's sympathies through art is of particular significance for the development of the Religion of Humanity in Britain because it was arguably through the novel that his ideas were most widely disseminated.

2

THE EARLY YEARS:
FIRST BRITISH FOLLOWERS

John Stuart Mill: Positivist reformer

The first and most famous of Comte's British followers was John
Stuart Mill, who emerged from initial enthusiasm through subsequent disillusionment to become a firm believer in the need for a
reformed religion of humanity, divested of its founder's authoritarian
politics and personal idiosyncrasies. He first encountered Comte's
work as part of the Saint-Simonian propaganda given to him by
Gustave d'Eichthal in 1828 and found his analysis of contemporary
spiritual needs convincing (Mill, *CW* XII 34–49, 70–1, 88–9). After
meeting the Saint-Simonian leaders in Paris in 1831 he wrote a series
of articles on 'The Spirit of the Age' in the *Examiner* propounding
some of their solutions. He even assisted in the drafting of their *Address to the British Public* the following year, presenting Saint-Simon
as the saviour of his time (Pankhurst 1957: 77).

The Saint-Simonian work Mill singled out for most praise was
Comte's 1822 'Prospectus' although even in 1829 he found it tainted
with the French vice of over-systematisation, attempting to apply the
same law of development to both France and England and over-
simplifying human progress (Mill, *CW* XII 35–7). He seems then to
have lost sight of Comte for several years before the *Cours* reawakened
his enthusiasm (Mill 1873: 166). The first two volumes, he wrote in
1837, represented 'one of the most profound books ever written on the
philosophy of the sciences' (Mill, *CW* XII 363), and he was almost
equally impressed by the third volume, which he read the following
year, urging his friends to read what he called 'very nearly the
grandest work of this age', written by the 'first speculative thinker of
the age' (XIII 487, 579). Alexander Bain was later to describe how Mill

gladly initiated both himself and Lewes into the absence of mystery of the Positive Philosophy (Bain 1882: 70–6). Mill himself recalled that his enthusiasm for Comte necessitated a rewriting of his *System of Logic*, two thirds of which had been written before he encountered the *Cours* (Mill 1873: 210).

Comte's influence upon the *System of Logic* is most noticeable in the final book, 'On the Logic of the Moral Sciences', which begins by accepting that human phenomena could be included within the hierarchy of positive science before expounding a Comtean belief in the modifiability of human character through the development of the habits of egoism and altruism. Mill advocates a separate science of the mind, psychology, independent of physiology, and an intermediate science of ethology, or the formation of character, based on the laws of psychology and leading to those of sociology. Unlike Comte, he retains a belief in political economy. But he calls Comte, 'the greatest living authority on scientific methods', dwelling in particular on the Frenchman's introduction to the study of history of 'the inverse, Deductive Method', the construction of hypotheses by *a posteriori* reasoning and their verification *a priori*, which enables generalisations from history to be tested against the laws of human nature (Mill 1843: II 564). He also accepts Comte's division of sociology into statics and dynamics, the laws which lead to order and progress, and gives an enthusiastic account of the law of the three stages (594–612).

Later editions of the *Logic* removed many of the eulogistic references to Comte. But a detailed comparison of the first with the eighth edition reveals that although Mill toned down his enthusiasm and cut out many of the tributes to Comte which he had added to the first two thirds of the book, his substantial reliance on Comte for the historical method remained unaltered. He replaced the motto for Book VI from Comte with one from Condorcet but preserved all the material quoted above. He added some criticism of Comte's recommendations for the future, which he regarded as greatly inferior to his appreciation of the past, but he also added a long footnote defending the law of the three stages. The changes were of tone rather than substance (Simon 1963: 275–9).

In November 1841 Mill wrote to Comte to express his admiration of the *Cours* and his desire to co-operate with the founder of Positivism. There were minor differences of opinion between them, which they could discuss, but he was struck by their complete agreement on scientific method. He remained diffident about his own work, mentioning the *Logic* only in his second letter and even suggesting that, had he known the *Cours* earlier, he would have translated that rather than write his own book. Comte returned the compliment by breaking his rule of cerebral hygiene to read the *Logic*, which he admired greatly. Mill regarded this as a sanction of his role in the propagation of Positivism. He hoped to contribute also to its elaboration. Comte had accepted an enthusiastic and deferential disciple, but was less prepared to receive Mill as a colleague, certainly not as a critic. Mill attempted early on to change Comte's historical bias against Protestantism and against England. They disagreed more fundamentally over psychology and the position of women.

Comte and Mill discussed the possibility of a science of psychology during the winter of 1841–2. Comte's insistence on the physiological basis of psychology stemmed from Gall, whom he made Mill read. Mill accepted that Gall had opened a new approach to the subject, but argued the need for introspection, the study of successive mental states, and ethology, the study of the influence of environment on the development of character. The discussion was adjourned inconclusively. Apart from this, Mill remained submissive until July 1843, when the same letter which claimed a larger role in the development of Positivism insisted on a frank discussion of differences. He accepted Comte's scientific method and social dynamics but not his social statics. In particular, he disagreed with Comte's strong defence of property and marriage. The subordination of women he regarded as an accident of history rather than an unchangeable relation between the sexes (Lévy-Bruhl 1899: 204–10). Comte argued on phrenological and historical grounds that women were, and had always been, inferior, dismissing Mill's disagreement as an example of the intellectual anarchy of the time (210–18). When Mill later showed the correspondence to Harriet Taylor, she was astonished at his apologetic tone towards 'this dry sort of man' (Hayek 1951: 114). Comte, for his part, adopted a tone of parental guidance and correction while Mill became increasingly reserved.

In spite of their differences, it was to Mill that Comte turned for financial aid when he lost his job as examiner for the École Polytechnique. Mill collected a subsidy for 1844 but found his friends unwilling to repeat their generosity the following year. Comte replied to this news with a long letter setting out his theory of patronage, forcing

Mill to explain that neither he nor his friends were disciples but sympathetic liberals prepared to support him through a crisis. The fundamental differences between them were raised again, with Mill reproaching Comte for his narrow-minded refusal to expand his own knowledge, especially in the area of psychology (520–4). Comte refused to accept this criticism and their correspondence gradually petered out. It is generally agreed that the dispute over the subsidy was the occasion rather than the cause of the break. The real cause was Comte's refusal to learn or modify anything. Mill realised that he would have to develop Positivism independently, without the aid of its founder.

On the question of religion, however, Mill remained entirely in agreement with Comte, the social purpose of whose scientific synthesis became increasingly clear to him on successive re-readings of the second half of the *Cours* at the end of 1842. He told Comte that he was convinced of the capacity of the Positive Philosophy to fulfil the social function hitherto played by religion but that his own position was extremely rare in England, since he had never believed in God but always looked instead to the idea of Humanity (135–6). Because he believed his own position to be so unusual Mill continually urged Comte to a more cautious treatment of religion in relation to England, where belief was much more deeply entrenched than in the rest of Europe. He opposed the idea of translating Comte's 1822 'Traité' in 1844 on the grounds that direct attacks on theology were still unacceptable in England (307–8). He gave the same reason for his rejection of Comte's 'Lettre philosophique' (later introduced into the beginning of the *Système*). The British were not yet capable of distinguishing between Comte's constructive approach and the negative attitudes of the eighteenth century (447–8).

Mill's recognition of Comte's personal limitations appears in his private correspondence (Mill, *CW* XIII 622, 653–4). The shock of seeing his mentor transformed into a 'patronized dependent' may explain the apparent harshness of some of Mill's later comments on Comte, who was by no means the first thinker he approached as a disciple and left with bitter disillusion on both sides (Mazlish 1975: 262). He continued to defend Comte against attacks on his professional reputation, for example Sir John Herschel's Presidential Address to the British Academy for the Advancement of Science in 1845 (Mill, *CW* XIII 673–7), and on his personal conduct, even to the extent of telling John Austin the palpable untruth that Comte's letters on their failure to renew the subsidy 'contained nothing like reproaches' (714). They were, as has been pointed out, 'one long reproach' and, as Mill himself admitted to George Grote, 'little creditable to his delicacy or gratitude' (690). Mill's work on the *Principles of Political Economy*, published in 1848 but begun in 1845, was taken by Comte as a personal affront. In fact, as Mueller has shown, it represented a modification of Mill's earlier position. Where he had believed in political economy as an isolable part of social behaviour, Mill's preface now agreed with Comte that it was inseparable from social philosophy as a whole (Mueller 1956: 116–18).

Two letters of 1848 clarify Mill's position at this time. When Littré approached him for a contribution to Comte's subsidy, he replied with a donation of 250 francs and a somewhat curt explanation of the distinction he drew between the positive method and the way Comte had applied it to social questions (Mill, *CW* XIII 741–2). He agreed with John Nichol that the *General View* was a strange but stimulating book whose utopian proposals were concrete enough 'to lay hold of' and consequently to reject. It did, however, establish

the grounds for believing that the *culte de l'humanité* is capable of fully supplying the place of a religion, or rather (to say the truth) of *being* a religion – and this he has done, notwithstanding the ridiculousness which everybody must feel in his premature attempts to define in detail the *practices* of this *culte*.

(738–9)

The letter goes on to elaborate areas in which Mill differs from Comte: on the formation of character, his restriction of liberty, his view of women and his reactionary politics. But it illustrates clearly the profound sympathy Mill felt towards the Religion of Humanity.

The extent of this sympathy with the Religion of Humanity emerges in Mill's letters and diaries of 1854. He assured a French Positivist who wrote to enquire about the position of his English counterparts that he knew of no-one who accepted all of Comte's ideas. The religion, he explained, was a stumbling block to most of his compatriots, although it was precisely this that he found most acceptable (XIV 236–7). A diary entry for 24 January confirms this preference for Comte's religion to other aspects of his thought. It is 'the best, indeed the only good thing (details excepted) in Comte's second treatise'. After outlining its main doctrines, solidarity and continuity, universal moral education and the cultivation of imaginative worship, Mill concludes, 'there is no worthy office of a religion which this system of cultivation does not seem adequate to fulfil' (Mill 1910: II 361–3). Other diary entries for this period reaffirm this belief (371–2, 379).

Mill's *Utilitarianism*, written in 1854 but not published until 1863, made his faith public: 'Mill here in effect adopts the Religion of Humanity' (Whittaker 1908: 70). He does not call it this, but he does refer specifically to Comte's *Système* as a demonstration of 'the possibility of giving to the service of humanity, even without the aid of the belief in a Providence, both the psychological power and the social efficacy of a religion' (Mill 1863: 48). The internal sanction of utilitarian morality, he argues, could be developed in exactly the same way as the conscience in the Christian tradition. 'Capacity for the nobler feelings', he admits, 'is in most natures a very tender plant, easily killed . . . by mere want of sustenance'. But these higher feelings can be developed by exercise into habits (15). Like Comte, he acknowledges the necessity for external sanctions, such as the opinion of others, to bolster the internal. But he rests his optimism on the belief that men's social instincts, the desire to help others and to unite with them, which may be weak, can be nourished by education and sympathy. Taught as a religion and backed by all the external sanctions, altruism could become a more dominant feature of Humanity.

Mill clearly felt unable to be more open about religion in the restricted intellectual climate of the 1850s. One of the reasons he gave to his wife for not accepting John Chapman's invitation to review Harriet Martineau's condensed translation of the *Cours* for the *Westminster Review* in 1854 was that he would not be allowed to write on Comte's atheism which he regarded as his best aspect. There were other reasons. He wanted nothing to do with Harriet Martineau, anyway, and Chapman would expect 'an article more laudatory on the whole, than I should be willing to write' (Mill, *CW* XIV 126). He had been against the project from the beginning, since Comte's politics were so 'very bad' and the book could be 'read in French by anybody likely to read it at all' (78). But he did feel the need 'to atone for the overpraise I have given Comte and to let it be known to those who know me what I think on the unfavourable side about him' (134). Mill abandoned for the time being the project of a review but not of an attack on the unacceptable face of Comtism, which forms a strong element in *On Liberty*, the joint venture on which he worked with his wife from 1854. It was a necessity, he wrote to her the following year, to bring people's attention to the '*liberticide*' aspects of contemporary social reformers, in particular Comte (294). Yet although he is the only contemporary thinker the book mentions by name, Comte was nothing like the menace to society Mill made out (Himmelfarb 1974: 90). The necessity was a personal one, the need to distinguish himself from such an easy target of ridicule.

On Liberty, written to define 'the nature and limits of the power which can be legitimately exercised by society over the individual', points to Comte's system as an example of the increasing belief in the necessity of state interference, which Mill calls the 'despotism of society over the individual' (Mill 1859: 7, 29). It also expresses an increased suspicion on Mill's part of the power of public opinion, which could only lead to 'collective mediocrity' (119). It is particularly critical of public interference in personal matters, which is often misinformed and 'is seldom thinking of anything but the enormity of acting or feeling differently from itself' (151). Mill was to write more favourably about public opinion in his *Considerations on Representative Government* of 1861, which argues against the secret ballot on the grounds that voting is not a personal right but a public duty and should therefore be performed openly. *On Liberty* concentrates on the need to protect the individual from the public. Yet it too rests man's hope for the future on the education of the feelings which Comte had systematised. Man's egoism, it asserts, must be subordinated to his altruism, 'the better development of the social part of his nature, rendered possible by the restraint put upon the selfish part' (114). Too much state interference, Mill argues, actually prevents men 'strengthening their active faculties' (196–7). Comte's ethics, in other words, are turned against his authoritarian politics.

The more theologically liberated 1860s gave Mill the opportunity of a full and explicit discussion of the Religion of Humanity. The appearance of Littré's book on Comte and Positivism in 1863 prompted him to agree to write two articles on Comte's life and works for the *Westminster Review*, which were developed into a book, *Auguste Comte and Positivism*. Mill divides Comte's work into two: the *Cours* is seen as 'essentially sound . . . with a few capital errors', the later speculations as generally unsound with 'a crowd of valuable thoughts' (Mill 1865: 5). Mill praises Comte's 'wonderful systematization' of the philosophy of science. He had provided excellent 'methods of investigation' though he failed to supply any 'test of proof' (53–5). In sociology, he had made the creation of a science possible by his conception of its method, although he had done nothing which did not 'require to be done over again, and better' (124). He had failed to understand the peculiar nature of England's development or the contribution made by Protestantism to the development of individual conscience. There were 'no fundamental errrors in M. Comte's general conception of history' but neither was there 'any scientific connexion' between his description of the past and his prescription for the future (113–18).

Mill expresses complete sympathy, however, with the aims of the Religion of Humanity, which provided both a creed and sufficient 'sentiment connected with this creed' to meet the requirements of a genuine religion (133). Comte's Great Being, he insists, a majestic concept appealing to men's deepest needs, is infinitely preferable to a Being who bribes devotees with promises of eternal happiness. Mill calls Comte 'morality-intoxicated' (139–40) for requiring the sacrifice of all egoistic pleasures, however innocent, criticises his obsession with unity and questions the need for a complete systematisation of life. He also pours scorn upon some of the details stipulated by Comte. He finds 'nothing really ridiculous in the devotional practices which M. Comte recommends towards a cherished memory or an ennobling ideal, when they come unprompted from the depths of the individual feeling'. They only became ridiculous when prescribed three times daily for two hours. Had he not been completely lacking in humour, Mill claims, Comte would have checked his characteristically French 'mania for regulation' (153). His utopia illustrated the 'melancholy decadence of a great intellect'. Yet he was finally to be ranked with other 'great scientific thinkers' who 'shrank from no consequences, however contrary to common sense, to which their premises appeared to lead' (199–200). His greatness was part and parcel of his absurdity.

Mill's writings of the late 1860s concentrated on areas in which he disagreed with Comte, such as psychology and the role of women. In 1869, for example, he published an edition of his father's *Analysis of the Phenomena of the Human Mind* and his own analysis of *The Subjection of Women*. The first of these rests within the tradition of introspection and association dismissed by Comte while the second repeats the arguments he had used in correspondence with Comte, that women had been conditioned over the centuries into being subordinate to men. His caricature of the view that he opposes, that 'it is the duty of women, and . . . that it is their nature, to live for others, . . . and to have no life but in their affections' (Mill 1869: 27), certainly fits Comte. Mill insists that the only way to discover the natural differences between sexes is to study 'the most important development of psychology, the laws of the influence of circumstances on character' (41). This harps back to the science of ethology which had been spurned by Comte.

Mill's *Autobiography*, published after his death in 1873 but largely written in the 1850s, is less than generous in acknowledging his debt to Comte. It highlights the unacceptability of Positivist politics, describing the *Système* as 'the completest system of spiritual and temporal despotism which ever yet emanated from a human brain' (Mill 1873: 213). Mill's posthumously published *Three Essays on Religion*, however, reiterate his sympathy with the Religion of Humanity. The second essay, on the 'Utility of Religion', first recognises that religion will always be necessary 'so long as human life is insufficient to satisfy human aspirations' then asks

> whether the idealization of our earthly life, the cultivation of a high conception of what *it* may be made, is not capable of supplying a poetry, and . . . a religion, equally fitted to exalt the feelings, and . . . still better calculated to ennoble the conduct, than any belief respecting the unseen powers.
>
> (Mill 1874: 104–5)

The Religion of Humanity, in fact, is seen by Mill to provide an object of devotion, the life of the species, which is superior to that of other religions in so far as it is disinterested and does not require the intellectual sophistry of ascribing perfection and omnipotence to the creator of this world and of hell. The third essay, on 'Theism', goes further than Comte towards indulging hopes in the superhuman, treating the prospect of individual life after death as a legitimate though uncertain aspiration, postulating the existence of 'an Intelligent Mind', limited in power and love but desiring our good, and refusing to rule out the possibility of Christ's claims being at least partly true. Devotion to his memory, when not contradicted by the evidence, is a legitimate indulgence which may help to 'fortify that real, though purely human religion, which sometimes calls itself the Religion of Humanity and sometimes that of Duty' and 'is destined, with or without supernatural sanctions, to be the religion of the Future' (255–7).

Mill's support for the basic tenets of the Religion of Humanity gave some encouragement to those of Comte's English disciples who were so committed to his system as to attempt the establishment of a

Church of Humanity along the exact lines he had laid down. Some of them, however, resented Mill's criticism of Comte so deeply that they came to regard him as more of an opponent than an ally. Congreve, for example, wrote to thank Mill for the endorsement of 'a simply human religion' in his *Westminster Review* essays, regretting, however, that he should have lent his 'powerful sanction to the ridicule so freely heaped' on their religion and objecting in particular to the sentence, 'We cannot go on any longer with this trash' (Bod.L. c 185, ff.58–60). Mill, who omitted the word 'trash' from the book, explained to Congreve the importance of recognising what was ridiculous in Comte's system, of balancing admiration with criticism. Without such discrimination, he argued, 'either the absurdities will weigh down the merits or the merits will float the absurdities' (Mill, *CW* XVI 1085–6). Neither eventuality appealed to Mill, whose uncommitted coldness antagonised Harrison, who felt that his erstwhile mentor and friend had become in some ways a bad influence in spite of his 'noble qualities' (FH 1899: 287). A similar ambivalence pervades Bridges' attitude towards Mill, whose temperament he compared with that of Comte himself, concealing 'springs of deep tenderness' beneath 'a cold and stoical exterior' (*PR* VII (1899) 90).

What the Comtists resented most in Mill was what they suspected as a take-over bid on his part. His strategy in dealing with other thinkers such as Bentham and Coleridge had been similar, to set himself up as the impartial critic who could select what was truly valuable in their work. Comte, as we have seen, enters many of Mill's texts, sometimes benignly and explicitly, as in the *Logic*, sometimes covertly, as in *Utilitarianism*, and sometimes, as in *On Liberty*, as a dangerous threat to liberal values. *Auguste Comte and Positivism* and Mill's *Autobiography*, employ the same strategy, presenting Comte as

a half-thinker, while Mill's persona exemplifies the whole thinker . . . A mismatch of thinker and poet, Comte and Clotilde stand in contrast to the shining example of John and Harriet in the *Autobiography*.

(August 1975: 181)

Ironically, it seems that Harriet's death, after a lifetime of warning Mill against Comte's illiberalism, intensified his awareness of the need for subjective worship of the beloved dead along Comtean lines.

There is evidently a psychomachia, an anxiety of influence, behind Mill's comments on the precursor who shared a similar intellectual, psychological and emotional growth from an eighteenth-century 'enlightenment' education to a nineteenth-century 'romantic' reaction through nervous breakdown and a consistent struggle to overcome depression. Mill's importance in the history of Positivism, however, lies in his providing a clear model for its development along lines which Comte had not envisaged. That aspect of Protestantism which to someone of Comte's French Catholic upbringing was so abhorrent, the encouragement of private judgement, emerges strongly in Mill's eclectic treatment of the Religion of Humanity. He was the great reformer of Positivism, modifying many of Comte's ideas but also giving them a much wider publicity than they might otherwise have achieved.

George Henry Lewes: 'Reverent Heretic'

Lewes was a man of many enthusiasms. Critic, biographer, novelist, philosopher and physiologist in turn, he declared allegiance to a number of different thinkers. One of Carlyle's 'young men' in the 1830s, when his main interest lay in German thought, he also acknowledged a strong debt to Herbert Spencer for encouraging his interest in science (Kitchel 1933: 150–1). To read through his journals is to realise the astonishing range of his reading and his continuing openness to new ideas, an openness that could be interpreted less charitably as trendiness. One of the labels constantly attached to him, however, both by his contemporaries and by later critics, is that of 'Comtist'. He was, according to Frederic Harrison, the 'chief representative to most reading Englishmen of the Positive Philosophy' (*Academy* XIV (1878) 543–4). His own version of the Religion of Humanity was certainly unorthodox, combined as it was with 'a rather indefinite though sincerely held form of Unitarian belief' (Kitchel 1933: 78) which caused consternation among the Positivists at his funeral when a Unitarian minister 'half apologised for suggesting the possible immortality of some of our souls' (Locker-Lampson 1896: 316). But recent biographers have agreed that his exposition and dissemination of Comte's ideas were his chief contribution to philosophy and that Positivism imparted clarity, structure and a sense of certainty to his criticism while providing him with what amounted to a religious faith (Hirshberg 1970: 190–1; Tjoa 1977: 34, 105).

Lewes caught his enthusiasm for Comte from Mill, at whose feet he used to sit in 1842, when he 'read the *Logic* with avidity, and took up Comte with equal avidity' (Bain 1882: 65, 76). Mill was less enthusiastic about Lewes, whose 'presumptuous . . . undertaking' of 'anything for which he feels the slightest vocation' left him open to the label, 'coxcomb' (Mill, *CW* XIII 499). Comte was more impressed with Lewes when they met in May 1842. Although not fully recovered from nervous illness, he seemed both loyal and interesting (Lévy-Bruhl 1899: 63–4). Mill commented somewhat disingenuously that Lewes's admiration for Comte was all the more creditable to his character and intelligence, considering the limits of his education (69). Lewes himself was soon trumpeting Comte's merits. An article of 1843 which recognised the need for a 'common creed' upon which to reorganise society called the *Cours* 'the most memorable work of the nineteenth century' in spite of its ponderous and repetitious style (*BFR* XV (1843) 353–406). Similar enthusiasm for Comte found its way into a letter to Michelet of December 1843 (Ashton 1980: 214–15) and into an article of 1844 crediting Comte with the discovery of 'the true historical method' and 'the fundamental law of human evolution'. In him, Lewes announced, 'History has had its Newton' (*BFR* XVI (1844) 85–98).

Similar grand claims are made in the final chapter on Comte in the *Biographical History of Philosophy*, which reached a wide audience through weekly issues in 1845 and 1846. Here Comte is described as 'the Bacon of the nineteenth century'. He alone aimed to construct a philosophy '*general* enough to embrace every variety of ideas, and *positive* enough to carry with it irresistible conviction' (Lewes 1845–6: IV 245–6). Lewes's unwavering enthusiasm for Positivism pervades the whole work. It seemed to Jowett 'a poor thing to have studied all philosophies and to end in adopting that of Auguste Comte' (Abbott and Campbell 1897: I 261), but that is precisely the claim Lewes made. His enthusiasm at this stage seems to have known no bounds. A rare series of political articles on 'The Coming Reformation' written in 1847 has been called 'uncompromisingly positivist . . . even to the extent of advocating the suppression of private judgement' in the interests of attaining the Comtean goal of intellectual and social order (Tjoa 1977: 37–9).

Lewes's correspondence with Comte reinforces the impression of fervent discipleship. It began with an exchange of letters on 1 April 1846, when Lewes called on Comte at his Paris apartment only to find him preoccupied with the final illness of his beloved Clotilde. He lost no time, however, in expressing his regard for the founder of

Positivism, 'vous à qui je dois tant' (AC, *CG* III 365; Lewes to AC, 1/4/46, MAC). They eventually met on 6 April, the day after her death, when Lewes gave Comte the first two volumes of the *Biographical History of Philosophy*, with which the Frenchman was duly impressed (AC, *CG* IV 20–1). Lewes returned the compliment, reporting that he was reading the final volume of the *Cours* 'for the fourth time with encreased admiration and assent' and looking forward to the forthcoming '*Cours de Politique*'. He signed, 'your sincere friend and affectionate pupil' (224–5). Comte renewed the correspondence in January 1847 with enquiries about Mill, more praise for the *Biographical History of Philosophy*, which had made him the most complete and explicit English adherent to Positivism, and suggestions for future work (98–102). Lewes replied the following month to report in Mill 'certain differences of opinion – certain deficiencies of sympathy on some points' and to give some advice on how Comte could improve his style (240–1).

Comte continued to urge Lewes to play an even greater role in the dissemination of Positivism, and repeatedly dangled before him the carrot of leadership of the English disciples. They rarely entered into discussion of Positivism itself. Lewes's letters were relatively short. He replied sympathetically to Comte's expression of devotion to Clotilde (148–51), reported the continued success of his *History of Philosophy* and recommended Comte to read Goethe, 'the eminently *positive* nature' of whose genius he was about to demonstrate (244–5). He arranged to meet Comte again in July 1847, and expressed interest in the forthcoming *Système* (250–1). When Comte sent him an advance copy of the *General View*, Lewes's reply of October 1848, headed 'Mon cher maître', expressed unbounded admiration, especially for the 'chapter on women'. The same letter boasted some successful evangelism: 'I have the satisfaction of making a great many *Comtists*' (Lewes to AC, 9/10/48, MAC). Comte objected to the personal nature of this title (AC, *CG* IV 194–8), but in terms hardly offensive enough to explain the ensuing four year gap in their correspondence. It is possible that some letters from this intervening period have been lost.

The next surviving letter from Comte to Lewes, of August 1852, while continuing to regard him as the leader of English Positivism, contains five pages of vitriolic attack on Littré as the leader of incomplete Positivism in France, followed by further complaints against Lewes for repeating the stories of his supposed affiliation to that charlatan, Saint-Simon (AC to Lewes, 12/8/52, MAC). Lewes was unable to provide good news from his side of the Channel. He reported that a number of prejudices, against subsidies, foreigners and infidels, had combined to reduce the size of the fund he was collecting for Comte (Lewes to AC, réçu 18/8/52, MAC). The correspondence degenerated into a rather sordid squabble over the size of the subsidy and the slowness with which it was sent. A final letter from Lewes, dated October 1853, accompanied a copy of *Comte's Philosophy of the Sciences* 'in which', he wrote, 'you will see what I have done in the way of popularizing Positivism in England', enabling the public 'to form a correct idea of the only true system of thought' (Lewes to AC, Oct. 1853, MAC). Comte's reply has been lost or destroyed. It was certainly not complimentary, for he claimed to have told Lewes that his book was 'often unfaithful' and seemed 'to have been composed in haste, to get the start of Miss Martineau's publication', which was 'much more satisfactory' (AC, *Letters* 33).

The change in Comte's attitude towards Lewes appears to have taken place in September 1853, for in August he was still calling him 'un homme intéressant; quoique fort incomplet' (AC, *CI* I 85). By 17 September, however, Comte had decided that Lewes's failure to contribute to the subsidy, although he was well off, confirmed the suspicion that his primary motive in the exposition of Positivism was opportunism: 'il ne s'intéresse au positivisme que comme domain d'exploitation' (269). He could still be useful to the cause, Comte wrote on 19 September, in spite of those grave defects of character only too common among Englishmen who gained their living by writing (87). But by the end of the month Comte's impatience for the subsidy Lewes had promised could no longer be contained. The man was clearly unreliable (96). Subsequent references complain of Lewes as a deist, to be lumped together with Mill as an intellectual Positivist only, a party to the conspiracy of silence which was preventing the *Système* from becoming well known in England.

In spite of these complaints, Lewes was largely responsible for the popularisation of Positivism in England in the early 1850s through the *Leader*, which he co-edited with Hunt from its foundation in 1850. All discussion of Comte in the *Leader* is likely to have been his, since he was the acknowledged expert on the subject. When George Eliot stood in for him in May 1854, for example, she specifically mentioned 'the absence of the writer to whom the exposition of COMTE in the col-

umns of the *Leader* peculiarly belongs' (*Leader* V (1854) 447). There
were references to Positivist religion as early as August 1850 (I (1850)
469–71) and the following January Lewes announced 'a series of
articles upon COMTE's philosophy' (II (1851) 15), which eventually
appeared from April to August 1852, along with advertisements and
information relating to the Comte fund. It will be considered in the
book form in which it was later published. Even outside this series,
Lewes continued to expound Positivist principles and to deplore the
failure of English publishers to produce a translation of Comte, whose
'importance', he insisted, 'it is impossible to overestimate' (609).

The appearance of new works by Comte always brought a prompt
response from the *Leader*, although its review of the first volume of
the *Système* in August 1851 was surprisingly harsh. Accepting that
the Religion of Humanity grew naturally from the Positive
Philosophy and discussing sympathetically the part played by
Clotilde de Vaux in the elaboration of Comte's religion, it expressed
the belief that it would 'find but few adherents'. The attempt to
regulate the *details* of the future had been 'an enormous blunder'
(731). This review has been attributed to Hunt or Pigott, since Lewes
was sick and away from London at the time (Kitchel 1933: 88), but
there does seem to have been a cooling on Lewes's part towards the
details of Comte's ideas as they became evident in the later volumes of
the *Système*. The political letters in the preface to the third volume,
for example, bound as they were to 'pain all his sincere friends', were
explained as the product of his 'hermit-like retirement' (*Leader* IV
(1853) 1048). A review of the *Catechism*, in December 1852, could not
resist a smile at Comte's conception of his work as combining that of
Aristotle and St Paul (III (1852) 1189–90) while the enthusiastic
welcome of Harriet Martineau's condensed translation of the *Cours*,
'the *opus magnum* of our century', also criticised her failure to rectify
Comte's scientific errors (IV (1853) 1171–2). There was never any suggestion in Lewes's defence of Positivism that Comte was infallible but
he was quick to defend Comte against unfair criticism, objecting, for
example, to Huxley's attempt to dismiss Comte as 'a mere bookman'
in biology (1023) at the same time as welcoming serious discussion of
Positivism, however antagonistic (V (1854) 330).

One area in which Lewes disagreed with Comte was on the need
for religion to cater for a sense of the mystery of the universe. His
unfinished novel which ran in the *Leader* from March to June 1850,

'The Apprenticeship of Life', began with an episode on 'The Initiation of Faith', in which the hero preserves his religious instincts in spite of a rationalist education partly through the example of a devout Catholic and partly through the arguments of a Christian Platonist, who teaches him that 'The Soul is Larger than Logic'. Although his Christianity is based on sentiment rather than dogma, the narrator insists that 'a new development of Christian principles' is preferable to the current attempts to found a new religion (I (1850) 17–18, 42–4). The following year, Lewes returned to the formula, 'The Soul is Larger than Logic', in a review of the *Letters on Man's Nature and Development* in which he objected to the deification of law by Martineau and Atkinson as ignoring the evidence of men's natural religious instincts in the face of 'the great Mysteries of the Universe'. Atheism, he agreed with Comte, was 'the product of effete metaphysics' (II (1851) 201–3). But he went much further than Comte in the indulgence of a sense of the infinite.

Lewes added three new chapters to his original articles in the *Leader*, which were themselves based upon abstracts of the *Cours* made by Walker and Bain in Aberdeen (Bain 1904: 157), to form the first part of a book entitled *Comte's Philosophy of the Sciences* which came out in 1853. The second part, 'Social Science', was completely new. A 'Biographical Introduction' announced its evangelical intent:

I owe too much to the influence of Auguste Comte, guiding me through the toilsome active years, and giving the sustaining Faith which previous speculation had scattered, not to desire that others should likewise participate in it.

This did not prevent him from 'dissenting' from some of Comte's opinions, he explained, since 'reverence is not incompatible with independence'. He made no attempt to conceal Comte's early insanity or his late devotion to Clotilde but strongly defended his 'grand religious aim' (Lewes 1853: 2–6). He offered little in the way of evaluation of the ideas he was concerned merely to expound but made it clear, in an added chapter on Comte's cerebral theory, that 'this abstinence from criticism is not to be interpreted into entire assent' (232). The 'Conclusion' of the book went so far as to describe Comte's 'attempts to reorganize society' as 'premature' and his religion as insufficient, since it made

Religion purely and simply what has hitherto been designated Morals . . . Humanity can only be the Supreme Being of *our* world – it cannot be the Supreme Being of the Universe.

Man's 'emotions of love and awe', he argued, were bound to wander beyond the limits of this world (339–42). But Comte's morality met with his full approval, especially his view of the role of the family in the development of altruism, a word which this book is credited with introducing into the English language (*OED* I 259).

Lewes's continual puffing of Comte in the *Leader* and elsewhere, even with these reservations on specific issues, wearied some of his friends. When Carlyle asked impatiently when the series on Positivism would come to an end, Lewes claimed that they were 'exciting great interest in the English Universities, and especially at Oxford' (D. A. Wilson 1927: 418). But he seems himself to have grown cooler in his espousal of Positivism in the second half of the 1850s. His reservations about phrenology, for example, developed into outright opposition. Whereas the first edition of his *Biographical History of Philosophy* had enthusiastically acknowledged the part played by phrenology in the destruction of metaphysics, the second insisted that it be subject to the process of verification which characterised positive science. A new paragraph in the chapter on Comte made a sharp distinction between the *Cours*, 'the grandest, because on the whole the truest, system which philosophy has produced', and 'his subsequent efforts to found a social doctrine', over which Lewes proposed drawing a discreet veil (Lewes 1857: 662).

A renewed concern for the propagation of all aspects of the Positive Philosophy, however, is apparent in Lewes's work during the second half of the 1860s, especially in the *Fortnightly Review*, whose first editor he became in May 1865. Advertisements announced that the articles were to be signed and their consistency to be 'one of tendency not doctrine' but it soon became 'extensively stigmatized . . . as "a positivist magazine" ' (*FR* ns VIII (1870) 118–20). Lewes praised Comte's 'earnest effort' and 'lofty aim' in the second number of the magazine, in June 1865, although he confessed, 'I have never been able either to accept the Religion, nor recognise it as a necessary outcome of the Philosophy' (*FR* I (1865) 251). Two long articles of 1866 went into further detail. The first was both biographical and critical, tracing Comte's development from discipleship of Saint-Simon to devotion to Clotilde and deploring his abandonment of the objective for the subjective method, when 'the philosopher brusquely assumed the position of a pontiff' (III (1866) 402). Because he made no secret of his opposition to the later system, Lewes complained, other

Positivists regarded him as a heretic. But he was, thanks to George Eliot, a 'reverent heretic':

> My attitude has changed now that I have learnt (from the remark of one very dear to me) to regard it as an utopia, presenting hypotheses rather than doctrines, suggestions for future inquirers rather than dogmas for adepts, – hypotheses . . . to be confirmed or contradicted by experience.
>
> (404–5)

Comte's disciples were partly to blame for the development of a 'pontifical spirit' in his later writing, but they deserved only praise for their courageous 'efforts to establish and spread the Religion of Humanity, undismayed by the ridicule and social persecution which awaits every religious movement at its outset'. They should, however, be more open to criticism: 'the Positivist need shrink from no discussion . . . because the system claims to rest on demonstrated truth, not on revelation or authority'. Positivism was greater than Comte and could only benefit from the combination of respect and criticism of which Mill provided so good an example (405–10).

The second article considers more closely the question of 'Comte and Mill'. Lewes distinguishes Littré and Mill, as Positivists, from Comtists such as John Bridges, 'a disciple of Comte from first to last'. He accepts some of Mill's detailed criticism of Comte, agreeing with both Littré and Mill against Bridges on the question of Comte's inconsistency. The difference between the early and the later Comte, Lewes argues, was not one of purpose but of method. Social reorganisation under a spiritual power had always been his aim, but in constructing his politics he 'forsook the Method which had organised his Philosophy'. In substituting the subjective for the objective method he was

> no longer subordinating his conception to the facts . . . but was calling in the avowed aid of fictions to assist him in the construction of a scheme deduced, without verification, from sentimental premises.   (VI (1866) 396–7)

Even in his later work, however,

> the constant presence is felt of a vast meditative mind, earnestly aiming to unriddle the great mysteries of life, and to make that life nobler by a wise subjection of the lower to the higher impulses.   (406)

The imperfections of contemporary scientific knowledge made it impossible for Comte to achieve a complete system but his was the groundwork on which Positivism should build.

These two articles were incorporated in the first two sections of a new chapter on Comte in the third edition of the *History of Philosophy* along with a third section examining 'The Transformation of Philosophy into Religion', in which the Religion of Humanity was seen as the natural development of Christianity. Comte's absurdly detailed and premature utopian prescriptions had obscured the fact that his system fulfilled the two essential roles of religion, to 'satisfy the intellect, and regulate the feelings'. Meanwhile, Lewes lamented, 'Anarchy continues, and the Faith is slow in growing' (Lewes 1867: 635–9).

The five prolix and unsystematic volumes of *Problems of Life and Mind* which appeared from 1874 to 1879 can be seen as Lewes's final attempt to bring Positivism up to date, adding Bain's associational psychology and Spencer's views on evolution and heredity to a basically Comtean methodology and morality. The first volume attempts to lay the foundations of a creed, beginning with an unequivocal statement of his religious purpose. While others argue that religion is extinct, Lewes places himself among those who believe that it will continue to regulate 'the evolution of Humanity'. But it must be 'a Religion founded on Science', the only kind of faith acceptable in the new era inaugurated by Auguste Comte (Lewes, *PLM* I 1–6). In attempting to establish some 'Psychological Principles' for the conduct of Positive Philosophy Lewes writes in Comtean terms of 'two classes of Motors: the personal and the sympathetic – the egoistic and the altruistic' (109), explaining in a long footnote how his ideas relate to Comte's:

They agree in regarding Science as a social product stimulated by social needs, and constructed by the co-operation of successive generations, so that civilisation and Humanity are developed *pari passu*. They agree in subordinating individual introspection to the study of the collective evolution . . . But they differ primarily in this: he holds that Humanity develops no attribute, intellectual or moral, which is not found in Animality (1.) 624, whereas I hold that the attributes of Intellect and Conscience are special products of the Social Organism.   (125)

This last idea he derives from Spencer, but the interesting thing is that he should make such an issue of this one disagreement with Comte.

The *Problems* are as permeated with Positivism as the rest of Lewes's work. Man's proper response to suffering, he argues, is to understand its causes, to 'modify them when they are modifiable, and resign himself to them when they are unmodifiable' (168). In describing the moral sentiments he employs variations on the Positivist motto, 'Live for others':

> Moral life is based on sympathy: it is feeling for others, working for others, aiding others, quite irrespective of any personal good beyond the satisfaction of the social impulse. (166)

His faith in the future rests like Comte's on the channelling of egoism into altruism and the extension of love from the family to all mankind. The second volume of *Problems* applies the positive method to metaphysics, the third to physiology. The fourth returns to *The Study of Psychology*, reiterating the belief that 'man is distinctly a social being' whose 'higher faculties are evolved through social needs', and acknowledging once more that the 'credit of this conception is due to Auguste Comte'. Again he expresses reservations about the details of Comte's system:

> His abstention from analysis and detailed investigation kept him from specifying the mode of operation of the social factor; and his 'cerebral theory', so unsatisfactory in its method, and so fantastic in its anatomy, could not supply what he left unspecified. (IV 5–6)

Comte remained nevertheless one of the 'three thinkers with whose general principles I am most in agreement' (59). The final volume treats *Mind as a Function of the Organism*, attempting a neurological explanation of associationism. Lewes explains in a lengthy 'Note' that he borrows some terms from Comte but changes their significance (V 239). But his description of the development of egoistic desires into altruistic emotions, 'the sentiments which constitute our moral, religious, and aesthetic life', keeps fairly close to Comte (387). The *Problems*, then, as James Sully remarked, were rather 'a fuller development of Comte's principles than a departure from them' (*NQM* II (1879) 372).

Some Positivists welcomed the *Problems* in this light (*PP* XIII (1874) 94). Harrison claimed that the first volume 'must be said to carry the religious claim of positive philosophy far higher than has yet been done by any English man of science' (FH 1907b: 103). Encouraged by Lewes to review the book 'from the positivist point of view' because he believed that his position had become 'more and more one of convergence towards Comte', Harrison's initial enthusiasm soon waned (HP 1/59, f.36). The official English Positivists in general treated Lewes with the same suspicious respect as that other heretic Mill.

Congreve took an instant dislike to him, regretting that he was so inseparable from George Eliot (Bod.L. e 51, ff.307v, 310) and never relinquishing the belief that he kept her from closer involvement with the Religion of Humanity. He noticed an improvement in 'tone' when discussing Positivism with Lewes in June 1864 and was 'gratified' by 'an unqualified retraction of his criticism on Comte's style in the *Politique*' (e 62, f.160). Articles such as Lewes's in the *Fortnightly Review* in 1866, however, he regarded as 'anything but a gain':

All such discussions from amongst our apparent ranks are of course a great hindrance in that they give so convenient a handle for those who do not wish to examine. The tone of the article is very respectful, as it was certain to be, but that does not make it the less hurtful to our cause.   (e 53, ff.80–1)

He detected 'a much less critical, much more discipular spirit' in the third edition of the *History of Philosophy* (BL 45232, f.142v) but the dogmatic Positivists could never accept Lewes as truly one of their number. Harrison's obituary of Lewes distinguished between the Positive Philosophy which he espoused and Comte's social and religious reconstruction which he repudiated. More than thirty years after his death, Beesly was still complaining to the French Positivist Hillemand of Lewes's 'desire to parade his own originality' and of his 'juggling about "atheism" ' when he was 'as completely emancipated from theologism as Comte himself' (ESB to Hillemand, 22/7/10, MAC).

Lewes, it seems, fell between two stools, being despised on the one hand as a Comtist, a populariser of unpopular foreign notions which he pressed upon his friends (Tjoa 1977: 19), and suspected on the other of not being orthodox enough. As a young man he jumped perhaps too swiftly on the Positivist bandwaggon, for which he incurred the disapproval of Comte himself, who complained of 'the hollowness of the self-styled judge who endeavoured to forestall' Harriet Martineau (AC, *Con* 439), and of Mill, who was later to admit that he found it unlikely 'that any book by Lewes would be profound either in philosophy or scholarship' (Mill, *CW* XVII 1913). But there is no denying the enthusiasm with which Lewes threw himself into four decades of discussion of the fundamental problems of science, philosophy and religion which Comte raised. And there can be no doubt that he was widely read, not only at the universities but by working-men such as those celebrated by George Eliot, who met together on a Sunday to discuss his work (GE, *GEL* II 389), and even, if we are to accept George Holyoake's account, by backwoodsmen in the United States 'by camp fires at night' (G. J. Holyoake 1893: I 244). The sheer persistence with which he made Positivism a living issue for the Victorian reading public for such a sustained period of time earns Lewes a prominent place among Comte's first British followers.

Critics, translators, corrrespondents and disciples

In spite of the work of Mill and Lewes the Religion of Humanity remained, before the establishment of the official Church of Humanity in 1859, the province of a few scattered and sometimes scatty enthusiasts. There were passing references to Comte in British periodicals of the 1830s (*WR* XVI (1832) 310; *FQR* XV (1835) 491) but nothing of any substance before David Brewster's review of the first two volumes of the *Cours* in the *Edinburgh Review* which drew attention to its new scientific method (*ER* LXVII (1838) 271–308). An article by one of Mill's pupils, William Smith, in *Blackwood's Edinburgh Magazine* in 1843 set Comte's 'originality and occasional profundity of thought' against his 'bold paradoxes' and 'egregious errors' (*BEM* LIII (1843) 397–414). A specifically theological objection was voiced in the *British Critic* by the Anglo-Catholic W. G. Ward, whose general admiration of Mill's *Logic* balked at his attack on delusions of providential interference in the laws of the universe. Such primitive belief in God, Mill had claimed, was 'fit only for the earliest of the three great stages of speculation', to which Ward appended a thunderous footnote explaining that this 'detestable sentiment' had been adopted from 'a French writer' who was clearly too evil to be named (*BC* XXXIV (1843) 413). Ward's *Ideal of a Christian Church* the following year included some surprisingly sympathetic references to Comte, Mill reported, interspersed with 'deep lamentations over our irreligion' (Mill, *CW* XIII 662).

Comte's name, as Mill told him in 1844, was beginning to crop up more often in British periodicals, and the *Cours* became difficult to obtain, according to Alexander Bain, as a result of 'a great and sudden demand for the book through the country' (Lévy-Bruhl 1899: 298). Mill placed great faith in Bain, of whose 'conquest' for Positivism he wrote excitedly to Comte in August 1843 (240–1), when at the age of twenty-six he already held the chair of moral philosophy at Aberdeen. He had spent the summer studying the *Cours*, yielding his strong religious beliefs to the seemingly irresistible logic of Positivism. By the following October Mill regarded him as his natural successor, on account of his powerful mind and scientific training (356). A paper he gave to the Aberdeen Philosophical Society in 1843 on 'The Classification of the Sciences', however, already contained the seeds of heresy, inserting psychology into the orthodox Comtean series (Bain 1904: 158). It was, of course, in this forbidden area that his most fruitful work was to lie. His *Autobiography* recalled reading and admiring the *Cours* in 1843 and actually meeting Comte in 1851 before being put off by the Frenchman's arrogance and lack of humour. Bain's later embarrassment about his youthful enthusiasm for Positivism made him highly sensitive to the mere mention of his name in connection with Comte (Vogeler 1976: 18–20).

Another potential disciple who never committed himself to the Religion of Humanity but who proceeded to expound the broad principles of Positivism was George Grote, who first met Comte in 1840 and became more closely acquainted with him during his long stay in Paris in 1844. Grote held out little encouragement for the growth of Positivism in England, where there was little taste for philosophy, even spiced with specialist facts and religious rhetoric (AC, *CG* II 432). He felt insufficiently in agreement with Comte's dogmatic sociology to continue his part in Mill's subsidy after 1845 in spite of his acceptance of the main idea of the *Cours*, the substitution of the scientific for the religious point of view (Lévy-Bruhl 1899: 403). After the publication of the *General View* in 1848, in which Comte's own philosophy was explicitly developed into a religion, Grote told Comte that his allegiance was restricted to Positivism as a philosophical method. The utopia he found unacceptable (Grote to AC, 13/10/48, MAC). He told others that he found Comte's conversation 'original and instructive' but could accept only the general idea of his 'philosophy of history'. Comte's only standard appeared to be 'his own taste and feeling', which had been powerfully affected by his Catholic upbringing; he seemed to have little respect for 'the *facts* of history' (Grote 1873: 158, 202–4; Clarke 1962: 183–4). Grote's *History of Greece*, published over five years from 1846 to 1851, reflects Comte's philosophy of history, tracing three stages in the evolution of Greek thought and acknowledging a debt to Comte for 'the most profound study of the human mind' (305–6). At least one contemporary reviewer placed it firmly within 'the positive school, as represented by M. Comte in France' (*ER* XCIV (1851) 204–28).

One of Comte's closest English friends appears to have been Sarah Austin, whose 'sociabilité presque française' he found very appealing (Lévy-Bruhl 1899: 256, 294). He expounded his ideal of womanhood to her as early as 1844, along with his vision of the possibility of a systematic development of the feelings in a new form of prayer (AC, *CG* II 242–6, *Letters* 1–5). For the most part, however, Comte regarded the English sympathisers with whom he corresponded in the 1840s as incomplete, merely intellectual Positivists. He told Congreve in 1853 that he was the first to confess adherence to the movement on grounds not exclusively intellectual, citing Mill and Grote among the distinguished minds whose Positivist sympathies remained sterile through failure to progress from philosophy to politics and finally to religion (AC, *LC* 14).

What notice Comte received in the British press in the late 1840s seems to have been predominantly critical. The presidential address given by Sir John Herschel at the British Association for the Advancement of Science in 1845, printed in the *Athenaeum*, apologised for troubling the Cambridge meeting with his refutation of Comte's attempted mathematical proof of the 'Nebulous Hypothesis', but found it necessary to offset the eager reception of the *Cours* in Mill's *Logic* and Chambers' *Vestiges of Creation* (*Athenaeum* (21/6/45) 612–17). The Reverend Adam Sedgwick, Woodwardian Professor of Geology at Cambridge, also attacked the *Vestiges* for its acceptance of phrenology and for its absurd belief in Comte as a 'great mathematician' (*ER* LXXXII (1845) 11–14, 22). Many of the prominent British scientists of the early Victorian period, of course, were ordained members of the Church of England and unlikely therefore to appreciate Comte's attack on theology. A writer in the *Quarterly Review* of 1849 made the point that English scientists tended to regard nature as the 'book of God's mind' in contrast with atheistic natural philosophers in France, such as Comte, who seemed to believe that he could make a better world than he found (*QR* LXXXIV (1849) 307–44). Comte accordingly remained unpopular and unread. In 1851, the *Eclectic Review* could still refer to his work as 'but little known in England' in spite of his 'original genius' and 'profound discoveries' (*Ec.R* I (1851) 392).

The first magazine to give extensive coverage to Positivism, apart from the *Leader*, was the *Westminster Review*, acquired by John Chapman in 1851. As James Martineau commented in 1855, it was 'saved from the hammer . . . only to be delivered into the hands of a Comtist coterie' (Haight 1940: 78). Whether it was George Eliot, who agreed to write 'the article on foreign literature for each number' (30), or whether it was George Lewes who was immediately responsible, for he often wrote the 'French Summary' (Haight 1968: 97–8), reviews of Comte's works in the *Westminster* were regular and sympathetic. Of the four summaries entitled 'Contemporary Literature of France' in the first year of the new series, three began by discussing Comte. The first, in April, emphasised the importance of the first volume of the *Système*, writing somewhat sentimentally of Comte's change of heart (*WR* I (1852) 346–8). The second, in July, welcomed Littré's popular exposition of 'the greatest of modern thinkers' on the ground that Comte himself was too verbose while his 'best known English disciples' disagreed with him 'on too many points, and those often essential points, to be properly regarded as apostles of his doctrine' (II (1852) 306). There were serious and sympathetic reviews of the *Système* (614–18), of the *Catechism* (III (1853) 318–20), and of the work of Comte's French disciples (IV (1853) 302). The 'Science' section of January 1854 included a more critical assessment of Comte by Thomas Huxley (V (1854) 254–6) and another article on the *Cours* which praised its general aims but objected to its historical inaccuracy and its sentimentality in politics and religion (VI (1854) 173–94).

The *Westminster Review*'s approach was neither uniform nor uncritical. John Chapman himself was flabbergasted that Congreve should spend so much money and time on translating Comte's 'extraordinary' *Catechism*, which seemed to him 'a melancholy exhibition of egotism, vanity and the marvellous ascendancy of a woman over a great mind' (HMP 216). But the *Westminster*'s review of the book was considerably less outspoken. The first part, written by Mark Call, claimed to represent

the numerous adherents of the Positive Philosophy who, while refusing to accept the religious elaboration of the 'Politique' and of the 'Catéchisme de la Religion Positive', yet recognise the moral ideal which they believe that philosophy evolves.

These 'Protestants of Positivism' reserved the right to decide for themselves 'what portions of the doctrines and ceremonial of the Positive religion are worthy of their acceptance' (*WR* XIII (1858) 305–24). The second half of the article, written by Chapman himself, attacked Comte's 'dogmatism and inflated egoism', his repression of women and his neglect of 'the realm of mystery' (324–50).

The *Westminster Review* was behind the earliest plans to translate the *Cours*, George Eliot confiding to John Chapman her preference for Call over Harriet Martineau, whose style might be popular but whose 'calibre of mind' was suspect (GE, *GEL* I 361). Call, however, backed down, generously allowing Martineau the use of the three volumes he had already completed (Haight 1940: 214–15), while a third potential translator, Edward Lombe, prevented by ill health from completing his own version, financed the venture, with George Eliot and Henry Atkinson being nominated as joint trustees (HM 1877: II 384; GE, *GEL* II 17).

Of Unitarian background, a firm believer in scientific laws, whether of association psychology or of political economy, a convert to Saint-Simonism and still more recently to the 'Mesmeric Atheism' of Henry Atkinson, Harriet Martineau recalled in her *Autobiography* that, although familiar with Comte's name for many years, she had only 'a vague notion of the relation of his philosophy to the intellectual and social needs of the time' before 1850, when a Yorkshire friend gave her a clearer view of Comte's system and suggested she study the *Cours* for herself. She sent away for a copy and studied Lewes's and Littré's expositions of Positivism. The first volume of the *Cours* arrived on 24 April 1851, and by 26 April she 'began to "dream" of translating it'. Once the details of publication had been arranged, a novel finished, and the imposing mathematical section completed, 'the work went swimmingly'. A 'perpetual succession' of guests throughout the summer of 1853 failed to distract her from her task. Her diary recorded the 'rapture' with which she worked, the 'blessed' relation she felt towards Comte and the 'delightful glow' of her mind as she worked through her twenty to thirty pages a day, often writing with 'tears falling into my lap'. She submitted the manuscript to her friend Professor Nichol for corrections of scientific detail but otherwise refused to spoil the freshness of her translation by any 'retouching'. A desire to 'put a stop to the mischievous, though ludicrous, mistakes about Comte's doctrines and work' added to her zeal and she was merciless in her manner of putting down those among her guests who cast aspersions on Comte's sanity or importance (HM 1877: II 371–96).

The 'Preface' of the *Positive Philosophy* made the enthusiasm of its translator public, claiming great influence for Comte over 'most or all of those who have added substantially to our knowledge for many years past', influence which had remained unacknowledged only because of their 'fear of offending the prejudices of the society in which they live'. In spite of its defects of style, which were partly a result of the mode of presentation in lectures, the *Cours*, Martineau claimed, could provide the firm convictions which were a defence against 'moral uncertainty and depression'. The detailed conclusions would be modified and amplified with the growth of knowledge, but she had taken the liberty of omitting what had already been disproved by subsequent scientific advance (AC, *Phil* I v–xv). She also omitted the final ten pages of the *Cours*, eventually to be translated and added to the third edition by Frederic Harrison, who pointed out that they provided crucial evidence of the unity of Comte's career since they contained his scheme for future work (AC, *Phil* 1896: xvi–xvii).

Comte was delighted with the translation, which he included in the Positivist Library in preference to his original version, so that it was subsequently retranslated back into French. He wrote a glowing letter of gratitude, expressing amazement that a woman should have had the breadth of knowledge necessary for the task. Their names, he believed, would be inseparably united, a marvellous example of the alliance of women and philosophers which would bring about the new religion. He sent her a copy of the *Catechism* and three volumes of the *Système* so that she could acquaint herself more fully with the Religion of Humanity with which he was confident she would sympathise (AC, *LD* I ii 143–6). She gave him little ground for such optimism, however. Her matter of fact letters of January and April 1854 contrast with his enthusiastic replies, emphasising the 'social persecution' which 'attends a rejection of all theology' and pointing out that there had been no 'thoroughly favourable public notice' of her translation (HM to AC, 16/1 and 1/4/[54], MAC).

The reviews of the *Positive Philosophy* in the British press were, for the most part, extremely hostile. The *Athenaeum*, the *Literary Gazette* and the *Quarterly Review* dismissed the work out of hand (Presswood 1935: 85). *The Times* referred sarcastically to 'Compte' (misspelt throughout) as 'the prophet, or rather the divinity of a new era' who was supposed to be offering 'an entirely new theory of the world' but whose treatment of the physical sciences was only 'the old dog in a new doublet'. What was new, and objectionable, in his work was the belief in universal regeneration to be brought about by the new 'master-science' of sociology. Comte's system was altogether too

Catholic and too French for *The Times*, which found his fatalism degrading, his atheism offensive and his denial of liberty frightening (*Times*, 23/12/53, 8–9). The *British Quarterly Review* also attacked his atheism, his 'sentimental nonsense' and his 'papal tyranny' (*BQR* XIX (1854) 297–376), an additional article by Herbert Spencer challenging his accuracy even in his treatment of the sciences (HS 1901: II 1–73). William Whewell, in the *North British Review*, was particularly caustic about the influence of Clotilde de Vaux on the development of Positivism from a sterile philosophy to a sentimental religion for which he could see little future (*NBR* XXI (1854) 247–95).

Harriet Martineau herself retained only the broadest faith in the 'positive philosophy' not as the 'particular scheme propounded by any one author' but as 'the philosophy of fact', of empirical science in general (HM 1877: III 323). Henry Atkinson claimed that she was 'losing confidence' in the founder of Positivism as early as 1857 (HH 859). But her correspondence is full of requests about Positivism or, in the case of Sara Hennell, reproaches of 'you, and "Positivists" in general, not excepting Comte himself' for neglecting the benefits of metaphysics (HMP 441). Her letters of 1874 to Trubner and Company, who bought up the remaining copies of the first edition of the translation with the intention of printing a second and politely pointed out that it had taken twenty-five years to dispose of the first 750 copies, indicate a continuing commitment to the propagation of Positivism. She corrected their figures (it was only twenty-one years) and insisted,

the book must be reissued. You will agree with me that there can be no question as to putting the work within the reach of the public, whose demand is likely to increase as the next generation comes forward.

She also passed on complaints from potential readers and from booksellers of the improcurability of the book (HMP 918, 920, 922).

George Holyoake was amazed that Harriet Martineau should have undertaken the translation of Comte in the first place, considering the risks it presented to her popularity and consequently to her financial position:

It is inconceivable why she should have run these risks except from the knowledge we have of her honourable devotion to truth. Neither she nor anyone else has succeeded in quite explaining what there was in Comte to any great number of people. It was because he bore a proscribed name, and was an original thinker, that she generously determined he should be known to the English people. Not being a Comtist, she did more for Comte than any other of his disciples have. (*Sec.R* II (1877) 49–50)

Holyoake, if anyone, should have known her motives. He was one of the first to whom she expressed her enthusiasm for Comte and her high 'expectations of the *eventual* influence of this book on the public mind' (BL 42726, ff.1–3).

Holyoake had himself grown enthusiastic about Positivism in the 1850s and so impressed Comte with his energy, sincerity and subordination on a visit of August 1855 that he was asked to translate the third volume of the *Système* (AC, *CI* II 182–3) and seen as a potentially stronger leader of the Religion of Humanity in England than Congreve (AC, *LPA* 23). Within a year, however, he had disappointed all these expectations and appeared to Comte no better than a revolutionary and agitator (36, 53). He had mellowed considerably since his imprisonment for blasphemy in 1842, working with Lewes on the *Leader*, whose motto he borrowed for his own paper, the *Reasoner* (HH 1153). What he meant by Secularism was what others called Positivism, the substitution of Christianity by a humanist religion based on the teaching of science. He himself tended to use the two terms interchangeably (McCabe 1908: I 296). He welcomed Harriet Martineau's translation of the *Cours* enthusiastically in the *Reasoner*, reaffirming her claim that Comte's ideas were everywhere though his name was seldom mentioned. The *Positive Philosophy*, he announced, could be taken as a detailed and definite manifesto of Secularism, an answer to those who accused it of having nothing constructive to offer (*Reasoner* XIV (25/5/53) 321–5), 'a scientific Bible of Secularism' which could save free thought from 'incoherence or a purposeless sentimentality' (XV (30/11/53) 363–5). From 1854 a motto from Harriet Martineau on the 'Positive Philosophy' appeared on the title page of the magazine, which two years later adopted the subtitle, 'Journal of Freethought and Positive Philosophy'.

The *Reasoner*, however, drew the line at the Religion of Humanity. A long obituary article on 'Auguste Comte and his Philosophy' in November 1857 deplored his impatient refusal to wait for science to prescribe the forms of the new religion. What he had instituted 'might justly be called a parody on Christianity'. He needed fewer 'disciples' and more 'apostles' to 'develop the system creatively and independently' (*Reasoner* XXII (18/11/57) 265). Holyoake maintained friendly relations, in fact, both with apostles such as Mill and Lewes, whom he admired tremendously, and with disciples such as Congreve and Harrison. Having described Congreve as 'another of those active and accomplished disciples of Comte, everywhere starting up' (XXII (1/2/57) 18) and advertised his 1860 lectures in Cleveland Street (XXV (29/4/60) 144), Holyoake elicited a friendly overture from the founder of the Church of Humanity to 'talk over several matters' and try to resolve their differences (HH 1375). Holyoake co-operated with Harrison on political issues of the 1860s and even preached at the Temple of Humanity in Liverpool in 1883. The 'Grand Old Man of English Free Thought', as Harrison dubbed him on his eighty-fourth birthday (3852), claimed he had 'always had the Comteian mind' (R. Harrison 1965: 319).

Within Secularism itself Holyoake was constantly having to battle against militant atheists such as Bradlaugh, with whom his espousal of Positivism was distinctly unpopular. He was interested in liturgy, receiving Harriet Martineau's 'Burial Service for Secularists' sympathetically and using it for his son, Austin, who helped to compile *The Secularists' Manual of Songs and Ceremonies*. His 'positive teachings' may not have cut much ice with the working-class core of the Secularist movement (Royle 1980: 328). He dismissed Positivism himself on one occasion as 'the natural religion of Capitalists' (Budd 1977: 195). But there is no doubt that the enthusiasm he displayed for Comte in the 1850s had a lasting influence on his particular brand of Secularism.

Holyoake's attractiveness as a potential disciple, from Comte's point of view, lay in his abundance of energy and enthusiasm. For Comte was constantly exhorting John Bull to shake off his 'Anglican torpor' and commit himself to Positivism (AC, *Letters* 15). He certainly exacted a severe standard of discipleship:

I can recognise as my true disciples only those who, renouncing the project of founding a synthesis of their own, regard that which I have constructed as essentially sufficient and radically preferable to any other. Their duty is to propagate and apply it, without aiming at criticising or even improving it. (72)

It is scarcely surprising, given these conditions, that Comte's early followers in Britain were limited both in number and quality. Most of his correspondents in the last years of his life were professional men, many involved in higher education, whose critical faculties were a constant source of irritation to Comte. It should be noted that the number of non-French subscribers to his fund actually declined from 26 in 1853 to 15 in 1857, the year of his death (Murphy 1968: 110–14).

Some of Comte's early followers were distinguished academics such as Alexander Williamson, the brilliant young chemist recommended by Mill as a mathematics pupil in 1845. After three years in Paris from 1846 to 1849, he was elected Professor of Practical Chemistry at University College London. Duing this period he came to admire Comte not only as a teacher but as a religious leader. He was a founder-member of the Positivist Society in Paris and wrote long letters to Comte accepting most aspects of his system apart from his attitude towards England. He must have reiterated his views at a meeting of the Positivist Society, for a long reply of Comte's, dated 19 November, takes him to task for his nationalistic and protestant prejudices, though still regarding him as the natural leader of the Positivist mission in England (AC, *CI* I 113–28). Williamson continued the debate with Laffitte, with whom he remained on friendly terms at least until October 1853. By 1855, however, he was regarded as no longer worthy of the presidency of British Positivism (II 188) and he seems to have had nothing more to do with the movement. An obituary, half a century later, described him as an outspoken and caustic critic of dogmatic ideas and a man who seemed 'not to brook contradiction' (*PRSL*, Series A, LXVIII (1907) xxiv–xliv), which probably explains why he did not remain a disciple of Comte for very long.

Three Irishmen figured prominently among Comte's correspondents: George Allman, Professor of Botany at Dublin University and subsequently of Natural History at Edinburgh University; Henry Dix Hutton, a Dublin barrister who was encouraged by Comte to aim at the priesthood and who later published a number of expositions of the master's leading ideas, remaining a figure of interest to later generations of Positivists on his occasional preaching visits as someone who had actually known their founder; and John Ingram, who became Vice-Provost of Trinity College, Dublin, and was regarded by his colleagues as 'the best educated man in Europe' (*Times*, 2/5/07, 9). Less familiar with Comte than the others, and slower to commit himself to the Religion of Humanity, Ingram became one of the most enthusiastic advocates of a full-blooded ritual for their religion. He delivered a celebrated attack on the pretensions of economics at the British Association in 1878. Retirement left him free to publish a whole stream of translations and expositions of Comte around the turn of the century. A young Scot, Alexander Ellis, also entered into correspondence with Comte in 1854, persuading him to incorporate Shelley in the Positivist Calendar (AC, *Letters* 188–9). He tried to combine an enthusiasm for the Religion of Humanity with a belief in God, advocating a broad and liberal version of Comte's religion when he spoke on the subject at South Place Chapel in 1880.

Some of Comte's most fervent English disciples, it must be admitted, bordered on the pathological. John Fisher, a melancholic medical student at Manchester who struck Comte as a natural leader of English Positivism, used to send him effusive letters beginning, 'Reverend Father and Master', into which he poured all his hopes and grievances. He produced an over-literal translation of the *Catechism* which no-one would recommend for publication before finally falling out with Comte over his treatment of Protestantism. James Winstanley, a convert of Congreve's who was doubly delightful to Comte on account of his wealth and devotion, used to genuflect before the portrait of Clotilde, to whom he wrote poetry of adoration. He planned to build a model Positivist village on his estate near Leicester and gave large sums of money to various Positivist funds. Bursts of manic energy and enthusiasm alternated with bouts of nervous prostration, however, until the anxiety from which he could never escape led him to drown himself in 1862 in the Rhine near Coblenz, where his unrecognisable body was identified because of its clothing by the distraught Richard Congreve. His Oxford contemporaries clearly felt that his initial hypersensitivity had been exacerbated by his contact with Positivism (Brodrick 1900: 89–92; Stebbing 1900: 73). The event sent Congreve into one of his 'fits of melancholy' (GE, *GEL* IV 52), made Bridges broody and was regarded by Harrison as 'a stigma on all of us' (HP 1/37, f.44). He was one of the first, and perhaps one of the weakest, of a long line of earnest Victorians who found, or thought that they could find, in the Religion of Humanity a definite and systematic answer to the problems of their existence. Whether it appealed to them because they were depressed or whether they became depressed as a result of its teaching is a moot point.

No readily identifiable pattern emerges from this mosaic of individual responses to Comte on the part of those who came into actual

71

contact with him. Their varieties of adhesion and sympathy, like those of opposition and ridicule, anticipate the complex attitudes adopted towards his ideas later in the Victorian era. Their involvement in Positivism was partly fortuitous, the result of visits to Paris or of casual recommendations of the *Cours*. Later in the century, partly as a result of their efforts and the activities of the Church of Humanity, it became almost impossible for educated people *not* to have encountered Comte's ideas.

3

ORGANISED POSITIVISM: CHAPEL STREET AND NEWTON HALL

Richard Congreve and the Church of Humanity

Richard Congreve, the founder of the Church of Humanity in England, was a product of Thomas Arnold's Rugby School, where he kept a journal 'very religious in tone' (BL 45261, f.7), and of the bastion of Oxford evangelicalism, Wadham College. He took a first in Greats in 1840, holy orders in 1843 and a fellowship at Wadham the following year. In Pisa that September he preached what was considered 'a most Protestant, evangelical sermon' (f.20). After spending three years as a master at his old school he returned to his old college as fellow and tutor in 1849, giving the University Sermon in 1852. At that time, as his pupil Frederic Harrison recalled, he was 'the best type of a College tutor', broad and thorough in his teaching of history (FH 1911: I 83). Richard Congreve was to Wadham what Mark Pattison was to Lincoln:

idolised by every Wadham undergraduate . . . the life and soul of a not very lively common-room, and generally considered to be on the high road to the highest preferment in the Anglican Church.   (Bod.M. d 487, f.52v)

To sacrifice such prospects in favour of the religion of Humanity was generally seen as heroically misguided. For 'to choose the Positive priesthood in England, under all the circumstances of that time, was to choose obscurity and isolation' without the possibility of the rewards, in heaven or on earth, which awaited Manning and Newman (Quin 1899: 18).

Congreve's change of allegiance from Christ to Comte was gradual. He first encountered Positivism in the mid-1840s through his friends Arthur Clough and John Blackett, and his reading of Mill's *Logic* and Lewes's *History of Philosophy*. He visited Comte in 1849 but did not then regard him 'as a guide in action or as a religious teacher' (BL 45259, f.2). Unimpressed by Comte's appearance, he felt 'the power of the man' in conversation (ff.4–5). But he was conscientious as a tutor to 'abstain most carefully, from shaking the belief of those under my tuition' (ff.15–16) and 'never once referred to Comte' in tutorials (FH 1911: I 87). His influence on three of his Wadham pupils, however, Bridges, Beesly and Harrison, was to prove powerful enough to draw them all into the Religion of Humanity.

1852 appears to have been the decisive year for Congreve. Brooding in solitude over 'disappointed hopes' and 'boiling with all sorts of fierce feelings', he became, according to Harrison, 'more murderously philanthropical than ever, more crabbedly benevolent' (HP 1/3, f.8). Harrison was later to argue that it was overwork at this time which 'broke down his very strong constitution and affected his whole temperament' (FH 1911: I 85). Congreve visited Comte a second time in September and entered into correspondence with him. By January 1853 he had read the *Catechism* and the following month was assuring Comte that his real attraction was to Positivism as a social and religious system (RC to AC, 19/1, 13/2/53, MAC). Comte was especially tickled by 'la prudence anglaise' evinced by the five pound note he sent as subsidy in two separate halves (AC, *LC* 14).

Congreve resigned his fellowship in June 1854 in order to marry his cousin, Maria Bury, in July and the following May they settled in South Fields, Wandsworth, where he gave private lessons and pursued his own research. His edition of *The Politics of Aristotle* and his Edinburgh lectures on *The Roman Empire of the West* both appeared in 1855. The following summer he saw Comte for the last time and accepted his commission to write a pamphlet on Gibraltar, dating his discipleship and 'English Positivism in the true sense, the complete sense, the religious sense', from this time (Bod.M. c 347, f.103). His letters of 1857, the last two of which address Comte as 'Maître', reveal an increasing commitment to Positivism as 'une véritable Église' with a spiritual power firmly lodged in Paris (RC to AC, 20/4, 7/7/57, MAC). Such devotion clearly touched the ailing Comte, whose attitude towards Congreve changed in the last year of his life. He had previously suspected Congreve's false position as an Anglican clergyman, his lack of independence and energy. When he formally resigned his orders, however, in 1857, Comte urged him to aim at the Positivist priesthood, expressing the hope that he would long remain the leader of British Positivism (AC, *LC* 39, 58–61).

Congreve made no attempt to disguise his allegiance to Comte

5   Richard Congreve, frontispiece to RC, *Essays* III

either in his edition of Aristotle or in *The Roman Empire of the West*, which was seen through Comtean eyes as a major step in the social progress of Humanity. The essay on Gibraltar called openly for a new spiritual power in Europe, a new harmony which could be initiated by the return of Gibraltar to Spain. Another pamphlet of 1857 announced, again with Comte's sanction, that there was no moral justification for the retention of India. These views, needless to say, antagonised the British press, a fierce attack in *The Times* portraying him as a naive disciple of Comte attempting, in a manner both un-patriotic and unchristian, to enforce the absurd principle that one should subordinate politics to morals (*Times* 16/1/58, 8). The hostile reception of his pamphlet on India forced Congreve to abandon all chance of getting pupils and live sparingly on the small income he derived from some investments. One of the few offers of pupils he received at this time came from Robert Browning, but Congreve's general prospects were bleak and his outlook pessimistic. The task of converting the 'commercial middle classes' among whom he lived seemed 'hopeless' (BL 45232, f.24).

Comte's death in 1857 had changed the whole position of his disciples, who were thrown back upon themselves for the propaga-tion and development of the Religion of Humanity. Congreve's own status within the movement had risen so much as a result of the complimentary remarks Comte had been making about him during the final year of his life that it was even suggested that he might take overall direction of the movement. But he urged the appointment of Laffitte, renewing his support the following year amid complaints of the Frenchman's lack of energy and enthusiasm. The personal and political manoeuvrings which were to lead to schism can be seen to have begun about this time, for his former pupils were already growing anxious that he had become 'the victim of a system' (HP 1/4, f.11). An 'iron mould' had clamped down upon him (f.35), turn-ing him into 'a man of formulas' (1/5, f.16). He had changed beyond all recognition from the confident, energetic tutor they had known (FH 1911: I 351).

Congreve, whose translation of the *Catechism* appeared in 1858, now decided that the time was ripe to launch the Religion of Humanity in England. In January 1859, on the anniversary of Comte's birth, he delivered his first sermon to a small audience in his home in Wands-worth. They could consider themselves a Church, he assured them, since they possessed 'a faith, the outlines of a ritual, and sufficient members' (RC, *Essays* I 279). The early ceremonies were very much family affairs, with Mrs Congreve playing Mozart on the piano to a select congregation of friends. But it was not only in his own home that Congreve assumed the role of Positivist priest. A letter on the building-workers' strike of 1859, addressed to the trade union leader George Potter and translated into French for Laffitte's benefit, explained that he was writing in his official capacity as 'un Ministre de la Religion de l'Humanité' (RC to Laffitte, 16/10/59, MAC).

Each year, from 1860 to 1863, Congreve delivered a series of lectures on Positivism in a room in the basement of the Institute in Cleveland Street, off Fitzroy Square. From his notes, which are now in the British Library, it is evident that he attempted to cover the whole religious system of Positivism. The seven lectures of 1860 were entitled 'Humanity', 'Human Nature', 'Society', 'Religion', 'Labour and Capital', 'Education' and 'Practical Conclusions'. This last lecture urged both material adhesion, contribution to the Sacerdotal Fund, and spiritual adhesion, the formation of a nucleus of believers (BL 45243, ff.3–10). In 1861 he delivered a comprehensive series of thirteen lectures, the following year a completely new series, also thirteen in number, and in May 1863 a shorter course of five lectures.

By this time, however, Congreve was struggling against fatigue and depression, the fruits of overwork and failure, exacerbated by the disappearance and suicide of his wealthiest disciple, James Winstanley. A triumphant return to Oxford, where the 'recreant priest' and 'crazy fanatic' was 'welcomed at every common-room' (HP 1/37, f.21), momentarily lifted the gloom. But by the end of 1863 he was so overworked and depressed, and so bowed down with sciatica that he could hardly stand. On medical advice he spent the whole winter abroad. For the next two years he worked hard to gain the medical qualifications necessary for the Positivist priesthood and was admitted as a Fellow of the Royal College of Physicians in 1866.

The next stage in the development of organised Positivism came in May 1867 with the official opening of the London Positivist Society, for which the conditions of membership included emancipation from theology and metaphysics and the acceptance of Comte's views on science and society (Bod.M. c 347, ff.107–8). Four days later Congreve began a new series of nine lectures at Sussex Hall, Bouverie

Street, off Fleet Street. Again he preached a fully-fledged Religion of Humanity, demanding of Comte's followers the attitude of disciples. Even on minor matters, he argued, it was 'the prerogative of genius to be recognised' (BL 45243, f.46). George Lewes estimated an attendance of seventy at the first lecture, though many of these were curious rather than convinced. George Eliot expressed reservations about Congreve's 'mode of lecturing' in the second of the series; the third she found 'chilling' though the fourth was 'rather better' (GE, *GEL* IV 360). Kate Stanley attended the second but thought it 'very dull indeed and very stupid' (B. and P. Russell 1937: II 40). Congreve himself dejectedly attributed his failure to elicit a more positive response to the fashionable and aristocratic nature of his audience (RC, *Essays* III 278).

Even Congreve's supporters, however, caused him problems. A minor crisis blew up within the Positivist Society over the remarriage of one of its founder-members, John Bridges, whose first wife had died soon after his emigration to Australia in 1860. He defended his remarriage eight years later in spite of Comte's recommendation of eternal widowhood, challenging Congreve's view that Positivism must 'proceed on the principle of staid and literal adherence to Comte's precepts' and arguing the need to develop 'the tradition of the Master' (BL 45227, ff.109–18). Congreve's sympathetic reply attempted to explain further his 'discipular frame of mind'. He had looked closely at Comte's major principles before accepting them while the minor details, such as the colour of the flag, were not worth questioning. Once the Religion of Humanity had been tried, he agreed, 'the experience of mankind will modify and enlarge' it, but for the moment unity could more easily be preserved by everyone's complete adhesion. The letter ended by expressing the hope that Bridges would continue to co-operate on social and political questions, as did Beesly and Harrison, who were also outside 'the pale' (Bod.L. c 185, ff.14–20).

Bridges questioned 'this pale . . . the degree of adherence necessary to constitute a Positivist', claiming to speak for many who were prepared to acknowledge

the gradual and organic growth of a new Spiritual Power, to whom yet the acceptance of a complete and detailed organization, not the result of centuries of growth, but springing at one jet from a single mind, is utterly impossible.

He suggested five basic principles of Comte's on which all could agree as a broader basis for Positivist allegiance (BL 45227, ff.120–4). Harrison, meanwhile, seems to have grown less critical of Congreve and agreed to join the Positivist Society in 1867 although he found Congreve's dry lecturing style no better than before. Beesly, who supported Bridges' remarriage, appearing 'rather glad that so foolish a rule should be broken' (Bod.L. e 53, f.168), joined the Positivist Society in May 1869.

All three of Congreve's former pupils co-operated with him in the establishment of the Positivist School at 19 Chapel Street, Bedford Row. At the inaugural meeting on 9 April 1870, Congreve explained the choice of the word 'School' rather than 'Church' or 'Club' to indicate the manner in which they were aiming to change public opinion. There would be no 'literary lectures', not even any 'single lectures', but coherent courses. The Positivist Society would meet there on Wednesday evenings, holding additional meetings of a 'religious character' on Sundays (BL 45243, ff.60–6). Harrison hoped they would continue as before and not come forward as apostles of a new church. His worst fears were confirmed when Congreve introduced into Chapel Street in July 1870 a tablet of white marble with the Positivist formulas engraved in bright green letters, 'a truly fantastic thing':

Religion of Humanity

Love for our principle
Order as our basis
Progress for our object

Live for others

Harrison promised to 'treat it with contempt' in order to show his dislike of all religion, complaining that Congreve was too indelibly a priest 'and what is once in a man who has had the bishop's hand on him can't come out'. He asked Beesly,

Do *you* worship the Great Being, do you publicly praise and bless him, do you privately pray to him, do you practise the sacraments?   (HP 1/16, ff.73–9)

Harrison clearly did not.

The differences of attitude between Congreve and Harrison continually flared up during the 1870s. In March 1872, Harrison wrote to explain why he did not wish to contribute to Sémérie's review. He felt that Positivism could be spread without 'a formal society':

I still retain as strongly as ever my old opinion that the real task before those who adopt Comte's conceptions is to work for the spread of Positivist convictions and Positivist life, and to leave the formation of a formal Church . . . to the spontaneous and natural result of a considerable society finding itself permeated with the same sentiments and faith.

They should avoid becoming 'a sect'. Positivism gave him 'a religious basis for life' in 'the conscious service of Humanity'. But he found no enthusiasm for the ritual envisaged by Comte and would 'wait to see how a sufficiently large body of opinion might show any disposition to adopt it' (BL 45228, ff.239–44).

The fragile foundations of the Positivist Society were further shaken by the scandal over a young French Positivist called Pradeau who came to England in 1871 with a young lady whom everyone assumed to be his wife. When it emerged after the birth of their son that she was his mistress and that he had left his wife in France, the Positivists were duly shocked, even more so when Congreve accepted the situation rather than insist on separation or excommunication. The atmosphere at the Positivist Society became so bad that Congreve anticipated 'a certain schism in our body' (Bod.L. e 63, f.50). Both Beesly and Bridges sent private letters to Congreve urging 'the severest condemnation' of Pradeau's behaviour (BL 45227, ff.47–52, 134–40) while a joint letter signed by a number of leading Positivists expressed concern about their public image, especially among women (45242, ff.15–20).

The immediate effect of the Pradeau affair, which Congreve eventually referred to Laffitte, director of Positivism in Paris, who characteristically left things as they were, seems, surprisingly, to have been to bring the English Positivists closer together. On 16 December 1872, Beesly called on Congreve to explain that his former pupils still supported him on everything but this one point. Congreve reported to his wife that they were all coming to accept the religious side of Positivism, even Harrison (Bod.L. e 54, f.65). Emboldened by this unexpected support, he began to make his lectures at the Positivist School 'more and more directly religious' (e 63, f.105). Harrison's increasing respect for the rituals of Positive religion is evinced by his offering his two sons for the Sacrament of Presentation in February 1874, the year in which Congreve was lecturing on the sacraments. He was still regarded by his former tutor as 'the most lukewarm Positivist among us' and partly responsible for their lack of success

(BL 45231, f.203v). But Congreve's annual addresses from 1875 to 1877 proceeded to expound Positivism as a form of 'Human Catholicism', which differed from Roman Catholicism only in abandoning belief in God. In other respects, in organisation and in social aim, the two were identical (RC, *Essays* II 225–320).

The Pradeau affair blew up again briefly in May 1876 when the children of the illicit union were put forward for Presentation. The following month Beesly expressed a difference of opinion on 'the degree of importance to be attached to forms, ceremonies and symbols of conformity'. But he avowed an increased support for 'the religious organisation of Positivism' (BL 45227, ff.56–7) and the following year suggested that the Positivist School should experiment with some liturgy. Congreve was overjoyed. He had been waiting till 'the time was ripe' and Beesly's encouragement spurred him into action (45242, f.181v). The first ordinary Sunday 'service' of the Religion of Humanity was held on 8 July 1877, when Congreve stressed that although the liturgy and ritual had not been fully developed, the meetings were services and not lectures (45246, f.4). Doctored passages from the *Imitation of Christ* were combined with excerpts from a wide range of other writers. Prayers, which Beesly found 'admirable', were introduced (ESB to A. Crompton, 28/11/77, BP 1).

Some of the French Positivists, eager to progress towards more religious observance and political involvement, were impatient with Laffitte's lethargic direction of the movement, and so when Congreve was in Paris in June 1877 it was suggested that he might stay there to 'strengthen the direction'. Audiffrent and Sémérie wanted him to take over from Laffitte, but, as Congreve himself came to realise, 'miscalculated the strength of the discontented party' (BL 45259, ff.53–60). Congreve issued a 'Circular', in both English and French, inviting all who agreed with him that Laffitte had failed to impart a religious character to the movement to group themselves around his leadership. Few, in fact, took the opportunity and the separatist group which was set up by Audiffrent soon severed the English connection altogether.

The crisis spread to England when on 1 May 1878, Congreve 'suddenly announced his withdrawal from the Positivist Society', declining to name a successor since 'he considered the society at an end' (LPS 1/1). At the following week's meeting of the society, on 8 May,

Beesly nominated himself President, whereupon Congreve's supporters withdrew. Throughout the year, various members of the
society circulated their opinions, in printed pamphlets and handwritten letters. Bridges' *Appeal to English Positivists* and Beesly's
Remarks on Dr Congreve's Circular placed the blame on personal
ambition rather than difference of doctrine. Congreve's *Answer to
Dr Bridges* attacked the intellectualism and disloyalty of his former pupils. A Positivist schism was inevitable. A practical problem
arose over the use of the room in Chapel Street, but after two
stormy meetings of the Positivist Society in October and November,
Beesly, Bridges and Harrison withdrew their claims to its un-
disputed use, which had been the only condition under which they
would have remained.

One of the first consequences of the schism was that the Positivist
School became known unequivocally as the Church of Humanity,
since Congreve no longer felt inhibited in his role as priest. His address on the anniversary of Comte's death in 1879, entitled 'De Propaganda Fide', insisted with evangelical fervour on 'the personality of
relation' to the founder of their religion, although he was to be
venerated as a model of religious cultivation rather than an object of
worship (RC, *Essays* II 683). His annual address for that year admitted
responsibility for the schism, claiming that it was his duty to make 'a
bolder, fuller, more direct assertion of the religious aspect of our doctrine' and reported 'the slow creation of a liturgy' in the course of the
year, although the services remained as yet 'rudimentary and tentative' (366–7). He was more optimistic in private, seeing 'the disappearance of the triumvirate' as 'a real gain to me and to the cordiality
and homogeneity of our meetings'. Both sides now had greater
freedom to spread Positivism in their own different ways (BL 45231,
f.254). The Festival of Humanity on New Year's Day, 1881, brought
the first use of the organ in Chapel Street, when Congreve promised to
bring a more overtly religious character to their services. The borrow-
ing of Anglican liturgy, he explained, was a temporary measure until
a distinctively Positivist public worship had developed (RC, *Essays* II
404–26).

Chapel Street soon became identified in the public mind with the
self-consciously clerical wing of Positivism. Congreve described it in
the *Pall Mall Gazette* in 1884 as 'a modern Catholic Church' with 'the
beginnings of a ritual' (*PMG* XXXIX (17/1/84) 1–2) while a series on

6   The Church of Humanity, Chapel Street, LPS 5/4

'Typical Churches' in the *Daily Mail* gave a full description of the building, complete with an altar at the east end 'draped in crimson velvet, edged with gold lace'. Above that, 'in the place of a reredos', was the tablet which had been introduced in 1870, and hanging over that an engraving of the Sistine Madonna. There were fourteen busts around the walls, representing Comte and his thirteen calendar saints, an organ, a lectern and a pulpit (*DM*, 13/9/87, 3). Malcolm Quin complained that it 'looked like an image writer's or phrenologist's shop'. Congreve's low-church background combined with the fastidiousness of his congregation, who 'considered hymn-singing a little beneath them' and never knelt for prayer, to produce a form of service whose frigidity offended the more liturgically adventurous. For Congreve had no feeling for art, no sense of ritual. 'He administered his sacraments,' Quin observed with astonishment, 'in an ordinary morning coat' (Quin 1924: 87). Sydney Style also found Chapel Street 'dry as dust' (McGee 1931: 198). The resemblance to 'any other church' was said to have been completed by the sight of Lord Houghton sleeping through the service (Pollock 1933: 100).

The 'Ordinary Morning Service' at Chapel Street was certainly a dry form of celebration. A recitation of the Positivist mottoes and of some quotations from the Bible and the *Imitation* led to a sort of bidding prayer which announced the intention of all 'believers in Humanity' to devote themselves to her service. A further rubric explained the function of the music, readings and petitionless prayers which preceded a lengthy invocation of the Great Power, Humanity. A reading from the *Imitation*, 'or some other religious book', introduced a variety of collects for the family, the country, and the west. A second reading, from the works of Auguste Comte, gave way to an 'Act of Commemoration' of the founder, which was followed by the sermon. After the sermon came a poetical reading, often George Eliot's 'Choir Invisible', a concluding prayer and then the 'Benediction'. A final rubric reveals that there was 'Music at the beginning and the end of the whole service and before and after the sermon' (RC 1898: 3–14). This was a concession on Congreve's part to what he saw as the weakness of his congregation.

A Positivist ecclesiastical year soon developed, with the Festival of Humanity as its highlight. This was graced with an 'Advent Collect' looking forward to 'the perfect day', when Humanity would be known to all, and a special liturgy of its own, complete with responses of the people to the priest (15–18). Additional festivals were introduced, such as the Day of All the Dead in 1879, the Festival of Holy Women in 1880, the Festival of the Virgin Mother in 1885 and the Commemoration of Auguste Comte's Birth in 1890 (McGee 1931: 117–18). All these were represented among the 'Prayers for Special Occasions' along with seven of the nine sacraments, although an additional note confessed that the sacraments of Retirement and Transformation had yet to be administered (RC 1898: 29). The commemorations of Comte's birth and death involved elaborate invocations of the

Great Teacher and Master, Auguste Comte, Revealer of Humanity to all her children, Interpreter of her Past, Prophet of her Future, Founder of her Religion, the One, the Universal Religion, to which all other Religions bear witness. (33)

84

A Positivist Creed.

I believe in the unity of science and religion demonstrated by Auguste Comte — real, useful, beautiful.

I believe in one great power, Humanity, ever growing, for whom the Gods have been regents — who now appears as the real principle of the world — for whose service we should perfect ourselves — in whose service we shall find true happiness.

I believe in immortality by our influence on the future, having derived our faculties from the past, we should live for others in the present, so as to live in Humanity after our death.

I believe in the innate benevolence of mankind; and in its ability, under the influence of Humanity, to discipline the selfish instincts and make them a source of good instead of evil.

I believe in duties, not rights — in mutual duty to respect the strong and protect the weak — in the duty of man to honour and maintain woman and to free her from all labour which prevents her exercising her holy influence on the family, the source of love.

I believe in the responsibility of every man for the due use of his faculties and of the property entrusted to him by society, and for the collective acts of the society in which he is a citizen.

I believe in the coming of the reign of Humanity — when love and duty shall finally conquer selfishness — when order shall prevail supported only by moral force — when all nations shall be united in brotherhood as children of Humanity.

7   A Positivist Creed, Bod. M. c 347, f. 176

As a final flourish, and 'a reminder that Italian is to be . . . the universal language', there was a translation of the Positivist mottoes into Italian and an adaptation of Dante's modification of the Lord's Prayer in the *Purgatorio*, 'O Madre nostra, che in terra stai', with three stanzas from the *Paradiso* (43–4).

The liturgy, Congreve had to admit, was not a tremendous attraction. 'The Sunday mornings', he confessed in 1887, 'are thinly and irregularly attended – our lukewarmness is to me astonishing' (Bod.L. e 67, f.246). But in numerical and geographical terms the Religion of Humanity continued to expand throughout his lifetime. Branches of the movement opened in Liverpool, Birmingham, Newcastle, Leicester and Cambridge, and Congreve was conscientious in visiting these provincial pockets of Positivism. He continued to refer to this expansion whenever he needed to reassure himself or others of the eventual triumph of their cause. But his letters to the Irish Positivist, John Ingram, reveal his awareness of the stagnation into which Positivism had sunk:

> We are in a curious movement, I suspect, a species of backwater. People who hoped for a more rapid advance than has taken place or could take place took an interest in Positivism for a time and on disappointment are warning others of the failure. The Timorous and Mistrust of the Pilgrim's Progress have their permanent counterparts.

He could not understand how others could think that the movement was growing (BL 45233, ff.46, 106).

The slowness of the Religion of Humanity to win popular support made Congreve's periodic bouts of depression deeper and more frequent. His letters refer repeatedly to headaches, tiredness and ill health, on account of which he was forever escaping to the Continent. His health grew steadily worse. An unspecified surgical operation of 1888 and a lithotomy followed by a paralytic stroke in 1896 led up to his eventual death from apoplexy on 5 July 1899. As he grew older and more infirm he seemed to gain in bigotry and narrow-mindedness. The last two volumes of his *Essays*, published in 1892 and 1900, chart this development in the form of his 'Annual Addresses on the Festival of Humanity' and other sermons delivered on various Positivist occasions. His emotionalism, his fundamentalism and his anti-intellectualism are constantly in evidence (Presswood 1935: 283). He continued, however, to attack 'that unlimited exercise of private judgment which is a fundamental dogma of Protestantism' (RC, *Essays* III 324) while his intolerance of incomplete adherence to the Religion of Humanity reached a peak in his opposition to the proposal to erect a statue of Comte in Paris in 1898, the centenary of his birth. It was, he complained, a suggestion from 'the official world of our time' to make 'a cheap atonement for their past years of neglect', involving a suppression of the truly religious nature of Positivism (339–41). Congreve's reaction to any recognition of Comte's importance on the part of partial sympathisers was to emphasise what they did not accept. He was not satisfied, for example, when in 1896 the *Revue des deux mondes* called Comte 'the greatest French thinker since Descartes'. 'What concerns us more than any literary expression', he insisted, 'is the question how far the Religion is making way' (382).

Congreve's coldness and formality, his habitual sadness and solemnity, seems to have been both a cause and a product of the failure of the Religion of Humanity to achieve any real success as an institution. 'He had no aptitude for making a popular appeal' (McGee 1931: 44). George Eliot soon discovered the coldness of heart under his 'beaming face' and 'benignant' look (GE, *GEL* III 53, 70). Bridges suggested to Laffitte that she was deterred from closer involvement with the Religion of Humanity by his narrow fanaticism and formality (10/2/81, MAC), a view endorsed by John Morley, who reported that she

more than once assured me that she saw no reason why the Religion of Humanity should not have had a good chance of taking root, if Congreve, its chief authority and expounder in our island, had only been blessed with a fuller measure of apostolic gifts.   (Morley 1921a: 62)

All who heard him speak seem to have been struck by his lack of enthusiasm. William Knight found him 'curiously desultory' (Carver 1976: 48), Moncure Conway 'curiously academic' (Conway 1904: II 345). The *Liverpool Daily Post* described him in 1880 as 'an exceedingly mild-spoken gentleman' whose voice, though 'weak and thin', revealed a mind 'thoroughly made up', never making an effort to be better heard or swelling 'into a current or even into an eddy of warmth' (*LDP* 30/3/80, 4). Malcolm Quin, although impressed by his piety and 'spiritual distinction' as well as his handsome face and white whiskers, could not conceal his disappointment at his coldness

(Quin 1924: 96–7). The failure of the Church of Humanity in England was at least partly due to the personal limitations of its founder.

The schism: problems of personality and liturgy

The Positivist schism of 1877–8, which led to the formation of Newton Hall as a rival centre to Chapel Street, presents one of the most fascinating aspects of the whole movement: 'In its absurd extravagance it throws light on the Soul of Man under Victoria' (R. Harrison 1965: 318). It is somewhat absurd, partly because of the contrast between the intensity of feeling it generated among the small body of men to whom it was of extreme importance and the amused indifference of the outside world. The combatants were certainly extravagant in the amount of energy they threw into the conflict, as a result of which there is a superabundance of printed and manuscript material relating to it. The dispute has generally been interpreted as an attempt on Congreve's part to take over from Laffitte as overall director of the movement and to impose a ritualistic form of the Religion of Humanity upon a number of other Positivists who were by inclination and temperament basically non-religious. It was, however, his dryness which many English Positivists found repellent. He had, it is true, a strong sense of the spiritual authority of the priesthood but was singularly unimaginative in evolving new forms of worship. An analysis of the correspondence between the leading Positivists and of the liturgical developments which took place at Newton Hall in the years following the schism reveal that, although Beesly, Bridges and Harrison had a different understanding of the 'religious' nature of Positivism, they were in many respects more alive to the liturgical possibilities of poetry and music than their more conservative counterparts at Chapel Street.

Part of Congreve's motivation for challenging Laffitte's direction of the international Positivist movement in 1877 had been sheer impatience with the Frenchman's easy-going inefficiency. Urged by Beesly to impart a more religious nature to the movement (ESB to Laffitte, 7/1/78, MAC), Laffitte proposed weekly meetings along the lines of the Positivist School in London, and proceeded to present the schism as an entirely personal rebellion on Congreve's part. But those who remained under Laffitte's direction were soon complaining about his inactivity, for instance his failure to condemn French imperialism in North Africa, although Harrison eventually became resigned to his inefficiency and developed a genuinely warm relationship with him.

The real problems of personality were within the English movement itself. The attitude of Beesly, Bridges and Harrison towards their former tutor had grown increasingly critical while his suspicion of them approached paranoia. Beesly's account of Congreve's resignation and attempted disbandment of the Positivist Society on Wednesday 1 May 1878 claimed an atmosphere of sweetness and light all round (ESB to Laffitte, 19/5/78, MAC). But this unnatural restraint could not and did not last. The debates that raged throughout the Positivist Society in the summer of 1878 were almost entirely personal. Harrison's letters to Congrevites such as Thomas Sulman and Joseph Kaines insisted that the case against Laffitte was 'not of moral obliquity, not of doctrinal error, but of administrative weakness' (BL 45242, f.141). The meeting of the Positivist Society of 2 October was occupied almost exclusively with a discussion of the relative merits of the two leaders, with supporters of Laffitte countering the attacks on his inefficiency by casting aspersions on Congreve's motives (ff.147–58; LPS 1/1).

Congreve in turn complained that his former pupils had failed to offer him 'the commonest respect and esteem', let alone 'any cordiality of co-operation' (BL 45242, ff.181–2). James Cotter Morison interpreted the schism as a deliberate move by Congreve to rid himself of his three former pupils, whom he could not accept as colleagues in spite of, or even because of the fact that they were better known to the public than he was himself (JCM to Laffitte, 19/10/78, MAC). Congreve often referred to Beesly, Bridges and Harrison together, as a conglomerate threat to his leadership of English Positivism, but there is a discernible difference in his attitude towards them as individuals. Beesly appears to have been the least objectionable, the most useful and most sociable among them, the one of whom he had the highest hopes, although this only made the break with him the more difficult to endure. Beesly dwelt on the contrast between Congreve's imposing exterior, worthy of a medieval Pope, and his narrowness of mind and personality (ESB to Laffitte, 4/11/78, 2/5/83, MAC) but paid tribute in an obituary to his former tutor's courage and commitment (*PR* VII (1899) 149–51).

It was the remarried Bridges, according to Congreve, who posed the greatest problem in the early 1870s (Bod.L. e 63, ff.116, 146). Bridges explained to Laffitte that Congreve's dominant personality could tolerate no form of opposition, even over minor details. His self-evident goodness and zeal tended to blind people, on first acquaintance, to his despotic leadership and his excessive formality, both of which repelled those who had to work with him (JHB to Laffitte, 12/10/77, 7/1, 10/2/78, MAC). As the schism widened, so Bridges' language increased in venom, until he was warning French Positivists against a dangerous and ambitious fool whose continued leadership of the English movement would have left Positivism stranded as a narrow fanatical sect.

Harrison was perhaps the most vitriolic in his attacks on the man he held responsible for the schism. He had to reassure Laffitte that these attacks were only made in private and to friends, to whom he indulged his feelings about Congreve's hypocrisy. In 1883, when Congreve donated some money to the central fund as a gesture of goodwill, Harrison warned Laffitte not to be taken in; there was no real abatement in his hostility and jealousy; he still forbade his supporters to contribute directly to the central fund and incited the women over whom he had influence to violate even the most common courtesies (FH to Laffitte, 21/3/83). Harrison grew increasingly hostile and suspicious, especially after the attacks on Laffitte in 1889 by Congreve's South American sympathisers. Congreve, he believed, would cling to his episcopal staff for ever and was quite capable of renewing war at any time (17/1, 5/7/89). By the 1890s Harrison had lost all vestige of sympathy for his former tutor's 'ridiculous mewling' and 'grotesque aping' of Catholicism (HP 1/40, f.26).

In the world beyond Chapel Street, of course, the Positivist schism was not treated with quite the same intensity of feeling. Congreve and his supporters continued to foster the general notion that it was a division between the 'religious' and the 'philosophical' Positivists, between those with Congreve's 'spirit of apostolic zeal' and 'the free lances' who preferred to operate independently in a broader sphere (BL 45242, ff.183–5). The 'free lances' themselves repudiated this label along with the suggestion that they were not truly 'religious'. Harrison insisted that religion had a wider meaning for Positivists than to 'utter praises to Humanity, and invocations to union' (ff.186–93). Disparaging the 'repetition of unmeaning formulas' and the identification of religion with outward forms, he claimed to detect 'a more religious atmosphere' in Paris than in London (f.142v).

The debate clearly hinged on the meaning of the word 'religion'. The supporters of Laffitte, accused of irreligion, adopted the tactic of redefining the word, insisting that this was central to Comte's thought. Bridges, for example, in his *Appeal to English Positivists,* denied Congreve's complaint that Laffitte had shown himself unable to implant 'a religious character' on the movement, pointing to the beginning of the *Catechism* for 'the only sense in which the word Religion has for the Positivist any meaning', a spiritual harmony of thought, feeling and action, united in the service of Humanity. Laffitte had accepted all along the necessity of a priesthood for social regeneration and the precedence of worship over doctrine. But he had seen 'the extreme danger of premature public manifestations when there was not a sufficient basis of conviction and feeling behind them'. Liturgical forms must spring from inner spiritual life (ff.168–72).

Even with regard to outward forms, Beesly claimed, the supporters of Laffitte had not been behindhand. The 'commencement of liturgical worship at the Positivist School on Sunday mornings' had been suggested by Harrison and himself (f.173v). His 'sonorous "Amen" ' to Congreve's first public prayer to Humanity was recalled years later (*PR* XXIII (1915) 173). His letters to Laffitte during and immediately after the period of the schism also indicate a genuine desire for increased religious observance. He sent Laffitte a copy of the order of service Congreve had introduced at Chapel Street with enthusiastic comments on its success (ESB to Laffitte, 7/1/78, MAC). The schism made no difference to Beesly's view that Congreve had been quite right in attempting to establish a proper church (29/12/78). When the supporters of Laffitte found a temporary home in the Strand, Beesly explained that the profane character of the room had led them to adjourn the question of a public cult. There were differences of opinion, anyway, about the precise form it should take, some supporting prayers, others quotations from poetry, while some preferred a talk, pure and simple. Beesly hoped in the end to develop a cult which would satisfy the heart without insulting the intelligence (14/1/79).

The whole question of worship was brought into the open by Beesly's annual address on *Some Public Aspects of Positivism* at the beginning of 1881. In describing their meetings, with readings and a discourse, he warned,

we shall be wise not to label this as 'worship' and 'service' as if it were the only or the principal way of worshipping and serving Humanity. Above all let us beware of making its performance a criterion of the religious character of Positivism.

Speaking for myself, I no longer see any way to an immediate development of liturgy, ritual, or ceremony, beyond what has been attempted by our co-religionists in France.

It was necessary first to build up a strong foundation of private worship, allowing outward forms to develop spontaneously from inner modes of thought. At the moment they ran the risk of a 'crude importation of terms, forms, and usages' from Christianity. Beesly wanted particularly to avoid the gloomy protestant gulf between sacred and profane, and to return to the civic ceremonial of polytheistic worship intimately connected with art and entertainment. The Positivist sacraments were to be envisaged as community occasions in this general sense. Comte, who had been so meticulously detailed about many aspects of Positivism, had wisely left no clear instructions about such festivals of the future (ESB 1881: 9–13).

Bridges was equally dubious about the value of a liturgy which was a mere parody of Christianity. He felt that some of Congreve's aims were valid, particularly his wish to see the Positivist body as a church rather than a literary coterie; if Laffitte made some steps towards a religious organisation, he insisted, he could avert a schism (JHB to Laffitte, 10/2/78, MAC) or at least place himself in the position of orthodoxy upbraiding a schismatic heresy (8/10/78). Congreve's obscurantism, Bridges argued, had plunged official Positivism into antagonism with the broad stream of contemporary thought, repelling sympathetic inquirers by his premature attempts to organise a cult which fell too easily into imitation and parody of the forms used to worship God (7/2/79). It had taken three centuries for the Catholic Church to achieve unity, he commented, and might take Positivism just as long (16/5/79). The Religion of Humanity under Congreve had degenerated into the repetition of formulas, whereas a more profound religious spirit was required, stemming from private prayer (26/5/79). Bridges became increasingly critical of the ossification of Positivism which he attributed to Congreve's clerical antecedents and his lack of scientific training. The liturgy repelled more than it attracted because it was a parody of Anglicanism, unconnected with its philosophical and scientific roots. Demonstrated religion should differ from revealed religion in accepting the limitations of its founder, who was the first of men, not the last of the Gods (26/8/79). Bridges remained sympathetic towards Christianity as a religion which had not reached the positive stage. He remained fundamentally opposed to irreligion and materialism (8/4/80).

Some of the issues raised in these letters reappear in Bridges' address on 'Prayer and Work' given on the Festival of Humanity in 1879, the year of his reluctant presidency of the London Positivist Committee established by Laffitte. Prayer, he explained, was the purification of feeling:

Communion with Humanity, then, that is to say, the attempt to bring before ourselves strongly and definitely that stream of continuous effort for good, whether material or moral, which has flowed from the first ages till now, and which is the source of our spiritual life, would seem to be the sole centre and stronghold of Positivist prayer.

Private worship centred upon the basic feelings of love within the family. He remained unenthusiastic about public worship. Comte himself had never attempted to construct a Positive liturgy and Bridges felt that it was possible to attend Christian services 'without hypocrisy, rather with deep and unfeigned sympathy' (JHB 1907a: 10–11, 16–18). He retained an aversion to reciting the Positivist formulas and complained bitterly when he thought Harrison was leading Newton Hall in the direction of Chapel Street in an imitation of Anglican practice, 'to go to church once, or twice, a Sunday, and to have a "Service" ' (HP 1/24, f. 37). Liturgy, he argued in the *Positivist Review*, did not 'grow up in the night like Jonah's gourd' but needed time to develop organically. To 'set up an artificial religion with rites and ceremonies borrowed from the Catholic Church' was like planting cut flowers in soil. The sacraments, he agreed with Beesly, should be based on the ancient Roman rather than the Christian model, as formal declarations of loyalty and devotion linking the private to the public life (JHB 1907b: 48–53).

Frederic Harrison's attitude towards the liturgical celebration of the Religion of Humanity developed from his initial violent rejection of Congreve's formulas in 1870 through participation in the sacraments in the 1870s to his even urging George Eliot to contribute something to Positivist liturgy in 1877. Two discourses given by Harrison immediately after the schism insisted that the change that had taken place within the movement was 'a change of persons only'; they retained the same faith in the Religion of Humanity (FH 1879: 5). On the Festival of Humanity, 1880, after repeating Comte's mottoes, he entered into a prolonged exhortation of the congregation and glorification of Humanity, recalling a variety of her benefactors and saints (FH 1880: 3–5). He insisted that their movement was neither 'a mere philosophical school' nor 'a political party' (10), neither a sect nor a social movement. It was rather 'a religious community', even if it interpreted religion in a broader sense than conventional piety (15).

In nominating Harrison as his successor to the presidency of the London Positivist Committee in April 1880, Bridges claimed that the principal phenomenon within their movement in the two years since the schism had been his increase in zeal (JHB to Laffitte, 8/4/80, MAC). Concrete proof of this was his erection of a small Positivist chapel or oratory attached to his house, in which his son, Austin, recalled that Sunday worship included prayers, collects and addresses (A. Harrison 1926: 86). Bridges described the proceedings there as more akin to ancient Greek and Roman traditions than Christian solemnities:

Quelques lectures saines et fortificantes, des aspirations très simples pour le progrès moral, privé ou public, quelques paroles commémoratives sur le saint ou le héros du jour – voilà tout, mais c'est beaucoup – parce que cela ne choque pas par des formalités ennuyeuses ou mystiques.

It was precisely by such natural and spontaneous means that Bridges hoped that the cult would gradually develop (JHB to Laffitte, 28/4/80, MAC).

Harrison had consulted Laffitte on the symbolic decoration of his oratory, which contained busts or paintings of the thirteen principal saints in the Positivist Calendar with Holbein's portrait of the Blessed Virgin Mary occupying a central position above a bust of Comte himself. There were nearly sixty additional busts of other Positivist saints and five prints representative of the principal phases of modern civilisation. He was more tentative about the decoration of the building in Fleur-de-lis Court, off Fetter Lane, Fleet Street, which was leased by the London Positivist Society from 1881 and renamed Newton Hall after Sir Isaac Newton, who had first acquired it for the Royal Society Museum. Laffitte was invited for the official opening on 1 May, and Harrison wrote anxiously to ask him whether or not to hang a large reproduction of the Sistine Madonna on the wall. He wanted to avoid offending protestants and atheists without being unduly timid (FH to Laffitte, 23/4/81, MAC). The result must have surprised Laffitte, who administered two of the sacraments there in order to emphasise 'the religious significance of the occasion':

8   Newton Hall, LPS 5/4

The interior was coloured a delicate green with cream-coloured pilasters and finishings; Positivist mottoes adorned the walls, and the busts, representing the thirteen months, were placed in brackets in order, while that of Auguste Comte stood on a pedestal in the position of honour.

In spite of these august surroundings, 'no ritual, or set service, was regularly observed at the Sunday meetings'. There was just a straight-forward talk. No prayers were addressed directly to Humanity, although the Positivist formulas and some passages of exhortation composed by Harrison himself were added to the proceedings on special occasions (*PR* XXXII (1924) 211–13).

Newton Hall was considerably more adventurous than Chapel Street, however, in its encouragement of music. In 1882, for example, they commemorated the anniversary of Mozart's death with a special concert. In 1883 they formed a choir for religious ceremonies for which Henry Holmes composed a cantata of George Eliot's poem, 'The Choir Invisible'. Other musical celebrations were arranged by

Vernon Lushington, the author of several Positivist hymns for various Positivist occasions, some of which were eminently singable if somewhat derivative. The opening hymn for 'The Day of Humanity', for example, began,

> Day of the opening year!
> Day when our Faith is dear,
> Day when our Hope is clear,
> Day of Humanity. (VL 1885: 1)

Others lent themselves more to recitation, such as the narrative poem in 'Commemoration of Auguste Comte', which told the story of his life in thirty pages of resounding rhyme. Harrison was pleased with their progress in this area, particularly with the poetic gifts discovered in his wife. A loyal Congrevite admitted they had 'advanced further in ritual than we at Chapel Street' (Sulman to Gouge, 4/6/90, MAC), but the hymns were not universally popular. Ethel Harrison, who produced an anthology of hymns and poems for *The Service of Man* in 1890, confessed,

I feel very uneasy about it. The hymns we have from outside are so didactic that they are not properly hymns at all, and those written from within are obviously on trial.

Hymns required 'generations of feeling' to attain depth and resonance. Their own, she feared, lacked 'grace and distinction, and are monotonous, and . . . too melancholy' (Bod.L. d 249, ff.125–6, 135v).

The Service of Man contains an odd mixture of traditional piety open to interpretation in a humanist sense, passages from the Bible and from well-known poets from Chaucer to Whitman accompanying more obviously Positivist productions such as two hymns for the sacrament of Presentation, one of which begins,

> Helpless, sweet Babe, thou art today
> As weed on wave that lies,

and the other, 'Hail to Thee! hail to Thee! Child of Humanity!' (EH 1890: 99–101). One of the favourites was 'La Marseillaise', a lively rendering of which deeply impressed Thomas Hardy on one of his visits to Newton Hall in 1889 (TH, *Life* I 288). A second edition appeared in 1908 containing additional poems, by Ingram and Quin in particular, and perhaps the most sentimental of all, by Thomas

Sulman, 'To My Mother', who, in spite of being 'beneath the daisy-roots', is implored,

> Sweet mother angel, kiss my brow
> Ere I this day the strife begin. (EH 1908: 56–7)

Charles Kegan Paul's address to 'Our Mother' appears to be an exercise in traditional Catholic piety until its final line, 'Though Christ be dead, great Mother come!' (2).

Newton Hall was by no means unanimous about these liturgical developments. When the choir took to singing 'Amen', a Mr Donkin announced that his conscience would not permit him to join them (Bod.L. d 249, f.136). There were complaints on the other hand that the activities of the Boy's Guild, which included boxing, dancing and gymnastics, were interfering with 'the reverential feelings which members feel or ought to feel for the Hall' (e 105, f.27). Ethel Harrison had formally to defend her hymn-book in a letter to the Committee, to which Bridges also submitted a report, 'Hymns at Newton Hall', which explained that the book was for private reading as well as for occasional use at public meetings. He would have preferred more patriotic ballads like the Marseillaise to distinguish it from 'a church or chapel hymn-book'. He thought that the regular use of hymns at their ordinary meetings had 'retarded rather than favoured the advance of our movement', tending towards giving them the character of 'a religious sect'. He himself, as a young student of Comte, would have been put off by such an organised cult (HP 3/7).

Harrison's attitude towards religious observance seems itself to have wavered. In spite of his evident enjoyment of the symbolic decoration both of his private oratory and of Newton Hall, he told Laffitte in 1883 that any reunion with Chapel Street would plunge them all into undesirable debate on the question of liturgy (FH to Laffitte, 23/2/83, MAC). He announced in his 1884 'Bulletin' for the *Revue occidentale*,

Ceux qui viennent à Newton Hall n'y trouvent aucune de ces manifestations qu'on est habitué à regarder comme inséparables de la religion et du culte: on n'y fait ni service, ni prières, ni invocations; rien qui rappelle, en paroles, gestes ou images, le rituel théologique. (*RO* vii (1884) 133–4)

Yet what could be more reminiscent of the *Book of Common Prayer* than the way Harrison ended his funeral address at the grave of Alfred Cutler in February of that year:

May faith in Humanity teach us how to live, may hope in Humanity strengthen us in need, may love for Humanity fill our hearts, giving peace with us and all men. (FH 1884)

Or what is more open to the accusation of biblical parody than his celebration of subjective immortality at the end of his address, *The Memory of the Dead*, on the last day of 1889:

Death is swallowed up in Humanity. O death, where is thy sting? O grave, where is thy victory? The victory is with Humanity, which has taken us up into herself for ever. (FH 1890: 19)

His New Year's Address of 1887 insisted once more that Positivism was not a 'religious sect', with 'arid formulas' and 'fantastic rites' (FH 1887: 5), stressing the difference between their worship and that of Christianity:

No unseen Power hears our hymns. They are meant only to raise the hearts of those who sing and those who hear them . . . The normal ideal of worship is an artistic social ceremonial, deepening the sense of moral duty. (13–14)

But it was difficult in practice to escape from the patterns of Christian worship in which they had all been brought up.

Harrison threw himself energetically into the liturgical activities of Newton Hall in 1887, describing for Laffitte's benefit the marriage ceremony he conducted in April, when the Hall was radiant with flowers. After the introductory music he pronounced the famous formulas along with 'quelques invocations'. There followed a song written by Vernon Lushington, 'une courte explication', and a reading from the *Système* on marriage, before he asked the couple to repeat the promises of the *Book of Common Prayer* with additional items referring to the providence of Humanity, their civic duties and the education of their children. Then came a second song, also written by Lushington, a short discourse in which Harrison explained that neither divorce nor second marriage was acceptable to Positivists, and a final song leading up to the official entry of their names in the Newton Hall registry. It was all very satisfying, Harrison reported, giving the effect of a religious rather than a civil wedding (FH to Laffitte, 4/4/78, MAC).

The following month Harrison outlined the programme for a visit by Laffitte with similar attention to detail. There would be a banquet at the Hotel de Paris followed by a formal reception at Newton Hall during which he would be installed in the throne of the high priest.

Speeches all round would then be followed by renderings of their respective national anthems and other songs before the formality gave way to general socialising (11/5/87). An equally elaborate protocol was observed on a Positivist pilgrimage to Paris, when they visited 'the humble set of rooms in which Auguste Comte lived, worked, suffered, and died', where they could touch the handrail that had felt the pressure of his emaciated fingers and even the chair upon which Clotilde had sat, before proceeding via the cemetery to an evening of dinner, punch and speeches (*PMG* XLIII (15/6/86) 1–2). The whole account oozes with an emotion which Harrison would have called religious. A notice he sent to Laffitte advertising the details of this visit refers to a number of similar pilgrimages to Westminster Abbey and to the tombs of Bunyan, Defoe and Milton and a variety of art galleries, along with additional talks, social meetings and concerts (FH to Laffitte, 27/5/86, MAC). All these activities made up Positivist worship as fostered by Newton Hall.

Harrison was not altogether happy, however, with the role of priest into which he seems to have been forced and was relieved to abandon plans for a formal consecration in 1889. He continued to attack the fundamentalist Comtists of Chapel Street, who spent their time genuflecting and repeating formulas. His valedictory address, '21 Years at Newton Hall', claimed that their religious celebrations had involved poetry, music and the inculcation of Positivist maxims but not '*services* in any special sense' (*PR* X (1902) 97–113). He grew increasingly despondent about the effect the premature attempt to create a formal liturgy had had on public attitudes towards their movement:

how injurious to the spread of Positivist philosophy and sociology are the silly so-called 'services' in the dingy hole so-called 'Church of Humanity'. This disgusts educated and thoughtful men from taking Positivism seriously and makes them (eg Times) treat us as a serio-comic and obscure sect, mumbling Catholic rites in a sordid hole. (Bod.L. c 260, f.156)

He told Marvin in 1916 that he read his late wife's hymn-book every morning and evening and felt that it was 'the best introduction to and explanation of the Religion of Humanity extant'. But he felt that 'in a few years the whole of our attempt to give shape and life and ritual to the new religion will have melted into air' (c 263, f.210v). In spite of some interesting liturgical innovations in Liverpool and Newcastle,

9   Frederic Harrison, LPS 5/4

to be described later in the book, Harrison's gloomy judgement seems nonetheless to have been correct.

Frederic Harrison: 'Happy Humanist'

Frederic Harrison, who achieved a certain notoriety as a vigorous campaigner for the trade unions, the Paris Commune and other radical causes and went on to win a more respectable if shortlived reputation as a man of letters, was known to others as the prophet of Newton Hall:

> It was one of the great experiences of life to pick one's way along the narrow and dingy purlieus leading out of the Strand and pass by an alley into the little hall with a grand name where Frederic Harrison, without any trick of gesture or rhetoric, made every mind and heart one with his own in sympathy, and for the happy hour one in thought. (Conway 1904: II 349)

He was a volatile man with what his son called 'A Victorian Temperament', the morbid depressions of his younger days giving way to later spates of temper in which his face would turn purple and his lips quiver (A. Harrison 1926: ch. 6). His easily aroused anger was partly a result of other people's refusal to take Positivism seriously but it was also part of that peculiarly 'impulsive' yet 'deliberate' frame of mind for which Comte seems to have had a special attraction (37). His complete commitment to Comte in the 1870s helped him to settle down and become productive (in literary terms) as did his marriage to his cousin Ethelbertha in August 1870, which transformed the rebellious spiritual wanderer choked by his own intensity into 'The Happy Humanist' of the later years (ch. 10). From then on his defence of the faith never wavered: 'no argument was sufficiently cogent, no ridicule sufficiently devastating, no indifference sufficiently discouraging to shake him loose' (Vogeler 1984: 5).

Harrison's continual need to let off steam amused opponents and worried his friends. He seems consciously to have modelled himself on 'that fuliginous old Polyphemus Carlyle' (HP 1/53, f. 34), 'the old Prophet at Chelsea' (1/54, f.3), who crops up in many of his letters. He certainly revelled in his physical strength and vitality, as he wrote one summer from Ventnor: 'I am as strong as a bull, life is a vivid animal pleasure to me every minute of the day and night' (1/57, f.54). Anthony Trollope described him at a hunt 'looking like a jolly butcher on a hippopotamos' while Wilfrid Blunt complained he had 'never had a pain or ache or sleepless night in his life' (Vogeler 1984: 89, 229). A life of fixed habits and regular devotion to his 'Clotilde', according to his son, turned him into 'the most consistently normal man who ever wrote books', 'the embodiment of common sense' and 'absolute wholesomeness' (A. Harrison 1926: 156, 182–3).

Harrison qualified and practised as a barrister, but his principal clients abandoned him after he had publicly defended the trade unions in the 1860s. Most of his writing for periodical publication was gratuitous, in accordance with Positivist principles. Only after his marriage and retirement from the bar did he accept what he was offered for his contributions to the *Fortnightly Review*. 'The balance *against* the books', he confessed, was enormous, and he failed to understand why Macmillans continued to publish them (FH to Gosse, 10/11/18, BC). But his father's stockbroking wealth enabled him to maintain a high standard of living, dining out regularly at the innumerable clubs to which he belonged, a subject on which Morley delighted in teasing him. Matthew Arnold also poked fun at the idea of 'Harrison, in full evening costume, furbishing up a guillotine', while Henry James was more severe on the 'provincial second-rate dandy' (C. Kent 1978: 95), whose espousal of the Religion of Humanity called for nothing like the sacrifice Congreve had made. On the other hand, his status in the community at large gave the activities of the Positivists more prominence than those of other small groups (Eisen 1967a: 589).

Harrison went to Oxford in 1849 with 'the remnants of boyish Toryism and orthodoxy' still about him but left after six years 'a Republican, a democrat, and a Free-thinker' (FH 1911: I 95). Apart from Congreve's teachings, whose source he soon recognised, he encountered Positivism indirectly through Mill, Lewes and Martineau. He confessed to Comte in an interview in 1855 that he could follow only the second volume of the *Cours* (on history and sociology) and that he still called himself a Christian, albeit of the Broad School (97–8). Having decided against holy orders he entered Lincoln's Inn in November to be called to the bar in 1858. Although opposed to British militarism and imperialism in the Crimea and India, he remained somewhat frightened of the rigidity of the Positivist system, fearing that Bridges was 'falling into the same maelstrom' as Congreve (HP 1/4, f.35).

Comte's death in 1857 seems to have provoked a mental crisis in

Harrison, which continued through 1858. He found himself increasingly attracted to the Positive Philosophy but alienated by the religion. He urged Beesly to join Bridges and himself in forming a new society, an extension of the college discussion group they had called 'Mumbo-Jumbo', based on their shared interest in Positivism. The Positivist Society, which Harrison visited in Paris in 1862, he dismissed as sentimental 'tomfoolery' and 'mere jargon' (HP 1/9, f.17). He was clearly seeking a more general religious and philosophical position as a basis for social and political action.

Harrison involved himself seriously in politics during his years at the bar, spending the summer of 1859 in Italy, from where he sent enthusiastic reports on the *risorgimento* to a number of British newspapers. He travelled north in 1860, 1861 and 1863 to observe working conditions at first hand, combining with the Christian Socialists to condemn the London builders in the disputes that raged from 1859 to 1861. He also lectured at the Working Men's College, where he helped to form a rival group opposed to its dominant Christian Socialist philosophy but grew increasingly sceptical of the usefulness of 'improving the style of semi-middle-class youths aspiring to be correct' and hankered after more definite 'convictions' (HP 1/36, f.35). Maurice suspected him of being 'a dangerous disciple of Auguste Comte', 'a sort of emissary of R. Congreve, i.e. of the Devil', especially when he attempted to impose a systematic methodology on the teaching of history (FH 1911: I 150–1). Undeterred, Harrison delivered his series of lectures on 'The Meaning of History', unashamedly based on the third volume of Comte's *Système*, at Holyoake's Free Thought Hall in Cleveland Street. He was unhappy about 'the whole atmosphere of the professional lecturer' and his own 'utter dumbness', awkwardness and 'incoherence' (HP 1/37, ff.3, 9) but published the two introductory lectures as a public avowal of his 'acceptance of the Positivist synthesis of human evolution' (FH 1911: I 266).

A combination of increasingly frequent visits to Congreve, reading the *Catechism* and listening to Maurice preach brought Harrison's final liberation from theological orthodoxy. He had earlier seen Maurice's intellectual honesty and moral commitment as redeeming features in an otherwise corrupt established church but now lost all respect for a mind he called 'utterly muddle-headed and impotent' (151). The Church of England, full of worldly bishops and incompetent curates, manifestly failed to meet Comte's ideal (142–6) and the appearance of *Essays and Reviews* in 1860 confirmed his growing disenchantment with the 'cynical insincerity' and shallow compromise of its latitudinarian theologians, who were attempting to find 'a spiritual meaning in an exploded mythology' (206–8). His intellectual respect for Jowett and Pattison did not prevent him from drawing attention to their 'personal position . . . as heretics within the Church' (Altholz 1977: 146).

Harrison's article on 'Neo-Christianity', which appeared in the *Westminster Review* in October 1860, pointed to the Positivist elements within *Essays and Reviews*: Temple took up the notion of the human race as a collective being; Williams, Baden Powell and Goodwin looked to the preservation rather than the interruption of universal laws; Pattison treated religious experience in a purely historical spirit while Jowett interpreted the Scripture like any other book. Dogmas and creeds disappeared; Christian ethics alone remained. But either Christianity was inspired, Harrison argued, or it was an entirely natural development, in which case it should rest on the surer foundation of science. His own faith in a personal God gradually evaporated in favour of 'a clearer perception of the Human Providence that controls Man's destiny on earth' (FH 1907a: 46). He still felt the beauty and inner truth of Christianity but his study of Comte's 'Social Statics', the second volume of the *Système*, for a projected translation, convinced him of the need for a completely new system of beliefs. He continued, however, to fight shy of the sort of misanthropic sectarianism associated with Congreve, favouring the formation of a 'school' for the diffusion of Positivist principles rather than a 'church' or 'sect' (FH 1911: I 280–3).

'Study of Comte' in 1862 led Harrison, like so many others, to 'Pessimism and Despondency in 1863' (278). He spent much of the summer of 1862 working on his translation but a reading of Bridges' version of the *General View* in October 1864 brought home the inadequacies of his own work, which needed to be rewritten and was not finally to appear until 1875. He became more concerned with applying the theories he had been translating to the practical details of British politics, especially 'the Positivist theory of capital and labour' (HP 1/9, f.42). He and Beesly became deeply involved in political journalism in the mid-1860s, making regular contributions to such working-class newspapers as the *Bee-Hive*. 'Beesly and I in the Bee-

Hive never touch religious questions or preach positivism', he assured Morley (1/57, f.24), but everyone knew the basis of their sympathy with labour. They were preaching implicit Comtism, 'presenting positivist theories under the garb of mere good common sense'. Harrison rebutted the charge of using the *Commonwealth* as a pulpit for Comtism and even rejected the offer of its editorship in order to preserve his independence (C. Kent 1978: 75–6). But it was an independence that allowed him, when he wanted, to preach 'Comte pure and simple' (R. Harrison 1965: 265).

Harrison also contributed to the first issues of the *Fortnightly Review*, pointing out 'The Limits of Political Economy', defending the function of 'Trades-Unionism' and advocating 'Industrial Co-operation' (FH 1908: 269–376) in articles littered with quotations from Comte. Harrison urged upon Beesly the importance of being seen to be 'occupied with a *system*' rather than 'taking it up in a *literary* way'. He should not therefore be content merely to defend Catiline but to 'explain the Positive theory of dictatorship' (HP 1/12, ff.7–9). He was extremely sensitive about any cuts, his letters containing frequent outbursts against 'hacks' and 'triflers'. Asking Beesly to look over the proofs of two of these articles, he insisted that Lewes should not 'cut or alter them or take out the motto from Comte' (f.76). His concern with industrial relations was broader and deeper than his desire to propagate Positivism. He was, for example, largely responsible for the final version of the Trade Union Act of 1871. But his involvement in politics was a direct result of his commitment to Comte.

Harrison became a founder-member of the London Positivist Society but found it difficult to follow Congreve's rigidly Comtist line, as he explained in an article on 'The Positivist Problem' in the *Fortnightly Review* in 1869. He was, he insisted, 'a disciple and not an apostle', believing that a Positivist synthesis was necessary but as yet premature, since it seemed to fall between two stools: 'Those whom the philosophy attracts, the religion repels. Those whom the moral theories strike shrink back from the science'. Students of Comte, persecuted as a 'malignant sect', were driven consequently to behave like one, 'to defend every statement of Comte's, as if it were a question of verbal inspiration'. He for one remained outside Congreve's church but within Comte's school (*FR* ns VI (1869) 469–93). His increasing distrust of Congreve did not prevent him from answering the scathing references to Positivism in James FitzJames Stephen's *Liberty, Equality, Fraternity* with a defence of the Religion of Humanity as he understood it, redefining religion as a state of harmony in which man's thought, action and feeling were all satisfied (XIII (1873) 677–99). The 'question of the existence of God,' he told Stephen, 'is a thing *I never could take the slightest interest in*!' (McLeod 1974: 167)

The translation of the *Système*, which was 'fearfully hard' work, proceeding at about thirty pages a week, continued to inspire him with enthusiasm. He spent the summer working on the proofs of the whole translation and even offered to make an index to all four volumes, rejoicing at this 'opportunity for what I have long intended, the complete rereading and reconsideration en bloc of the Positive system and religion' (HP 1/60, f.29). His increasing commitment to Comte shocked and horrified Morley, who regarded the translation as a total waste of time and energy since those who wanted to read it would be able to do so in French (1/80, f.74). 'You have sunk into the Comtian morass', he complained, attempting alternately to bully and to cajole Harrison out of his faith (f.79). 'Would a gig', he asked, on the occasion of their pilgrimage to Paris, 'be enough to hold the orthodox church?' (f.87). But Harrison remained adamant, announcing the following November, 'I have made up my mind to give it entirely to Comte and to Positivism' (HP 1/60, ff.48–9).

Relations between the two men had deteriorated since Morley's attempt to tone down Harrison's attacks on Bismarck's Church Laws in the 'Public Affairs' section of the *Fortnightly Review*. The whole issue of Harrison's commitment to Comtism now became the subject of another violent row. 'You do wrong to tell me that I am giving myself up to "a sect" ', remonstrated Harrison:

The spirit of sect is the surrender of the character to an idea manifestly too small to embrace the field of life, and the conventional adoption of an exclusive temper. I am confident that I am doing neither of those things.

He accused Morley of scepticism,

the attitude of mind which holds itself degraded by adopting (on conviction) any set of general truths, on the ground that they have been found by some other mind . . . that form of so-styled culture which vaunts its superiority to *any* scheme of thought.

He claimed to have made a 'step forward . . . during the last six months' by abandoning the liberal qualms which still held Morley back from full discipleship (ff.50–3).

Harrison expounded his new position more fully in two articles on 'The Religious and Conservative Aspects of Positivism' which he annoyed Morley by sending to the *Contemporary Review*, along with 'A Socratic Dialogue', a reply to Mark Pattison's criticism of Comte. The first article claimed that most of the attacks on Comte's system applied to 'any definite organization of religion'. Harrison himself found the vagueness of neo-Christianity and the 'higher Pantheism' unacceptable, sneering at the phrases of Spencer and Arnold, 'the Unknowable' and 'the stream of tendency that makes for righteousness'. Religion remained subjective and personal unless founded on 'a *coherent scheme of doctrines*, as the basis of an *organized code of practice*'. It had to be both '*definite*' and '*systematic*' (*CR* XXVI (1875) 992–1012). Theology had been so battered by science, he argued in the second article, that it now laid claim to only a small area of life. Positivism, in contrast, claimed 'to do what for centuries Theology has ceased to do; to make religion again the basis and the end of man's thoughts' (XXVII 141). 'A Socratic Dialogue' presents the alternatives in the form of a dialogue. Phaedrus, a London barrister who is given all the best lines, refuses to live in 'a phantasmagoria of dissolving creeds', insisting on a real 'faith which can explain and guide my life', while Sophistes, an Arnoldian 'son of sweetness and light', finds man too evil and Humanity too feeble an object for devotion. Phaedrus, of course, has the last word, accusing Sophistes of cynicism and despair and offering in their place the optimism of the Religion of Humanity (FH 1907a: 158–94).

Harrison now found himself 'in a literary sense at any rate, in the position of Congreve', the target of much ridicule and derision (HP 1/61, f.18). The political essays he collected under the Comtean title, *Order and Progress*, which contained an extended comparison between Comte and Carlyle (FH 1975: 31–42) but whose Positivism was otherwise mainly implicit, received a rough ride in the press (xx). He vowed, however, to devote the rest of his life to the propagation of Positivism, whatever the 'gibbering tribe' of 'hired baboons' might say (HP 1/63, f.74). 'If one of us were to make remarks about the horses for the next "Derby" ', he complained, 'there would be a hullabaloo about Clotilde de Vaux, Priestcraft, monkeys and protoplasm' (f.21). Partly out of sympathy for Harrison and his persecuted fellow-Positivists

Morley agreed to write the article on Comte in the *Encyclopaedia Britannica* rather than let him 'fall to some denigrator' (HP 1/82, f.20). But his rereading of Comte left him baffled:

how *you* of all men on this bright planet have gone over to such an idol doth perplex me by day and by night. The whole thing has provoked a 'crise cérébrale'. All night I toss and tumble and water my bed with my tears, and moan, 'And does Harrison find a key to this stuff – this dreary – '. No more – or we quarrel.   (Hirst 1927: II 16)

Matthew Arnold also urged Harrison not to spend all his 'life and talents over Comte' (FH 1975: xx). But there was no going back. He became fully involved in all the activities of the Positivist School, taking on the presidency of the London Positivist Committee in 1880, a post he held for twenty-five years.

Newton Hall under Harrison was not only a chapel but a school and a club, a centre for general education, political agitation and social celebration. A women's guild was started in 1884, led by Ethel Harrison, and a young men's guild five years later, under the tutelage of S. H. Swinny. The former arranged flowers, tea parties and dances while the latter played football and cricket (Harrison himself bowling fierce off-cutters). The Harrisons entertained all and sundry in their own house. They arranged concerts, dinners, pilgrimages to the tombs of various 'saints of Humanity', visits to museums and art galleries and talks, endless addresses on history, science, literature and religion, all of them, of course, from a Positivist standpoint. Harrison boasted,

Many a clerk, workman, and man of business, who had neither time nor money for a college, has been able in twenty years to get a general conception of history, science, and literature, such as many a B.A. has never heard of.

Much of the historical material, he added, found its way into the *New Calendar of Great Men* in 1892, which contained biographical studies of the 558 saints of Comte's calendar, edited and many of them written by Harrison himself (FH 1911: II 274). He wrote a regular 'Bulletin' of the activities at Newton Hall for the *Revue occidentale* and became a major contributor to the *Positivist Review*.

Harrison's literary output in defence of Positivism was quite staggering. Hundreds of pamphlets and periodical articles propound the basic principles of his faith with the same energy, clarity, sense of humour and fundamental lack of originality. The best of these found their way into various volumes of collected essays published by Macmillan in the later years of his life: *The Creed of a Layman* and *The Philosophy of Common Sense* (both of 1907), *National and Social Problems* and *Realities and Ideals* (both of 1908) and *The Positive Evolution of Religion* (1913). These volumes contain many of the same ideas, endlessly rephrased and reiterated. They are worth brief consideration, however, as representative of the contributions Harrison made to the fields of religion, philosophy, politics and literature in the years following his complete submission to Positivism.

The Creed of a Layman, the earliest of Harrison's volumes of collected essays, begins with an autobiographical piece entitled 'Apologia pro Fide Mea' before reproducing what Harrison regarded as his most interesting essays on matters of religion. There are several items from 1881, the crucial year in which Newton Hall was founded, including the title essay, which explores the three aspects of Comte's religion (belief, worship and action) before ending with a prophetic vision of society under the Religion of Humanity. It also includes representative samples such as 'A Positivist Prayer', several sermons preached on the celebration of various sacraments at Newton Hall, a report of the activities there in 1885 and the 'Valedictory' address given on the removal of the Positivists from Newton Hall in 1902.

The Positive Evolution of Religion consists entirely of discourses given at Newton Hall, some of them reprinted from the *Positivist Review*. Some introductory remarks on the faith of the future give way to an attempt to answer a number of 'orthodox' and 'deistical' objections to the Religion of Humanity, the position of the Roman Catholic, Anglican and Dissenting churches being examined in turn. 'Neo-Christians' are once more attacked for stopping half-way along the critical process. The Religion of Humanity, in fact, is 'Neo-Christianity carried out to a strictly logical conclusion' (FH 1913: 185). *The Philosophy of Common Sense* traces without irony 'how I came by degrees to solve the main problems of Thought' (FH 1907b: xii), mainly, it seems, through reading and regurgitating Comte and Lewes. Most of the essays are papers first delivered to the Metaphysical Society refuting metaphysical concepts such as 'The Absolute' and 'The Soul' or explaining 'The Basis of Morals' from the Positivist point of view. The problem, as Harrison sees it, is that 'morality will be undermined if based on a theology which is not true' but that 'morality without religion is insufficient for general civilization'. Common sense taught that the solution was 'a non-theological religion' (151–6). The book continues with similarly clear-cut answers to the objections to Positivism raised by Spencer, Huxley and Balfour in controversies to be considered in the following chapter.

The two prongs of Positivist political agitation, on an international level opposition to imperialism, and on a national scale raising the dignity of labour, are reflected in Harrison's discussion of *National and Social Problems*. 'National Problems' take up the first part of Harrison's book, beginning with attacks on 'Bismarckism' and celebrations of the liberation of Italy and continuing with attacks on British imperialism in Afghanistan, Egypt, Northern Ireland and South Africa. The 'Social Problems' of part two involve a defence of the trade unions and of the co-operative movement and an elaboration of 'Moral and Religious Socialism', the term Harrison uses for the political side of Positivism. His simplification of all political problems elicited from Morley an ironic restatement of the Positive hierarchy of the sciences: 'Mathematics at the bottom; hysterics at the top' (HP 1/78, f.3). They brought even more severe censure from more conservative circles. Robert Lowe denounced 'that strange, exotic band of *philosophes*, the English Comtists', who remained 'free from those complicated, embarrassing, and troublesome considerations of the collateral and future effects of measures which perplex ordinary mortals' (Martin 1893: 280), while Admiral Maxse portrayed Harrison as a dangerous but 'brilliant writer' who wanted the English people to be 'dragooned' into accepting 'national dismemberment' (*PMG* LV (4/10/92) 3). Harrison himself admitted to preferring 'the principles of Positivism' to the perpetual compromise of practical politics (FH 1906: 14), although this did not prevent him becoming first an alderman and then a member of the London County Council.

Harrison was the eternal amateur forever railing against professionalism of all kinds, especially in literature. His generally cordial relations with Lewes and Morley, successive editors of the *Fortnightly Review*, were liable to explode at any moment into violent hostility. 'Literature is like pitch,' he exclaimed in 1872; 'no man can touch it and not be defiled' (HP 1/54, f.2). It was 'only one more degree honourable than "the stage" – a questionable amusement for idlers' (1/57, f.5). His attitude mellowed over the years. He continued to make extreme moralistic judgements, condemning both Zola's 'morbo-ology' and Sterne's 'schoolboy smut' (FH to E. Gosse, 9/11/96, 26/2/14, BC). But he also wrote numerous introductions to novels and other literary ventures as well as publishing a whole series of historical and literary monographs. He even produced what he described to Hardy as 'a historical romance of the old-fashioned "Bow-wow" style' (FH to TH, 23/2/03, DCM), *Theophano*, which he transformed into a melodrama entitled *Nicephorus*. These writings have little or nothing to do with Positivism:

> when he writes on literature, in fact, it is odd how small a part his Comtean sympathies seem to play. He might be almost any well-to-do old-fashioned radical, who just happens to have one rather large bee in his bonnet.
>
> (Gross 1969: 112)

He was not even above criticising Comte for contributing to the overshadowing of the 'literary, poetic, and romantic interest' by the 'scientific and sociological' (Vogeler 1984: 302).

Harrison was thus transformed from a dangerous radical to a grand old man of letters, a relic of the Victorian period to be patronised by the more sophisticated, less earnest Edwardians. It is difficult to give this metamorphosis a precise date. Perhaps it was the extraordinarily successful tour of the United States early in 1901, from which he returned full of renewed confidence and vigour. He was not unaware of the irony of this late recognition. Having been shrieked at by the Warden of Wadham in 1868 as one of the 'infidels, atheists, backbiters and strifemakers coming down from London to disturb the harmony of a happy family' (HP 1/15, f.27), he marvelled at the clerical authorities in Oxford bringing their pupils to hear him preach Positivism in the first Herbert Spencer lecture in 1905 (FH to Hillemand, 25/5/05, MAC). He retained an extraordinary vigour and vitality till late in life, rushing from one social engagement to another in retirement at Bath like 'a sort of Positivist Beau Nash' (Bod.L. d 262, f.289), boasting of the variety of his achievements. Maurice Bowra and Gilbert Murray were astonished at his continuing vigour when they met him in his nineties (Bowra 1966: 137; MP 501, ff.97–106). When he eventually died in 1923, the national papers treated the 'knight-errant of Positivism' as a major literary figure (*PR* XXXI (1923) 34–5). With his death, however, the Positivists lost not only their most energetic champion but perhaps the last claim which they had to national attention (McGee 1931: 226).

Beesly, Bridges and company

Edward Spencer Beesly, Professor of History at University College London from 1860 to 1893, was a born controversialist, a man who stood out as a hard hitter even in 'the day of the fighting Professors' (*MG*, 10/7/15, 11). He cut a 'striking figure' at George Eliot's salons with his imposing stature and 'handsome features' but never quite fulfilled the expectations raised by his early success in the academic world (*WG*, 15/7/15, 2). No-one was more aware of the disproportion between his early prospects and his final achievement than Beesly himself. In the sixties and seventies he had been as prominent and productive as Harrison, but while Harrison grew steadily in stature Beesly dropped quietly out of the main stream of cultural and political life, a contrast in fortunes which he found hard to accept.

Coming from an aggressively evangelical background, Beesly was said to have won a Bible clerkship at Wadham in 1849 because it was the only book he knew well. His father was a clergyman and his mother remained convinced on her death-bed that her son would go to hell. After graduating from Wadham in 1854 he taught as an Assistant Master at Marlborough College before being appointed Principal of University Hall at the age of 28 in 1859. The chairs of History at University College and of Latin at Bedford College followed in 1860 but his annual private income easily exceeded his professional salaries and he wrote for propagandist rather than professional reasons. Whether he was attacking Kingsley's heroic view of history (*WR* XIX (1861) 305–36), defending Catiline as a systematic thinker and revolutionary hero inevitably opposed by mere 'literary men' such as Cicero (*FR* I (1865) 167–84), or criticising the class basis of British imperialist naval policy (ESB 1866: 155–222), he never missed an opportunity to preach Positivism.

From the moment of his arrival in London, Beesly espoused the cause of the working class. His activities in the Labour Movement, in defence of the trade unions, as President of the International Working Men's Association, and in support of numerous international causes, brought him rapid notoriety. After his famous speech in Exeter Hall in July 1867, when he denounced Governor Eyre as a 'greater murderer' than Broadhead and those associated with the Sheffield outrages, *Punch* suggested he should 'apply to HER MAJESTY for leave to insert a "T" between the "S" and the "L" of his name' (*Punch*,

13/7/67, 14). *The Times* described his speech as 'an offence against public and private morality' (*Times*, 4/7/67, 8) and the Council of University College was only just persuaded not to remove the professor from his chair. Beesly enjoyed causing a commotion:

When I think that there are some half dozen of us that make all this stir, I must say that we manage wonderfully well. We run here, and peep in there, and tread on this man's toes and stick a pin in that man and bonnet the next and so they are all hitting about wildly as if they were assailed by a legion.

(ESB to H. Crompton, 5/10/67, BP 1)

His energetic defence of the Paris Commune led to further attacks on 'Comtist agitators . . . unscrupulous in the machinations of turbulence' (R. Harrison 1959: 212–13). His courage and unflagging energy on behalf of the oppressed earned him the praise of Karl Marx, who was fully aware of the source of his ideas (57, 214, 241). His regular contributions to the *Bee-Hive* and the *Labour Standard* applied unmistakably Positivist principles to contemporary affairs. The many volumes of Positivist pamphlets now in libraries at Keele and Liverpool, some unsigned, some written by Beesly and many more which were originally sent to him, attacked without ceasing what he considered the two most dangerous political tendencies of the age: oppression of the working class and imperialism.

Beesly had attended Congreve's lectures as early as 1860 and kept in contact with the high priest of Positivism throughout that decade, joining the Positivist Society in March 1869. He presided over the fortnightly evening meetings at the Positivist School from its opening in April 1870 until they were discontinued at the end of the following December. Having played a prominent part in the various disputes leading up to the schism, he nominated himself President of the Positivist Society in May 1878 and took on much of the responsibility for steering it through the awkward years before the founding of Newton Hall, even to the extent of holding meetings in his own house. The difference between his position and that of Congreve lay not so much in his attitude to the Religion of Humanity in general as in the authority he was prepared to invest in Comte. Beesly refused to take the *Système* as the Positivist Leviticus (ESB 1881: 14), acknowledging Comte's personal imperfections and arguing in the first issue of the *Positivist Review*, which he founded in 1893, that to call oneself a 'disciple' of the 'master' was not to submit oneself to 'slavish subjection' and obedience but to accept his ideas unless or until they were contradicted by 'empirical good sense'. The foundation of a Positivist periodical was itself a classic example of Comte's disciples growing to understand that his denunciation of journalism was a direct result of his own disastrous experience, not a permanent element of the faith (*PR* I (1893) 73–7).

Setting up the *Positivist Review* fulfilled one of Beesly's oldest ambitions. As early as 1867 he had expressed the need for 'a newspaper of our own wherein to hurl defiance at our enemies' (ESB to FH, 19/8/67, BP 1) and by 1893 he could afford to pay for the privilege. The *Positivist Review* was undertaken solely at his expense, at least in its early years, but he soon grew dispirited with the problems of preparing a monthly number. He claimed to sell about 300 copies a month and to 'distribute another 300 gratis to clubs and libraries' (Bod.L. e 108, f.104). The main problem was a lack of contributors. Of those Positivists who were qualified to write, the Congrevites dared not antagonise their leader while too many of those at Newton Hall stood aloof (e 109, f.70). By 1900 he felt an urgent need for 'fresh blood': 'I feel that I, for one, have said in seven years pretty nearly all that I have to say and that I go on repeating myself' (MP 7, ff. 100–1).

That certainly is the impression given by the *Positivist Review*, with its endless reiteration of Positivist principles. Beesly occasionally indulged in discussion of contemporary politics, as in his editorial of August 1895 deploring Morley's election defeat at Newcastle and pushing him for the leadership of the Liberal Party (*PR* III (1895) 151). There were, of course, reviews of recent publications but the predominant type of contribution was a short article by Bridges, Beesly or Harrison on a particular aspect of Positivism, on an individual's relation to Positivism, or on Positivism in general. There was simply not enough variety. 'If I ever became solely responsible for a Positivist organ myself as the Professor has been', Harrison told Marvin the year after Beesly's resignation as editor in 1901, it would have to be much broader 'both in contributors and in topics'. It might include reviews of plays, even a short story. 'But all this would cause growls from the Professor and constant remonstrances from the stricter set' (Bod.L. d 255, f.208).

Even in retirement Beesly continued to devote himself to the cause. His translation of Comte's *Discourse on the Positive Spirit*, designed for workmen, with 'Explanatory Notes', a 'Translator's Preface', an 'Explanation of Philosophical Terms' and an 'Analytical Table of Con-

tents', appeared in 1903. He continued to write occasionally for the
Positivist Review, pleading for a broad and balanced understanding of
the faith. His private letters reveal an increasing distaste for Comte as
a person, partly due to the publication of successive volumes of his letters but he remained faithful to the Religion of Humanity right up to
his death in 1915.

John Henry Bridges, by contrast, suffered a dramatic breakdown at
the end of his life which involved a repudiation of his Positivist
beliefs, although in other respects his career affords a close parallel to
Beesly, his lifelong friend and exact contemporary at Wadham. He
was born in the same year, 1831, into a famous puritan family. His
father, too, was an evangelical clergyman in the Church of England.
After being head-boy at Rugby, Bridges won a scholarship to
Wadham, which he entered in October 1851. He recovered from a
disastrous third-class degree in 1854 to win an Oriel Fellowship in
1856. The same year he entered St George's Hospital, gaining admission to the Royal College of Physicians after three and a half years as
opposed to the usual five. After marrying his devout cousin, Susan
Torlesse, in February 1860, he emigrated to Australia only to return
with her dead body, a victim of typhoid, six months later. Both
families were too frantically evangelical for Bridges to live with, so he
moved up to general practice in Bradford in the neighbourhood of
another cousin, Georgina Hadwen, whose daughter Mary he married
in 1868. He returned to London the following year, as medical inspector to the Poor Law Board, for whom he waged a ceaseless battle for
health and sanitation in the city until his retirement in 1891.

Bridges was the earliest member of 'Mumbo' to commit himself to
Comte. He started subscribing to the Positivist Society in Paris in
1856, and it was his friendship with Laffitte, he was later to claim,
which kept his faith alive in the face of Congreve's over-literal interpretation of the Religion of Humanity (JHB to Jeannolle, 18/5/02,
MAC). It was clearly Congreve, however, who first aroused his
interest in Comte. He made a thorough study of Comte in 1857 and
wrote a long letter to Laffitte in 1860, bearing witness to his firm
belief in Positivism as a religion (JHB to Laffitte, 8/3/60, MAC). He
began his excellent translation of the *General View of Positivism*,
which was finally to appear in 1865, on the return journey from
Australia, assuring Harrison that 'the religion of Humanity stands the
test of sorrow' (Liveing 1926: 85). Harrison was impressed by his

friend's courageous response to bereavement, which he saw as a vindication of the Positivist doctrine of subjective immortality. But it was he who saved Bridges from complete nervous breakdown, listening to all his troubles and arranging for him to take pupils abroad (104–8).

Bridges continued to preach Positivism with undiminished zeal and applied to Laffitte in 1864 for the sacrament of destination. The following year he defended the unity of Comte's teaching against Mill, who, he pointed out, had accepted most of Comte's religion, apart from the need for a spiritual power, and that had been a major component of Positivism from the beginning. Seeing the western world in the grip of paralysing religious doubt Comte had supplied a definite creed and an authority on which men could rely. The appearance of Bridges' translation of the *General View* in the same year was virtually ignored in the press, but Bridges continued to preach Positivism in courses for workmen in Bradford. He also contributed an article on 'England and China' to a collection of Positivist essays entitled *International Policy* in 1866. Congreve's hostile reaction to his desire to remarry, however, as we have seen, caused him to question the whole notion of literal adherence to Comte's system and to propose a broader understanding of the Religion of Humanity. To the more sympathetic Laffitte he admitted that he no longer fulfilled all the conditions of Positivist priesthood but hoped nevertheless to continue to propagate Positivist doctrine (JHB to Laffitte, 12/5/68, MAC). His return to London gave him the opportunity to participate fully in the Positivist School, although Beesly clearly felt that he was not pulling his weight, especially after his removal from Gower Street to Wimbledon in 1873 (ESB to H. Crompton, 10/7/73, BP 1).

Bridges was reluctantly persuaded to accept the presidency of the London Positivist Committee for the year following the schism and continued to command great respect within the movement even after his resignation. His intellectual pre-eminence and religious intensity impressed even the most ardent Congrevites. He was, by all accounts, a brilliant conversationalist and his rigorous scientific training equipped him to incorporate new scientific discoveries into the Positivist synthesis. He steadfastly rejected any tendency to treat Comte as God or Pope or to parrot forth the Positivist formulas without criticism or modification (JHB to Hillemand, 28/10/89, MAC). He also exercised a calming restraint upon Beesly, who he felt went in for too much 'rotten egg throwing and the amenities of the hustings' (Liveing 1926: 121).

Bridges was a regular contributor to the *Fortnightly Review* on scientific and medical subjects as well as specifically Positivist themes. But his published work is disappointing. The problem is that for all his assertion of the need to develop Comte's ideas, much of his work is content merely to repeat them. Many of his addresses at Newton Hall, for example, were straightforward exercises in exposition, designed to clarify the basic teaching of the faith for the less gifted members of his audience. One of his *Five Discourses on Positive Religion* explains eighteen 'Positivist Mottoes' one after another, like a Brontë nightmare. The others also expound fundamental Comtean doctrines: prayer and work, order and progress, science and solidarity. Yet they seem to have been popular, going into a second edition in 1891 and being reprinted in a posthumous volume of Bridges' *Essays and Addresses* along with a number of 'Commemorative Addresses' delivered on the festivals of various saints.

Many more of Bridges' addresses survive in pamphlet form. One of the most interesting is that on 'The New Testament', the third of a series of lectures on *Positivism and the Bible*, in which he risks a few of his own thoughts, for instance his reasons for not accepting the Christian assessment of Jesus:

The brevity of his career, our extremely imperfect knowledge of the facts of his life, and the insufficient exercise of many virtues which would seem essential to the highest moral excellence.   (JHB 1885: 64)

Bridges apparently contributed 194 of the entries in the *New Calendar of Great Men* and Harrison was so impressed with the quality of his work, which 'made an altogether new thing of it', that he delayed its publication for a year in order to improve some of the other entries (Bod.L. d 251, f.106). He was less impressed with Bridges' edition of the *Opus Majus of Roger Bacon*, which was riddled with errors caused by his ignorance of palaeography and the rustiness of his Latin and Greek. It was so savagely attacked that the publishers withdrew it from sale in 1898, to reissue a revised and re-edited version two years later.

Some of Bridges' best work appeared in the *Positivist Review*, to which he contributed over a hundred essays, a selection of which appeared in another posthumously published volume entitled *Illustrations of Positivism*. He was in a position to write informed critiques of some of the major scientists whose views diverged from the Positivist line: Darwin, Spencer and Huxley, for example. He reviewed theological debates, such as the Lambeth Conference of 1897. But there were also many articles expounding once more the basic principles of Positivism: 'The Meaning of the Word "Positive" ', 'Faith in Humanity', 'Altruism', 'Order and Progress in Science', 'Catholicism and Science' and so on. These were not designed to be read one after the other, of course, but as separate articles over a long period of time. His work continued to pad out the pages of the *Positivist Review* long after his death in 1906. The last ten years of his life were filled with sorrow and anxiety, personal bereavements and public disappointments. The Boer War came as a particularly strong shock to his faith in Humanity and he grew to envy the simple faith of Roman Catholics. He raved during his final illness about being Judas destined for hell and was eventually given a Christian funeral, much to the disgust of his fellow-Positivists, who arranged their own Commemoration Service in South Place Chapel, attended by about two hundred people, a mark of the general respect in which he was held (Torlesse 1912: 241–4).

There were a number of prominent barristers among the Positivists, including two pairs of brothers, the Cromptons and the Lushingtons. Henry Crompton, whose brother Albert was to play an important role in the development of Positivism in Liverpool, was a founder-member of the society, a friend and political associate of Beesly and Harrison throughout the sixties and seventies, and Attorney General to the TUC. He tried for a long time to remain neutral in the Positivist schism before eventually siding with Congreve partly out of personal loyalty but primarily because he believed in the Religion of Humanity as it was practised at Chapel Street. His obstinate defence of Comte used to amuse friends such as the Amberleys, who enjoyed teasing him 'about the woman in green' and other aspects of his faith (B. and P. Russell 1937: II 417). Lord Arthur Russell called him 'one of the biggest fools I ever met', only for Lord Amberley to come to the Positivists' defence, poking fun at the 'reasonable men' in whom they provoked such unreasoning hostility (II 462–77). Crompton wrote much more extensively on legal, social and political questions than on the Religion of Humanity, which he saw as 'strengthening the moral fibre', revelling in pious Positivist sentiments such as, 'Humanity is the Heaven we look to' (HC 1893: 4).

The sermons he delivered in his short term of office as successor to Congreve exude religiosity, being full of pious hopes and solemn blessings. He believed wholeheartedly that the Positivist sacraments would replace their Catholic counterparts and Humanity supplant the traditional objects of western piety, Jesus and Mary. Preaching, however, was something of a strain on his dwindling reserves of energy and he gave up responsibility for Chapel Street in 1901, three years before his death.

The Lushington twins epitomise another variety of upper-crust Comtism. Sir Godfrey was 'both the most respectable and the most latitudinarian of Positivists' (R. Harrison 1965: 289). A contemporary of Bridges at Rugby, where he was a hearty games player and head-boy, he gained a double first at Balliol and a fellowship at All Souls in 1854. From 1856 he taught at the Working Men's College where, it was recalled, 'Maurice was the prophet, Ruskin the poet, and Lushington the gentleman' (*WMC* X (1907–8) 53–4). He was already having 'religious difficulties' at this time, but Congreve scrupled to take advantage of his personal influence over the young man (C. Kent 1978: 58). Called to the bar in 1858, Godfrey Lushington became first legal adviser and later permanent under-secretary to the Home Office, working with Harrison on the draft of the Trade Union Act of 1871. He and his twin brother Vernon were founder-members of the Positivist Society, siding with the triumvirate in the schism. They participated in most of the activities of Newton Hall, although Godfrey exasperated Harrison by holding aloof from their more radical activities and eventually withdrew his subsidy because of their violent protests over the Boer War (FH to Jeannolle, 30/10/01, MAC). According to Beesly, he thought Comte had been 'over-sanguine, over-dogmatic, and . . . often premature' (*PR* XV (1907) 70–1).

Vernon Lushington, county-court judge for Surrey and Berkshire from 1877 to 1900, also taught at the Working Men's College from 1855, but 'the devotion of his life', as their journal recalled, 'was given to Positivism, which was to him a true religion' (*WMC* XII (1911–12) 270–1). A letter of his to Harrison in January 1884 bears witness to the way in which the Religion of Humanity sustained him after the death of his wife (HP 1/47, ff.26–7). An active member of the London Positivist Committee from May 1878 until his resignation in November 1897, he gave frequent lectures at Newton Hall and composed his own *Positivist Hymns*. Other Positivists called to the bar included Alfred Cock, treasurer of the London Positivist Committee from 1884 to 1896 and Hardy's friend from Dorchester, Benjamin Fossett Lock, another county-court judge who served as secretary on the committee until resigning after a wrangle over Home Rule in 1886. His sister Jane married Sydney Style before moving to the Church of Humanity in Liverpool. Francis Otter, who studied at Rugby under Congreve and became a brother-in-law of George Eliot's husband, John Cross, was another barrister to join the Positivist Society, shortly after a visit from Bridges (JHB to Laffitte, 2/9/82, MAC). It was clearly through family connections and friendships such as these as much as through their formal propaganda that Positivism made inroads into the upper middle classes.

One of the most interesting although least successful of the Positivist barristers was William Knight. Forced by bronchitis to cease practice in the late 1870s, Knight was an avid student of Comte who attended both Chapel Street and Newton Hall. He was equally unimpressed by the preaching of Congreve, Laffitte, Bridges and Harrison but an otherwise disappointing evening he spent at Newton Hall in March 1888 was partially redeemed by Vernon Lushington's condescension in accompanying him home third class after the service (Carver 1976: 48–50). The evangelical background and temperament common to so many Positivists is very much in evidence in Knight's letters of courtship urging his future wife to read Comte. Her reluctance to read the long passages he copied out for her or even to listen to him talking about Positivism were a source of contention between them until they reached a compromise which left them free to worship in their own way:

For him, it was the Religion of Humanity that gave meaning to her Anglican Communion Service. She did not misunderstand his offering when he laid a flower in front of the statue of the Virgin Mary, in a poor little Roman Catholic Church where they went sometimes to say their prayers.   (65)

The Positivist significance of this act was carefully explained to their daughter. The Religion of Humanity, however, could not sustain William Knight's spirits in the face of continuing ill health and financial insecurity or prevent him from committing suicide soon after the turn of the century.

Knight's disappointing visit to Newton Hall in March 1888 found its members lamenting the untimely death of James Cotter Morison and the publication of his final book, *The Service of Man*, which they considered 'very unsatisfactory – fragmentary – put together when he was not up to such work' (49–50). Morison's contribution to Positivism, however, was altogether fragmentary. Enabled to live comfortably and to wield influence in the literary world by the proceeds of his father's famous pills, he was one of the founders of the *Fortnightly Review*, for which he sometimes wrote and whose editorship he procured for his Lincoln College friend, John Morley. Morison lived in Paris in the early 1870s, where he offered himself as an amanuensis to Laffitte before disagreeing with him over his refusal to allow access to key documents for an abortive biography of Comte. Returning to England in 1873, he wrote regularly to Laffitte about lectures at Chapel Street and his wife's dramatic derangement, which led to her tragic death in November 1876.

Morison sided firmly with Laffitte in the schism, complaining bitterly of Congreve's profoundly egoistic, hard and arrogant nature (JCM to Laffitte, 3/9, 19/10/78, MAC). He became for a while a key figure in the London Positivist Society, which waited for his return from France in January 1879, for example, before making a decision about hiring a room (LPS 1/1). His lecture of that year, *On the Relation of Positivism to Art*, discussed the five great arts in the order in which Comte arranged them. He was a regular attender throughout the early 1880s, although his health soon began to suffer from the hectic social life he led, full of the sort of 'roaring gabble-gobble' Meredith attended at his house in July 1883 (GM 1970: II 705). He gave a series of lectures at Newton Hall in 1885, but the last few years of his life seem to have been mostly bed-ridden. His reputation as a writer rests mainly on his lives of Gibbon, Macaulay and, above all, St Bernard.

Congreve had always regarded Morison with suspicion as 'a literary person' who remained uncommitted to 'the system' (BL 45235, f.171). Even his Newton Hall colleagues, while being grateful for his legacy of £500, were disappointed with his final work, *The Service of Man*, with its tentative subtitle, *An Essay Towards the Religion of the Future*. It was, Morison confessed in private,

largely founded on Positivist principles, but by no means exclusively so. And as a matter of fact Comte is never referred to or even named. Great harm has been done to Positivism by forcing Comte crude and simple down people's throats and winding up every paragraph in the Liturgy with a 'Through

Auguste Comte our Lord' . . . I differ often so deeply and completely from
Comte that I cannot take him as my sole authority.   (Clodd 1916: 115)

The Service of Man was not meant as 'a Positivist utterance', Harrison
explained, but as 'a sort of "Whole Duty of Man", from the Positivist
point of view' (FH 1888: 20–1). It caused something of a stir when it
first appeared, being denounced from the pulpit on the one hand and
hailed on the other as 'the most powerful attack on Christianity that
has been produced in England during this generation' (*Athenaeum*,
29/1/87, 153). It is a striking book. After stressing the impossibility of
reconciling benevolence and omnipotence in the Creator of such an
evil world and disputing the assumption that the disappearance of
Christianity would lead to a period of universal licence, Morison
discusses the possibility of a new religion emerging to replace it. He
resists the claim that any individual could invent a new faith, which
would need to grow organically over a period of time. But the final
chapter, 'On the Cultivation of Human Nature', postulates a future
Religion of Humanity divested of its Comtean details.

   Another 'literary person' to frequent the Positivist Society in the
years immediately after the schism was the publisher, Charles Kegan
Paul, whose 'faith in revealed religion' when chaplain at Eton was
undermined by a reading of the *Cours* (C. K. Paul 1899: 203–5). He
eventually resigned his living in 1874 only for his daily study of *The
Imitation of Christ* to lead him to a fully-fledged Roman Catholicism,
which looked on Positivism as 'Catholicism without God', a misdirec-
tion of devotional zeal, 'a fair-weather creed' which had 'no message
for the sorry and the sinful' and 'no succour in the hour of death'
(365–7). Positivism had, in fact, been hit by a number of deaths in the
late 1880s, including that of the much-travelled William Frey, who
left his native Russia in 1868 in order to establish a Comtean community in Kansas (Billingham 1960: 814). He came to England in
1884, preparatory to returning to preach Positivism in Russia, and
spoke frequently at the Positivist Society in the four years up to his
death.

   Newton Hall could boast the services of 'a brilliant array of
teachers' (Cohen 1959: 363), including F. S. Marvin, ·S. H. Swinny
and F. J. Gould, who shouldered the responsibility for the continuation of organised Positivism into the twentieth century along with
some of the distinguished professors who were to be seen at Newton
Hall in their younger years: F. G. Fleay, A. J. Grant, Patrick Geddes,

Gilbert Murray, Percy Harding and C. H. Herford. Their story will be told in chapter six. Charles Gaskell Higginson was another teacher who abandoned the profession in order to devote himself to Positivist study and propaganda before succumbing to the Positivist disease, neurasthenia or depression. A small pocket of Indian Civil Servants remained loyal to the Religion of Humanity as they had learnt it from Congreve. Samuel Lobb propounded a simplified form of Positivism in the *Calcutta Review* and the *Bengalee*. James Geddes, who married Congreve's niece, Emily Bury, in the first ever Positivist marriage ceremony, was regarded as a potential successor to Chapel Street until his early death. Henry Cotton, another fervent supporter of Congreve in the schism, held full-scale Positivist services in his Calcutta apartments in the 1880s, working towards a synthesis of Positivism and Hinduism, a task which was continued by one of his disciples, Jogendra Chandra Ghosh (Forbes 1975: 32–49).

The men who achieved prominence in the Positivist Society, as one might expect, belonged mainly to the professional, well-educated middle and upper classes. There were clerks in the movement, men like Joseph Kaines, who left Chapel Street after a dispute over music to set up the North London Positivist Society, and Henry Ellis, who remained convinced that the working classes would come to Positivism in the end (*PR* I (1893) 146–50). There was a bookseller, Edward Truelove, which was useful, and a coppersmith, John Overton, the proletarian novelist, who brought along his union's president, Charles Rogers. Both Truelove and Rogers resigned in the 1870s but Edmund Jones, a basket-maker, stayed with the faith until his death in 1881. F. W. Bockett, a compositor, contributed several articles to the *Positivist Review* from the point of view of someone who knew his place and sought duties rather than rights. Another compositor, Henry Tompkins, acknowledged that he owed his education to Positivism (LPS 3/1).

The lack of more widespread working-class support for Positivism, however, was a worry to both Congreve and Harrison. Congreve blamed the class system itself for separating workmen from the lives of active believers in the Religion of Humanity. They had no chance to see the faith in practice (R. Harrison 1965: 320). Harrison was occasionally prepared to blame the workmen themselves, for instance when he agreed to change his lectures at Newton Hall to seven o'clock in order to suit their convenience:

It seems that the 'working man' will not come at 11 a.m. because he likes to lie in bed and cook his Sunday dinner comfortable. He will not come at 3 p.m. because he has not finished his dinner. He says he cannot keep awake at 4 p.m. because he takes an extra glass of beer at dinner and feels rather heavy. He objects to 8 p.m. because he likes to get home early on Sunday night and go to bed comfortable by 9 p.m. But he says . . . that he will come at 7 p.m. because he has his tea at 5 p.m. and can keep awake for an hour, and get home by 8.30.

(HP 1/40, ff.1–2)

The Newton Hall Guilds attempted to accommodate the working man's need for recreation with a combination of football, cricket, boxing, dancing, music and drama (McGee 1931: 175–7).

The Positivists' work for the trade unions brought them into close contact with a number of their leaders who themselves developed an interest in Comte. George Odger, the shoemaker, attended the Positivist School regularly in the 1870s and one of his friends, William Chatterton, formally joined the society. Robert Applegarth and George Howell both looked back with gratitude and admiration to the services rendered to their unions by Beesly, Crompton and Harrison (R. Harrison 1965: 323–8). Howell had read and discussed Comte with his dying son and with Henry Crompton during 1879 and 1880 and seemed to be on the brink of formal adhesion. His manuscript 'Autobiography' recalls an initial attraction to Positivism through personal contact with its leaders being subsequently repelled by the religiosity of a New Year's Eve service at Chapel Street, at which, incidentally, he met George Eliot (BI). Neither he nor any of the other trade union leaders committed themselves permanently to the propagation of Positivism and this failure to lay deep roots among the working classes was a major factor in the suddenness with which Positivism was to decline. Another important reason for this was the damning criticism of Comte launched by his many and varied opponents.

4

THE MIDDLE YEARS: A MATTER
OF CONTROVERSY

The press: from ridicule to respect

It is impossible, of course, to give a full and systematic account of the reception of the Religion of Humanity in the British press. Such was the proliferation of periodicals in the Victorian period that Harrison could boast a hundred notices for a single address (FH to Hillemand, 23/9/91, MAC). But in the best known periodicals and in those articles which were preserved by the Positivists themselves there does seem to have been a development from unthinking rejection and ridicule to more serious consideration, whether critical or sympathetic. To begin with, the treatment accorded to Comte during his life, which with the notable exceptions of the *Leader*, the *Reasoner*, and the *Westminster Review* has been seen to have been unanimously hostile, continued in dismissive announcements of his death (*LG*, 12/9/57, 882) and in the howls of derision which greeted Congreve's translation of the *Catechism*, which the liberal Catholic *Rambler* called

the result of a boundless conceit, an inordinate love of theoretical system, a deep-seated weakness of character, a feebleness of passion properly so called, an admiration for many things in Catholicism, and an utter absence of belief in a personal God.

Comte himself was described as a 'religious emotionist' of 'the sugar-and-honey, or the milk-and-water description' without that 'perception of the absurd' which would have alerted him to 'the astonishing folly of his whole system' (*Rambler* X (1858) 164–73).

Similar attacks came from the Congregational *British Quarterly Review*, which had earlier called the *Système* the product of a 'laborious and long-winded genius' (*BQR* XXI (1855) 423). The *Catechism*, it claimed, was 'so puerile, so silly, so drivelling' that it could only have been the product of an insane mind and Clotilde was to be thanked for bringing into the open the latent assumptions of his early writings (XXVIII (1858) 422–46). Mill, Littré and Lewes were later praised for covering 'with a decent veil of silence the shame of their master' in producing such a 'melancholy parody' of Christianity (XLIV (1866) 59–89). The *Athenaeum* also found the *Catechism* ridiculous, poking fun at Comte's pontifical pretensions and his idea of worship, to conjure up an image of 'the handsomest woman of one's acquaintance' (*Athenaeum*, 10/4/58, 463). Bridges' translation of the *General View* was praised only for clarifying Comte's 'unfitness for the English mind' (4/3/65, 312). Congreve's essays were described in relatively generous terms (4/7/74, 9–10), but the completed translation of the *Système* was welcomed once more because it helped 'to show up the absurdity and shallowness' of the original. There was some 'good sense and generous thought mixed up with the absurdities', however (11/8/77, 171–3). By 1885, when Positivism was clearly doomed to failure, the *Athenaeum* could even afford to praise Caird's sympathetic treatment of Comte as 'a wholesome corrective to that tendency to deprecate him altogether to which not a few English writers have yielded' (25/4/85, 531–2), particularly, it failed to add, in its own pages.

The writers of the *Saturday Review*, who 'specialised in enthusiastic exposures of shoddy thinking or defective scholarship' (Gross 1969: 63), warmed to this role in relation to the Religion of Humanity. Positive Philosophy they could follow, but not the product of Comte's later years. James FitzJames Stephen, who was probably responsible for a comic depiction of the Positivist Calendar in 1857, began his review of the *Catechism* by observing that Comte, who had recently 'become subjective', was now being 'invoked as the patron of utterly wild and extravagant fancies'. An unsympathetic account of the details of the Positive religion, interspersed with suggestive nudges and winks about Comte's relationship with Clotilde, led on to a denunciation of Congreve for taking it seriously (*SR* III (10/6/57) 567–8). Congreve's first sermon, a 'somewhat dull discourse', came in for additional ridicule (VII (12/3/59) 304–5), as did Harrison's attack on *Essays and Reviews*, in which he 'disposed of Christianity and everything connected with it, and turned humanity out stark naked in search of a new creed' all in thirty-eight pages. Comte's own writing was described as 'the most portentous exhibition of egoism in literature' (XI (2/2/61) 114–15).

Comte's philosophy was treated with respect in Stephen's review of

Mill's 1865 *Westminster Review* articles but 'that strange parody upon religion which might be described as Popery conducted upon atheistic principles' continued to suffer ridicule for being both papist and foreign (XIX (15/4/65) 431–3). 'Comte', explained a review of the Positivist essays on *International Policy* of 1866, 'copied everything French and when he invented a religion and a Utopia took care to have in it an imitation of the Romish priesthood in France' (XXII (16/8/66) 177). The *Saturday Review* never ceased to attack the Religion of Humanity, though by 1877 it felt that there was no longer any point in dwelling on its details. Clotilde had suffered quite enough from 'excessive idolatry on the one hand and from unworthy ridicule on the other' (XLIII (23/6/77) 773–4). Harrison, who had come to expect a 'hullabaloo about Clotilde de Vaux' from the *Saturday Review*, was still complaining about its 'ill-natured ribaldry to please the parsons' in 1892 (Bod.L. d 252, f.196).

The *Spectator* was another paper which refused to take Positivism seriously. Even in 1867 it saw little danger of Comtism becoming an influential creed in England, proficient in politics though its followers had proved to be (*Spectator*, 3/8/67, 857). It defended Positivism against misrepresentation in 1871 (5/8/71, 952–3), but it depicted Harrison as immature and Congreve as positively mad (8/11/73, 1403–4). Congreve's *Essays* were described as 'the most eccentric structure of insane and sanctimonious vanity ever fashioned outside of a mad-house'. The 'real object of Comte's own worship', the review claimed, 'was the *grand être* who lived at 10 Rue Monsieur-le-Prince'. Laffitte and Congreve completed the unholy Positivist Trinity. The *Essays* comprised 'such a book as might be written by a pious and benevolent but misanthropical Atheist' after twenty years as a recluse (12/9/74, 1142–3). By 1877 the *Spectator* could write complacently about the peculiar appeal afforded by the Positivist combination of 'all the pleasures of aristocratic scepticism with all the pleasures of a glowing faith' (17/11/77, 1429).

The *Saturday Review* and the *Spectator* excepted, there seems to have been a deepening seriousness in the treatment of Positivism towards the end of the 1860s. *The Times*, for instance, which had been so dismissive of the *Positive Philosophy* in 1853 and so vindictive towards Congreve in 1858, wrote much more sympathetically in 1868 of Comte's 'great force of intellect' and 'marvellous genius for scientific method'. Even the later works were worth reading, it argued, in spite of their tedious style, for 'the rich though broken lights of truth which they reveal amid masses of astounding self-assertion and even downright nonsense' (*Times*, 21/4/68, 5). Godfrey Lushington was one of the leader-writers for *The Times* at this juncture and William Stebbing, who took over its editorship in the 1870s, was an old schoolfriend of Harrison's. Harrison himself featured regularly on the letter page of *The Times*, which treated the 'high priest of the Positivist Church . . . and eulogist of the Paris Commune' with a slightly patronising but affectionate irony (27/10/92).

Harrison came in for much more savage treatment at the hands of the *Edinburgh Review*, which detected in his article on 'Neo-Christianity'

an almost fanatical desire to inveigle those who stood on more secure positions to the narrow ledge of the precipice on the midway of which he himself was standing . . . in order to adopt the mixture of Paganism and Catholicism in which the followers of M. Comte have found a refuge. (*ER* CXIII (1861) 464)

By 1868, however, the *Edinburgh Review* found the Religion of Humanity too serious for ridicule. A sustained analysis of its principal components ended with a furious attack on its 'wild impiety' and 'dismal and monotonous superstition' (CXXVII (1868) 303–57). There was an equally harsh attack on Positivism in the *London Quarterly Review* the following year (*LQR* XXXI (1869) 328–48). The increased seriousness of these reviews probably reflects the seriousness with which Positivism was discussed in places like the *Westminster Review*, which continued its earlier policy of openness to the movement, so that even the secondary offerings of Congreve and Bridges were assured of sympathetic notices.

The *Fortnightly Review* became so widely associated with Positivism that its second editor, John Morley, felt obliged to insert an explicit denial of the *Saturday Review*'s insinuation that it was 'the effective and consistent organ' of 'the followers of Comte'. The last eighteen numbers, he wrote in July 1870, contained

no less than three deliberate, exact, and powerful assaults on Comte and his system. The truth of the matter is that the *Fortnightly Review* is, with the exception of the *Westminster Review*, the only English organ in which Positivism has been treated seriously and had fair play, and in which it has never been either attacked or defended except by competent persons. (*FR* ns VIII (1870) 119–20)

Two of these assaults came from Thomas Huxley and will be examined along with other scientific criticism of Comte in the final section of this chapter. The third involved Professor Cairnes, who argued that Comte was ignorant of political economy (ns VII (1870) 579–602). Morley always allowed the Positivists the right of reply to these attacks so that Harrison ended up by contributing more than sixty articles, Beesly fifteen, Morison thirteen and Bridges eight. Almost every monthly issue of the *Fortnightly* from the appearance of Huxley's original attack in February 1869 to Morley's editorial comment the following July included an article on Positivism (Everett 1971: 93). The following four years, by contrast, contained half as many as these eighteen months (101). Public interest, it could be argued, had been exhausted and Positivism over-exposed. From 1870 onwards, while continuing to give generous space to the propounders of Positivism, the *Fortnightly* represented a variety of positions linked only by the broadest kind of positivism, a general 'faith in science and empiricism' (323).

The *Fortnightly Review* was the nearest thing to a Positivist periodical before the foundation of the *Positivist Review*, but it was by no means alone in treating Positivism seriously and sympathetically in the 1860s and 1870s. Another vehicle of Liberal thought, the *Contemporary Review*, whose publication of Harrison's articles on Positive religion so angered Morley, also published a number of intelligent assessments of Positivism from a Christian point of view. The first of these came in 1866 in a review of the Positivist essays entitled *International Policy*, which disputed 'their great assumption that Christianity is a thing of the past, doomed and rapidly passing away' (*CR* III (1866) 477–98). There were subsequent essays by Brooke Westcott in 1868, Mark Pattison in 1876 and Edward Caird in 1879, to be considered later in this chapter. The *Nineteenth Century*, founded in 1877 by James Knowles after a disagreement with the owners of the *Contemporary Review*, to be 'an open court for the free handling of all forms of serious thought', also paid serious attention to Positivism and printed forty-one essays by Harrison in its first fifty volumes. It was in the pages of the *Nineteenth Century* that Harrison did battle with the two major scientific opponents of Positivism, Huxley and Spencer.

Many of the contributors to the *Nineteenth Century* were deeply opposed to Positivism. The majority of the members of the

Metaphysical Society, for example, whose papers were normally published in the *Nineteenth Century*, clearly denied Comte's premise that unprovable concepts such as immortality and the existence of the soul were meaningless (A. W. Brown 1947: 94–5). Much of the discussion was not explicitly Positivist. The famous question, 'Is Life Worth Living?', posed to the society in 1877 by W. H. Mallock, involved an attack on positivism with a small 'p' with 'no special reference to the system of Comte or his disciples' (Mallock 1879: xxxiii). Other attacks were both specific and malicious, for example the Bishop of Carlisle's expressions of horror at 'Comte's Famous Fallacy', the law of the three stages (*NC* XX (1886) 473–90), and 'Comte's Atheism' (XXI (1887) 873–82). But the *Nineteenth Century* generally tended to review Positivist publications with discriminating sympathy. Wilfrid Ward found much to praise in Morison's *Service of Man* and welcomed the broadening of attitudes at Newton Hall to which he believed the book bore witness:

The really interesting issues which Positivism raises are divorced in it from the extraordinary theological phraseology concerning the great Being Humanity, the nine sacraments . . . and so forth, which Comte adopted when his mind commenced to fail, and which Mr. Frederic Harrison at one time attempted to perpetuate . . . it is satisfactory to note that the Positivists are now ready to enter the arena unencumbered by this strange and embarrassing attire.   (XXII (1887) 413–14)

The *New Calendar of Great Men* also received a sympathetic review in the *Nineteenth Century* from John Morley (XXXI (1892) 312–28).

The transition in public attitudes towards Positivism from general ridicule and contempt to sympathetic criticism and respect is also evident in a paper such as the *Pall Mall Gazette*, which began in 1865 and 'soon took a place among daily papers similar to that which had been occupied by the *Saturday Review* in the weekly press' (LS 1895: 212). Having vilified the Positivists in the 1870s for political activities such as the defence of the Commune, they printed sympathetic articles in the 1880s under the editorship first of Morley and then W. T. Stead, who also gave space to critics of Comte such as Canon Liddon. But he allowed Harrison the right of reply (Vogeler 1984: 199). This new-found respectability was partly a tribute to the stature Harrison had achieved within the literary establishment as a personal friend of the editors of many of the periodicals. It may also indicate a relaxation of orthodox vigilance in relation to the attacks of rationalism and science in general. The Positivists were no longer regarded as a threat to society.

Oxford men of letters: Arnold, Ruskin, Pater, Morley

Between Newman's Catholicism and Green's idealism, according to Mark Pattison, the dominant philosophy in Oxford was Mill's positivism (MP 1885: 165–7). There was a well-trodden path 'From Oxford to Comte' (C. Kent 1978: ch. 4) which can sometimes be traced still further back to Thomas Arnold's Rugby. Matthew Arnold and Arthur Clough, who were friends and contemporaries of Congreve at both Rugby and Oxford, also interested themselves in Positivism. Matthew Arnold never took the Religion of Humanity seriously. As early as 1848 he teased his friend Clough about his interest in Comte, who had been 'quite passé these 10 years' (Lowry 1932: 74). But then, as Harrison complained, Arnold never took anything seriously and could never be tied down. He was a different kind of Oxford product: urbane, sociable, scholarly and detached (FH 1911: II 112).

It was an attack by Harrison on the type of culture that Arnold represented which brought about the good-humoured but deeply-felt controversy which provides one of the most interesting strands of *Culture and Anarchy*. Harrison's original attack formed part of a general warning to the middle classes that tinkering with reform would not avert the coming revolution (*FR* ns I (1867) 261–83), a warning which made him a suitable target for Arnold's final lecture as Professor of Poetry, in June 1867, on 'Culture and its Enemies'. This lecture, which was incorporated into the first chapter of *Culture and Anarchy*, identifies 'Mr Frederic Harrison and other disciples of Comte' as exponents of 'Jacobinism', a violent rejection of the past in favour of some systematic blueprint for the future. Culture, however, has little time for systems or system-makers:

A current in people's minds sets towards new ideas . . . and some man, some Bentham or Comte, who has the real merit of having early and strong felt and helped the new current, but who brings plenty of narrowness and mistakes of his own into his feeling and help of it, is credited with being the author of the whole current, the fit person to be entrusted with its regulation and to guide the human race.

Against such dogmatic narrowness and the 'fierce exasperation which

. . . hisses' through Harrison's work Arnold sets 'the pursuit of sweetness and light' as the aim of culture (MA, *CPW* v 109–12).

Harrison responded quickly with 'Culture: A Dialogue', in which he posed as a defender of sweetness and light against the rigorous attacks of Arnold's blunt German, Arminius von Thunder-ten-dronck, the friend of *Friendship's Garland*. Arminius criticises Arnold's 'flabby religious phrases', demanding to know by what methods culture is to be attained and then tested. In a world of suffering and evil he finds Arnold's fastidious detachment unsatisfactory. Informed by Harrison of Arnold's misrepresentation of Comtism, which differs from Jacobinism in its reverence for the past, its hatred of revolution, and its belief in education, Arminius feels that Arnold should study Comte more closely, since they appear to hold much in common (*FR* ns II (1867) 603–14). Arnold, who was so amused by Harrison's article that he laughed till he cried (G. W. E. Russell 1895: I 372), reported that his German friend had finally abandoned him for 'a much better-dressed man, with whom he is pursuing researches concerning labour and capital' (MA, *CPW* v 7, 314).

Arnold himself, far from accepting a close connection between Comte and culture, went out of his way to attack both his system and its English exponents. The longest passage to be omitted from the five essays on 'Anarchy and Authority' in the final version of *Culture and Anarchy* shows Arnold revelling in his ability to play 'the cat with Harrison's mouse' (E. K. Brown 1935: 21). Distinguishing between 'the Rabbi' himself and his English disciples, he finds the former guilty of 'system-mongering' and the latter of flattering the populace in a manner directly contrary to the *Catechism* '(Congreve's translation, authorized version)'. He warns the Comtists against setting too great a store on ceremony, claiming that they should have 'more reason to be pleased with me than annoyed' for this friendly piece of advice (MA, *CPW* v 504–6).

That this was not the Comtists' response is the probable reason for Arnold's omitting this passage from *Culture and Anarchy* in 1869. The following year, he actually met Harrison, who reported 'how much better I like Arnold in the flesh than the spirit' (HP 1/52, f.20). He continued, however, to dismiss the products of Arnold's pen as 'dilly dallying stuff' (1/53, f.17) and to warn Morley not to follow in the footsteps of this 'literary juggler' (1/57, f.6). Arnold, for his part, advised Harrison through the dying words of Arminius 'to do more in literature – he has the talent for it; and to avoid Carlylese as he would the devil' (MA, *CPW* V 347). He also tried 'to make our peace with the Comtists' by quoting Littré in *Literature and Dogma* (VI 174).

Arnold continued to interest himself in Positivism in the seventies, copying passages from the *Philosophie positive* into his diary, where, in reply to Harrison's argument that 'Streams of Tendency' took us 'a very short way' in religion and politics and that it was 'the pedantry of sect' to claim the monopoly of terms such as the 'soul' and the 'spiritual' (*CR* XXVI (1875) 1010–11), he reasserted his belief that 'the power of religion does of nature belong, in a unique way, to the Bible and to Christianity' (MA, *CPW* VIII 134). The real pedant, Arnold claimed in two essays of 1885, was Comte, who assumed that he possessed the necessary 'religious genius' to create a completely new set of beliefs (X 231–2). Harrison also came in for ironic pity for having 'weighted himself for the race of life by taking up a grotesque old French pedant upon his shoulders' (207).

Harrison in turn poured scorn on the celebrated phrases by which the apostle of culture had attempted to preserve religion and literature from dogma and dissent,

these 'indescribable eternals that make for righteousness,' and all the other phrases by which clever men try to escape from the obvious difficulties they feel in saying God when they do not mean God.   (FH 1879: 9)

His final estimate placed Arnold on a pedestal as a poet and critic while condemning his other writing. His ignorance of Positivism, which he had masked with an 'air of laughable superiority', prevented him from recognising that he was 'constantly talking Comte without knowing it' (FH 1899: 111–34). There were certainly similarities in their aims. Both set out to regenerate a decaying society by replacing its theological creed with an ethical humanism based on the highest achievements of art and science. There was a world of difference, however, between their respective solutions. Arnold's urbane concept of culture was far too nebulous for the more eager evangelical temperament of Harrison and his Comtist colleagues (Vogeler 1962: 454–8).

Another Victorian prophet and product of Oxford to cross words with Frederic Harrison was John Ruskin. Once again, Harrison claimed that 'Ruskin and Comte are constantly saying the same thing' (FH 1899: 101), while Ruskin continually denied any such affinity. Harrison met Ruskin at the Working Men's College in 1860 and urged him to study the 'social and economic principles laid down in the *Positive Polity*'. But 'John would take no ideas from the Angel Gabriel himself'. Eight years later Harrison tried once more to explain that Positivism provided a scientific basis for Ruskin's own economic theories, but his friend was not prepared to read Comte just to see if he had been anticipated (FH 1911: I 229–33). What he heard from Harrison of this 'supposed religion of Humanity' seemed to him absurdly elitist, 'one of the most microscopic "isms" which have ever become particles of coagulation for the wandering imaginations of the Sons of Men' (HP 1/101, ff.8–9). *Fors Clavigera*, in June 1876, attacked Harrison's whole notion of progress, whether in art or nature, statues or pippins, especially in the human race: 'An aggregate of men is a mob, and not "Humanity" ', he proclaimed (JR, *Works* XXVIII 618–25). Throughout the ensuing controversy, however, he tempered these 'public denunciations' with private letters full of affection (FH 1911: I 238), some of which were included in an appendix to *Fors Clavigera*. They explain 'the real reason' for his attack on Harrison, 'the unconsciousness' displayed by the Positivist of the 'misery' brought by the loss of faith in God (JR, *Works* XXIX 565–9). When Harrison complained that he misrepresented Comte, Ruskin admitted with characteristic frankness that he had 'never read a word' of Comte and had 'no idea what Positivism means' (XXVIII 662–4).

Harrison had no wish to continue the controversy but objected to being addressed, 'Human Son of Holothurian Harries':

when he says look what a mudlark and slug this Positivist is – I am willing to show cause. The real thing behind Ruskin is Carlyle, and behind Carlyle is God – who still has a following and may yet give trouble.   (HP 1/62, f.35)

Their unpublished correspondence reveals personal strains beneath the surface of their public dispute. Ethel Harrison's mother had died on 8 July 1876, and Ruskin's letter of consolation to Harrison could not resist the remark, 'Religion with *me* means, belief in the Resurrection.' Harrison replied with a sermon on subjective immortality in which he reproached Ruskin with blasphemy against Humanity (FH 1911: I 239–40), whereupon Ruskin labelled the 'entire school of modern rationalists . . . a mere fungoid growth of semi-education' led by a 'loathsome cretin', John Stuart Mill (HP 1/101, f.27). Ruskin continued to dismiss 'positivism with its religion of Humanity', for instance in the 1882 preface to *Sesame and Lilies*, where it is seen as a contributory factor to the 'dust-cloud' of new ideas thrown up by a well-meaning but vulgar age (JR, *Works* XVIII 50–1). 'What is Positivism', he asked Harrison in 1884, 'but the Everlasting Me?' (Vogeler 1975: 92). Harrison, however, lived long enough to have the last word, including among the weaknesses of 'Ruskin as Prophet' his ill-informed denunciation of Comte (FH 1899: 77–110), some of whose ideas he unwittingly and unsystematically repeated (FH 1902: 73, 112).

Another prophet to rise from Oxford, William Morris, seemed to see more of a future for the Religion of Humanity. At least, the old man in *News from Nowhere*, speaking at the beginning of the twenty-first century, voices the belief that humanity is now worthy of worship. 'In times past', he confesses, 'men were told to love their kind, to believe in the religion of humanity and so forth' but were immediately repelled by the hideousness of the individuals who made up the mass they were supposed to worship. They could only overcome this basic problem 'by making a conventional abstraction of mankind that had little actual or historical relation to the race'. Now that men have been freed from all the constraints upon their innate goodness which capitalist society had imposed, no such problem exists (Morris 1973: 298–9). Quite how ironic Morris is being is not certain. In a sense he is voicing an obvious objection to the Religion of Humanity. But he does seem to take it seriously as a possible religion of the future.

A somewhat surprising Oxford sympathiser with the Religion of Humanity was Walter Pater, who delivered a paper on 'Subjective Immortality' as early as 1864 (Monsman 1970: 359–89). His published work gives little indication of his interest in Comte, although he criticised Coleridge in 1866 for attempting to resist the inevitable advance of the 'relative spirit' fostered by 'the influence of the sciences of observation' (WP 1973: 1–2) and for insisting that a belief in the supernatural was essential for the development of 'the spiritual element in life'. Pater advocates 'the broader spiritualities' of systems opposed to Christianity, such as 'positivism' (21), praising the 'historical method' in particular as 'one of the applications . . . of the relative spirit', which could help in the interpretation of religious dogmas as 'memorials of a class of sincere and beautiful spirits . . . in a past age of humanity' (23–4). But the humanism propounded in this essay, although clearly drawing from Comte, is more reminiscent of Arnold than of the Positivists:

The humanist, he who possesses that complete culture, does not weep over the failure of a theory ... nor shriek over the fall of a philosophical formula. A kind of humour is one of the conditions of the true mental attitude in the criticism of past stages of thought. Humanity cannot afford to be too serious about them. (6)

His description of the Mona Lisa in *The Renaissance* suggests that it could be taken as a 'symbol of the modern idea ... of humanity summing up in itself, all modes of thought and life'. But she encompasses 'the animalism of Greece, the lust of Rome' and 'the sins of the Borgias' as well as 'the reverie of the middle age' (WP 1901: 125–6). The famous ending of the book insists on an aesthetic detachment from all systems, 'never acquiescing in a facile orthodoxy of Comte' or any other thinker (237).

An essay on 'Wordsworth' in the *Fortnightly Review* of 1874, in which Pater wrote approvingly of the fetichism involved in attaching religious sentiments to particular places, encouraged Harrison to claim, 'Positivism has made a triumph in capturing a man so naturally antipositivist as he' (HP 1/59, f.17). There are even more specific references to Comte in *Marius the Epicurean*, which has been seen to 'move toward a somewhat sentimental and self-indulgent "religion of humanity" ' (DeLaura 1973: 348). The hero's mother allows her late husband

that secondary sort of life which we can give to the dead, in our intensely realised memory of them – the 'subjective immortality,' to use a modern phrase, for which many a Roman epitaph cries out plaintively to the widow, or sister or daughter, still in the land of the living. (WP 1910: I 20)

His friend Flavian, it is true, derives little comfort from the notion of Marius weeping over his dead body, while the Christian catacombs offer the greater hope of resurrection. But Pater interprets Christianity in a decidedly positive spirit. He has more time for the person of Christ than Comte, but the real centre of his attention is the Church, in which Marius finds 'that regenerate type of humanity' for which he seeks (II 110). Their worship takes Christ as a moving idealisation of the notion of Humanity, 'a figure which seemed to have absorbed ... all that was deep-felt and impassioned in the experiences of the past' (134). Pater's review of *Robert Elsmere*, which celebrated the virtues of renunciation as taught in *The Imitation* and saw the priest as 'one of the necessary types of humanity', maintained the 'possibility' that Christianity might be true but continued to present it

in a Positivist light, pleading for a much broader Church than orthodoxy could allow (WP 1973: 135–41).

The unpublished and fragmentary essays of Pater's last decade confirm the strength of his interest in Positivism. An essay on 'Plato's
Ethics', for example, refers to 'egoistic' and 'altruistic' instincts (WPP
1) while two other philosophical essays contrast 'positive knowledge'
with 'metaphysical systems' (2, 3). An essay on 'The Aesthetic Life'
advocates a religion free from the tyranny of science, focussing instead
on art, which reveals the 'successive stages of the story of humanity'
(7). A further fragmentary essay on 'Art and Religion' takes up the
idea from Mill's 'gloomy essays on religion' that contemplation of
Christ could be indulged as an ideal, 'one of those whom humanity has
sanctioned' (11). His most explicit discussion of the Religion of
Humanity occurs in a set of notes which he was thinking of using in an
introduction to an edition of Plato's *Ethics* or else in *Marius the
Epicurean*. This finds the idea of cultivating 'sympathy with a body of
persons outlived but perhaps vaguely in our minds . . . the most effective sanction of morals', half-paraphrasing, half-quoting Comte's
definition of Humanity, which is presented as the culmination of a
long tradition of western thought. Pater goes on to discuss the 'church
of the future organised around the cultus de ce vrai Grand-être',
governed more and more by the dead, which he feels capable of
meeting men's religious needs:

This cult, so ideal, so religious, with such char[acteristic] notes of ideality
and rel[igious]ness, while it will direct a new organisation of benevolent sentiment and activity towards the present and future generations has on the
other hand undeniably added to the feeling of friendly reverence for the past
by the generation of that more liberal air through wh[ich] we are allowed to
see the rel[igio]ns of the past, not as Voltaire saw them, but as stages of
growth in wh[ich] especially the rel[igio]n of the Ch[urch] of Rome fills a
great place.

Pater calls the Positivist Calendar a 'quaint imitation' of the Christian
ecclesiastical year but accepts the notion of hero-worship derived
from Carlyle (17). His treatment of Comte is altogether sympathetic
and full of respect. He cannot accurately be described as a Positivist,
but the Religion of Humanity undoubtedly contributed to his very
liberal interpretation of Christianity.

Perhaps the most important Oxford man of letters, from the
Positivist point of view, was John Morley. Introduced to Comte's

ideas by Morison at Lincoln, Morley worked on the *Leader* shortly before its expiry 'of dullness and Comte' (Hirst 1927: 141). He admired Lewes for his wit and positively worshipped George Eliot, by whom he was 'brought into an outer ring of sympathisers' (55, 72). For a time, he recalled, he was 'not far off from a formal union with this new church' (JM 1921a: 162–3). But he was all along a protestant Positivist in the Millite mould, first attracting Mill's attention in 1865 by an attack on those who rejected Comte's ideas simply because they were unusual. His first issue as editor of the *Fortnightly Review* distinguished between 'catholic' readiness to accept a whole religious tradition and 'protestant' refusal to accept any system uncritically, a distinction he repeated in a letter to Congreve (Hamer 1968: 21–3), who liked Morley, regarding him as 'one of the most useful men to our cause . . . more useful to us in fact than if he were more fully with us', because of his 'position amongst the scribes of the day' (BL 45233, f.207v).

Morley's biographical studies of the 1860s and 1870s present a basically Comtean view of the intellectual background to the French Revolution (Willey 1956: 256–9). Comte entered his study of Burke as 'a great thinker of a later day' who had substituted the relative and positive for the absolute and abstract (JM 1867: 23). He also appeared in an article of 1867 as 'the thinker who has done more than any other towards laying the foundation of scientific history' (*FR* ns II (1867) 229). But his relegation of Voltaire to a secondary place in his calendar, and then only as a dramatic poet, is seen as a failure to appreciate the essential work of destruction typical of 'those with systems to defend' (JM 1923a: 37). Comte was basically too conservative in modelling his ideal of a future society on 'the ancient or medieval constitution' which it was to replace (177–9).

The first of these two passages in *Voltaire* has a long footnote replying to 'one or two private critics' who accused Morley of misrepresenting a philosopher to whom he acknowledges 'numerous . . . obligations, direct and indirect', a phrase taken from a letter from Harrison (HP 1/53, f.87), to which Morley had replied with an admission that three-fifths of what he said about Voltaire had been influenced by Comte. He had, he claimed, omitted a preface defining these obligations on the grounds that it was irrelevant to Voltaire and unnecessary, since critics already treated him as a disciple of Comte. Reviews of his previous book had thrown 'Clotilde de Vaux and all the rest . . . systematically into my very innocent face', in spite of his dislike of everything associated with her name. He insisted, 'I agree with you and Bridges and Beesly and Crompton five million times more than I differ from you'. But if he had to define his position he was 'not Comtist but Positivist', accepting Harrison's statement of the Positive problem but not his solution, 'certainly not Comte's new organisation, which I entirely dislike'. His mind was not yet made up, but he would probably become 'more and more Millite, less and less Comtist'. If the Positivists wanted more support, however, he would give it (Hirst 1927: I 199–200). Harrison and 'the brethren' remained nonetheless suspicious and resentful of the 'Positivist Heresiarch' (201, 193), while Morley continued to decline invitations to speak at the Positivist School and to express his distaste for sectarianism, urging Harrison to escape from 'that narrow Comtist pinfold' and to shed his Positivist 'blinkers' (179).

Morley was a frequent visitor to Paris, where he found Laffitte's relaxed brand of Positivism more congenial than Congreve's. A Sunday discourse at rue Monsieur-le-Prince early in 1872, he reported to Harrison, 'was totally free from Sectarian jargon, and from the technical pedantries in which your London chief delights' (206). He enjoyed meeting 'the whole positivist church, catholic and universal' in Morison's Paris flat (HP 1/79, f.52) and responded favourably to Congreve's Annual Address in 1873, agreeing that religion was 'the key to Comtism and its strength' (1/80, f.2). But his letters to Harrison of that year continue to criticise some of Comte's 'silly and pedantic' ideas (f.5) and to poke fun at the Religion of Humanity. They also discuss the idea of God, printed in *Rousseau* with a small 'g', which Morley could accept as 'a stream of tendency' but not as a person. He agreed with Laffitte that Positivists were necessarily atheists since they could not conceive of God (Hirst 1927: I 246–8).

Morley was depressed by the lukewarm reception of some lectures he delivered on Positivism in the summer of 1873 which Harrison of all people called 'too Comtist' (249). But he remained on good terms both with Laffitte and with Congreve, no mean feat in itself. An obituary article on John Stuart Mill expressed Morley's belief that the coming religion would 'rest upon the solidarity of mankind' (*FR* ns XIII (1873) 676), although a review of Mill's *Autobiography* compared his admirable caution with Comte's 'rash and premature' attempts at social reconstruction, which contained some ideas of great beauty and power, some of extreme absurdity, and some which would be very mischievous if there were the smallest chance of their ever being realised. (ns XV (1874) 11–12).

Harrison was alarmed by this 'angry bite at Comte', which seemed to him symptomatic of an anxiety 'to rub off the label of Positivism' (HP 1/59, f.77). He urged Morley to make 'a tabula rasa' of his opinions and 'rebuild the edifice anew on true Positive lines' (f.48).

Morley's subsequent work, however, reveals an increasing lack of respect for the Religion of Humanity. He criticised Flint's underestimate of Comte's contribution to history (*FR* ns XVI (1874) 351–2) but made no mention of the Religion of Humanity in his long review of Mill's *Essays on Religion* (634–51; ns XVII (1875) 103–31). It has been argued that 'the Comtist problem of the separation of powers' is the central theme of his essays *On Compromise* (C. Kent 1978: 126). The basic principles proposed in the introductory chapter clearly derive from Comte. Moral principles are 'registered generalisations from experience' and therefore 'rest on the same positive base as our faith in the truth of physical laws' (JM 1874: 15, 21). But he departs completely from Comte in favour of Mill on the question of liberty. He believes that 'self-regarding acts' should be free from state interference: 'Whether the lawmakers be laymen in parliament or priests of humanity exercising the spiritual power, it matters not' (210–11).

Harrison was delighted with *On Compromise*, which he took as evidence that his friend remained 'a Positivist if not a Comtist' (HP 1/60, f.24). By the end of 1874, however, he was forced to recognise Morley's language as that of 'the literary mind of the liberal or unattached sort' (f.52). Morley himself distinguished between the man of letters and the man of systems in his study of Diderot the following year:

the man of letters has his work to do in the critical period of social transition. He is to be distinguished from the great systematic thinker, as well as from the great imaginative creator. He is borne on the wings neither of a broad philosophic conception nor of a lofty poetic conception. He is only the propagator of portions of such conceptions, and of the minor ideas which they suggest.

It was a modest role whose dangers had been pointed out by a 'deep observer' identified in the footnotes as Comte (JM 1878: I 17–18). It was the role Morley himself chose to adopt.

Before committing himself to this role, however, Morley carried out the task Harrison had long been urging upon him. He re-read much of Comte's work in order to write the section on Comte for the ninth edition of the *Encyclopaedia Britannica*. An overjoyed Harrison offered him 'a "study" to yourself with the works of Comte in all forms' (HP 1/63, f.35), but was less pleased when he heard Morley's verdict. The article begins by placing Comte in the perspective of the eighteenth-century critics with whom Morley was so familiar and proceeds to give a clear outline of Comte's life and thought, defending his consistency of purpose. 'Comte's immense superiority' over revolutionary utopians is seen to lie in his emphasis on the moral progress which must precede social and political change. The Religion of Humanity, however, is described as 'utilitarian crowned by a fantastic decoration'. Comte had managed to clothe an 'intrinsically conciliatory' doctrine in a most unattractive fashion. The article ends by expressing the hope that 'the world . . . will take what is available in Comte' and ignore his peculiar aberrations (*EB* VI (1877) 229–38).

Similar reasons for Morley's final rejection of the Religion of Humanity emerge in his 'Commonplace Book', which discusses the possibility of Positivism leading a 'strong moral and spiritual reaction' against the prevailing 'luxury, materialism, and secularity' of the age. Morley concluded that it would not achieve this aim because it lacked an inspiring text, a 'history of martyrs and high examples' and an ascetic strength: 'It does not strike the imagination enough to catch any of the vast mass of indifferents who can only be seized by the external' (Hamer 1968: 388–9). Morley himself withdrew from any involvement with Positivism. He remained on friendly though less intimate terms with Harrison and continued to review such Positivist productions as the *New Calendar of Great Men* with sympathy and understanding. But he wrote no more about the Religion of Humanity, contenting himself with putting some of its principles into practice. He became increasingly pessimistic about Humanity, which he felt was 'becoming *rebarbarised*' (Quin to Grant, 14/10/99, BLUL), and was to resign from the Cabinet in protest against the nationalism and imperialism he detected in the First World War, when the Victorian attempt to unite rationalism and sentiment took on additional attraction. Mill and Comte had been left stranded by later developments in science and history (JM 1908a: 145–67). But Morley preferred to be linked with them than with their successors. 'If I were to have a label,' he confessed, 'I should be a Positivist' (JM 1921a: II 253).

Cambridge critics: Sidgwick and the Stephens

Had he gone to Oxford rather than Cambridge, Leslie Stephen claimed, he too 'might have been a Positivist' (Annan 1951: 148):

I did read Comte and was much impressed – I still have elaborate notes of the Philosophie Pos[itive]. But I had no companions in my interest and so escaped or missed conversion.   (HP 1/108, f.36)

For while Congreve was 'finding his chief proselytes at Oxford . . . Cambridge looked on with a comparative indifference, and congratulated itself upon its intellectual calm'. The Positivists, he admitted, had 'too much reason for thinking that I sat in the seat of the scorner', for he was aware of the 'comic side' as well as the 'important truths' of the new religion (LS 1924: 139–40), but his work can be seen as another significant attempt to winnow the Comtean chaff from the positive grain. Having lost his fourth-generation evangelical faith and resigned his fellowship, he left for London at the end of 1864 to earn his living by writing reviews. He continued to study Comte, especially in the mid-sixties, when he also discussed religious and political questions with 'Fred. Harrison and some of his positivist friends' (LS 1977: 8). He offered 'an acceptable worship' at George Eliot's feet in the seventies (30) and later became a close friend of Judge Vernon Lushington and his family.

By 1869 Leslie Stephen felt confident enough to undertake 'a judicial account of Comte's philosophy' in order to correct some of the misunderstandings from which it suffered (LS 1924: 57). His unsigned article on 'The Comtist Utopia' claimed that although committed Comtists were to be 'counted by tens rather than hundreds', the progress of Positivism had been as rapid as anyone apart from its founder could have hoped. Its ideas had sunk 'deeply into public opinion'. Its moral code seemed to Stephen, as it had to Mill, 'one-sided and exaggerated' and the system as a whole he found 'in many ways chimerical and absurd' but it contained some 'valuable ideas' which he hoped might find 'general acceptance'. The opponents of Positivism, he concluded, should recognise that 'opinions which sway many minds owe their power not to the falsehoods, but to the truths which are in them' (*FM* LXXX (1869) 1–21).

Throughout the seventies, when he was editor of the *Cornhill Magazine*, Leslie Stephen continued to row 'with the positivist tide' (Gross 1969: 91). He found much valuable teaching in Harrison's *Order and Progress* in spite of its visionary tendencies and untenable assumption that Comte had spoken the last word (*FR* ns XVII (1875) 820–34). His own articles of this period, which were occasionally reviewed and translated in Littré's *Philosophie positive*, reinforce his claim to have made a judicious selection of what was valuable in Positivism. The human predicament is presented dramatically in one of Stephen's *Essays on Freethinking and Plainspeaking*, 'A Bad Five Minutes in the Alps', in which a climber spends what he thinks are his last moments imagining the possibility that first the Christians, then the spiritualists, and finally the Positivists are right. The thought of being 'a mere atom in the great current of humanity' fails to provide much comfort. He tries to tell himself that his work will outlive his life and contribute to human progress:

The Social Science Association will gradually extend its soporific influence over the face of the world . . . We shall have a Pope, only in Paris instead of Rome, and he shall preach scientific instead of theological dogmas. Providence will be superseded by the 'three bankers' of the future.

Such a religion, of course, lacks conviction. Humanity is 'too big and distant' to afford comfort in any crisis and he is forced back to an 'obscure sense of honour' in playing out the game of life to the final whistle (LS 1877: 156–97). 'An Apology for Plainspeaking' spells out the moral: no new creed can replace the old forms of worship hallowed by deep and long association or hope to obliterate the wish for personal immortality. The only possibility is to lay the foundations of the new faith which time alone will complete (359–62).

Leslie Stephen continued to mingle respect for Comte's 'reasoning power' and 'view of history' (*FR* ns XXVII (1880) 672–95) with amazement at his arrogance in attempting to 'dictate a complete system to the world' (LS 1893: 205–31). *The Science of Ethics*, published in 1882, in spite of its basic aim to provide a scientific basis for morals and the obvious debt to Comte of the chapter on 'Altruism', which is divided into separate sections on 'Egoistic Instincts', 'Sympathy', 'Altruism' and 'The Rule of Conduct', omitted the founder of Positivism from its list of influential thinkers. Reprimanded by Henry Sidgwick for this neglect, Stephen acknowledged a great debt to Comte which he had overlooked only 'through carelessness of expression' (Maitland 1906: 352). Even this book, then, can be seen as 'a by-product of Comte' (Annan 1951: 212). His addresses to various ethical societies also tended to preach positivism with a small 'p'. His tribute to 'Forgotten Benefactors', delivered shortly after the death of his beloved wife, Julia, took a distinctly Comtean line on the reverence due both to great men in history and to angels in the house:

Every religion has its saints . . . But that man is unfortunate who has not a saint of his own − some one in whose presence, or in the very thought of whom, he does not recognise a superior, before whom it becomes him to bow with reverence and gratitude, and who has purified the atmosphere and strengthened the affections in a little circle from which the influence may be transmitted to others.

This influence, he claimed, could continue after death in a form of subjective immortality, 'as if those who left us had yet become part of ourselves' (LS 1896: II 264−5).

Leslie Stephen's *Mausoleum Book* instructed his children to worship the memory of their mother, to 'fix her picture' in their minds and so 'to feel all that is holy and all that is endearing in human affection' as well as allowing her to continue to live in their lives (LS 1977: 96−8). The children themselves did not see things quite in this light. Virginia Woolf, who was thirteen when her mother died, rebelled against her father's Comtean teaching: 'All these tears and groans, reproaches and protestations of affection, high talk of duty and work and living for others', she complained, 'for long did unpardonable mischief by substituting for the shape of a true and most vivid mother, nothing better than an unlovable phantom' (VW 1978: 45). She was only too aware of the other side of her father's worship of women, his tendency to tyrannise over them. Her sister Vanessa braved his wrath by refusing to 'accept her role, part slave, part angel of sympathy' (125).

Leslie Stephen emerges somewhat battered from Virginia Woolf's autobiographical writings and from the novel which she wrote to exorcise the memory of her parents. He is clearly the model for Mr Ramsay in *To the Lighthouse*, with his insensitive pursuit of truth at all costs, his outbursts of temper, his 'acting the part of a desolate man, widowed, bereft', and above all his fears of his own mediocrity, of only reaching 'q' on an alphabetical scale of intellectual achievement (VW 1927: 54, 254−6). The editor of the *Dictionary of National Biography*, who contributed some 378 articles bestowing an official subjective immortality on their subjects, feared that his own name would soon pass into oblivion (LS 1977: 93). His later works, such as *The English Utilitarians*, continued to criticise the 'later vagaries of positivism' (LS 1900: III 368) but he was in a good position to recognise George Eliot's indebtedness to Comte (LS 1902: 199–200).

Leslie Stephen's brother, James FitzJames Stephen, took an entirely different stance on the Positivists, whose political activities he denounced from the standpoint of patriotic common sense. He enjoyed nothing so much as an intellectual dog-fight with Harrison at the Metaphysical Society. Harrison recalled one particularly 'hot debate over the religion of Humanity' in which Stephen maintained 'that he would rather worship an African ape or a bull-dog' than Humanity (FH 1911: II 87–8). Their argument spilt over into print in 1873 when Stephen published a harsh attack on the Religion of Humanity as it had found expression in Mill, a faith which might be all right for the elite but would never appeal to the ignorant masses:

The real truth is that the human race is so big, so various, so little known, that no one can really love it. You can at most fancy that you love some imaginary representation of bits of it which when examined are only your own fancies personified. A progress which leads people to attach increased importance to phantoms is not a glorious thing, in my eyes at all events. It is a progress towards a huge Social Science Association embracing in itself all the Exeter Halls that ever were born or thought of. (JFS 1967: 241)

Stephen's dislike of all evangelical earnestness emerges in this passage as it does throughout the book.

Harrison, of course, could not resist a reply. He told Morley that Stephen was partly right in his attack on Mill's metaphysical notions of liberty, equality and fraternity. This was precisely why Comte had propounded so exact a creed. There was, however, something unpleasant about Stephen's attitude to the masses, 'a sense of "300,000,000 niggers" to be kept quiet', which spurred Harrison to attack what he called 'The Religion of Inhumanity' (HP 1/55, f.50). Stephen seemed to regard religion as a matter of effective bribing and threatening, 'as if the problem of life were a contested election, and Mr Stephen the agent of Omnipotence'. He had clearly failed to read Comte, where he would have found an attack, on 'the popular sophisms about Liberty, Equality, and Fraternity' as harsh as his own and a religion rather more succulent than his 'maxims of worldly wisdom' (*FR* ns XIII (1873) 678–9).

Stephen renewed his attack on the Religion of Humanity in a second edition of *Liberty, Equality, Fraternity*, which likened Harrison to 'a woman who, having lost her real child, dresses up a doll, and declares that it does a great deal better, as there is no fear of its dying'. Humanity could be seen inclusively, in which case it was so vague and abstract as to be virtually meaningless, or exclusively, pruned of its bad elements, in which case it was 'simply I writ large' (JFS 1967: 40). Harrison was so 'thin-skinned' that he smelt 'blasphemous allusions to his prophet in passages which had not the slightest reference to him' (126). Stephen continued to attack the idea of Humanity as shadowy and insubstantial (*NC* XV (1884) 905–19) even after he had abandoned his belief in religion as a necessary support for morality, when he confessed to his brother that there was little difference between his own position and that of Harrison apart from the Positivist's 'more enthusiastic view of human nature' (LS 1895: I 454).

Henry Sidgwick, 'the outstanding personality in the Cambridge philosophical world in the nineties' (*CR* CLXXXIX (1956) 27), was an altogether milder and more earnest student of Comte. As a young lecturer in classics in the early 1860s, he had been 'the only man in Cambridge' to have studied the Positive Philosophy for himself rather than 'through the medium of Mill's *Logic*' (Sidgwick 1906: 136), although even he confessed to seeing Comte 'through Mill's spectacles' (39). A notebook begun in October 1861 admits,

The strongest conviction I have is what Comte calls 'altruisme': the cardinal doctrine, it seems to me, of Jesus of Nazareth . . . Whether a Comtist or not I feel as if I should never swerve from my cardinal maxim, which is also his. 'L'amour pour principe'/'Le progrès pour but.' (TCC d 70, f.2)

The ten years between taking his degree in 1859 and resigning his fellowship in 1869, Sidgwick recalled, brought harrowing oscillations between enthusiastic attraction and violent repulsion towards Comte (42). He spent the Christmas vacation of 1861–2 in Cambridge precisely 'to have a quiet study of Auguste Comte', whose life he could still admire even if he could not bring himself to worship 'Gutenberg, the inventor of printing'. In March he reported,

I am reading Comte too again, and am just now by way of taking long solitary constitutionals in order to unravel a violent reaction from Comteism which at present holds me. I cannot swallow his Religion of Humanity, and yet his arguments as to the necessity of Religion of some sort have great weight with me. At present I am much more a disciple of Herbert Spencer than of Comte: but I am thinking of enunciating the formula 'God is Love' as a scientific induction to form the basis of a religion.

By June he admitted that his conversion back to Christianity, 'a violent reaction into a yearning after the Spiritual, after soaking myself in much Comte', had 'ended in smoke' (Sidgwick 1906: 74–81).

Jottings in Sidgwick's notebook under the heading, 'Vie d'Auguste Comte', show that this inner struggle between Positivism and Christianity continued through the mid-sixties. One passage, after accepting Littré's view that Comte's method had changed and questioning the Positivist assumption that all religions sought human unity, makes a direct comparison between the Religion of Humanity and Christianity (TCC d 70, f.6). Later notes reveal close study of the Positivist philosophy of history as expounded in the second chapter of the *General View* (f.65v). In 1866 he announced, 'I have finally parted from Mill and Comte . . . not without tears and wailings and cuttings of the hair' (Sidgwick 1906: 158). All these inward doubts and debates came to a climax at the end of the decade, when, finding it no longer possible to assent to the Apostles' Creed, Sidgwick resigned his fellowship. This 'miserable bit of legal observance,' he complained, was all that he could 'lay on the altar of humanity'. 'Even my Positivism is half against me', he lamented. 'If I had been a hero and had perfect confidence in myself I might have been even as Harrison or Beesly' (199–200). But he could neither commit himself entirely to the Religion of Humanity nor cut himself off completely from Christianity. His ambivalent position is encapsulated in a paper given to a discussion group in Cambridge, probably the Apostles, in February 1869, 'Is Prayer a Permanent Function of Humanity?', which studies 'the germs of what is now called "Positivism" ' in Ancient Greece, before concluding that religion had yet to find its final form (TCC c 95, item 5).

Sidgwick continued to discuss Comte and to keep in touch with his disciples in the seventies and eighties. Reviews he wrote in the *Academy* recognised 'the powerful influence of Comte on Mill' and rebuked James FitzJames Stephen, among others, for his ignorance of Positivism. Sidgwick criticised Comte, not for excluding notions derived from introspective observation, as Mill had complained, but for 'employing them uncriticised' (*Academy* IV (1873) 193). His journal records a visit to the Positivist Francis Otter in April 1885 at which they discussed recent developments in Positivism, including the

schism and the publication of Comte's private correspondence with
Clotilde de Vaux:

It certainly is not adapted for the profane. Some of the letters − just before the
crisis *manqué* of their love affair − would be thought a grotesque caricature if
they appeared in a 'Tendenz-Roman' *against* Comtism . . . Still, I like Comte,
so far as one can like any one so portentously devoid of a sense of humour.

(Sidgwick 1906: 409)

Sidgwick re-read Comte that summer, 'lazily' by his own standards, in
preparation for his presidential address to the British Association, a
reply to Ingram's attack on political economy in the *Encyclopaedia
Britannica*. He was reluctant to resort to ridicule: 'I do not like jeering
at a great man's foibles'. But he resented the 'fatuous self-confidence'
Comte shared with Spencer, even if this was 'a defect inseparable
from their excellencies'. He was in the end dissatisfied and 'rather
ashamed' of his 'sterile criticism', which contrasted Comte's extravagant predictions about the future of religion with those of other
sociologists in order to disprove the supposed objectivity of sociology
(419–22).

Such open and public discussion of Comte is rare in Sidgwick's
published work. His many volumes on ethics make little explicit
reference to Positivism, which seems to have 'dropped off him' (to use
a phrase of Kegan Paul's on a visit Sidgwick paid him in 1888). The
work published before his death maintains a strictly Positivist silence
about metaphysical questions, but his posthumously published
studies of the nineties have been interpreted as an idealist 'Refutation
of Positivism', insisting on an introspective rather than a sociological
approach to ethical questions (Havard 1959: 59–89). His *Philosophy,
Its Scope and Relations* rejects the claims of sociology to 'an exclusive
right of deciding as to truth and falsehood on all matters of interest to
men', theology and metaphysics having been dismissed as 'different
stages of error'. Comte's objections only applied to 'crude theology'
and 'bad metaphysics'. Sidgwick felt that it was possible to reconcile
'belief in a Divine Will with invariable law', pointing out the
teleological elements in Comte's view of the development of Humanity
and being particularly severe on his notions of perpetual widowhood
(Sidgwick 1902: 218–31).

By 1894 Sidgwick was denying that Comte had been anything more
than a sedative for his religious doubts:

I never came near to accepting either dogmatic Agnosticism or the worship of the Grand Être, Humanity. Still, it tranquillized me in the midst of scepticism to feel that, 'After all, there is Positivism to fall back on' – meaning by 'Positivism' practical direction of science and human progress.

(Schneewind 1977: 23)

It should be clear from his struggles of the sixties, however, that the Religion of Humanity had offered him a very real alternative to Christianity. The form of neo-Christianity he eventually adopted, by his own confession, was a more comfortable choice than that made by Congreve and the other Positivists. When in 1889 he invited Harrison to lecture at the Cambridge Ethical Society, of which he was President, he explained that their attitude was not aggressively anti-theological and that they included orthodox Christians among their number (HP 1/105, ff.33–4). It was by compromises such as this that he was able to remain safely ensconced in Cambridge to the end of his life.

Theological sympathy and secular dislike

The earliest theological considerations of the Religion of Humanity, by Christian Socialists and liberal Christians, seem to have been motivated by a need to distinguish their own position from that of the Positivists. John Ludlow, for example, in a curious dialogue with Godfrey Lushington in *Tracts for Priests and People*, accused Comte of kneeling to Humanity beneath Clotilde's amputated arms (Masterman 1963: 189). F. D. Maurice seems initially to have held Comte in similar contempt but his attitude had mellowed enough by 1868 for him to recognise 'the Christian aspects of Comtism', deprived though it was 'of such a Father of the whole Family as Christ revealed, of such a Redeemer and Centre of Humanity as He is' (F. Maurice 1884: II 578). Comte loomed large in Maurice's Cambridge lectures on *Social Morality* the following year, which expanded from 'Domestic Morality' and 'Family Worship' through 'National Morality' and 'National Worship' to 'Universal Morality' and 'Human Worship'. A chapter entitled 'The Modern Conception of Humanity' included a fulsome expression of Maurice's 'unspeakable obligations' to Comte and his followers, who were 'men of the highest worth and honesty', devoted to the service of Humanity, even if it was 'a headless Humanity', lacking Christ as its true centre (FDM 1893: 355–67). But Maurice retained

149

doubts about their idealisation of women (414), blamed them for stirring up national and class animosities (FDM 1884: II 619) and denied any personal inclination towards 'the philosophy which is called positive' (FDM 1873: I xxxv).

Mark Pattison was sympathetic to the positive spirit, praising Congreve in an 1857 review of Buckle (MP 1889: II 418) and arguing in *Essays and Reviews* that 'good sense' could construct a religion and an 'ethical code, irreproachable in its contents and based on a just estimate and wise observation of the facts of life', without heavy reliance on revelation (85). His wife 'turned to Comtism . . . for a while' (Peterson 1976: 66), finding in the Religion of Humanity a refuge from the tedious routine of university life. As Lady Dilke she was even allowed to write on a subject which seems to have been a source of disagreement in her first marriage (Vogeler 1984: 145, 423), since Mark Pattison himself was unable to accept 'The Religion of Positivism', on which he wrote at length in the *Contemporary Review*. For religion was a matter of 'individual consciousness' and its relationship to God rather than 'social regulation'. No single intellect, he argued, was 'capable of embracing and codifying all truth' and no system of philosophy could explain the mysteries of life. The 'positive spirit' which had distinguished Comte's early work was altogether absent from the later volumes, which were all law and no spirit, appealing only to a particular mentality, 'powerful and educated, but ill-grounded in science or philosophy', which could be taken in by its 'plausible completeness and superficial systematisation' (*CR* XXVII (1876) 593–614). Pattison's dislike of all definite creeds, which Harrison attributed to a 'morbid spirit of criticism, suspicion, and mental timidity' (FH 1911: II 92), lasted to the end of his life. His career and depressive temperament afford a direct comparison with Congreve, whose energies were similarly 'paralyzed' by anxiety and doubt in a neighbouring common room in the 1850s. Pattison, however, remained at Oxford, retaining the most tentative of faiths in a divine providence.

Benjamin Jowett 'made a special study of Comte' as early as 1850 and carefully re-read him in 1882. It was presumably the sad decline of his friend Congreve and the tragic death of Winstanley which made Jowett fear that 'Comtism destroys the minds of men' (Abbott and Campbell 1897: I 130–1). Generously coming to Harrison's support and treating him as an ally in the fuss over 'Neo-Christianity', Jowett explained exactly where he differed:

I agree with you in thinking that great religious changes are needed and that religion must be much more based on fact. Only fact and demonstration must not exclude right and conscience – or the hope of a future life – or communion with God or the sanctifying and elevating influences of the N[ew] T[estament] – or the 'fact' of the religious and moral nature of man will rise up and condemn them. Above all any religious movement must take into account the poor and uneducated.

He respected Comte as a thinker but felt that he had gained 'a false and absorbing hold on some minds'. His 'enormous generalizations' could be 'a stimulus and help to thought' but they could also lead people to 'warp or overlook facts' (Abbott and Campbell 1899: 15–16). Jowett seems to have disliked Comte as a person 'as much or more than he disliked his philosophy'. Mishearing Comte for Kant when his colleagues were discussing the offer of a new bust for the college library, he is supposed to have exclaimed, 'You would not put a fellow like that in the Library, would you?' (Abbott and Campbell 1897: II 187–8). The Positivists resented the 'bitterness' of some of the references to Comte in his posthumously published letters, which they attributed to jealousy over his pupils and to a sense of guilt at clinging hypocritically to his privileged position (*PR* V (1897) 125–9).

Jowett's 'Recollections of Comte', a notebook set aside for the study of the *Cours*, illustrates his eagerness to find weaknesses in Positivism. Straightforward annotation is interspersed with critical comments, as when he charges Comte with being the 'slave' of abstractions which, unlike those of Catholic theologians, 'have no real hold on men's minds' (JP, f.5). Theological ideas, he insists, raise men's minds; without them 'we should have continued orang-outangs' (f.13). Jowett's list of 'Objections to Comte' includes the impossibility of women living without religion, the abstract nature of his system and his partiality for medieval Catholicism (f.14). Later lists point to Comte's inadequate treatment of fetichism and of Judaism and to the limitations of his reading, especially in German philosophy. A detailed comparison with Hegel reveals Comte as 'more positive and real' but 'inferior in critical power' and 'more fatalist'. Comte's interest is seen to lie in the 'political element of all religion', Hegel's in the 'metaphysical and spiritual' (f.21). 'The chain that Comte winds round you', Jowett claims, is 'not really based upon facts but metaphysical' (f.20v). He continued, however, to allot him a prominent position in his 'Lectures on the History of Philosophy'.

151

The Positivists were much happier with Jowett's successor at Balliol, Edward Caird, whose sympathetic articles of 1879, entitled *The Social Philosophy and Religion of Comte*, saw in Comte 'that unmistakable instinct for truth which renders even the errors and inconsistencies of men of genius more instructive' than the orthodoxy of others who needed no repentance (Caird 1885: xx). Concentrating on the *Système* rather than the *Cours*, Caird gave a serious account of the Religion of Humanity without dwelling on its more exotic details. Like Kant, he argued, Comte had been 'broken into inconsistency' by the transition from the old world to the new, but his systematic and rigorous thinking helped to clarify the great questions of religion (247–9). A later analysis of 'The Problem of Philosophy at the Present Time' defended Comte's abandonment of the objective for the subjective synthesis (Caird 1892: I 197–204). Caird finally rejected Comte's concept of Humanity as affording an insufficient object for worship (II 526–30) but his Gifford lectures, *The Evolution of Religion*, explained why modern thinkers such as Comte found it difficult to accept or even conceive of a transcendent deity (Caird 1893: I 196–7).

Theological interest in the Religion of Humanity was not restricted to Oxford. At Cambridge Brooke Foss Westcott claimed that there was 'no fundamental antagonism between the Positive method and Christianity' (*CR* VIII (1868) 371–86). Comte misrepresented Christianity, overlooking St Paul's devotion to the Person of Christ, underestimating the Greek fathers, and treating the faith too much as a system instead of 'a spirit of life'. But he demonstrated the religious nature of mankind, whose needs Christianity alone could meet (VI (1867) 399–421). For Westcott, as for Caird, it was the later Comte who provoked most interest. His 1886 sermons, entitled *The Social Aspect of Christianity*, expressed 'deep gratitude' to the *Système* for its 'powerful expression' of the 'social ideal' of the gospel (BFW 1900: xii). The mother clasping the infant in her arms, he claimed, had found 'the secret of life', which was to 'live for others' (viii) and he repeated this Positivist motto in his explanation of the growth of morality in family life. But he added a Christian twist to the Comtean progression from 'The Family' through 'The Nation' and 'The Race' to include the largest community of all, 'The Church'. There are echoes of Comte in some of Westcott's other work, for instance in his discussion of Christianity's separation of spiritual and temporal powers in one of the essays appended to his edition of *The Epistles of St John* (BFW 1886: 267). Comtism, he confessed, also had a tendency to 'come out' in his letters (1903: I 268). His Cambridge colleague, Fenton Hort, claimed to have taken 'the *Politique Positive* when it first appeared' (Hort 1896: II 76) and although deploring the 'fanaticism of those sweet youths' (85), the contributors to *International Policy*, he found their faith on the whole 'refreshing and hopeful' (100). Among other clergymen sympathetic to the Religion of Humanity were Beesly's friend, Dean Farrar, and the Revd Llewelyn Davies, who like Beesly was a brother-in-law of Henry Crompton.

A limited amount of fraternal feeling was expressed when Positivism appeared before the Church Congress in Manchester in 1888. The evening session of the second day (2 October) was divided between a discussion at the Free-trade Hall on 'The Needs of Human Nature and their Supply in Christianity', at which the Archbishop of York dismissed the Religion of Humanity as 'raving' (*Times*, 3/10/88, 7), and a closer examination of 'Positivism: Its Truths and Its Fallacies' at the Concert Hall, at which a Cambridge college chaplain spelt out some of the resemblances between Christianity and Comtism. The Religion of Humanity, he argued, was 'systematic and complete' but afforded 'a meagre incentive to noble feeling' in comparison with 'conscious personal relationship with the Eternal'. Christianity also had the advantage of showing more hope to those afflicted with guilt (Dunkley 1888: 163–9). Other contributors to the debate admired Comte's 'deeply stirred emotions', preferred Positivism to 'that kind of scoffing infidelity which has no robust faith in anything', and included among the lessons the Church had to learn from Positivism the cultivation of altruism by exercise, the recognition of the importance of art and the celebration of the great 'heroes of humanity'. There had been an element of 'genius' in Comte, even though he died in 'mental darkness' (170–9).

The highlight of the evening was undoubtedly Lord Balfour's address, the basic thrust of which was that life was so dreadful that it could hardly be supported except by a belief in God and immortality. Positivism was ill equipped to face 'the problem of evil'. Its reliance on public opinion as a replacement for the doctrine of hell struck Balfour as utterly inadequate. Nor could he find much to excite religious veneration in the contemplation of 'a race with conscience enough to know that it is vile, and intelligence enough to know that it is insignificant'. The Religion of Humanity, he concluded, was all right for conscientious upper-middle-class agnostics but had little to offer the working masses (180–9). Balfour's performance was apparently greeted with 'loud cheers' (*Times* (3/10/88) 7), but the ensuing discussion contained more sympathy than hostility towards Positivism. One delegate challenged the idea that Positivism was a 'fading force' while another spoke of the corrective effect it had had on Christianity. Another saw Positivist worship as embodying 'feelings after God'. The concluding remarks of the Bishop of Carlisle, however, while conceding the impossibility of living in the world of thought without imbibing 'some measure of Positivism', insisted that 'the old story is true' (Dunkley 1888: 189–94).

The general seriousness and respect with which 'these good men' had treated Comte, 'erroneous and superannuated as are their beliefs', earned even Beesly's praise, although he resented Balfour's morbid query whether life was worth living, 'an idle question, which any man who is not a sickly dreamer ought to be ashamed to put to himself, and still more ashamed to put to other people' (ESB 1888a: 2–16). Balfour continued to offend the Positivists by trotting out 'the old, cloudy, sceptical, sub-cynical pessimism . . . in the interests of the established creed' (FH 1907b: 323–34) well into the twentieth century. So did the man who had placed before the Metaphysical Society the question, *Is Life Worth Living?*, W. H. Mallock, who believed that the Positivists were exceptional in maintaining morality without supernatural sanctions and that society as a whole would degenerate into anarchy and sexual indulgence if it were not for the fear of eternal punishment. Their failure to see how unworthy Humanity was of their worship was a credit to their generosity but not their intelligence (Lucas 1966: 88–143).

By the end of the century the Anglican Church could afford to take a more relaxed attitude to Positivism. *Lux Mundi* openly welcomed the 'new knowledge' that science could bring, advocating a positive openness to the truths contained in 'the new social and intellectual movements' (Gore 1890: ix). J. R. Illingworth, who had defended Comte at the Church Congress, claimed,

It is impossible to read history without feeling how profoundly the religion of the Incarnation has been a religion of humanity.   (211)

Belief in the Incarnation, it was affirmed at the Church Congress in

1896, conferred an obligation on all Christians to concern themselves with 'everything that interests and touches human life' (Bowen 1968: 173–4). The Positivists, of course, were outraged at having their best ideas baptised, especially Harrison, who objected violently to Benn's prediction that 'Neo-Christianity is more likely to absorb the religion of Humanity than to be absorbed by it' (*PR* XIV (1906) 253).

One of the most surprising sympathisers with the Religion of Humanity was Cardinal Manning, who found 'the real spirit of Catholicism' in Harrison's attack on Stephen (HP 1/56, f.57) and 'nourished hopes' of his conversion (1/49, f.31). Manning, who felt that Comte's Catholic upbringing had resurfaced in old age, described Positivism as 'a noble torso from which the head had been cut off' (FH 1911: II 89). Newman was frankly worried by Positivism, although he derived some comfort from the fact that its founder 'considered religion *necessary* for the mind' and expressed such profound admiration for the medieval Church (Newman, *Letters* XXIV 129–30). It was difficult to enter into controversy with the Comtists, he complained, because there was no common ground on which to base discussion. He objected in particular to their assumption that 'our race can produce a great moral type without the actual incarnation of deity' (XXVIII 146) and was gratified when Wilfrid Ward braved Harrison's wrath by criticising both him and Spencer for stripping religion of a personal God (*NRev.* III (1884) 554–73).

Unitarian interest in the Religion of Humanity emerged in the voluminous works of Sara Hennell, for whom the ideal figure of Jesus was the 'cherished image of Divine Humanity' (Hennell 1860: 53) and God 'the essence of the Species of Humanity' (65). But she earned the Leweses' displeasure with a careless dismissal of Comte (GE, *GEL* III 320) and compounded her error later in the sixties by insisting that Christianity was 'set in NECESSARY ANTAGONISM TO POSITIVISM' (Hennell 1869: title page). Harriet Martineau's brother James expressed admiration for the scientific aspects of Positivism but scorn for Comte's later 'puerilities' (*NRev* VII (1858) 184–220). His *Types of Ethical Theory* allotted a lengthy chapter to Comte's mixture of profundity and pretension before dismissing his 'grotesque scheme of ritualism' and inverted reverence (J. Martineau 1885: I 472). Genuine religion, he insisted, required personal relationship with a Divine Being (J. Martineau 1889: ix-xiv). Adept as any Anglican theologian, however, at incorporating into his own faith what he admired in others, he included a chapter on 'God in Humanity' in his book on *The Seat of Authority in Religion*.

Philip Wicksteed, who succeeded James Martineau at the Unitarian Chapel in Little Portland Street, deplored his predecessor's attempt to make Comte 'look ridiculous' (Herford 1931: 81). Such was his sympathy for the Religion of Humanity as a student at University Hall that he had to assure his father that he was not 'going to make Beesly my father-confessor and turn Positivist'; his interest lay in the practical and moral rather than the intellectual aspects of Positivism (41-3). His sympathetic review of the *Système* drew letters of thanks from Beesly while visitors to Portland Street Chapel, including Mrs Beesly, claimed to detect Positivism in his teaching (185-9). He tended, however, to turn to poets such as Dante, Wordsworth and Ibsen rather than Comte's official calendar saints for 'a veritable religion of humanity' (190-4).

Positivism influenced the development of some other varieties of religious humanism which surfaced in Victorian Britain. South Place Ethical Society, which developed from a Unitarian foundation, decorated its chapel with tablets of great moral teachers, including Christ; and their most famous leader, Moncure Daniel Conway, compiled a *Sacred Anthology* from Buddhist, Hindu, Muslim and Christian texts. The Positivists remained on good terms with South Place, where Beesly, Harrison, Henry Crompton, Patrick Geddes, William Knight and Leslie Stephen were among the preachers. Conway in turn paid the occasional visit to the Church of Humanity, recalling one service at which 'some fine-looking young men arose and stood with open eyes and without bowed heads' while Congreve addressed Humanity. Conway admired Congreve yet found the service 'pathetically picturesque, but no more' (Conway 1904: II 346-7).

The leading light of the Ethical Movement, Dr Stanton Coit, who had been Conway's successor at South Place before moving to the West London Ethical Society, which became the Ethical Church at Bayswater (Ratcliffe 1955: 55), was equally unimpressed by the Positivist ritual of his own wedding. His own church developed a form of 'ethical High Anglicanism', complete with stained glass windows and anthems. Coit was more radical than the Positivists and more of a political activist, although the nationalist strain in his thinking increasingly dominated the political (Budd 1977: 224-43). The Ethical Movement involved men who had studied Comte carefully, such as John Seeley, Henry Sidgwick and Leslie Stephen, but it should be seen as a deliberate alternative to Positivism, offering a less rigorous and systematic creed, a more idealist philosophy and a more colourful ritual.

The Secularists, who were of longer standing than the Ethicists, were mostly more hostile to the Religion of Humanity. Holyoake, as we have seen, lost his early enthusiasm for Comte while Charles Bradlaugh, who founded the National Secular Society in 1866 on a distinctly anti-religious basis, seems to have taken no interest in him at all, although he co-operated with the Positivists in a series of meetings to whip up support for the French against the Prussians in 1870. Annie Besant passed through a Positivist phase in the mid-seventies, although it has been suggested that her refusal to allow 'any slur on the frank and noble love which bound these two great souls', Comte and Clotilde, was partially motivated by her own love for Bradlaugh (Nethercot 1960: 105). Her series of articles on Comte in the *National Reformer* in 1875 began with a clear expression of her respect for Comte, whose sufferings she recorded with a certain sentimentality (*NR* XXV (21/3/75) 186–8). But there were 'peculiarities in the Religion of Humanity' which she could not accept. His system was 'rigid' and 'unbending' while to follow his rules exactly would be 'to live in leading-strings' (XXVI (3/10/75) 210–11). H. G. Atkinson assured readers of the *National Reformer* that 'Comte was not quite so original and great a thinker as his admirers would have us believe' (XXV (6/6/75) 359), dismissing altogether his 'foolish notion of a religion of humanity' (XXVI (19/9/75) 182–3).

Annie Besant produced her own *Secular Song and Hymn Book* in Leicester in the 1870s but was to move on to theosophy in the 1880s. She and Holyoake represent the softer side of Secularism which produced such converts to Positivism as Malcolm Quin and F. J. Gould. Many of their colleagues were hard-bitten atheists who enjoyed nothing so much as a good laugh at Bible miracles and episcopal salaries (Royle 1980: 117–19). G. W. Foote's exposition of *Secularism* recognised some affinities with the Positivists but complained of their having rejected theology only to 'make a god of Comte' (Foote 1879: 29). He also complained that Positivism, although numerically much weaker than Secularism, had managed to make itself better heard in 'circles of highest education' (5). J. M. Robertson poured scorn on the notion of humanist worship, believing that religion of any kind brought 'intellectual atrophy' (Robertson 1891: 238). Positivism clearly had more in common with Christianity than with Secularism of this virulently anti-religious strain.

Comte and the science of history

Comte quickly became the focus of a continuing debate on the possibility of a science of history in which even historians who owed no allegiance to his system found it hard to avoid being tarred with his brush. As early as 1850 the anonymous *Theory of Human Progression* was rebuked by at least two reviewers for plagiarising Comte's ideas (*Ec.R* I (1851) 392–3; *BQR* XIV (1851) 6). In 1864 it was suggested that the Positive Philosophy was behind all attempts to treat history as a science (*LQR* XXI (1864) 462–5). It was the appearance of the first volume of Buckle's *History of Civilization* in 1857, however, which really began the debate. Buckle has often been called 'the English Comte' (Aubyn 1958: 163). He referred enthusiastically both to the *Cours* and to its author (Buckle 1857: I 4–5). But although he read Comte with some care he has been shown to have taken up differing positions on such fundamental matters as methodology, psychology, economics and the relation between mind and morals (Simon 1963: 219–21). Most importantly, because he believed that progress came about through the intellect rather than the emotions, Buckle maintained that religion was not 'a decisive influence in the onward movement of humanity' (Bury 1921: 310). The Positivists themselves resented what they saw as an attempt to capture some of their master's glory (*PP* II (1868) 54–8) and poured scorn on Buckle's 'unsystematic and haphazard' methods (Robertson 1895: 45). Buckle in turn expressed distaste for Comte's 'monstrously and obviously impracticable' utopia (Buckle 1872: I 24). The British public, however, were convinced that Buckle and Comte were alike in propagating the impersonal and irreligious notion that history was a science. They were attacked together both in reviews and by the Professors of Modern History at Oxford and Cambridge.

Without actually naming Comte, Charles Kingsley's inaugural lecture at Cambridge in 1860 on *The Limits of Exact Science as Applied to History* made the target of his attack quite clear, disparaging the fashion for philosophies of history fostered by French historians and the expansion of the inductive sciences. While accepting the principles of 'order and progress', he felt that history belonged to moral rather than 'positive science'. Human progress came about through the action of great individuals inspired by God (Kingsley 1860: 60). Goldwin Smith's *Lectures on the Study of History*, delivered at Oxford from 1859 to 1861, were more specifically directed at Comte. His inaugural lecture, too, denied the possibility of a science of human progress. His second lecture poked fun at the 'copy of the Church of Rome' put forward by Positivism in its 'mystical' phase (GS 1865: 60) while the third attacked the Comtean jargon of 'social statics' and 'dynamics' (84), calling the idea of Humanity 'a desperate attempt to satisfy the religious instincts of man'. The very

fact that the blankest scientific atheism has been compelled to invent for itself a kind of divinity and a kind of spiritual world, and to borrow the worship of the Roman Catholic Church   (92–3)

he regarded as a powerful witness to men's need for religion. But those disciples of Comte who had any sense of the grotesque, he observed in the final lecture, were turning away from his travesty of Catholicism, with its 'whimsical Calendar of historical characters' from which Christ was omitted while the butcherous Caesar occupied a prominent position (141–61).

Beesly's scathing review of Kingsley's lecture was toned down on Harrison's insistence but Goldwin Smith's 'blundering arrogance and unfairness' (HP 1/8, f.39) led Harrison himself to protest against 'sneering religion into favour'. Merely to mention Comte in the current climate of opinion, he complained, was to cry 'mad dog!' (*WR* XX (1861) 293–334). The controversy spilled over into the *Daily News*, where Goldwin Smith claimed that Comte, who was undoubtedly insane, was 'the real though disclaimed author of the "Westminster" philosophy' (GS 1865: 173). Harrison decided not to pursue the matter further since he genuinely admired Goldwin Smith, who became increasingly friendly towards the Positivists and even travelled up to London in order to offer Beesly his personal support when his Chair was under threat. He renewed his public differences with Positivism in the *Bystander* in the 1880s (Wallace 1957: 217), but his private correspondence reveals a certain sympathy for their cause. He was full of pity for the 'almost tragical' fate of Congreve (GS, *Sel* 84) and although he confessed, 'I don't feel any inclination to worship Space, except when I am in a crowd and somebody's elbow is in my rib', he accepted that he was not 'very far from certain Positivists who are essentially theological' (91). He contributed to Comte's centenary memorial out of respect for him 'as a thinker and still more as a servant of humanity' (355) and the liberal theism which Smith preached in the last part of his career even echoed some of Comte's ideas. A late work entitled *In Quest for Light*, for example, looked forward to 'a new religion independent of tradition' (GS 1906: 130), referring to Jesus as 'the Great Teacher of Humanity' (165). This is yet another example of Comte's phrases becoming acceptable currency even with his critics.

A similar development can be seen in the attitudes of many Cambridge historians, although Kingsley's attack on the science of history was followed by sneering references to Comte in the second of a series of articles on 'The Study of History' by his professorial predecessor, James Stephen, the father of Leslie and James FitzJames Stephen (*CM* IV (1861) 25–41). Kingsley continued to preach a heroic divinely-inspired version of history in *The Roman and the Teuton* (1864) and four sermons on *David* (1865) but 'greatly feared the influence of Comte on undergraduates' (Rothblatt 1968: 169) and devoted his final course of lectures to a comparison of Comte's ideas with those of Carlyle, Maurice and Bunsen. 'We shall all drift together into some sort of Comtism', he told Maurice while 'hard at work on Comte' in September 1868; 'it is difficult not to be cowed by his self-sufficient glibness and cheerfully naive sophistry' (Kingsley 1879: II 213–14). Kingsley claimed to have spent nine months studying Comte and to have been 'half-witted' by the time he delivered these lectures, of which there is no record apart from one undergraduate's statement that they made a good impression, 'especially the grand concluding one on Comte' (224). Later letters of Kingsley dismiss Comte as one of those fools who cannot conceive of God 'because they cannot condense His formulas into their small smelling-bottles' (237), while continuing to fear the influence of 'a loose maundering kind' of Positivism and to defend the established Church as the only bastion against atheism in general and Comte in particular (297).

Gladstone, keen to appoint a successor capable of combatting both Comte and atheism, asked Kingsley to sound out John Seeley, who did not at first

feel equal to the task of opposing Comte . . . just at present Comtism seems so irresistibly triumphant, that I have contented myself with pointing out that it is in a sense a Christian movement and with trying to induce the Church to appropriate what is good in it.   (Wormell 1980: 25)

Seeley shared an evangelical background and temperament with many of the Positivists. He had taught with Beesly at Marlborough College and with Harrison at the Working Men's College before rejoining Beesly in 1863 on assuming the chair of Latin at University College London. It has been suggested that his close personal contact with the Positivists in the 1860s led him to overestimate the importance of their creed and to become himself 'a small-p positivist' (32). One of the chapters of *Ecce Homo* preaches a 'Positive Morality' while another expounds 'The Enthusiasm of Humanity', that altruistic love for mankind which it was Christ's achievement to have revealed.

This enthusiasm was only partially toned down in Seeley's historical work. His inaugural lecture at Cambridge in February 1870 followed the pattern of his inaugural lecture at University College London (Rothblatt 1968: 165–8), expressing a similarly Positivist belief in the consolation afforded by an individual's study of 'the great process of which his own life is a moment' (JS 1870: 297). He continued to seek for a reconciliation between Christianity and Positivism in *Natural Religion*, in which he claimed that new experiments in worship, with Humanity as its object and Greek Paganism as its model, 'may be less subversive than they seem'. For the 'worship of humanity . . . belongs to the very essence of Christianity' (JS 1891: 69–76). Like Comte, he postulated three stages in the development of 'the higher life' from Higher Paganism through Primitive Christianity to Science, in which final stage religion had to admit necessity and abandon immortality (136–72). His writings display an unusual 'blend of Cardinal Newman and Comte' (*PR* XIV (1906) 271), romantic in his fervent need for religion but agnostic about the possible object of belief.

Seeley's successor as Professor of Modern History at Cambridge was John Acton, who had helped initiate the whole debate about history as a science. As editor of the *Rambler* he used to set off 'a salvo every few months' against the Positivists (Schuettinger 1976: 58). He included the *Cours* among a list he drew up for Mary Gladstone in 1884 of the hundred books which 'had most moved the world', because it had put 'scientific observation in place of God' (Fasnacht 1952: 143–6) and he warned her father against the threat to the 'Ethical order' posed by the 'shocking things in Comte' (Figgis and Laurence 1917: 211). He deplored Comte's influence upon George Eliot; he and Feuerbach comprised 'what was worst, ethically, in all

European thought' (290). But he recognised Comte's contribution to the development of scientific historical methods. This respect for Comte as an historian was maintained by his successor, J. B. Bury, and by the contributors to the *Cambridge Modern History*, which Acton founded, encouraging them to treat history as a positive science and to treat major movements of thought, such as Positivism, as 'other religions or substitutes for religion' (Schuettinger 1976: 174). Comte certainly emerges well from the original *Cambridge Modern History*, which describes him as 'the most powerful thinker of his half-century' (*CMH* XI 526), the final chapter of *The Latest Age*, by G. P. Gooch, ending with a tribute to his 'attempted formulation of the laws of mental and social evolution' as an important element in 'The Growth of Historical Science' (XII 850).

Historians elsewhere held decidedly mixed views on Comte. Robert Flint claimed to have avoided the 'extremes of idolatrous adulation and the most scornful compassion' in his 1874 *Philosophy of History in Europe*, professing admiration for Comte's treatment of the Middle Ages but disdaining to discuss his 'flimsy and fanatic' religion which he left to the 'commonsense and sense of humour in humanity' to reject (Flint 1874: 259–84). W. E. H. Lecky regarded Comte as one of the 'most suggestive *seminal* minds of England and France' of his century (Hyde 1947: 10), referring to him with respect in the *History of Rationalism* (Lecky 1865: I 208, 303). But there were many areas of difference between them. Lecky cast doubt on the importance of definite arguments as opposed to general currents of thought in the intellectual development of mankind. He was a great admirer of the Reformation, stressing the link between protestant rationalism and the development of conscience, and contrasting the spirit of dogma with the spirit of truth. The *History of Rationalism* ends with an attack on the defects of rationalism, utilitarianism, materialism and the whole 'philosophy of experience' identified with Mill in England and with Comte in France (II 404–9). Lecky anticipated the hostility of the Comtists in particular to his 1869 *History of European Morals* (Hyde 1947: 75), which attacked all ecclesiastical despotism and referred somewhat offensively to the prostitute as 'the eternal priestess of humanity' (Lecky 1869: II 300). *Democracy and Liberty* was scathing about Comte's ingratitude to Saint-Simon, from whom he had 'simply copied' so much (Lecky 1896: II 209).

It is difficult to draw a definite line between those historians who studied Comte for themselves and others who merely reproduced similar ideas. Draper's *History of the Intellectual Development of Europe*, for example, was seen as a product of the Positive Philosophy (*WR* XXVII (1865) 100–1) although it contains no specifically Comtean features. There is no mention of Comte in Winwood Reade's popular account of human progress, *The Martyrdom of Man*, which appeared in 1872. But Reade, who had studied at Oxford in the 1850s, reproduced such Positivist notions as a three-stage religious development, the division of temporal and spiritual powers, the medieval worship of women and 'one great human mind which grows from century to century' (Reade 1948: 190). He referred specifically to the development of 'the religion of humanity' from family love and patriotism (355–6) and looked forward to the total harmony of an ever-improving species devoted to the 'service of humanity', instructing his readers to remember past labours with gratitude and to 'pay to the future the debt which we owe to the past' (412–37). Edward Tylor drew on Comte for his study of *Primitive Culture* (Peckham 1970: 197), recognising that anthropologists of his generation 'owe much to Comte' (*Mind* II (1877) 145). James Fraser's *Golden Bough* has also been placed in a Comtean tradition (Baumer 1960: 150–1). Even where it is impossible to prove direct influence, however, it is important to recognise the way in which Comte's view of history and his belief in humanity could filter through to those who never read his work.

Scientific disavowal: Spencer and Huxley

Some of the most severe criticism of Positivism came from professional scientists eager to protect themselves from the stigma attached to Comte. When Herbert Spencer found himself the target of Comtean claims of plagiarism in 1864 he had little difficulty in persuading a number of fellow-scientists, including Thomas Huxley, John Tyndall, Charles Lyell, John Herschel, Charles Babbage and Michael Faraday, to sign a testimonial, never actually published, denying that Comte had exercised any influence over their scientific thought (Eisen 1967b: 56–7). Thomas Huxley finally put paid to the popular linkage of science and Positivism with a ferocious attack on Comte in 1869. From then on, it appears, the scientific movement ceased to be associated automatically with Comte (Presswood 1935: 299), although Spencer and Huxley continued to have periodic skirmishes with the most belligerent exponent of the Religion of Humanity, Frederic Harrison.

Spencer was a close friend first of George Lewes, whose *Biographical History of Philosophy* he read in shilling volumes after meeting him at Chapman's house in 1850, and then of George Eliot, whom he met there the following summer. He later denied either having loved George Eliot or having shown much interest in Comte, who 'was hardly ever spoken of between us', he claimed, since she knew 'that I had no sympathy with his Religion of Humanity'. He had required her help to read the introduction to the *Cours* in French 'sometime in 1852' and could recall two occasions when Comte was discussed in front of others. She once 'sought to enlist my sympathy with the Comtean religion, but, meeting with no response, never raised the subject again' (HS to Cross, 31/1, 12, 24, 27/10/84, Yale). His *Autobiography* repeated the claim that Positivism had become 'a tacitly tabooed topic' between them as a result of his refusal to sympathise with her 'strong leanings to the "Religion of Humanity" ' (HS 1904: II 364–5).

Spencer's difficulty in dissociating himself from Comte had been increased by his casual and unconscious adoption of a Comtean term in the title of his first book, *Social Statics*, in 1851. At this stage, he insisted, Comte was only a name to him (I 359–60). Two years later, partly to rectify this damage, he asked the editor of the *North British Review* if he could review the forthcoming translation of the *Cours*, 'having much to say on his system – mainly in antagonism to it'. He promised not to touch on 'the theological aspect of his doctrine' but to restrict himself to its scientific accuracy (Duncan 1908: 72–4). The first few months of 1854 found him 'busy reading Comte', as translated by Martineau and Lewes, and 'getting up a very formidable case against him' (HS 1904: I 444). The resultant article, 'The Genesis of Science', eventually appeared, not in the *North British Review*, which entrusted its onslaught on Comte to William Whewell, but in the *British Quarterly Review*. Misinterpreting Comte's conception of the classification of the sciences as rigidly linear, like a ladder, Spencer proposed the alternative image of a tree in order to represent the organic nature of their evolution (HS 1901: I 1–73). He developed this concept of the filiation of ideas in his *Principles of Psychology*, published the following year, an example of the way in which his disagreement with Comte seems to have stimulated the development of his own ideas (Eisen 1967b: 54). He actually visited Comte in 1856 in order to pass on the profits from the translation of the *Cours*, but the meeting was not a success. Spencer's French was only sufficient for 'very slipshod' argument and he found Comte 'a very undignified little old man', perhaps because he ventured to suggest marriage as the best cure for nervous exhaustion (HS 1904: I 493; Duncan 1908: 82).

As early as 1862, in *First Principles*, the first part of what eventually became *A System of Synthetic Philosophy*, Spencer attempted to reconcile 'Religion and Science' (the title of the first chapter) by postulating 'The Unknowable' as the basis of life. Ultimate ideas, he argued, were unattainable, in religion and science alike. He undertook to expound the laws of phenomena, 'The Knowable', but was again diverted from this massive task by his 'compulsion to discredit Comte' (Eisen 1967b: 54–5). Reviews of *First Principles* in America and France had likened his aims and methods to those of Positivism, and he determined to set the record straight, sending a letter to the *New Englander* officially repudiating any suggestion that he was a follower of Comte:

On all . . . points that are distinctive of his philosophy, I differ from him. I deny his hierarchy of the Sciences. I regard his division of intellectual progress into three phases, theological, metaphysical and positive, as superficial. I reject utterly his religion of humanity. And his ideal of society I hold in detestation. Some of his minor views I accept; some of his incidental remarks seem to me profound; but from everything which distinguishes Comtism as a system, I dissent entirely.   (Duncan 1908: 113)

Another review linking him with the Comtean school early in 1864 provoked Spencer into yet another exposition of his *Reasons for Dissenting from the Philosophy of Comte* in which he disputed Comte's authority as an 'exponent of scientific opinion' and deplored the lumping together of all scientists as 'positivists'. He shared with Comte the belief that all knowledge derived from experience and was accordingly relative and accepted that the task of science was to formulate the laws underlying such knowledge. However, he disagreed with a number of fundamental Positivist principles: the law of the three states, the inaccessibility of causes, the dominance of ideas in human progress, the immutability of species and the rejection of introspective psychology. Passages from his own work and from Comte were placed in parallel columns to highlight these differences. The biggest disagreement was over politics: Comte advocated the utmost exten-

sion of the powers of a centralised government which Spencer wanted
to reduce to a minimum. The proper object for religious sentiment for
Comte was Humanity but for Spencer it was 'the unknown source of
things', the 'universal agent' or 'the Infinite Unknowable'. There
were 'sundry minor views' in Comte which Spencer could accept,
many of which possessed 'great depth and value', but their differences, which would doubtless increase 'were I to read more of his
writings', remained fundamental. The greatest debt he owed to Comte
was the stimulus provided by their disagreement towards clarifying
and developing his own views (HS 1901: 118–44).

Writing the *Reasons for Dissenting from the Philosophy of Comte*
brought on a 'fit of excitement' in Spencer, exacerbated by a dispute
with Lewes, to whom he showed the proofs (HS 1904: II 111).
Spencer's paranoid fear of Positivism was certainly not helped by
being surrounded by Positivists. What there was of his social life
seems to have centred on Chapman's soirées in the 1850s, frequented
by Bridges and the Leweses, and Mill's dinner parties at Blackheath
in the 1860s, where he had to defend his position to men such as
Morley. The basic distinction Spencer made to Lewes between his
aims and those of Comte was that while the Positivist was concerned
to give 'a coherent account of the progress of *human conceptions*' and
was accordingly relative and subjective, his own system gave an
account of 'the progress of the *external world*' and was thus both objective and absolute (488).

Spencer succeeded only in antagonising Lewes and extracting from
Mill a double-edged acknowledgement that he could have read little of
Comte's work, since 'several of the things which you urge as objections to his theory, are parts of the theory' (Mill, *CW* XVI 1219). Mill
went on to defend Comte's classification of the sciences against
Spencer while further comments in the third edition of Lewes's
History of Philosophy and in John Fiske's Harvard lectures on
'Positive Philosophy' impressed upon him still further the need to
distinguish his own system from that of Comte. It was primarily for
this reason that he adopted the term 'Synthetic Philosophy' for subsequent volumes on the principles of biology, psychology, sociology
and ethics (Duncan 1908: 131, 156–7).

Spencer's religious views were not in fact very remote from the
Religion of Humanity. When a friend's mother died in 1878 he wrote,
'There would be something like a justification for the Comtist religion

– "the worship of Humanity" – if there were much humanity like her' (195). The following year he wrote to George Holyoake about the need for a 'positive creed for the guidance of life', to be based upon science and to replace the old superstitions (HH 2523). Part VI of his *Principles of Sociology*, 'Ecclesiastical Institutions', speculated on the continuation of religious observance and religious consciousness after the loss of faith in a knowable God. The final chapter of this section, appearing in the *Nineteenth Century* in January 1884 under the title, 'Religion: A Retrospect and Prospect', was to spark off one of the first of Spencer's celebrated controversies with Frederic Harrison.

Spencer's article, attempting to apply the principle of evolution to religious belief, came to the conclusion that religious awareness, far from diminishing, would increase as a result of centring on the 'Ultimate Mystery' at the heart of the universe (*NC* XV (1884) 1–12). Harrison refused to accept such vague agnosticism as a religion; it was rather 'The Ghost of Religion'. What kind of liturgy, he asked, could be based upon the unknowable? Religion required an object and Humanity was 'the grandest object of reverence within the real and the known' (XV 494–506). Spencer called the Religion of Humanity 'Retrogressive Religion', poking fun, among other things, at Comte's anti-evolutionary stance. He found it impossible to worship so warped a creature as Humanity, but he could feel reverence for the 'Ultimate Cause' of life (XVI 3–26). Harrison replied with another defence of the Religion of Humanity in which he insisted that Comte's suggestions were hypothetical and not binding. He was even prepared to abandon the capital 'H', since Humanity was not to be worshipped as a deity but revered as a symbol of all that was good in mankind. He poured scorn on Spencer's 'Agnostic Metaphysics', his sociological research-es and his ignorance of Comte, to him 'the Absolute Unknown' (353–78). Both here and in his address at Newton Hall on the anniversary of Comte's death, which was given wide circulation in *The Times* and the *Standard*, he resurrected the spectre of Spencer's debt to Comte, which Spencer immediately and heatedly denied. His 'Last Words About Agnosticism and the Religion of Humanity' picked up some of Harrison's misrepresentations and pointed out that he had been engaged in the business of making sociological observations and predictions rather than establishing new cults (826–39). The whole debate on the future of religion, personal and inconclusive as it was, excited widespread interest in the press, where it was described as the most important discussion of the subject since Mill's posthumous essays (Eisen 1968: 48–9).

Harrison claimed that he finally abandoned the controversy partly because the public had 'had enough' but also because he had heard rumours that Spencer was contemplating suicide (48). This, however, did not prevent the second phase of their dispute from becoming even more bitterly personal. It was initiated by an American reprint of the original disagreement published without Harrison's permission but with a preface supporting Spencer and a satirical account of one of Congreve's services. An enraged Harrison wrote to *The Times* complaining about this new 'form of literary piracy' and demanding a financial report on the venture. A long public correspondence ensued during which Spencer ordered the plates to be destroyed and Harrison finally apologised for his temper. Another American publisher thereupon brought out an edition even more sympathetic to Spencer in which Harrison was portrayed as a 'pampered, saucy, lively little poodle' who had dared to attack 'a big sedate Scottish collie' (49–52; HP 6/3–5).

Friendly relations between these two unbelieving old dogs took some time to revive. But Spencer found in some of the arguments deployed by Harrison against Huxley in 1892 echoes of his own notes for the concluding chapter of his *Ethics*, on the duties and pleasures of working for one's children and the future of mankind. The only difference seemed to be that Harrison regarded as religion what he placed under ethics (Duncan 1908: 324). A letter of 1900 expressed his pleasure that their 'extensive differences' had not obscured their 'more extensive agreements' (HS to FH, 28/4/1900, CUL). He became a regular reader of the *Positivist Review*, to which he contributed articles on evolution and the unknowable. Harrison, who always spoke of Spencer with 'bated breath' (A. Harrison 1926: 72), later claimed that he had finally come to 'Faith in Humanity and the Service of Man' (*PR* XVI (1908) 148–9). He presented Comte and Spencer as the two great synthetic philosophers of the nineteenth century in the first of the Herbert Spencer lectures at Oxford in 1905 and in his presidential address to the Sociological Society in 1910.

The most damaging criticism of Positivism emanated from a more practical scientist and a more ferocious controversialist than Spencer, Thomas Huxley, who launched a succession of attacks on Comte's scientific credentials. As early as 1854 he showed that the *Cours* was already out of date, antagonising Lewes by calling his mistake-ridden attempts to update *Comte's Philosophy of the Sciences* inexcusable even on 'the plea of mere book-knowledge' (*WR* v (1854) 256). Harrison reported having been 'frightfully pounded' at the Century Club in 1866 when he ventured to oppose Huxley's assertion that Comte's actual knowledge of the natural sciences was a 'mere smattering' picked up at second hand (HP 1/18, f.75). Huxley was spurred into a more public denunciation of Comte three years later by the Archbishop of York's casual association of scientific empiricism with Positivism. He announced to the world, in the *Fortnightly Review* of February 1869, precisely what he thought of Comte's 'dreary and verbose pages', which contained 'little or nothing of any scientific value, and a great deal which is as thoroughly antagonistic to the very essence of science as anything in ultramontane Catholicism'. The Positive Philosophy, in his opinion, could best be described as 'Catholicism *minus* Christianity' (*FR* v (1869) 141–2).

The Positivists were appalled. 'You have dealt us a very hard and damaging blow', complained Beesly while Vernon Lushington persuaded his friend Darwin to pass on a 21-page letter urging Huxley to read Comte more carefully (Eisen 1964: 342–3). Congreve undertook to reply for the Positivists in the April issue of the *Fortnightly Review*, pointing out that they fully accepted their debt to Christianity. A more appropriate description of their faith, he suggested, was 'Catholicism *plus* Science'. Scientific specialists only attacked Comte because they feared his threat 'to put an end to their indiscipline' and to recall them to their social function. He could not believe that Huxley preferred to be one of their number rather than belong to the 'new scientific clergy', suspecting that Huxley's remarks stemmed from a cursory inspection of Comte's treatment of his own subject, biology, and craving 'a more deliberate judgement from the Professor' (*FR* v (1869) 407–18).

Huxley accepted Congreve's challenge. The strength of his feeling on the subject can be gauged from a letter to Kingsley, in which he called Congreve 'no better than a donkey', claimed that 'Comte knew nothing about physical science', described the law of the three states as 'a bad way of expressing' men's tendency to personification, dismissed the classification of the sciences as 'bosh' and expressed 'sheer disgust' at Comte's treatment of his wife. The worship of Humanity, he concluded, was 'as big a fetish as ever nigger first made and then worshipped' (L. Huxley 1900: I 300–1). He was apparently indebted to his wife for the comparatively moderate tone of his published reply to Congreve, which pointed to inconsistencies in the exposition of the law of the three states, even within the *Cours*, and followed Spencer's critique of Comte's classification of the sciences, stressing once more the 'unreality and mere bookishness of M. Comte's knowledge of physical science', his 'arrogant dogmatism and narrowness' and his 'spirit of meddling systematisation'. It was a fundamental duty of scientists, he argued, to doubt precisely what Comte expected them to accept without question, the 'principles established in the sciences by competent persons'. The only achievement with which he was prepared to credit Comte was in impelling others 'to think deeply upon social problems and to strive nobly for social regeneration' (*FR* V (1869) 653–70).

The Positivist response to Huxley's second article was relatively subdued. Harrison, who claimed that he was 'never less angry in his life', defended Huxley's right to deny any connection with Positivism (THP XVIII 46). He was less confident, however, about Congreve's ability to tackle the 'very nasty opponent' he had 'goaded up' (HP 1/15, f.64). Both Harrison and Lewes complained about inaccurate critics of Comte (*FR* V (1869) 483; Lewes 1871: II 687–9) while opponents of Positivism rejoiced at their discomfort. Darwin, who had made notes on Comte as early as 1838 (Beer 1983: 263), was delighted to be relieved of his 'vague wish' to read him (Darwin 1903: I 313). Huxley renewed the onslaught on Comte in 'A Modern Symposium' arranged by the Metaphysical Society in 1877, where he called Positivism 'a half-breed between science and theology, endowed, like most half-breeds, with the faults of both parents and the virtues of neither' (*NC* II (1877) 340).

Harrison's real complaint was that Huxley offered nothing to replace what he destroyed, a point he repeated in an article on 'The Future of Agnosticism' in 1889, which stirred Huxley to 'boiling pitch' (L. Huxley 1900: II 221). 'Of all the sickening humbugs in the world', he wrote to Edward Clodd, 'the sham pietism of the Positivists is to me the most offensive' (229). His own article on 'Agnosticism' took Harrison to task for scientific ignorance, philosophical platitudinising and absurd optimism about the evolution of mankind, a subject which he personally found 'unutterably saddening'. Positivism ranked with Mormonism as 'remarkable phenomena ... of religious self-delusion'. The difference was that Joseph Smith was 'a low-minded, ignorant scamp' while Auguste Comte, though 'repulsive' in dullness and revealing only 'an amateur's acquaintance' with science, wrote 'good things here and there'. The Mormons had thrived through persecution while the Positivists were deprived even of that privilege (T. H. Huxley 1895: V 209–62). Harrison and Huxley remained on friendly terms, in spite of these attacks, regarding polemical frankness as a sign of respect.

A final clash between Huxley and the Positivists was inaugurated by a review of Huxley's *Essays upon Some Controversial Questions* in which Harrison argued that the fact that he could agree with nine-tenths of their content showed that Huxley was 'a rudimentary Positivist'. Harrison admitted that Comte had been proved wrong on certain scientific issues, such as evolution, and described himself as an agnostic, like Huxley, rather than a Comtist. 'Why cannot we Agnostics', he asked, 'kiss and be friends?' (*FR* ns LII (1892) 417–37). Huxley responded with 'An Apologetic Irenicon', explaining how far apart they still were. He disliked all parties and sects, particularly those which purveyed a facile brand of optimism. The doctrines of 'original sin, of the innate depravity of man' and 'the essential vileness of matter' he found much nearer the truth than 'the "liberal" popular illusions' of the Positivists (557–71). Harrison was forced to admit that 'Mr Huxley's Ironicon' separated him totally from the Religion of Humanity (713–21). He resented, however, Huxley's deliberate mistaking of his disavowal of the Comtist label for a renunciation of the Positivist faith (*PR* II (1894) 77–8).

The difference was really one of temperament. Huxley held 'a grim and terrible view of life', a Carlylean Calvinism *minus* Christianity (Cockshut 1964: 86–98). His famous Romanes lecture of 1893 on 'Evolution and Ethics' made a clear distinction between the 'cosmic process', the competitive struggle for survival which had evolved man's aggressive, selfish instincts, and the 'ethical process', the arti-ficial product of human energy and intelligence, which attempted to soften the harshness of the external world (T. H. Huxley 1894: IX 46–116). Harrison, who held a similar view of the need to combine resignation and action, tended to look on the bright side of things, stressing the innate goodness of man. Huxley never missed an oppor-tunity to ridicule Comte, for instance in his life of Hume, for 'pro-pounding solemn nonsense' in 'vilipending psychology' (VI 62), words which once more delighted Darwin (Darwin 1903: I 382). Huxley was apparently working on some further criticism of Comte in his final years and contemplating the publication of an alternative summary of scientific and philosophical progress in which the Middle Ages would fare considerably worse than they had under Comte (L. Huxley 1900: II 425–6).

Huxley can be seen to have articulated the scorn which most practising scientists seemed to feel for Comte. They clearly resented his warnings against specialisation and his belief that the whole of science was capable of summary. The Positivists in turn disliked them, as Darwin commented to Spencer:

How curious and amazing it is to see to what an extent the Positivists hate all men of science; I fancy they are dimly conscious what laughable and gigantic blunders their prophet made in predicting the course of science.

(Darwin 1887: III 149)

Early Victorian scientists had been attracted initially by Comte's attempted summary of the sciences. But as early enthusiasts such as Bain, Allman and Williamson pursued their respective researches in psychology, botany and chemistry, they came to realise the shortcomings of his system and to drop the Positivist connection. Among practising scientists it was only men like Lewes, who found merits in Comte's later work, which made no claim to scientific certainty, who could continue to revere the founder of Positivism, and men like Bridges, with a special temperament and background, who continued to subscribe to the Religion of Humanity.

5

LITERARY POSITIVISM: NOVEL IDEAS

George Eliot and Positivism: the facts

George Eliot was not a disciple; she could not 'submit' herself, she said, 'to the guidance of Comte' (GE, *GEL* I xlvi). She regarded him as 'a great thinker' (III 439), to whom she acknowledged a 'great debt' (GE, *Life* III 369), and studied his ideas very carefully, playing a major part in their propagation. The extent of his influence upon her has always been a controversial subject from the first reviews by Christian critics, who used the Positivist stigma to beat her dogma, to recent more sympathetic accounts of her work (T. R. Wright 1981: 257–8). She encountered him relatively late in her philosophical development, first referring to him in a review of January 1851 which reveals an ignorance of the importance of history to his system (GE, *Essays* 28). Later that year she was involved in Chapman's plans to publish a condensed translation of the *Cours*, and the year after that found her helping Herbert Spencer to read the French original and failing to enlist his sympathy with the Religion of Humanity. Her familiarity and sympathy with Positivism stems, therefore, from her early thirties, long after she had been acquainted with Bray's philosophy of necessity, Combe's phrenology, the philosophical theism of the Hennells, Spinoza and Strauss, Feuerbach's more impulsive religious humanism, Mill's *Logic* and Carlyle's fervent belief in historical continuity.

George Eliot's association with Positivism cannot really be separated from her relationship with George Lewes, although the influence was by no means one way. When she wrote on Comte for the *Leader* in May 1854, as we have seen, she apologised for assuming a role that was really his but twelve years later he attributed to her his increased respect for the Religion of Humanity. The Congreves certainly regarded her as the sounder disciple, blaming him for 'keeping

Marian back from better things' (L. and E. Hanson 1952: 210). When she took over the 'Literature' section of the *Leader* during April and May 1854, she continued his defence of Comte against the charges of plagiarism and of 'unblushing' unbelief, which she interpreted as 'a eulogy on his moral strength' (*Leader* V (1854) 377). Another article in the *Leader* welcomed the percolation of the positive *a posteriori* method into Germany (GE, *Essays* 153) while an essay of 1856 in the *Westminster Review* gave an unmistakable paraphrase of Comte's classification of the sciences (290). Her attacks on the baptised egoism of Dr Cumming and Edward Young owe as much to Feuerbach as Comte, but maintain a strong humanist position.

George Eliot's interest in the Religion of Humanity received an additional stimulus when the Leweses became neighbours of the Congreves in February 1859. The two pairs of social outcasts soon became firm friends, the women confessing their mutual love that May (GE, *GEL* III 53). The Congreves, however, distrusted Lewes while the Leweses found Congreve rather cold (70). Their journals record frequent discussions of the Religion of Humanity between the two households and by March 1860 George Eliot was singled out by Maria Congreve as the nearest thing to a complete sympathiser they had gained (MC to Mrs Edger, 30/3/60, MAC). What survives of their correspondence, most of which has been destroyed, apparently because of its intimate nature (Haight 1968: 496), reveals George Eliot's continuing interest in Positivism. She rejoiced over the success of Congreve's lectures that summer (GE, *GEL* III 293) and even after their move from Wimbledon to Blandford Square in July, she continued to worship Maria's 'image', associated as it was 'with some of my most precious and most silent thoughts' (460). Full of admiration for Congreve's decision to leave Oxford and dismayed by Winstanley's suicide, she reported a 'long chat' with Congreve in November 1862 (IV 52, 67), at which she committed herself to an 'Acceptance of Humanity' and a 'Promise of subscription' (BL 45261, f.62). The accounts of the Sacerdotal Fund from 1864 to 1891 mention a payment from Lewes or Cross every single year except 1878, where some pages are missing, and 1880–1, the time of her death. From 1868 the reference is pointedly to 'Mrs Lewes' (45257, ff.2–77), who remained, in Congreve's eyes, 'on the religious point very satisfactory' (Bod.L. e 62, f.160v).

George Eliot's support for Congreve's cause appears to have

deepened in 1865, when there was an increase in visits between the two households. A letter from George Eliot in January described a recent visit to Comte's house and wished them success in commemorating Comte's birthday, a gathering she likened both here and in an unpublished 'leaf from her notebook' to the last supper (GE, *GEL* IV 174; *HLQ* XXXIX (1966) 356). In January 1867 she wrote from Biarritz to tell Mrs Congreve how much she and Lewes were enjoying their joint study of the 'Politique', which, she claimed, gave her a 'moral glow' for the whole day, filling her with 'gratitude . . . for the illumination Comte has contributed to my life', even if there was 'still much to learn and to understand' (GE, *GEL* IV 333). This is clearly a polite way of saying that they still felt some reservations about the system as a whole, reservations which were increased by their attendance at Congreve's lectures in Bouverie Street in May. When Lewes left for Germany, George Eliot complied with his wish that she should not attend on her own lest his absence be misinterpreted (363, 413).

George Eliot continued to defend both Congreve and Comte against misrepresentation. They were not atheists, she assured one friend: 'There is no denial of an unknown cause, but only a denial that such a conception is the proper basis of a practical religion' (367). In April 1868 she offered to share the expenses of publishing Congreve's translation of the *Système* (430) and in December passed on good news about the sales of 'that "mass of Positivism", in the shape of "The Spanish Gypsy" ', news, she added, 'which concerns the doctrine, not the writer' (496). Congreve, who attended many of her Sunday afternoon gatherings, resented her comparatively hectic social life but his wife kept in close touch. 'Marie sends her best love and a circular', wrote her sister in 1874 (Emily Geddes to GE, 24/7/74, Yale). The two came together, so that it is difficult to separate George Eliot's affection for Mrs Congreve from her sympathy with the movement. Congreve himself appears not to have recognised the Positivist significance of her work. 'She is most useful to our cause', he conceded in 1867, 'as she is decidedly with us' (BL 45232, f.150), but he seems not to have grasped this from the novels themselves. He found *Middlemarch* 'gloomy' (Bod.L. e 54, f.82), saw no reason to encourage his adopted daughter to persevere with *Romola* (e 67, f.26v) and resented the time other people spent on 'such works' as *Daniel Deronda* (BL 45235, f.22).

George Eliot met other leading Positivists, such as Harrison, Beesly and Bridges, through the Congreves. It was at their house, for example, on New Year's Day, 1860, that she first encountered Harrison, who was as impressed by her as she had been by his attack on 'Neo-Christianity' (FH 1911: I 204; GE, *GEL* III 353). Her admiration for his early contributions to the *Fortnightly* led her to request his help with the legal aspects of *Felix Holt* and she was later to support his stance against Matthew Arnold in 1867 (GE, *GEL* IV 395), 'Bismarck-ism' in 1870 (V 125) and FitzJames Stephen in 1873 (421–2). Although initially 'jarred by the more personal part at the close' of his article on 'The Positivist Problem' in 1869, she gained 'a stronger impression of its general value' on a second reading and apologised for her own 'unreasonable aversion to personal statements' and 'decided "deliverances" on momentous subjects' (75–6).

Harrison found it difficult to comprehend such reticence and continually urged her to commit herself more completely to Comte, interpreting Lewes's article on Comte of January 1866 as 'the first announcement of *her* Positivism' (HP 1/14, f.3). His suggestion of July 1866 that she should write a directly Positivist novel received a patient reply explaining the distinction between propaganda and aesthetic teaching (GE, *GEL* IV 300–1). Referring in June 1877 to Congreve's use of her poem, 'The Choir Invisible', in their recent services, he pressed her for further contributions to their liturgy and a clarification of her own position on the Religion of Humanity: 'why should you so long abandon Religion for Art?' (Haight 1968: 506–7). This correspondence, combined with long discussions with Harrison at Witley Heights, spurred her into polishing and publishing 'A College Breakfast-Party' and into rethinking her position on Positivist liturgy, waiving her original objections to 'the Prayers we spoke of' so long as they kept 'within the due limit of aspiration and do not pass into beseeching'. She agreed that 'a ritual might bring more illumination than sermons and lectures' (GE, *GEL* VI 439). In April 1880, after the schism and before her marriage to Cross, she sent five pounds 'towards your branch of Positivist work' along with excerpts from various poems which expressed the worship of Humanity (VII 260–1).

Harrison, like Congreve, seems not to have appreciated how much of the Religion of Humanity found expression in her novels. His letters to her offered nothing but praise. It gave him great pleasure, he claimed, to recognise in *The Spanish Gypsy* 'the profound truths and sacred principles' of 'the Faith of the Future . . . for the first time truly idealised' (IV 484). But he told Beesly that it was 'a fiasco' (HP 1/15, f.18) and was even more outspoken about *Daniel Deronda*:

Knowing all I do of her, and how she recently spoke to me of 'us Positivists', I am quite indignant at the silly playing about Judaism, and the unfair appeal to Theistic prejudice . . . when I think of the Positivist view of her art which she perfectly understands and professes to embody in art, I am quite grieved to see her career end in a poor literary aim, . . . to mince at the applause of a sycophantic group. (HP 1/63, ff.48–9)

Harrison, who 'took practically no interest in the analysis of motive', tended to prefer the more boisterous Dickens to the psychological complexity of George Eliot or Gissing (A. Harrison 1926: 111–12, 143).

Bridges and Beesly were also frequent guests at the Priory, where the Leweses lived from 1863. Bridges' friendship with them dated from his days at Chapman's in the late 1850s and it was he who was partly responsible for the breakdown of George Eliot's anonymity. Beesly introduced Henry Crompton into their circle in 1865, when they found publishers for the volume of Positivist essays entitled *International Policy*. George Eliot came to Beesly's defence at the time of the Sheffield outrages but disagreed with him over the Franco-Prussian war (GE, *GEL* IV 374, 378; V 118). Other visitors to the Priory included the Lushingtons, Morison, Geddes, Kaines and Sulman. All these friendly relations, however, were shattered by her decision to marry John Cross, which was seen as an abrogation of the Positive duty of eternal widowhood.

The Positivists' reaction bordered on the hysterical. Harrison wrote a double-edged letter of congratulation and veiled excommunication, conceding that the doctrine of eternal widowhood rested 'upon a whole system of truly religious ideas, ways of looking at life and its meanings' which he could not 'presume to think of imposing . . . on those who stand entirely aloof from our ways and our thoughts' (VII 271–2). Congreve, who had been nursing high hopes of George Eliot once removed from the influence of Lewes and her literary 'milieu' (Bod.L. e 55, ff.156, 165–77), expressed disbelief. If it were true, he added, with immediate thought for the party image, 'we may rejoice that her adhesion to Positivism has not been more open and complete'. 'The world will taunt Positivism with it', he realised (e 56, f.145v), but attempted to calm others down by underplaying her involvement in the movement:

Remember always that she is not nor ever has been more than by her acceptance of the general idea of Humanity a Positivist – so that she will not harm
our cause as much as she might have done, had she given a more complete as-
sent.   (e 67, ff.119v–20)

They could derive some comfort, he insisted, from 'the fact that so
powerful an intellect adopts the doctrine – the central idea of our
system – the religion of Humanity' and that any diminution of her
support could now be seen as a consequence of her 'weakness'
(ff.122v–4).

George Eliot's case was complicated by the fact that she had not
actually married Lewes. The Positivists, who had made such a fuss
about the Pradeau affair, accepted the special circumstances surrounding Lewes. But for George Eliot to marry a younger man so soon
after the death of her lifelong companion, raised all their old suspicions. Mrs Beesly, who felt that it merely confirmed Ethel Harrison's
belief that George Eliot 'had got tired of Mr Lewes and had liked Mr
Cross before he died', urged her husband to condemn her (Mrs ESB to
ESB, 27/12/[80], BP 5). The Congreves were sufficiently reconciled
to dine with the Crosses shortly before George Eliot's death and to
accept her husband's continued subscription until 1892 but Harrison
adamantly refused to meet 'that epicene woman' who 'got to loathe
the very memory' of the 'poor dear old boy' with whom she had lived
so long (Vogeler 1981: 421–2).

There were, however, public acknowledgements of George Eliot's
intellectual contribution to Positivism by Laffitte and Beesly (Laffitte, *CA* 1881: 13; ESB 1881: 7–8), while Harrison endowed her with
subjective immortality. As the Newton Hall choir sang a cantata of
'The Choir Invisible', he claimed, on the Day of All the Dead, 1881,
she would be 'living tonight in us' (FH 1907a: 94). His review of
Cross's *Life* argued that her 'genius' was 'saturated' with Comte's
ideas (*FR* XLIII (1885) 321) and later essays noted her 'careful study'
of Comte and 'entire sympathy' with his religion (FH 1895: 66–78;
1906: 143–60). Other Positivists also claimed her for the movement,
describing her novels as 'Positivist poems' (*PR* IX (1901) 28). But they
never forgave her for violating one of their most sacred rules. The
Positivist Society of North London held a series of conferences on the
Positivism in her novels, at which it was proposed that the main lesson
to be drawn from her work was the importance of fulfilling the moral
obligations she had neglected in her life (*RO* XIV (1891) 76–88). The

Positivist Review felt it right to 'temper moral reprobation by gratitude for great services' (*PR* XXV (1917) 66) and went on accordingly to celebrate the centenary of her birth (XXVII (1919) 279–81).

There can, however, be no doubt about George Eliot's close study of Comte. Her annotated copy of the *Catéchisme* is cluttered with marginal linings and comments, particularly on the sixth conversation, on private worship, where she summarised Comte's theory of 'Guardian Angels', noticing even his recommendation of 'substitutions or compensations in case of unfitness' and his times for 'Prayer: morning, mid-day, evening' (AC *Cat* [1852]: 186–92, DWL). She copied the names and dates of all the Positive sacraments, the 'Symbol of Humanity, Madonna and Child' and the Positive banner: 'Madonna on the white ground. Formula on green – Love, Order, Progress' (193–201, 207–8). Details of Comte's utopia, the duties of the priesthood, the 'Industrial Hierarchy' and the 'Gratuitousness of Labour' all receive attention (299, 304). The final page contains a short index and a chronology of Comte's life. It is difficult to draw conclusions from evidence as slight as this. It is possible, for example, that the details were selected on account of their absurdity but she was at least familiar with them.

George Eliot's study of Positivism continued unabated throughout the 1860s. She read the 'survey of the Middle Ages' in the *Cours* in July 1861 in preparation for *Romola* and observed, 'few chapters can be fuller of luminous ideas' (GE, *GEL* III 438). Her 'Italian Notes' of 1862 are punctuated with comments such as this:

Influence of egoism in determining formulae.
Necessity of strong theistic feeling as a preparation for
the Religion of Humanity.   (Bod.MS Don. g 8, f.22)

She told Mrs Congreve in November 1863 that she had been greatly moved by the *Discours préliminaire* and that she had been positively 'swimming in Comte' (GE, *GEL* IV 111, 116). Her study of the *Système* is evident not only from her diary but from her Commonplace Book, into which she copied the tables of contents for each volume and a long passage on the influence of the living and the dead (GECB, items 225, 227). Her notebook for *Felix Holt* includes an interesting discussion taken from Comte on the extent to which theological faith encourages egoism (GE, '*FH* Notebook', Yale, f.[33]). The day before she began the novel itself she started once more 'Comte's Social

Science in Miss Martineau's edition' (GE, Diary, 28–9/5/65), which she also sent for while working on *Middlemarch* (GHL to Charles Lewes, 28/5/71, Yale). A complete copy of the Positivist Calendar is included among other notes taken at this time (Pratt and Neufeldt 1979: 234–43).

The appearance of the English translation of the *Système* in 1875 seems to have stimulated George Eliot into further exhaustive study of Positivism. A notebook now at Nuneaton, entitled 'Greek Philosophy, Locke and Comte', selects almost exactly the same quotations as another notebook now in New York (Pforzheimer 707). Their main theme is his attempted reconciliation of the objective and subjective methods. But attention is also paid to his opposition of will and necessity and his description of fatalism as the 'necessary corrective of theology'. His definition of Humanity and description of the feeling of solidarity with that Great Being, an extension of family and national feeling, are also copied, as is the tabular form of his cerebral theory, together with an explanation of the way in which moral habits are supposed to be developed. The late composition of these notebooks rules out the detailed study of Comte to which they bear witness as an influence on any of her novels apart from *Daniel Deronda*, but they provide yet more evidence of her veneration for the founder of the Religion of Humanity.

George Eliot and Positivism: the fiction

All the elements of the Religion of Humanity examined in the opening chapter of this book can be found in some form in George Eliot's work. Such philosophical themes as the importance and limits of verification by experience and the need for a subjective synthesis of knowledge to give unity and meaning to life and to compensate for such unpleasant facts as death, recur throughout her work. Equally pervasive is the constant recommendation of resignation to the unalterable and action where change is possible, along with such concepts as solidarity and continuity with Humanity in the past, present and future. Many elements of Comte's detailed historical and sociological analysis can also be found in the novels, whose moral framework is based upon Positivist principles, in particular the channelling of egoistic instincts in altruistic directions by habits of prayer and worship and the need to live openly and rely on the beneficent influence of public opinion. Eliot's fiction, then, can be considered as a critique of Comte, a set of 'experiments in life' (GE, *GEL* VI 216) in which Positivist concepts are examined and sometimes found wanting. Conversely, the religion of Humanity provides an important key to her mythologies, clarifying the significance of several aspects of her work.

'The great conception of universal regular sequence' (GE, *Essays* 413) is too pervasive a theme of nineteenth-century philosophy to be linked exclusively with Comte. But George Eliot frequently uses some of the synonyms Comte enumerated for the word 'positive': real, exact, precise. Many of her characters are judged by their failure to recognise the operation of the law of consequences, that certain actions lead to inevitable results. Their belief in providence is seen as a baptised form of egoism and their resort to mysticism as an abandonment of 'real' phenomena open to observation and verification. The mind of St Ogg's, for example, is well beneath the positive stage. Opinions, such as those of Mr Riley on education, are not 'based on valid evidence' (GE, *MF* I 35) and Maggie Tulliver remains

quite without that knowledge of the irreversible laws within and without her, which, governing the habits, becomes morality, and, developing the feelings of submission and dependence, becomes religion. (II 31–2)

The idea of a religion based upon scientific laws finds its most clearly Comtean expression in George Eliot in *Daniel Deronda*, where Gwendolen is reprimanded by Klesmer for her failure to know things 'exactly' (GE, *DD* I 381) while Deronda himself uses another of Comte's synonyms for the word 'positive': 'Some real knowledge', he tells her, 'would give you an interest in the world beyond the small drama of personal desires' (II 266). Her study of sugar-canes parallels Dorothea's poring over maps of Asia Minor in this respect. Mathematics is the foundation of the positive sciences and is therefore an entirely appropriate subject for Deronda to study at Cambridge, although they are ignorant there of 'the principles which form the vital connections of knowledge' (I 269). For it is only 'your dunce who can't do his sums', as Felix Holt complains, who languishes after the infinite (GE, *FH* I 184).

The need for a subjective synthesis to perform the binding function of religion can be seen in Milby, where the evangelical revival leaves each convert 'no longer a mere bundle of impressions, desires and impulses' but a person whose thoughts, feelings and actions are united in the service of others (GE, *SCL* II 163). Maggie Tulliver's need is religious in this Comtean sense. She wants 'something that would link together the wonderful impressions of this mysterious life' (GE, *MF* I 369) and it is precisely this impulse which justifies the narrator's comparison of her sufferings with those of more heroic contributors to the progress of Humanity: 'does not science tell us that its highest striving is after the ascertainment of a unity which shall bind the smallest thing with the greatest?' (II 6). Esther's life too is 'a heap of fragments' before Felix comes along 'to bind them together' (GE, *FH* I 256). The sense of law he brings her is the 'first religious experience of her life' (II 45), although the narrative admits that she is too early for Positivism as such:

It is only in that freshness of our time that the choice is possible which gives unity to life, and makes the memory a temple where all relics and all votive offerings, all worship and all grateful joy, are an unbroken history sanctified by one religion. (286)

Unless this passage is ironic, it must surely refer to the Religion of Humanity.

Dorothea's temperament and aspirations are also religious in this Comtean sense. She has a passionate desire for solidarity and continuity, an

eagerness for a binding theory which could bring her own life and doctrine into strict connection with that amazing past and give the remotest sources of knowledge some bearing on her actions.

Knowledge for her must combine with 'sympathetic motive' to produce 'action at once rational and ardent', the Positivist synthesis of thought, feeling and action (GE, *MM* I 128–9). But the best exemplar of the subjective method is Mordecai, whose visionary power, we are told, is an 'emotional sequence' of his 'firmest theoretical convictions' (GE, *DD* II 308). His joy when Deronda fulfils his visions by appearing in the Thames sunset is that of a scientist celebrating predicted results (327–8). A later passage, again likening his abnormal insight to the formation of scientific hypotheses, contends that 'enthusiasm may have the validity of proof, and, happening in one soul, give the type of what will one day be general' (358–9). This is precisely the defence made by Comte's disciples against the Millite charge of having abandoned the principle of verifiability.

The understanding of the Cabbala exemplified by *Daniel Deronda* accords remarkably closely with the Positivist concept of 'subjective assimilation'. Comte believed,

> Intellect and emotion . . . may pass into another brain so as to be fused with the results attained by that other brain itself, supposing the two beings to be in sufficient harmony. (AC, *Pol* IV 90)

Mordecai speaks in similar terms of 'spiritual perpetuation' and the fusion of souls, which enables him to pass on his acquired wisdom to Deronda (GE, *DD* II 332, 398). The originally Jewish notion assumes a distinctly Positivist shape. The whole concept of subjective immortality, in which the dead are believed to live for ever in the minds of others, recurs throughout George Eliot's letters and novels. Milly Barton's love lives on in Milby, Annette's in Rufus Lyon's heart. Only when the belief in subjective immortality is extended to the duty of perpetual widowhood do her characters, like their creator, rebel. Dorothea, for instance, refuses to be bound by Casaubon's will, seeing 'a deep difference between that devotion to the living and that indefinite promise of devotion to the dead', between the 'ideal' and the 'real yoke of marriage' (GE, *MM* II 314–17).

George Eliot's favourite form of subjective immortality was literary, finding its clearest expression in the poem so widely used as a Positivist hymn:

> O may I join the choir invisible
> Of those immortal dead who live again
> In minds made better by their presence. (GE, *LJ* 301)

'The Death of Moses' describes the manner in which the Jewish prophet lived in his people through the Ten Commandments while the legendary Jubal is persuaded to forsake individual existence for his eternal share in the 'growth of song' (41). It is Tito's mistake, Romola explains to his son at the end of the novel, not to have used his learning more positively, 'so that he might still have lived in his works after he was in his grave' (GE, *R* II 444).

Comte's dictum, 'Notre vraie destinée se compose de *résignation* et d'*activité*', quoted verbatim in two of George Eliot's letters (GE, *GEL* II 127, 134) and echoed in many more, seems to lie behind her discussion of tragedy in her 'Notes on *The Spanish Gypsy*', which dwells on

> The dire strife
> Of poor Humanity's afflicted will,
> Struggling in vain with ruthless destiny.

The inheritance of some grave disease, for instance, requires a balance of the two Comtean qualities:

large resignation and acceptance of the inevitable, with as much effort to overcome any disadvantage as good sense will show to be attended with a likelihood of success.

What some call the 'divine will' is, in fact, 'so much as we have ascertained of the facts of our existence which compel obedience'. Just as Comte rested his belief in progress on the possibility of developing innate altruistic instincts by private worship, George Eliot proclaims 'the all-sufficiency of the soul's passions in determining sympathetic action', especially if those faculties have been developed 'by an imagination actively interested in the lot of mankind generally'. Titian's 'Annunciation' is taken as an idealised example of the call for submission to a required duty (GE, *Life* III 34–40). This image, together with that of disease or maiming, recurs throughout the novels, reinforcing their dramatisation of the need for resignation.

The world of invariable law to which George Eliot's characters are required to resign themselves is often personified. 'The imperious and inexorable Will' insists there can be no forgiveness for Don Silva (GE, *SG* 340), while a clause from the Lord's Prayer, 'Thy will be done', comprises Milly Barton's epitaph (GE, *SCL* I 122). But the 'Divine Will' is only a term used by men like Mr Tryan as a focus for their 'feelings of trust and resignation' (II 254), feelings which Janet Dempster and Adam Bede learn through suffering. The key which enables Maggie Tulliver to accept the harshness of the world is supplied by the book Comte recommended all Positivists to study, substituting Humanity for God. Maggie takes up the copy of *The Imitation of Christ* given to her by Bob Jakin and reads those passages, conveniently marked in pencil, which advocate resignation. As if to confirm that hers is a Positivist reading of the book, the narrator explains that the *Imitation* 'remains to all time a lasting record of *human* needs and *human* consolations' (my italics), illustrating society's need for 'an emphatic belief' in something that 'lies outside personal desires, that includes resignation for ourselves and active love for what is not ourselves' (GE, *MF* II 36–8).

The Comtean duty of resignation comes to Romola as to Maggie through medieval Catholicism. Savonarola, like à Kempis, is made to sound curiously similar to the priest in Comte's *Catechism* when he explains, 'The higher life begins for us, my daughter, when we renounce our own will to bow before a Divine law' (GE, *R* II 100–8). Romola is visited by no angels, Titian or otherwise, but faced with a choice between 'the path of reliance and action' or that of 'inaction and death' she sees that her duty lies in a Positivist balance of resignation and action (54). This balance is crucial. In *Felix Holt*, for example, Jermyn and Mrs Transome go to one extreme, attempting to make life 'delightful in spite of unalterable external conditions' (GE, *FH* I 329) while Felix himself attacks the other, the 'Byronic-bilious' school which is 'more given to idle suffering than to beneficent activity' (II 34). Esther achieves the correct balance, overcoming her 'resignation' to a life of 'middling delights' (281) in order to reject her inheritance and marry the man she loves. Dorothea Brooke reaches a similarly active decision. It is not that she lacks Mrs Garth's 'rare sense which discerns what is unalterable, and submits to it without murmuring' (GE, *MM* I 369). But while Lydgate wavers between resignation, fatalism and rebellion, becoming cynical in the end and complaining about the irresistible empire of chance, she encourages resistance to what he thinks 'unchangeable' (III 354). For a time 'she thought only of bowing to a sad necessity which divided her from Will' (15), seeing his separation from her as 'irrevocable' (402). But her benevolent action in returning to Rosamond modifies their position, enabling Will in the end to triumph over Destiny. Many of the other characters in the novel, however, have little choice but resignation to physical and spiritual maiming.

Images of maiming and annunciation recur in *Daniel Deronda*, in which Gwendolen is taught to submit to the inevitable 'as men submit to maiming or a lifelong incurable disease' (GE, *DD* II 264). At the end of the novel, when she has to resign herself to Deronda's absence, the scene is likened to the annunciation, although on this occasion the angel is departing. It is one of those moments, we are told, when

the submission of the soul to the Highest is tested . . . and a religion shows itself which is something else than a private consolation.   (III 398–9)

The discussion in the 'Hand and Banner' revolves around this question. Deronda asks how far the laws of development which Lilly has outlined are inevitable and to what extent they can be hastened or retarded, warning the others against 'the danger of mistaking a tendency which should be resisted for an inevitable law that we must adjust ourselves to'. Mordecai argues for powerful action, for instance to resist the decline of national feeling, a process which can only be reversed by determined resistance to determinism (II 378). In this novel especially, Positivism provides the framework of the narrative: a world of verifiable laws, which can be subjectively synthesised in a religion based on resignation and action.

The essential ingredients of Positivist piety, a sense of solidarity and continuity with Humanity in the past, present and future, recur throughout George Eliot's letters. The main function of church services, she believed, was to make 'the past vividly present' and the individual 'feel part of one whole' (GE, Journal 14/4/58, 30/8/65), encouraging 'the delightful emotions of fellowship' (GE, *GEL* V 448). One of her notebooks analyses the 'collective consciousness' developed by such religious observance in terms of the twin Positivist virtues, '*Continuity* (in human history) and *Solidarity* (in the members of the race)'. Continuity, although affording a less powerful motive for the egoist, who was more immediately affected by what happened to his neighbours than his ancestors, could be developed by family love:

The widening of sensibility through the love of children, even the care for a son in its lowest form of transferred egoism, is a stage on the way to a care for posterity in general.

Comte's uncritical acceptance of the organisation of the medieval Catholic Church as a model for the philosophical priesthood of the future, however, ignored his own distinction

between the Static and Dynamic − between what is an inherent quality or characteristic or need of the human being . . . and what is modifiable or doomed to disappear under successive changes.

George Eliot envisaged 'a sort of universal congregationalism' developing out of a split between liberal and conservative clergy (Pinney 1966a: 364–76).

The liberal clergy in George Eliot's novels certainly stress the virtues of solidarity. Mr Irwine preaches human interdependence while Dr Kenn's analysis of the breakdown of the old order of society points to the absence in St Ogg's of any sense of community, calling Maggie's wish to return to her closest ties 'a true prompting, to which the Church in its original constitution and discipline responds'. The Church, he continues, 'ought to represent the feeling of the community', binding it together like a family, and 'must ultimately recover the full force of that constitution which is alone fitted to human needs'. The 'relaxation of ties' and forgetfulness of the past illustrate the community's abrogation of solidarity and continuity (GE, *MF* II 358). That Dr Kenn should talk in these terms is an anachronism as far as the setting, but not the writing, of the novel is concerned. His preaching closely resembles the 'Human Catholicism' of George Eliot's new neighbour, Dr Congreve, as does his character, full of reserved, cold-seeming benevolence, spiritual conflict and 'devoted service to his fellow-men' (361).

The most powerful preacher of solidarity in George Eliot's novels, Felix Holt, bears more than an initial resemblance to another bearded, priggish and hot-tempered muscular Positivist, defender of trade unions and advocate of 'commonsense', Frederic Harrison, who was in constant correspondence with George Eliot over the legal aspects of the novel. Felix Holt, who was dubbed 'the Chartist of Positivism', deserves the title 'Radical' as little as Harrison (Holyoake 1905: I 92). The roots to which they both refer are moral rather than political, 'roots a good deal lower down than the franchise' (GE, *FH* II 44). Both in the novel and in his 'Address to Working-Men', published in *Blackwood's* in 1868, Felix Holt preaches undiluted Positivism: the ideal of solidarity, the importance of remaining within one's own class, the need for education in the sciences and the moral power of public opinion. He, Esther and the miners represent the alliance sought between philosophers, women and workers for the regeneration of society (Myers 1966: 5–33).

Felix captures his audience, as Comte had recommended, over their drinks, winning them over by the magnetism of science and insisting on their showing solidarity with their fellow-miners in Newcastle, before attempting to establish a school. His speech at Duffield on nomination-day insists that they abandon 'thoughts that don't agree with the nature of things', the laws revealed by science, and put their faith in the power of public opinion to exert moral control over politicians (GE, *FH* II 85–92). His 'Address to Working Men' also advocates 'the turning of Class Interests into Class Functions or duties', controlled by public opinion, which would supervise a gradual channelling of egoism and personal ambition into the service of others. The spiritual and temporal powers, he insists, must be kept separate, so that life can be 'regulated according to the truest principles mankind is in possession of'. There can be little doubt about the identity of 'that religion which keeps an open ear and an obedient mind to the teachings of fact', distinguishing at all times 'between the evils that energy can remove and the evils that patience must bear' (GE, *Essays* 415–30).

If *Felix Holt* demonstrates the extent of George Eliot's general agreement with Comte at the end of the 1860s, *Middlemarch* dramatises her doubts about the details of his utopia. Comte had seen one of the functions of art as the construction of utopias and Harrison was pressing her in the late sixties to produce a novel to illustrate the 'normal relations' within a Positivist society, in particular the influence of the local physician (GE, *GEL* IV 284–9). She explained the difficulties she experienced in making 'certain ideas thoroughly incarnate' but kept his letter constantly 'at hand' and 'read it many times' (300–1, 448), even following his suggestion to study Becker's *Charicles*, an historical novel Harrison claimed to be of value 'exclusively to the actual student of Comte' (Pratt and Neufeldt 1979: xxxviii). When she began *Middlemarch*, she claimed, 'The various elements of the story have been soliciting my mind for years – asking for complete embodiment' (GE, *GEL* V 16). Her diary for July 1869 records her reading about utopian ideas in general and those of Saint-Simon in particular while her '*Middlemarch* Miscellany' quotes two important extracts from Saint-Simon (Pratt and Neufeldt 1979: 20, 113). She also turned to Littré in July, presumably for details of Comte's life, which would also have been furnished by Comte's letters to Valat, which she read in 1870, the year in which they were published (GE, Diary, 25/7/69, 27/10/70).

Of the many characters in *Middlemarch* who cherish utopian ideals Lydgate can be linked with Positivism through the men on whom he is modelled, who include Maria Congreve's father, Dr Bury, and Dr Allbutt, whose career had been decided by a reading of the *Cours* and with whom George Eliot had discussed the religion of humanity in 1868 (Kitchel 1950: 2–5). Lydgate himself is supposed to have spent some time in Paris in 1829, when 'he had thought of joining the Saint Simonians' (GE, *MM* I 227), and is motivated by the Positivist 'ambition of making his life recognised as a factor in the better life of mankind – like other heroes of science' (251), whose memory he cultivates as 'patron saints, invisibly helping' (II 278). Thoughts of Vesalius, reviled as a body-snatcher in his own time but revered by posterity as a benefactor of mankind, revive his flagging spirits. Rosamond refers scathingly to these 'great heroes' but he finds sympathy from Dorothea, the guardian angel he substitutes for his unworthy wife, and his meditation upon her 'voice of deep-souled womanhood' fulfils the same function, in terms of Positivist worship, as 'the enkindling conception of dead and sceptered genius' (III 91).

Lydgate shares not only Comte's aspirations but some of his weaknesses, being forced like him to move from the grand lodgings occupied immediately after his marriage. More significantly, his ideals are shown in the novel to be as unrealistic as those of Comte's utopia. The alliance between physician and capitalist founders on their own frailty as well as the prejudice of their community, which is simply not ready for advanced scientific ideas. Public opinion has the power to hound the hypocritical banker from his position but requires much more time to overcome the weaknesses of human nature (J. F. Scott 1972: 59–76). Hypocrisy, the narrative insists, is not confined to Bulstrode but 'shows itself occasionally in us all', even those who 'believe in the future perfection of our race' and the 'solidarity of mankind' (GE, *MM* III 132).

Many of the features of Comte's historical model of human progress, however, can be detected in George Eliot's novels. *Middlemarch* itself portrays a particular stage of the Western Revolution, the intellectual and social disintegration of the feudal system founded in the Middle Ages. Neither the rector, Casaubon, nor the squire, Brooke, command the respect of their parishioners and tenants. *Romola* goes back to the beginning of that process of disintegration while *Silas Marner* depicts the sense of alienation such breakdown of the community has brought (McLaverty 1981: 318–26). Silas Marner's feeling for his old brick hearth and brown pot is described as a form of 'fetishism', the origin of all religion (GE, *SM* 212). He is eventually nursed back to a sense of solidarity with the Raveloe community and continuity with his own past through his adopted daughter.

Romola has also been seen as a Positivist allegory in which the heroine passes through all three of Comte's stages, thereby tracing in her own life the history of Humanity (Bullen 1975: 425–35). She certainly fits Comte's symbolic picture, appearing as she does at the end of the novel as a widow of about thirty with a child in her arms, preaching altruism and the cultivation of human saints. She represents all that is admirable in the moral development of mankind from the 'intellectual elaboration' of classical scholarship through the 'affective evolution' brought by her medieval Catholic faith to the Religion of Humanity she teaches in the epilogue. Tito, by contrast, carries into oblivion all that Comte regarded as unworthy in human history. The novel's portrait of Savonarola also fits Comte's analysis of the way in which the moral influence of medieval Catholicism began to decay because of its failure to preserve the separation of the spiritual from the temporal powers. Savonarola makes the mistake of entering politics but remains worthy of Positivist veneration: 'the victim is spotted, but it is not therefore in vain that his mighty heart is laid on the altar of men's highest hopes' (GE, *R* I 358–60).

If *Romola* recognises the place of Catholicism in the moral development of Humanity, *Daniel Deronda* dramatises her debt to Judaism, a debt of which George Eliot felt that Christians ought to have been more aware (GE, *GEL* VI 301–2). The sense of continuity which inspired such gratitude to the past was what George Eliot admired most in Judaism, along with its 'feeling of race, a sense of corporate existence, unique in its intensity' (GE, *TS* 270). One of her notebooks for the novel praises the 'unknown teacher to whom we are indebted for the Book of Daniel' for grasping the essential truth that 'the history of the world' was 'one great whole' (GE, Pforzheimer 710, f. [14]). Her own Daniel has a similar belief in historical tradition which emerges at King's Topping, where he is mocked for taking off his hat to the horses which now occupy the ruined abbey (GE, *DD* II 218) and in the Jewish synagogue in Frankfurt, where 'the splendid forms of that world's religion . . . were blent for him as one expression of a binding history' (137). Mordecai himself presents the notion of continuity in Comte's image of the family: 'the past becomes my parent, and the future stretches towards me the appealing arms of children' (381), adding crucial words such as 'binds' and 'dutiful' to the quotation from Jehuda Halevy: 'Israel is the heart of mankind, if we mean by heart the core of affection which binds a race and its families in dutiful love' (384–5; Baker 1975: 177). His explanation of the Shemah embodies a similar sense of 'the ultimate unity of mankind' (GE, *DD* III 289). The Wordsworthian epigraph to chapter 69, which celebrates

> The human nature unto which I felt
> That I belonged, and reverenced with love,

was one of the extracts George Eliot sent to Frederic Harrison for incorporation into the Positivist liturgy (GE, *GEL* VII 261). She clearly appreciated its Comtean significance.

Theophrastus Such is even more explicit in advocating the sense of 'corporate existence' and 'common descent'. If we cannot yet feel strongly bound to a 'common humanity', Theophrastus argues, we can at least cultivate a sense of national identity, which is one step on the altruistic path to universal benevolence (GE, *TS* 264–5). George Eliot's novels constantly celebrate any faith which takes people outside themselves, giving them a sense of belonging to a wider community with historical traditions. In *Adam Bede* it is Wesleyan Methodism which gives its followers 'a rudimentary culture, which linked their thoughts with the past' (GE, *AB* I 52). In St Ogg's that past is swept into oblivion like the ruins on the bank of the Rhone instead of belonging like the castles along the Rhine to 'the grand historic life of humanity' (GE, *MF* II 4). Dorothea, too, lacks the historical understanding which could have enabled her to appreciate Rome, 'the spiritual centre and interpreter of the world' (GE, *MM* I 296), and she is not helped by Casaubon's dry antiquarian researches, which lack any connection with 'the general life of mankind' (301). She learns instead from Ladislaw to make the 'vital connection' between the world's ages (325), just as Romola learns from Savonarola to link the present with the past and to see herself as part of 'the history of the world' (GE, *R* II 107). The exact nature of the tradition is unimportant. What matters is that the individual is incorporated into a life wider than his own.

The Positivist belief in the moral benefits to be derived from a developing commitment to the family, the nation and the race forms part of a cerebral theory which figures prominently in George Eliot's novels. Both she and Lewes exasperated Bray by preferring Comte's cerebral theory to his phrenology (Bray 1863: 145, 149). Her letters of the sixties constantly describe both the general 'need for the education of mankind through the affections and sentiments' (GE, *GEL* IV 13) and her own attempts to channel egoism into altruism. Her editing of the final two volumes of Lewes's *Problems of Life and Mind* included an important passage in her handwriting explaining the development of 'The Moral Sense' from animal instincts such as attachment and another passage on the origins of altruism in the nutritive and reproductive instincts (Collins 1978: 492).

191

The 'affective motors' set out in Comte's diagram of Positivist cerebral theory, which George Eliot copied into two of her notebooks (Pforzheimer 707, f.37; Nuneaton f.34), form a scale against which the characters of Geoge Eliot's novels are measured, a ladder up which they climb (when there are no snakes to cause them to fall). Egoistic instincts can be broadened by careful exercise and meditation into altruistic attachment and universal love. Maternal love, for example, which comes into Comte's category of an egoistic instinct which can be purged of its selfishness and developed into altruism, is celebrated in 'Janet's Repentance' as capable of making 'selfishness become self-denial' and giving 'even to hard vanity the glance of admiring love' (GE, *SCL* II 186). It provides a ray of hope for Mrs Tulliver but cannot redeem Mrs Transome, who is unable to make the transition from egoistic to altruistic love:

> The mother's love is at first an absorbing delight, blunting all other sensibilities; it is an expansion of the animal existence; it enlarges the imagined range for self to move in: but in after years it can only continue to be joy on the same terms as other long-lived love – that is, by much suppression of self, and power of living in the experience of another. (GE, *FH* I 32)

Maternal love is only one aspect of family life, of course, but is taken here as a specific example of an innate propensity which can be cultivated into a higher sentiment.

Egoistic instincts such as sexual attraction and vanity are seen to conflict with altruism in Hetty Sorrel, who is indisputably vain and deficient in 'any warm, self-devoting love' (GE, *AB* I 236). Her attachment to Arthur educates her feelings, at least to the extent that she blushes at a kindness from Adam that would have 'found her quite hard before' (332). Arthur too relishes admiration and praise but even he has a modicum of altruism, being 'at once affectionate and vain' (II 13), a mixture of 'egoism' and 'sympathy' (33). A similar battle between egoism and altruism takes place within Maggie Tulliver, who revels in Philip's admiration before learning from him that 'love must suffer before it can be disembodied of selfish desire' and grow into 'that enlarged life which grows and grows by appropriating the life of others' (GE, *MF* II 371–2). Her attraction to Philip, unlike her infatuation with Stephen, involves an appeal to her good qualities rather than to 'her vanity or other egoistic excitability of her nature' (225). The reiteration of Positivist terminology is less conspicuous in the text, of course, where it is supported by more complex characterisation.

Pride and vanity reappear in *Daniel Deronda* in the persons of Grandcourt, whose one aim in life is to exercise power, and Gwendolen, whose 'wounded egoism' resents all criticism (GE, *DD* I 68). These egoistic instincts, however, so horribly clear to the enhanced perception of Latimer in 'The Lifted Veil', are balanced by the existence of innate benevolence. Even someone as degenerate as the alcoholic wife-beating lawyer Dempster is shown to possess 'stirrings of the more kindly, healthy sap of human feeling, by which goodness tries to get the upper hand in us whenever it seems to have the slightest chance' (GE, *SCL* II 121). His love for his mother reveals 'the deep-down fibrous roots of human love and goodness' (128), natural 'channels of pity, of patience and of love' which, properly exercised and strengthened, can 'sweep down . . . our clamorous selfish desires' (271). Physiological metaphors here provide a hypothetical description of the processes at the heart of Positivist cerebral theory.

Love and reverence are the two fundamental altruistic instincts on which George Eliot built her faith in humanity: 'The first condition of human goodness is something to love; the second, something to reverence' (264). The words recur throughout the novels. In *Adam Bede* there is even a hint of cerebral localisation: Adam's 'tenderness lay very close to his reverence, so that the one could hardly be stirred without the other' (GE, *AB* II 157). Romola struggles to unite the two qualities while Esther Lyon shudders at the prospect of a life such as Mrs Transome's, deprived of the joy which 'sprang from the unchanging fountains of reverence and devout love' (GE, *FH* II 349). *Daniel Deronda* positively bulges with these gifts, which are defended by Theophrastus Such as the 'moral currency' of humanity, not to be debased by flippancy or irreverence (GE, *TS*, 149).

The altruistic instincts are best developed, according to Positivist cerebral theory, through family relationships, which are supposed to foster a sense of solidarity with wider communities such as the nation and the race and continuity with past and future generations. Filial reverence, the one healthy feature in Lawyer Dempster and one of the few virtues that Adam Bede lacks, is central to *The Mill on the Floss*, in which Maggie realises that breaking the bonds of family relationship involves the destruction of her sense of continuity: 'If the past is not to bind us', she asks Stephen, 'where can duty lie?' (GE, *MF* II 329). Esther Lyon rejects a life at Transome Court on similar grounds, recognising its 'incongruity' with 'that past which had created the sanctities and affections of her life' (GE, *FH* II 186). Silas Marner's removal from Lantern Yard brings about a destruction of all sense of belonging. That 'the sap of affection was not all gone' is evident from his tears over his broken pot and his meditation on future guineas as 'unborn children' (GE, *SM* 29–31). What he needs is a real child on which to exercise his weak and distorted affections and this is provided by Eppie, who connects him not only with his present community but with his past family relations, since she reminds him of his little sister. The absence of close family ties is all too evident in the Red House, which lacks 'that presence of the wife and mother which is the fountain of wholesome love and fear' (34). It is no surprise, therefore, that both sons turn out ill, although Nancy Lammeter manages to restore to the house 'the habit of filial reverence' by preserving various relics of the squire after his death (226).

Tito, that exemplar of egoism, loses all sense of 'the love that is rooted in memories' (GE, *R* I 151), selling first Baldassare's ring, a symbol of 'a claim from the past' (216), and then Bardo's library, leaving Romola with a genuine dilemma. For the marriage tie is itself binding:

> the light abandonment of ties, whether inherited or voluntary, because they had ceased to be pleasant, was the uprooting of social and personal virtue.
>
> (II 272)

'Social' and 'personal', of course, are the Positivist synonyms for altruistic and egoistic. Tito is called 'one of the *demoni*, who are of no particular country' (I 294). When he suggests that she should leave her beloved Florence, Romola quite rightly suspects the sincerity of a man who 'professed to appropriate the widest sympathies and had no pulse for the nearest' (436), echoing the same complaint in the *Système* (AC, *Pol* I 189).

Another element of Comtean ethics which finds frequent expression in George Eliot's novels is encapsulated in the motto, 'Live openly, live without concealment'. To live openly is to expose oneself to what Theophrastus Such calls the 'wholesome restraining power of public opinion' (GE, *TS* 189). Concealment, on the other hand, fosters evil desires, which lose some of their power once confessed. Arthur Donnithorne's failure to confess his love for Hetty has a progressively corrupting effect, in contrast with Dinah's redemptive openness and absence of secrecy. Maggie Tulliver realises that her secret meetings with Philip destroy 'the simplicity and clearness of her life by admitting a ground of concealment' (GE, *MF* II 91). As an openly avowed friend, however, he becomes a source of strength, 'a sort of outward conscience' (225). She is particularly in need of such 'outward help' as 'a reflection of her own conscience' when she returns to St Ogg's (340), but public opinion there fails to perform its proper function. The final chapters of the book suggest 'both the power of public opinion and the need to develop it more consistently to a higher level of social sympathy' (Levine 1965: 405).

Silas Marner dramatises the blighting effect of Godfrey Cass's 'long concealment' of his secret marriage (GE, *SM* 238) before he resolves to be 'plain and open for the rest o' my life' (246). Concealment contributes to Latimer's problems in 'The Lifted Veil' and also hastens Tito's moral degeneration. Romola, who cannot bear even the duplicity of the nun's habit in which she attempts to escape from him, pleads with him to be open. The Transomes positively treasure their secrets but Rufus Lyon rectifies his 'initial concealment' of his past by being completely open with Esther's mother (GE, *FH* I 116). The power of public opinion also prevents Harold Transome from accepting Christian's offer to sell his information about Esther's parentage and to leave the country. He envisages the way his action would look if it ever became public knowledge: 'Thus the outside conscience came in aid of the inner' (II 155).

Middlemarch, for all the backwardness of its public opinion, illustrates the benefits of openness. Fred Vincy is enabled to recover because he confesses his follies both to his father and to Caleb Garth. Farebrother, too, secures himself against the temptation to take advantage of Fred's stupidity by talking openly of his own love for Mary. Lydgate, who constantly reproaches Rosamond for her secrecy, has finally to confess to Dorothea, 'I ought to be more open' (GE, *MM* III 358). The theme recurs throughout *Daniel Deronda*. Grandcourt's life is 'full of secrets' such as Mrs Glasher (GE, *DD* II 239) while Gwendolen gradually loses her habits of concealment and secrecy. Having suffered himself from the lack of 'open daylight' on his life, he sees 'concealment as a bane of life', choosing instead 'that openness which is the sweet fresh air of our moral life' (160–3, 177). There seems here to be an echo of the French version of the Positivist motto behind all this teaching, 'Vivre au grand jour'.

George Eliot could be a fierce advocate of Positivist prayer (Hamerton

1897: 324), priding herself on her ability 'to recall beloved faces and accents with great clearness' and claiming that 'in this way my friends are continually with me' (GE, *GEL* IV 80–1). 'Contemplation of whatever is great', she argued, 'is itself religion and lifts us out of our egoism' (104, 108). Her 'worship' of Lewes, she claimed, was her 'best life' and she permitted others beside him to worship her (184; VI 27). When they had the opportunity to see the original painting of the Sistine Madonna, that central symbol of Positivist worship, on a visit to Dresden in 1858 she and Lewes were both overwhelmed. She sat on the sofa opposite Raphael's painting in 'a sort of awe, as if I were in the living presence of some glorious being'. He gazed at it until he 'felt quite hysterical'. They returned to the gallery frequently during their six-week stay for 'quiet worship of the Madonna' (II 471–2). George Eliot's letters abound with references to 'guardian angels' as well as such saints as the Newman brothers whose good deeds would 'live in others' after their death, providing 'a *partial* salvation, a *partial* redemption of the world', less complete than Christianity but also less illusory (IV 158).

'Paint us an angel', exclaims the narrator of *Adam Bede*, but 'paint us yet oftener a Madonna' (GE, *AB* I 270). George Eliot's novels are full of idealised portraits of suitable objects of worship. Amos Barton only recognises the worth of his wife, 'a large, fair, gentle Madonna . . . with large, tender, short-sighted eyes', after her death (GE, *SCL* I 24). Arthur Donnithorne says of Dinah Morris, 'I could worship that woman' (GE, *AB* II 275), while the Bede brothers literally meditate upon her virtues. Unhappy in her absence from the Donnithorne dance, Seth gains strength to put up with his querulous mother merely by thinking of her:

Dinah had never been more constantly present with him than in this scene, where everything was so unlike her. He saw her all the more vividly after looking at the thoughtless faces and gay-coloured dresses of the young women – just as one feels the beauty and the greatness of a pictured Madonna the more, when it has been for a moment screened for us by a vulgar head in a bonnet. But this presence of Dinah in his mind helped him to bear the better with his mother's mood.   (I 423–4)

The notion of subjective presence and the reference to the Madonna clinches the association of such morally beneficial meditation with the Religion of Humanity.

The worship of women is treated more humorously in *The Mill on the Floss* when Tom accepts Aunt Glegg's gift of linen 'but evaded any promise to meditate nightly on her virtues' (GE, *MF* II 297). It appears in the angelic imagery used of Eppie throughout *Silas Marner* and in Romola's being mistaken for the Madonna by starving Florentines and plague-stricken villagers. Felix Holt too gazes at Esther 'very much as a reverential Protestant might look up at a picture of the Virgin, with a devoutness suggested by the type rather than the image' (GE, *FH* II 39). She is, to begin with, somewhat reluctant to accept this Comtean mould but comes round to returning his devotion, preserving his memory 'embalmed and kept as a relic in a private sanctuary' (177). Fedalma inspires worship in Don Silva, who

> enshrines
> Her virgin image for the general awe
> And for his own − will guard her from the world,
> Nay, his profaner self, lest he should lose
> The place of his religion.   (GE, *SG* 37)

Fedalma also exercises angelic influence over her father, who acknowledges her as the source of his pity for the Duke's circle, whom he selects for decent burial. 'Widowed' of Don Silva's 'touch', she eventually fulfils the mission unfolded to her by Zarca, 'to be the angel of a homeless tribe' (373, 147).

Dorothea Brooke's affinities to Madonna and angels inspire both Lydgate and Ladislaw to meditate upon her virtues, while Daniel Deronda is so eager to worship women that he has to be reprimanded by Sir Hugo for gazing at them so tenderly. Once Mirah has taken 'her place in his soul as a beloved type', however, her 'indwelling image' protects him from Gwendolen's glamour (GE, *DD* III 306). The woman who occupies his thoughts perhaps most of all is his mother, with whom he has 'ideal' meetings and whom he addresses as a representative of the Great Being: 'Mother! take us all into your heart − the living and the dead. Forgive everything that hurts in the past. Take my affection' (135). Her refusal to play this role leaves him 'conscious of a disappointed yearning − a shutting out for ever from long early vistas of affectionate imagination' (145), making 'the filial yearning of his life a disappointed pilgrimage to a shrine where there were no longer the symbols of sacredness' (176). Passages like these, of course, tend to provoke amusement or annoyance in modern readers. Their effect, whether intended or not, is to highlight the sheer impracticality of Positivist worship.

197

Many of George Eliot's characters practise a form of Positivist prayer in that they purify their feelings, strengthening their altruistic instincts by meditation upon the needs of others. Dinah, for example, tells Hetty how she sits alone with her eyes closed in order to conjure up the sight and sound of people she knows, laying them with love 'before the Lord' (GE, *AB* I 211). The 'children of God', she tells Seth, 'bear one another about in their thoughts continually as it were a new strength' (II 61). The point, for George Eliot at least, is that it is immaterial whether God hears these prayers; they still succeed in strengthening Dinah's capacity to live for others. The same can be said of Maggie Tulliver, who tells Philip, 'I think about everybody when I'm away from them' (GE, *MF*, I 288). Even Rufus Lyon's 'prayerful meditation' on his daughter is given a Positivist interpretation:

He was striving to purify his feeling in this matter from selfish or worldly dross – a striving which is that prayer without ceasing, sure to wrest an answer by its sublime importunity. (GE, *FH* II 185–6)

The answer to his prayer, of course, will come not from God but in the form of increased altruism.

Similarly, when Casaubon refuses Dorothea's sympathetic arm after hearing from Lydgate of the seriousness of his condition, it costs her 'a litany of pictured sorrows and of silent cries' to overcome her initial feeling of indignation (GE, *MM* II 234). Her night of prayer after surprising Rosamond and Ladislaw together also strengthens her capacity to help them:

All the active thought with which she had before been representing to herself the trials of Lydgate's lot, and this young marriage union . . . all this vivid sympathetic experience returned to her now as a power: it asserted itself as acquired knowledge asserts itself and will not let us see as we saw in the day of our ignorance. (III 391)

Deronda too sits up 'half the night' reliving his discovery of Mirah through 'emotive memory' and 'inward vision' (GE, *DD* I 306). He considers future possibilities carefully and so prepares himself for any eventuality, indulging in 'passionate meditation' in which 'Mirah and Mordecai were always present' (III 211). He explains to Gwendolen that she too can learn to develop and purify her feelings through 'fixed meditation' (II 268).

The same principle lies behind Comte's belief in the importance of art as a form of 'moral exercise . . . calling sympathies and antipathies into healthy play' (AC, *Pol* I 228). This central feature of Comtean aesthetics, explained in a series of articles in the 'Contemporary Literature' section of the *Westminster Review* under George Eliot's editorship in 1852–3 (Stang 1959: 146–8), also found expression in an article of 1856 in which she discussed 'the extension of our sympathies' and the development of 'moral sentiment' which art could bring (GE, *Essays* 270). George Eliot's novels can be understood in this way as an attempt to improve her readers by exercising their altruistic instincts. She made a number of explicit references to the Positivist purpose of her work. Her Comtean hymn to the 'Choir Invisible' not only records her desire for subjective immortality but describes her work as a contribution to Positivist worship, establishing an ideal image which can help mankind to moral improvement:

> our rarer, better, truer self,
> That sobbed religiously in yearning song,
> That watched to ease the burthen of the world,
> Laboriously tracing what must be,
> And what may yet be better – saw within
> A worthier image for the sanctuary,
> And shaped it forth before the multitude
> Divinely human, raising worship so
> To higher reverence more mixed with love.   (GE, *LJ* 302)

Her novels, she confessed, were 'deliberately, carefully constructed on . . . my conviction as to the relative goodness and nobleness of human dispositions and motives', attempting to clarify 'those vital elements which bind men together and give a higher worthiness to their existence' and to dissociate 'these elements from the more transient forms on which an outworn teaching tends to make them dependent' (GE, *GEL* IV 472). Her function, as she explained to Harrison, was 'that of the *aesthetic*, not the doctrinal teacher – the rousing of the nobler emotions . . . not the prescribing of special measures' (VII 44). But even this description fits very closely into the Positivist view of art.

George Eliot seems to have regarded her poetry as more overtly propagandist than her novels. Each poem, she told John Blackwood, 'represents an idea which I care for strongly, and wish to propagate as far as I can' (VI 26). No-one has ever doubted the seriousness and sincerity with which they were written. 'A Minor Prophet', for example, which begins as a satire on an American crank, soon goes on to celebrate those who preach true religion, the sense of solidarity and continuity, the qualities of 'order, justice, love', and a recognition of invariable law, before culminating in a vision of 'better things on earth', which includes reverence and love, the subordination of egoism to altruism, and 'thoughts, like light, that bind the world in one' (GE, *LJ* 186–94). 'Self and Life' teaches resignation and reverence for the heroes of 'the solemn, splendid Past' (273), while 'Brother and Sister' assume their proper Positivist roles: he behaves chivalrously towards her, exercising control over his more aggressive instincts, while she recognises 'My present Past' as 'my root of piety' and learns to subject fantasy to fact, 'by "What is," "What will be" to define' (202–6).

Comte is actually named in 'A College Breakfast-Party', which recounts the earnest discussion of a group of undergraduates who derive their names from *Hamlet* and some of their views from Comte. Guildenstern, the most Positivist, attacks a priori 'rainbow-bridges' of thought, as George Eliot had done in her essay on Riehl. When Rosencrantz attacks 'relativism' and the worship of progress, he claims that 'binding law' and an enthroned 'Ideal' can only be provided by recognition of invariable law in the universe, resignation to the unalterable 'Outward', and amelioration of human nature, 'Urging to possible ends the active soul'. A sense of solidarity can be generated by the study of sociology and a new religion built on the ruins of the old. The poem ends, however, on a characteristically uncommitted note, with Hamlet going down to the river to ponder what they discussed and dreaming 'so luminous' a dream that he wakes convinced, only to withhold his secret from the public (232–61).

Some of George Eliot's unfinished projects were clearly designed to continue her investigation and exposition of Positivist ideas. From the late 1860s, for example, she intended to write about the Greek hero Timoleon and her '*Middlemarch* Miscellany' contains notes from Grote's partially Positivist *History of Greece* on 'Fetichism', 'Worship of the heroes of Marathon', 'Family sacred rites', the power of 'public opinion' and 'Spiritual power beside the Temporal' (Pratt and Neufeldt 1979: 9–11). Her Napoleonic novel was to include a widow, a teacher, an 'Ideal Working Vicar' (GE, Card Calendar for 1876, Yale) and a young scientist whose 'chief ambition, the most fervid yearning of his life, is to complete the development of a philosophic system which will make an epoch in the advancing thought of mankind' (Beaty 1957: 175). These sketchy notes, like those for her completed novels, as well as shedding light on the processes of her imagination, provide evidence of the prominent position Positivism seems to have held even in the initial stages of her writing.

There are areas where George Eliot clearly disagreed with Comte. She had a much keener sense of mystery, for instance, which emerges both in the letters and the novels. The basic human need for 'the blessed possibility of mystery' is most dramatically revealed in 'The Lifted Veil', whose hero clings to the one 'oasis of mystery in the dreary desert of knowledge' (GE, *SM* 322). George Eliot, it has been argued (Adam 1975: 95–9), attempted to 'stabilise' this story in 'acceptably positive terms' in 1872 by giving it a new motto:

> Give me no light, great Heaven, but such as turns
> To energy of human fellowship;
> No powers beyond the growing heritage
> That makes completer manhood.   (GE, *SM* 276)

But it continues to disturb any complacent Positivist with its portrait of the horror of knowing everything.

George Eliot was altogether less fond of systems than Comte. 'Human beliefs', we are told in *Silas Marner*, 'like all other natural growths, elude the barriers of system' (236). Her letters are full of diffident disclaimers of her own powers of understanding, making it necessary for her to probe philosophical formulas by clothing them in 'some human figure and individual experience' (*GEL* VI 216–17). Perhaps the most important difference between Comte's religion and George Eliot's lies in their concept of Humanity. For Comte the Great Being did not include all human beings but only those worthy of incorporation. He had little sympathy with the mass of mankind. George Eliot, on the contrary, could not place too much emphasis on the mediocrity of her characters. One of her greatest strengths as a novelist is her ability to show the moral significance of the smallest acts. For 'it is in these acts called trivialities that the seeds of joy' are to be lost or found (GE, *MM* II 231). her novels consistently display the qualities of humility, tolerance, sympathy and humour so noticeably absent from Comte's writing. His Religion of Humanity, it might be said, gained in her work the quality of humanity.

Thomas Hardy: Positive pessimist

Thomas Hardy has often been compared with George Eliot precisely because of his use of Positivist terminology. When the *Spectator* attributed *Far From the Madding Crowd* to her he blamed the mistake on the fact that 'he had latterly been reading Comte's *Positive Philosophy*, and writings of that school' (TH, *Life* I 129). George Eliot's death also 'set him thinking about Positivism', whose failure he attributed at least in part to a tactical mistake:

If Comte had introduced Christ among the worthies in his calendar it would have made Positivism tolerable to thousands who, from position, family connection, or early education, now decry what in their heart of hearts they hold to contain the germs of a true system. It would have enabled them to modulate gently into the new religion by deceiving themselves with the sophistry that they still continued one-quarter Christians, or one-eighth, or one-twentieth, as the case might be. This is a matter of *policy*, without which no religion succeeds in making way. (189)

The original draft of this passage stipulated John the Baptist and St Paul as examples of Christians who could have been included, even 'to the exclusion of greater men' (Taylor 1978: 223). Like George Eliot, Hardy insisted that his novels presented no systematic 'philosophy of life': 'Positive views on the Whence and Wherefore of things have never been advanced by this pen as a consistent philosophy' (TH, *Jude* 444). He objected to critics treating *Jude the Obscure* as 'a religious and ethical treatise' (25) and refused to join the Rationalist Press Association in case this led to his being 'misread as propagandist' rather than 'artistic' (TH, *Life* II 83).

Hardy was, however, deeply attracted to the Religion of Humanity. A letter to Lady Grove in 1903, full of admiration for Frederic Harrison's latest 'New Year's Address', disclaims the title of Positivist for himself but agrees with Anatole France that 'no person of serious thought in these times could be said to stand aloof from Positivist teaching and ideals' (TH, *Letters* III 53). He seems to have encountered the Religion of Humanity for the first time in the mid-1860s, the period during which he lost his Christian faith. He read John Stuart Mill avidly in the summer of 1865 and went carefully through a copy of Bridges' 1865 translation of the *General View* given to him by his friend and mentor, Horace Moule, a contemporary of the Wadham

Positivists at Oxford who followed Beesly to Marlborough College before committing suicide in Cambridge in 1873. Some of the numerous marginal notes in this volume were made by Moule 'but others are certainly Hardy's and show that he was particularly familiar with the chapters on "The Intellectual Character of Positivism" and "The Influence of Positivism on Women" ' (Millgate 1982: 91). He maintained his interest in Positivism through the 1870s, embarking like George Eliot upon a systematic study of the English translation of the *Système* as soon as it was published, paying particular attention to the third volume, which expounds the 'General Theory of Human Progress' (Gittings 1980: 21).

Hardy's *Literary Notes* contain more material from the *Système* than from any other single work (Björk 1974: 286). Like George Eliot's notes, they seem to have been designed to concentrate his mind, to take firm hold of the ideas. There are few critical comments, although a warning by Bacon against over-simplification in French thinkers (119) and a passage from Henry James on Balzac's 'French passion for completeness, for symmetry, for making a system as neat as an epigram' (124), suggest that he was not uncritical of Comte. He also copied a passage in which Comte explains the difficulties of working out 'new conceptions in the old language' without falling into the opposite extremes of 'diffuseness and obscurity' (137). His main concern, however, seems to have been to understand precisely what Comte had to say.

Hardy saw Positivism as a 'complete Synthesis', retaining the basic principles of the 'Objective method' while resurrecting '*Subjectivity in a regenerated form*'. At the heart of the Religion of Humanity, he observed, were the principles of 'unity' and 'order', clearly visible in the positive hierarchy of the sciences, which became increasingly complex and correspondingly more susceptible of modification (73–8). He reproduced Comte's view of history in his own diagrammatic form (138), being especially interested in the image of 'the looped orbit' by which progress was supposed to take place. He noticed the complexity of the law of the three stages and the link between the development of the individual and that of the race, and he seems to have been fascinated by 'Fetichism'. He copied several of Comte's remarks on Greek philosophy (78–80) and the French Revolution also features prominently in these notes.

Hardy devotes some space to Comte's attack on the concept of God and to the struggle between monotheism and science, recognising that it is somehow safer to attack monotheism than Christianity. Some 'gratitude', he notes, is 'due to its ancient services', especially in its medieval Catholic form, with its worship of saints and anticipation of the worship of Humanity. A number of annotated passages deal explicitly with the 'Positive religion'. Positivist ethics, with their emphasis on '*Feeling* – the great motor force of human life', also make an appearance. Hardy observes the 'Biological dependence' of the 'nobler phenomena' on the 'grosser', 'the cerebral functions on the nutritive economy' (70–8).

Other Positivists who feature in Hardy's notes include Harrison, Bridges and Morison, extracts from whose *Service of Man* Hardy copied into his 'Literary Notes' for 1887 or 1888 (265). There are also passages from Leslie Stephen, George Henry Lewes and John Morley. The extensive marking of Hardy's copy of *Diderot* has been seen to reflect 'his general acceptance of Morley's positivism and "religion of humanity" ' (263). One passage that Hardy copied from *Diderot* criticises the failure of Voltaire, Rousseau and others 'to recognise this important truth, that the founders of religions satisfied a profound need in those who accepted them' (61). These notes provide no evidence of commitment to the Religion of Humanity, of course, but they prove Hardy's thorough familiarity with its basic concepts.

Hardy knew many of the Positivists personally. Judge Benjamin Fossett Lock, a childhood friend from Dorchester, invited him to his daughter's Presentation at Newton Hall (Millgate 1982: 219). He may well have met Beesly as early as 1865, when he was studying at King's College (Sherman 1953: 167–8) while his first contact with Leslie Stephen, 'the man whose philosophy was to influence his own for many years', came in 1874 (TH, *Life* I 132). He was saddened by the death of James Cotter Morison, whose *Service of Man* he thought unfairly treated by the critics (TH, *Letters* I 173) and was a frequent guest of Vernon Lushington and his family. His friendship with Frederic Harrison, 'whose cast of mind he once found extremely attractive' (xi), dates from his London visits of the mid-1880s, when he used occasionally to attend Newton Hall. He was particularly impressed by one of Harrison's lectures there in 1885 and urged him to renew his attacks on 'the New Christians' three years later (134, 176).

Encouraged by such sympathy, Harrison immediately attempted to bring Hardy and his writing into the Positivist fold, finding *Tess* so 'saturated with human and anti-theological morality' that it read 'like a Positivist allegory or sermon' (FH to TH, 29/12/91, DCM). He sent Hardy a copy of the *New Calendar of Great Men*, receiving in return an assurance that the first draft of *Tess* had contained 'much more on religion as apart from theology' (TH, *Letters* I 251). When their correspondence was renewed in 1901 Harrison informed Hardy of the fate of Newton Hall, which was due for demolition (FH to TH, 18/10/01, DCM), while Hardy was full of praise for Harrison's 'New Year's Address' (TH, *Letters* III 46), attributing to 'the Positive view of the Universe' expressed in *The Dynasts* the *'odium theologicum'* it had raised among the critics (98). He even praised Harrison's novel (191–2). Philosophically, he claimed, they were in agreement:

I, too, call myself a 'meliorist', but then, I find myself unable to be in such good spirits as you are at the prospect . . . The fact is that when you get to the bottom of things you find no bed-rock of righteousness to rest on – nature is *un*moral – and our puny efforts are those of people who try to keep their leaky house dry by wiping off the waterdrops from the ceiling. (231)

Harrison continued to urge Hardy, as he had urged George Eliot, to take a fuller part in Positivist activities. He admitted, after a visit to Max Gate which left him lamenting that they had not seen more of each other earlier in life, that he had been 'a keen G. Eliotan' mainly 'because she read and understood Comte' and helped in their work, but preferred Hardy as a novelist. He pressed him, as he had pressed her, to 'tell us in plain words' what he believed 'about Creation – God, Immortality, Worship, and Duty'. 'Such a deliverance', he continued, again picking up her terminology, 'would be the most important of your Wessex Tales to the Twentieth Century' (FH to TH, 11/11/13, DCM). But Hardy, like George Eliot, steered clear of such unequivocal statements.

The temperamental differences between the two men came to the surface when Harrison attacked the consistent pessimism of Hardy's 'Lyrics' in a review of 1920 (FH 1921: 27–34). Hardy defended himself in an 'Apology' to his *Late Lyrics and Earlier* in 1922, insisting that his 'pessimism' was only a matter of ' "questionings" in the exploration of reality', a 'series of fugitive impressions which I have never tried to co-ordinate' but which was best described as 'evolutionary meliorism'. Human and animal suffering, he believed, could be

kept down to a minimum by loving-kindness, operating through scientific knowledge, and actuated by the modicum of free will conjecturally possessed by organic life when the mighty necessitating forces . . . happen to be in equilibrium.

He looked to 'religion, in its essential and undogmatic sense' to provide a 'forlorn hope' for the future, quoting Comte to the effect that apparent retrogression may herald real progress, since 'advance is never in a straight line, but in a looped orbit' (TH, *CP* 525–32). Harrison appears to have been quite happy with this limited affirmation of sympathy, wishing him 'a happy and still hopeful 82nd birthday' later in the year (FH to TH, 23/5/22, DCM), while on Harrison's death the following year Hardy looked back with gratitude on forty years of friendship (Björk 1974: 362).

Hardy's religious position remains difficult to pin down. A long letter to Morley in November 1885, regretting not having met him at Harrison's the previous summer, speculates on the possibility of a Church which would meet 'the religious wants' of 'thoughtful people who have ceased to believe in supernatural theology . . . an undogmatic, non-theological establishment for the promotion of that virtuous living on which all honest men are agreed' (TH, *Letters* I 136). A letter to Edward Clodd of 1897 attacks 'dogmatic ecclesiasticism – Christianity so called (but really Paulinism *plus* idolatry)' (II 143), a phrase illustrating his familiarity not only with Comte but with the controversies to which his ideas had given rise. He returned to the same theme five years later:

If the doctrines of the supernatural were quietly abandoned to-morrow by the Church, and 'reverence and love for an ethical ideal' alone retained, not one in ten thousand would object to the readjustment, while the enormous bulk of thinkers excluded by the old teaching would be brought into the fold, and our venerable old churches and cathedrals would become the centres of emotional life that they once were. (III 5)

Hardy contemplated a more public declaration of his views, making notes in 1907 for an article on religion which was to advocate 'services at which there are no affirmations and no supplications', falling between the two extremes of 'Rationalists' and 'Mystics':

Religious, religion, is to be used in the article in its modern sense entirely, as being expressive of nobler feelings towards humanity and emotional goodness and greatness, the old meaning of the word – ceremony or ritual – having perished. (TH, *Life* II 121)

The article was never published but Hardy remained, by his own confession, irredeemably 'churchy', delighting in services and hoping for the 'giving of liturgical form to modern ideas' (176). His hopes for a rationalised Church were resurrected in the 1920s by rumours of a revised Anglican liturgy acceptable to 'the majority of thinkers of the previous hundred years who had lost all belief in the supernatural' (225). But he was once more to be disappointed.

Hardy's novels are full of positivists with a small 'p', characters who are up to date with modern thought and seeking a secular faith to replace their lost theological convictions. Henry Knight, like Leslie Stephen, writes 'social and ethical essays' (TH, *PBE* 96). The episode in which he is suspended on the cliff-face parallels almost exactly Stephen's 'Bad Five Minutes on the Alps' and performs a similar function, forcing him to confront death and the meaning of life (Hyman 1975: 42–3). Positivism seems to be among the 'strangest notions about things' which Clym Yeobright brings back from Paris (TH, *RN* 132). 'Yeobright loved his kind', we are told, wanting to lead it into the 'wisdom' and 'ennoblement' he had gained from 'his studious life in Paris, where he had become acquainted with ethical systems popular at the time' (196). He eventually finds a vocation as a preacher, delivering 'a series of moral lectures or Sermons on the Mount' which are 'sometimes secular, and sometimes religious, but never dogmatic', omitting all 'creeds and systems of philosophy' (422–3). It has been argued that his role as 'humanitarian reformer' is 'not an altogether natural extension of his character', expressing not what Hardy really believed but what he wanted to believe (Paterson 1960: 65–6). At least part of Hardy, however, seems to have been attracted to the Religion of Humanity at this time.

Angel Clare presents a less attractive aspect of Positivism. A 'sample product of the last five-and-twenty years' (TH, *Tess* 309), he believes that 'improved systems of moral and intellectual training' will 'elevate the involuntary and even the unconscious instincts of human nature' (206). Priding himself on his own moral superiority, he cannot forgive Tess, whom he positively worships, 'creating an ideal presence that conveniently drops the defects of the real' so that her fallen self seems to him a totally different person (287). She is no longer a Comtean Madonna and with her the whole race is diminished:

'humanity stood before him no longer in the pensive sweetness of Italian art, but in the staring and ghastly attitudes of a Wiertz Museum, and with the leer of a study by Van Beers' (304). The rigid ethical code with which he supplants Christianity is seen to narrow rather than to broaden his sympathies. His idealisation of Tess actually dehumanises him, causing him to forget 'that the defective can be more than the entire' (310).

Jude Fawley's quest for self-improvement brings him into contact with some Positivist members of the Artisans' Mutual Improvement Society from which he is forced to resign, rather like Pradeau, for failing to uphold their moral standards. He too worships his Comtean angel, Sue Bridehead, making 'an ideal character' out of her, kissing her photograph, which 'seemed to look down and preside over his tea', and erecting her into such a 'divinity' that her 'real presence' can only disappoint him (TH, *Jude* 108, 165, 185). He continues to claim that he is 'elevated' by her (285), asking her to stay with him 'for humanity's sake' as his 'guardian angel' (373). It has been claimed that 'the terms she uses show her to be a follower of the Positive Philosophy of Auguste Comte', especially when she condemns Oxford as 'a place full of fetichists' and tells Jude that he is in the 'Tractarian stage' (Gittings 1978: 140–1). Like Ethelberta Petherwin and Elizabeth-Jane Henchard, she is a devoted student of John Stuart Mill.

Two of the main features of the Positive Philosophy, the denial of metaphysics and the recommendation of resignation, find frequent expression in Hardy's novels. Hardy himself had little time for metaphysics, referring to Comte in order to dismiss it as a 'sorry attempt to reconcile theology and physics' (TH, *Life* I 234). Much of this dislike of metaphysics falls upon Fitzpiers, who, having abandoned any serious attempt at investigation and experiment, finds himself superfluous as a physician in a strong healthy community. He prefers 'the ideal world to the real', 'abstract philosophy' and romantic literature to 'the books and *matériel* of science' (TH, *W* 144, 153). His immorality is presented as a product of his false and dangerous philosophy (DeLaura 1967: 392–4).

The objective method, however, was less important for Hardy, as for the later Comte, than the subjective human perspective, which saw the world in terms of human needs and aspirations. *Two on a Tower*, as its preface explains, presents 'the emotional history of two infinitesimal lives' as more important than 'the stupendous background of that stellar universe' against which it takes place (TH, *TT* 29). Swithin St Cleeve, like Lydgate, begins with massive scientific aspirations, combining 'scientific earnestness' with 'melancholy mistrust of all things human' (38). He stands as a 'priest' on the 'temple' of 'sublime mystery', the tower from which he pursues his investigation of the universe (84), but his 'goddess Philosophy' fails to protect him against the despair engendered by the discovery that his work has been anticipated (92). For, as his insensitive treatment of Lady Constantine reveals, the man 'who was stable as a giant in all that appertained to nature and life outside humanity, was a mere pupil in domestic matters' (253). The narrative pours increasing scorn on 'this indefatigable scrutineer of the universe' who is so infatuated with 'sublime scientific things' that he ignores the sacrifice made by his lover (275), partaking with other scientists in 'the cruelty of the natural laws that are their study'. This hardness of heart is somewhat softened by his attempt at 'loving-kindness' on returning to her at the end of the novel (291). But he is never fully converted from the objective to the subjective point of view.

It is sometimes suggested that Comte was too optimistic for Hardy (W. Wright 1967: 30) but their view of life was remarkably similar. The trouble with 'venerable philosophers' such as Hegel, against whom Hardy quoted Comte, was that 'they cannot get away from a prepossession that the world must somehow have been made to be a comfortable place for man' (TH, *Life* I 234). Hardy believed, on the contrary, that the world was not 'adequate' to 'humanity' (TH, *Letters* III 113) and that the only remedy for this lay in resignation to the inevitable, combined with determined action toward the progress of the race.

Gabriel Oak's powers of endurance dominate *Far From the Madding Crowd* while a similar dogged resignation is required of the inhabitants of Egdon Heath, a place whose 'sombreness' may have been 'distasteful to our race when it was young' but is 'in keeping with the moods of the more thinking among mankind' at a later stage (TH, *RN* 34). Typically, when 'Humanity appears upon the Scene', in the title of the second chapter, it is 'Hand in Hand with Trouble'. But whereas Eustacia Vye makes no attempt to curb her raging passions in accordance with these conditions but harbours a 'smouldering rebelliousness' against the heath, which leaves her, 'as far as social ethics were concerned', at the 'savage state' (120), Clym's 'view of life as a thing to be put up with' makes his resigned expression 'the typical countenance of the future, replacing that zest for existence which was so intense in early civilizations' (191). To see him calmly chopping away at the furze in order to make faggots, the only occupation his fading eyesight will permit, enrages Eustacia. Hardy himself seems torn between emotional sympathy with her and intellectual recognition of the need for resignation.

Most of Hardy's admirable characters learn 'the sad science of renunciation' (TH, *L* 342) as the novels grow progressively more pessimistic, placing increasing emphasis on the horrors of the world and their incompatibility with an omnipotent and benevolent providence. The positive beliefs which rescue Hardy from utter pessimism, however, lie in Humanity, its progress in the past and the possibilities of its future amelioration. A sense of continuity, a conscious identification on the part of an individual with the historical progress of the race, is one of the features that mark his sympathetic characters. The prime cultivator of continuity in Hardy is Jude Fawley; meditation upon the worthies of Christminster also stimulates his 'faith in the future' (TH, *Jude* 106–7). Disappointed in the university, he can still read the 'book of humanity' in such historic monuments as Fourways (137).

Ethelberta Petherwin also cultivates a sense of continuity. Just as Harrison's earliest surviving letter to Hardy is an invitation to accompany the 'Newton Hall pilgrimage to Milton and Penn' (FH to TH, 15/6/85, DCM), so Hardy makes his heroine suggest 'a pilgrimage of an unusual sort' to Milton's tomb. 'We ought to quicken our memories of the great', she insists, although she fears her upper-class friends may regard the suggestion as sentiment. As she solemnly intones a passage from *Paradise Lost* in Cripplegate Church, 'she could be fancied a priestess'. And as if to indicate that he himself had made a similar pilgrimage, Hardy adds a footnote about the changes that have taken place in the monument (TH, *HE* 209–12). Ethelberta is also glad to visit Corvsgate Castle, to place her own 'social fight' against the 'great struggles' of history (245) and justifies her marriage to the lecherous Lord Mountclere because the peerage appeals to 'our historical sense' (383). She looks forward to exploring his library, 'which contains all that has been done in literature from Moses down to Scott' (324), an odd choice of authors possibly deriving from the Positivist Calendar, the first month of which is named after Moses while the eighth is devoted to Modern Epic Poetry, ending with

Milton and including Scott. The point is not that Ethelberta is a Positivist but that some aspects of her character derive from Hardy's close study of Comte in the year in which the novel was written. It was not only because his wife was called Ethelbertha that this novel became an especial favourite with Harrison (FH to TH, 10/11/13, DCM).

Comte's 'looped orbit' of progress, Hardy realised, took place in accordance with 'essential laws' which did not always conform to the 'social expedients' devised by 'humanity' (Orel 1967: 127). This notion seems to underlie Clym Yeobright's insistence that an 'awkward turning' can lead to a happy outcome, in contrast to the popular belief 'that there is no progress without uniformity' (TH, *RN* 228). Egdon Heath is certainly a primitive place, encouraging a 'fetichistic mood' to imagine it has a spirit of its own (81). Its inhabitants are pagan, their bonfire at the beginning of the novel and their maypole celebrations at the end containing residues of ancient rites. There is 'something fetichistic' too, about Henchard's primitive superstitions (TH, *MC* 49) while Swithin St Cleeve continues to worship the sun in 'a very chastened or schooled form of that first and most natural of adorations' (TH, *TT* 36).

The process of development through Comte's three stages finds dramatic expression in *Tess*. The Durbeyfield family is full of superstition and 'fetichistic fear' (TH, *Tess* 50) and Tess's rendering of the Psalms is described, in terms taken from Hardy's annotation of the *Système*, as 'a Fetichistic utterance in a Monotheistic setting', redolent of 'Pagan fantasy' rather than 'the systematized religion taught their race at a later date' (141). The Christianity Tess encounters in the sign-painter is 'the last grotesque phase of a creed which had served mankind well in its time' (115). The first edition of the novel added scenes with him, the unsympathetic vicar and Angel Clare's father which bring out more fully the anti-theological bias of the novel (Laird 1975: 167–9).

Passages which seem to clarify Angel's Comtean attitude towards Christianity were also printed for the first time in the first edition, for instance where he baffles the dairy hand by referring nostalgically to 'mediaeval times, when faith was a living thing' (TH, *Tess* 148) and explains to his father,

I love the Church as one loves a parent. I shall always have the warmest affection for her. There is no institution for whose history I have a deeper admiration; but I cannot honestly be ordained her minister, as my brothers are, while she refuses to liberate her mind from an untenable redemptive theolatry. (153)

He has, however, gone beyond the negative or metaphysical stage: 'My whole instinct in matters of religion is towards reconstruction'. Quite what his 'desultory studies' entail we are not told but he emerges from them 'wonderfully free from chronic melancholy which is taking hold of the civilized races with the decline of belief in a beneficent Power', enabled to see 'something new in life and humanity' (154–7). Jude too passes through similarly Comtean stages, bowing down to his horse and the moon under the influence of a 'polytheistic fancy' inspired by Horace (TH, *Jude* 53) and passing through what Sue calls his 'Tractarian stage' in Christminster, 'a place full of fetichists and ghost-seers' (171), before emerging as a representative of the modern spirit.

Hardy's belief in altruism as the unifying quality of mankind (TH, *Life* I 294) emerges in the novels as part of a cerebral theory derived at least in part from his reading of Comte (Page 1980: 108–13). His essay on 'The Profitable Reading of Fiction' posits a highly Positivist hierarchy of human faculties: 'The higher passions must ever rank above the inferior – intellectual tendencies above animal, and moral above intellectual' (Orel 1967: 114). The 'basic pattern' of his novels involves setting 'the evolution of altruism in one character' against the egoism of others (Hyman 1975: 39). The preface to *Two on a Tower* draws attention to 'the growth of the social sympathies' illustrated by that novel (TH, *TT* 29). Lady Constantine struggles hard to rise above 'self-love' to 'altruism', rejoicing that her 'self-centred attitude . . . was becoming displaced by the sympathetic attitude', enabling her to sacrifice her own happiness to Swithin's career (244). The shock of discovering that she is pregnant, however, resurrects her 'instinct of self-preservation', stifling the 'altruism' which had been evident in 'subjecting her self-love to benevolence' (257). Swithin's astronomic pursuits, as we have seen, provide him with 'little food for the sympathetic instincts' (281), although he is eventually capable of 'loving-kindness' (291). There is a contrast evident throughout the novel between the 'personal' and the 'social', the 'selfish' and the 'sympathetic', 'self-love' and 'altruism', terminology which derives directly from Comte (Salter 1981: 79).

Not all of Hardy's characters, of course, succeed in regulating their emotions. Eustacia Vye suffers from a lack of the self-control by which she might have 'attenuated the emotion' she feels for Clym (TH, *RN* 143) while Henry Knight's cultivation of his feelings only makes him fastidious and morbidly introspective, his poetic study tending to 'develop the affective side of his constitution still further, in proportion to his active faculties' (329). John Loveday quite infuriates readers of *The Trumpet-Major* by keeping his feelings 'so religiously held in check' (TH, *TM* 308), allowing his more impetuous brother, the lines of whose mouth 'showed that affectionate impulses were strong within him – perhaps stronger than judgement well could regulate' (125), to win Anne Garland's hand. There is a specific reference in the text to 'the phrenological theory of Gall' (320) but Hardy seems here to be questioning the practicality of a morality based upon such a cerebral theory.

'Modern ethical schools' also play a part in *A Laodicean* (TH, *L* 230), in which Captain de Stancy attempts to starve his sexual instincts, 'rigidly incarcerating within himself all instincts towards the opposite sex', only to find this 'chamber of his nature . . . preserved intact' and open to stimulus (201). Similar phrenological terms recur throughout *The Hand of Ethelberta* to describe the development and retardation of basic human instincts. Picotee finds that Christopher Julian has 'enlarged her capacity' for love (TH, *HE* 153) while the more volatile Ethelberta struggles to control the 'animal spirits' observed in her at the beginning of the novel (34). Fitzpiers fails to control his instincts or to develop his emotions, which 'differed from the highest affection as the lowest orders of the animal world differ from advanced organisms' (239).

Tess of the d'Urbervilles illustrates both sides of Hardy's attitude towards Comtean cerebral theory, an acceptance on the one hand of its evolutionary meliorism, looking to the increased subordination of egoism to altruism, combined with a recognition of its insufficiency to cope with human sexuality. Angel Clare, as we have seen, holds a Positivist belief in moral progress. He struggles hard to suppress his own sexual instincts, first impressing but later horrifying Tess with his exaggerated sense of duty. Hardy himself seems to have been unsure about this aspect of Clare's character. The variant manuscript versions of this passage refer to his 'purity of mind', 'slight coldness of nature' and 'chivalrous sense of duty'. Similar indecision seems to have surrounded a later passage describing his 'fastidious emotion' for Tess: 'he was, in truth, more spiritual than animal' (Laird 1975:

133–5). His refusal to forgive her bears out the suspicion sown here, 'that with more animalism he would have been the nobler man' (TH, *Tess* 287), and he learns later to reject 'the old appraisements of morality' as well as 'the old systems of mysticism' (388). His rigidity, however, need not be seen as a product of his Comtean moral scheme but of a failure to realise the capacity for regeneration for which it allows (Paris 1969: 62).

The preface to *Jude the Obscure* promises a similar portrait of the 'deadly war waged between flesh and spirit', of the problems that 'press in the wake of the strongest passion known to humanity' (TH, *Jude* 23). The antagonism between nature and grace, translated into Comtean egoism and altruism, dominates the novel. Tricked into marriage by the 'animal' attractions of Arabella (59), Jude seems to have ruined his chances of 'showing himself superior to the lower animals, and of contributing his units of work to the general progress of his generation' (82). He aims for a time at 'the ecclesiastical and altruistic life', the cultivation of his 'nobler instincts', his innate 'altruistic feeling' (148–9) but these aspirations too are undermined by his strong sexual instincts. He still believes that his love for Sue is not altogether egoistic and the responsibility of fatherhood brings 'a new and tender interest of an ennobling and unselfish kind' (308) which the tragic ending of the novel does not altogether undermine. The problem is not resolved but what needs to be recognised is the extent to which it is stated in terms derived from Comtean cerebral theory.

Positivist worship also features prominently but ambiguously in Hardy's work. Giles Winterborne becomes the object of 'worship' and 'devotion' on the part of Grace Melbury and Marty South (TH, *W* 371). Grace soon abandons her visits to his grave but the novel ends with Marty's passionate assertion that he will live for ever in her memory because of his goodness. Hardy's heroines are subject to constant idealisation. Elfride, for example, having been 'worshipped' by Stephen Smith (TH, *PBE* 86), finds herself the centre of 'a religion' in Henry Knight's heart (356). Bathsheba elicits devotion from both Gabriel Oak, who keeps her image 'vividly' and 'tenderly' before him during sleepless hours (TH, *FMC* 105), and from the unfortunate Farmer Boldwood, in whose morbid mind she achieves an unhealthy dominance. Since no 'mother existed to absorb his devotion, no sister for his tenderness, no idler ties for sense' (154), she becomes the central focus for his worship. Another somewhat morbid example of devotion is provided by Christopher Julian, who discovers that

> a woman who has once made a permanent impression upon a man cannot altogether deny him her image by denying him her company, and that by sedulously cultivating the acquaintance of this Creature of Contemplation she becomes to him almost a living soul. (TH, *HE* 326)

He eventually escapes from the ideal to the real world by transferring his devotion from Ethelberta to her more accessible sister. Jocelyn Pierston's idealisation of *The Well-Beloved* verges on the absurd because of the complete divorce between the real objects of his desire and his own 'ideal or subjective nature' (TH, *WB* 26). The deaths of his wife and mother leave Clym Yeobright free to cultivate their memory with regular visits to their graves. He is depicted at the end of the novel sitting on one of his mother's chairs and meditating upon the virtues of 'the sublime saint whose radiance even his tenderness for Eustacia could not obscure' (TH, *RN* 421). The dangers of a similar idealisation of Tess and Sue by Angel and Jude have already been discussed. Hardy seems loath to deny his characters the delights and rewards of such worship but he clearly illustrates its dangers.

Hardy's poetry, unlike George Eliot's, is less explicitly Positivist than his prose. Encouraged by the references to Comte in his 'Apology' to the *Late Lyrics*, some critics have pointed to his general acceptance of the Positivist principle that 'all real knowledge is based upon observed facts' (Paulin 1975: 91) while others have found in his poems such Comtean concepts as subjective immortality and fetichism (Pinion 1976: 18, 99–100, 162; Salter 1981: 77). But surprisingly few of the 'starry thoughts' which sustained him 'In the Seventies' (TH, *CP* 430–1) seem to have survived his growing disenchantment with life. Even his early poems rage against the empire of 'Crass Casualty', detecting little sign of purpose or of progress in the world (7). The whole point of the poem, 'Her Immortality', is that it is so short-lived. The spirit's claim to subjective immortality, 'By living, me you keep alive', is limited to one life-span (48–50). 'His Immortality' grows progressively fainter as his friends die, shrinking finally to 'a feeble spark' of memory in the dying poet (130–1). Human values, it is true, remain better than nature's:

> There, now and then, are found
> Life-loyalties. (57)

But the positive claims of Hardy's poetry are at best muted; there is not much to celebrate 'in the monotonous moils of strained, hard-run Humanity' (302).

Two poems on the death of God come closest to expressing a faith in the Religion of Humanity. 'A Plaint to Man' ends with the divine figment of human imagination instructing mankind to face up to the 'fact of life' that future happiness depends entirely on human 'brotherhood' and 'loving-kindness' (306). The observer of 'God's Funeral' dimly discerns a 'pale yet positive gleam' of light on the horizon, a replacement for the older more confident faith (307–9). Even this faint hope, however, disappears from the later poems. The words of Hardy's Positivist friend, Benjamin Fossett Lock, 'Nothing Matters Much', spoken presumably as an expression of resignation, acquire added bitterness when recalled after his death (779–80). Hardy's own 'Winter Words' abjure all faith in mankind, whose many faults and weaknesses are enumerated in 'Thoughts at Midnight'. 'We are getting to the end', he announces, of all dreams 'that our race may mend by reasoning' and he finally resolves to 'load men's minds' no more with the awful and unwelcome truth of their predicament (886–7).

Hardy's epic verse-drama, *The Dynasts*, comes closer to a Positivist view of history. Hardy himself mentioned Comte as one of the philosophers he had read more than Schopenhauer, often seen as the major influence on the poem (W. Wright 1967: 38). His identification of the Pities with 'Humanity' is borne out by notes from the period of its preparation which refer to 'Humanity' as 'a collective personality' with an 'ubiquitous' intelligence 'like that of God' (TH, *Life* II 222). The poem itself dramatises the conflict between sensitive human awareness and the mechanical laws of the universe. The Pities, Hardy explains in his preface, represent 'the Universal Sympathy of human nature', the Years represent the 'Insight of the Ages' (TH, *Dynasts* xxv). The Pities are young and full of compassion, eager to increase their sympathy by taking on the 'feverish fleshings of Humanity' (17). Their thoughts and feelings are 'the flower of Man's intelligence' (137). Their Spirit, who is addressed as 'young Compassion' by the Spirit Ironic (467), complains bitterly about human suffering, which seems rather the product of 'some mean, monstrous ironist' than of the 'Unmaliced, unimpassioned nescient Will', but is told by the Spirit of the Years not to be 'too touched with human fate' (304). The Pities celebrate human qualities, the 'limitless love' of 'motherhood' (356) and the heroism shown in war.

Humanity, however, battles from the beginning against an 'Immanent Will' which works 'unconsciously' through 'clock-like laws' (1).
This Will is impassible and illogical, lacking purpose or conscience.
Everything in life is determined by its unfathomable purpose, the 'living masses of humanity' which are the characters in the drama being
shown on two awful occasions to be but transparent puppets of its will
(36, 118). That these human 'figments' ever became conscious,
'emerging with blind gropes from impercipience', seems to have been
an unhappy chance (77, 100). Yet the poem ends optimistically (for
Hardy) with a vision of the Immanent Will itself gaining consciousness. 'Men gained cognition with the flux of time', argues the
Spirit of the Pities, 'And wherefore not the Force informing them?'
The Chorus of Pities then sings a kind of Magnificat to the Will as
'Great and Good', full of the human quality of 'tendermercy' as its
heart and consciousness awakes (522–5). Hardy claimed that this
ending was his own idea,

at which I arrived by reflecting that what has already taken place in a fraction
of the whole (i.e. so much of the world as has become conscious) is likely to
take place in the mass; and there being no Will outside the mass – that is, the
Universe – the whole Will becomes conscious thereby: and ultimately, it is to
be hoped, sympathetic.   (TH, *Life* II 125)

The idea of a Great Being comprising the highest human qualities,
however, comes close to the central object of the Religion of
Humanity.

It would be wrong to overestimate Hardy's debt to Positivism.
He was not interested in the best human qualities alone but also the
'shoddy humanity' encountered by Jude (TH, *Jude* 49). The tension
between the individual and the community in his writing, as
Lawrence observed, remains unresolved. He 'must stand with the
average against the exceptional' and 'represent the interests of
humanity, or the community as a whole' but he also sympathises with
the individual against the destructive community (Lawrence 1978:
439). Humanity, for Hardy as for George Eliot, has a wider meaning
than it had for Comte. The novelist has no need to tidy everything into
a complete system. Both his novels and poems present life as more
painful and more puzzling than the Positivists liked to admit. But the
view of the world, of human history and morality, which emerges
from his novels has much in common with the Religion of Humanity.

George Gissing: Positivist in the dawn

Gissing's involvement with Positivism was brief but intense. As a young man in London in his early twenties he read Comte eagerly, attended meetings of the Positivist Society and looked on the Religion of Humanity as the only hope for the future. His loss of faith in Comte, a result of temperamental as much as philosophical disaffinity, led to a rejection of all creeds. When the 'ecclesiastical buzzards' boasted of his death-bed conversion, his friend Morley Roberts announced that he had held no 'creed whatsoever' and that his 'temporary Positivist pose' had been 'entirely due to his gratitude' to Frederic Harrison (M. Roberts 1958: 221, 96). Positivism, according to Roberts, was 'a disease . . . rarely fatal to the young' from which Gissing had 'speedily recovered' when its 'plaster deity' was shattered by the reality of London (Coustillas and Partridge 1972: 209). He was later 'disturbed and shocked' when presented with the evidence that he had for a time dated his letters by the Positivist Calendar (M. Roberts 1958: 100).

That Gissing's faith in the Religion of Humanity was genuine, however, is shown by letters to his family which precede any contact with Harrison (Donnelly 1954: 10). Although Positivist ideas are most obviously present in his first novel, *Workers in the Dawn*, they can also be found in his later writing, on which Comte remains one of the 'major ideological influences' (Goode 1978: 143). The influence is not always positive; sometimes the novels satirise the sort of 'agnostic optimism' associated with Comte. The part played by Positivism in the later novels is difficult to identify with precision because it was absorbed into more general themes. But the struggle of mankind against evil which they portray takes place against a philosophical background in which the Religion of Humanity retains an important presence.

That Gissing had read the *Cours* by November 1878 is clear from the detailed description of the positive hierarchy of the sciences in a letter to his brother Algernon full of enthusiasm for Comte's 'wonderful *résumé* of all human knowledge' as the basis for a solution to their state of social anarchy (GG to Algernon, 9/11/78, Yale). He had to admit the following January that Comte's hopes of preaching in Notre Dame had been 'too sanguine'. But having 'pierced so deeply into the secret of history and gained so clear an insight into the future of the human race', Comte could be excused for expecting others to be convinced by his 'clear proofs and statements' (GG, *LMF* 42). 'I have adopted the Positive Philosophy of Auguste Comte', Gissing announced to his brother in May, going on to give a lengthy account of its scientific methods and humanitarian ends. The trouble with Christianity was that it attempted to answer 'impossible questions as to the *origin* of the world and life, of which man *can know nothing*'. Concentrating on the essential question, 'How shall I conduct my life?', Positivism constructed a synthesis of human knowledge, including a '*history of the world*', sufficient for the regulation of the individual and society and for the 'elevation of humanity' (GG to Algernon, 9/5/80, Yale). Another letter of this period expresses a belief in the subjective 'immortality' to be gained by a beneficial influence on 'those living in contact with us', spreading 'like the circles . . . in a pool . . . to the whole future human race' (GG, *LMF* 69).

Desperate at the lack of success of his first novel, Gissing turned to the one person he felt might understand the spirit in which it was written, the man whose own writing had led him to Comte, Frederic Harrison, who proceeded to puff the book among his influential friends. Grateful for this, and for Harrison's encouragement, Gissing explained that the 'light of Positivism' shone all the more gloriously for him since it was the first faith he had ever held. But he repeated the warning implicit in the novel, 'the necessity for a personal invasion of these realms of darkness' by those who wished to impart that light to the poor (GG to FH, 23/7/80, Pforzheimer). Gissing himself clearly enjoyed the patronage and the meals he began to receive from Harrison, with whom he was soon boasting of 'constant intercourse' (GG to Algernon, 3/11/80, Yale). The same letter records his first visit to the Positivist Society, when, as at subsequent visits early in 1881, the main topic of discussion was Home Rule. He began teaching Harrison's two sons in December and Vernon Lushington's four girls the following January. Beesly meanwhile found him a regular space in a Russian journal, *Vestnik Evropy*, in which his eight 'Letters from London' showed a Positivist concern about Government cruelty in Ireland and imperialism in Africa (*VN* XXIII (Spring 1963) 12–15).

The enthusiasm for the Religion of Humanity which runs through Gissing's letters to his brother of 1881 goes much further than gratitude to the Positivists. He began dating them according to the Positivist Calendar, which he explained for his brother's benefit, at the end of January (GG, *LMF* 90–1). He tried to restrict references to Positivism to its '*intellectual* side' rather than 'press' the religion upon him. But for himself, he confessed, 'its emotional side, the so-termed Religion of Humanity', had 'vast influence' and he felt 'this enthusiasm for the Race to be a force perfectly capable of satisfying the demands usually supplied by creeds, confessions, etc.' (GG, *LMF* 92). The belief that supernatural religion was necessary for humanitarian zeal and that its abandonment would lead to unrestricted egoism was 'all nonsense', he exclaimed: 'in times to come the mere enthusiasm of humanity will inspire generosity and self-sacrifice in no respect yielding to this of the religionists' (GG to Algernon, 19/6/81, Yale). A letter to his sister Margaret of September preaches a similarly Positivist belief in the twin duties of acquiring 'positive knowledge' and living for others (GG, *LMF* 104).

Gissing's enthusiasm for the Religion of Humanity seems to have waned in 1882. He continued to be impressed by the 'inexhaustible kindness' of the Harrisons, who, having heard of his illness, insisted on his having lunch with them twice a week (108). But a combination of domestic problems, deteriorating health and growing distaste for public meetings of any kind led him to cease attending the Positivist Society after May 1881, when he met Laffitte (GG, *Essays* 16). His doubts about the Religion of Humanity found expression in an article on 'The Hope of Pessimism' which 'developed into nothing more nor less than an attack on Positivism' (GG, *LMF* 120). The Religion of Humanity is taken as the most philosophically respectable representative of that 'unconscious optimism of humanity' which so amazes 'deep-pondering minds'. It is 'the first serious attempt to replace the old supernatural faiths', which were fundamentally pessimistic, with a coherent system built upon the advances of science. It is the last bastion of 'philosophical optimism': demolish this and you are left with pessimism alone (GG, *Essays* 76–9).

This Gissing proceeds to do. He describes the appeal of the Religion of Humanity to 'practical, energetic minds' (such as Harrison) and even 'for a season, – to less easily satisfied intelligences' (such as his own). 'It is the philosophy of cheerful resignation' and accordingly worthier of respect than coarser forms of optimism. But its basic tenets, that man can eradicate his metaphysical tendencies, accept the limitations of his intellect and find rest in a common-sense 'realistic' interpretation of the universe, cultivating his innate altruistic instincts in the service of Humanity without any supernatural sanctions, are far too optimistic for Gissing, who finds them neither possible nor desirable. He cannot accept that the positive stage will be the final stage of evolution, for natural science is striking at 'every moment against the barriers of the unknowable' while the mass of mankind, incapable of remaining agnostic, will find solutions to the mystery of life in mysticism, pantheism or some form of superstition. The 'struggle for mere existence' absorbs so much of their energy that they are unlikely to devote themselves to abstract study or to cultivate their altruistic instincts. These high ideals falter before the facts of suffering and 'the convincing metaphysics of death' (80–7).

Gissing turns with a lament to the object of Positivist devotion, the supposed stimulus to altruism:

Alas, and can we really persuade ourselves that man will ever worship man in spirit and in truth? Granting that Humanity is the highest we can ever know, that it is vain to seek after another God, are we not too fatally conscious of the distance between the utmost human goodness, and that ideal which we are capable of conceiving?

Since such an 'ideal embodiment of man's noblest faculties and attainments . . . will never find its avatar in human flesh', Gissing suggests that 'our only guide' should be 'our own good instincts'. And since they have proved so ineffectual against the 'flagrant social misery' which even the belief in a divine Father failed to prevent, he can hold no hope that 'our painfully excogitated philosophy' will achieve 'final regeneration for all mankind'. The world, he concludes, 'is synonymous with evil' and the conviction that this is the only world there is, combined with all the pressures of capitalism, could only lead to 'the strengthening of the natural forces of egotism'. The only solution to the suffering which was the inevitable lot of humanity lay with Schopenhauer: the extinction of the will to live and the cultivation of compassion for the generations which remained (88–97).

Gissing, who felt understandably 'uncomfortable at the thought of Harrison reading' this essay (GG, *LMF* 120), did not even submit it for publication. The Harrisons continued to look after him, inviting him to their house in Surrey, building up his strength with daily meals and lending him money. But the contrast between their world and his, between their middle-class respectability and the sordid details of his daily life, between Harrison's temperament and tastes, optimistic towards life and didactic in art, and Gissing's preference for pessimism and naturalism, surfaced in fierce quarrels. When Harrison attacked his unpublished novel, 'Mrs Grundy's Enemies', Gissing dedicated the work pointedly 'to those to whom Art is dear for its own sake' (Donnelly 1954: 53). He apologised for the shock caused in the Harrison household by *The Unclassed* but insisted on his duty as an artist to 'wallow and describe' (A. Harrison 1926: 83). By 1885 he felt that his 'intercourse with the Harrisons' was 'as good as over'. They were too conventional for him while to them he was merely 'an enemy of society' (GG to Algernon, 31/1/85, Yale). Their relationship had undergone additional strain when a chance encounter with a former college friend forced Gissing into a full confession of his expulsion from Owen College (Gettman 1961: 230). Gissing tended at best to be 'unnerved' by the high society to which the Harrisons introduced him and towards the end of 1884 opted for the squalor and loneliness of his lodgings without the demands upon his time and energy made by teaching and socialising. He continued to spend the occasional day with the Harrisons in Surrey but remained sensitive to their difference of class. When he sat down to his own 'squalid meal' he would speculate sardonically on Harrison's likely reaction to it (M. Roberts 1958: 89). He was annoyed not only when they did not invite him to dinner properly (Donnelly 1954: 86) but also when they did, since it interrupted his work (GG, *Diary* 146–7).

Gissing seems to have got on rather better with Ethel Harrison than with her husband, although the sympathy he received from her brought out his worst self-pity. He would describe for her benefit the symptoms of his nervous condition as well as the evils of London while she sent him photographs of herself and her husband and invited him to stay. It has been suggested that he 'entertained fantasies' about her, taking her as a model for *Isabel Clarendon*. His short story, 'The Lady of the Dedication', certainly seems to depict his relations with the Harrisons, its starving hero scraping a living by tutoring the children of an industrious writer and his gracious wife (Vogeler 1984: 187). Gissing expressed his gratitude to Harrison in 1895 for fifteen years of support, assuring him that he kept abreast of his work (GG to FH, 7/11/95, Pforzheimer), but when he met the Positivist at a Cosmopolis dinner the following year, 'after a lapse of 6 or 7 years', found his speech 'sadly dull' and 'ponderous' (GG, *Diary* 414). They seem never to have met again. After Gissing's death Harrison undertook to write a more acceptable preface to his posthumously published historical novel *Veranilda* than that produced by Wells but his characteristically incautious remark that it was 'by far the most important book' he ever wrote stirred up a storm of critical protest. Harrison claimed to have 'a deep sympathy' with Gissing's 'genius' (Coustillas 1968: 588–610) but maintained a private conviction that *Workers in the Dawn* was his best work (GG, *LC* 25). He combined with Wells and Gosse, however, to provide a pension for Gissing's children (Vogeler 1984: 325).

Traces of Gissing's development away from Positivism can be observed outside his relationship with the Harrisons. As early as 1883 he told his brother that 'Philosophy . . . scarcely interests me any more' (GG, *LMF* 128), although he assured him the following year, sending him a parcel of Positivist pamphlets, that there was 'much in Positivism of which you can make use' (GG to Algernon, 15/5/84, Yale). His few friends included James Cotter Morison, the wasting of whose talent, 'ruined by luxury', he could only deplore (GG, *LB* 205). But certain passages in *The Service of Man* made his 'nauseous', he confessed in 1887: 'I cannot tell you how I loathe that positivism at present' (4). *George Gissing's Commonplace Book*, which characteristically quotes Lecky's comment on the prostitute as 'the eternal priestess of humanity' (GG, *CB* 50), speculates on the possibility that 'humanity will make place for something else, just as the individual, the family, and the nation' (61). Quite what this larger entity might be he refuses to elaborate. For he was unable to accept 'any of the solutions ever proposed' to the mystery of the universe (Clodd 1916: 180–1). The section on 'Religion' in the *Commonplace Book* certainly ruled out Christianity, for which he could find only contempt (GG, *CB* 47–9). But he described his early years in London as 'a time of extraordinary mental growth, of great spiritual activity' (23), and Positivism, which he encountered and explored during this period, must rank as one of the most important factors in this development. It was a creed he grew away from but could not altogether forget.

The Religion of Humanity plays a large part in Gissing's first novel, *Workers in the Dawn*, which was written 'to show the nobility of a faith dispensing with all we are accustomed to call religion, and having for its only creed a belief in the possibility of intellectual and moral progress' (GG, *LMF* 73). The character in the novel who dares most to alleviate the suffering of the poor, Helen Norman, is certainly motivated by a Positivist faith. Introduced to Comte's work by her

German mentor, Dr Gmelin, she is immediately attracted by his principle that 'the true destination of philosophy must be social' and by his insistence 'upon the development of sympathetic instincts for the human race at large'. Four months' study of the *Cours* leaves her convinced of the need to abandon metaphysics, 'delighted . . . with his [Comte's] masterly following of the history of mankind', eager to help with 'the progress of humanity' through the 're-modelling of all social theories in a purely scientific spirit' and altogether anxious to play her part 'in the service of that true religion, the Religion of Humanity' (GG, *WD* I 325–9). 'I have faith in Humanity', she declares, a faith which is bolstered by Schopenhauer and Shelley (333–5). She admits to the liberal-minded Dissenting minister Mr Heatherley that his faith offers more 'sources of consolation' but cannot accept it as true (II 223).

Helen is 'the goddess' first of Edward Norman's hearth (I 27) and then of Arthur Golding, who compares her to Raphael's Madonna (384) and makes his own portrait of her as a 'Madonna' or 'goddess' (II 91–3), to which he turns for inspiration in hours of need. Under her influence and that of the printer, Mr Tollady, who treats him as 'a young and promising bud on the great tree of humanity' (I 179), teaching him to abandon theology for history and to admire only those heroes 'whom fate has ordained as instruments to *advance* humanity' (242), Arthur becomes something of a Positivist himself. His wife, however, refuses to become a Goddess of Humanity, preferring to remain 'A Priestess of Venus' (III ch. viii).

The struggle between the altruistic and egoistic instincts, a central feature of this novel as of all Gissing's work, is portrayed in terms of Positivist cerebral theory although Gissing remained less optimistic than Comte about the power of good to overcome the massive obstacles in its path. Helen's ardent humanitarian ideals are fully tested by the grim realities of East London which her guardian takes a delight in showing her. The 'fine organs of virtue', he explains, 'have absolutely perished from their frames' (II 6) while their egoistic instincts have strengthened through frequent exercise. Arthur is forced to admit 'how much of the sincerest love is pure egotism' (162) and, in despair, attempts 'to brutalise his own nature' (III 123). Even the angelic influence of Helen Norman fails to survive her death, the news of which deprives Arthur of his remaining will to live. Schopenhauer can be seen to be replacing Comte even in this novel, which contains the seeds of his later 'disillusion with Comtism' (Francis 1960: 58).

Some of the characters in Gissing's later novels struggle to preserve a faith in humanity in the face of bitter experience. Osmond Waymark, the hero of *The Unclassed*, is a conscious backslider, speaking with distaste of his early enthusiasm for 'The Gospel of Rationalism' into which he used to sublimate his 'starved passions' (GG, *U* 54, 201). He finds Christianity too pessimistic, Christ 'representing Humanity' in abnegation and self-denial, in contrast with Prometheus, who affords a more attractive type of 'the triumphant aspiration of Humanity' (214). Of the unholy trinity which inspired Helen Norman, it is Shelley rather than Comte and Schopenhauer who seems to have had most impact on Waymark. Ada Warren actually reads 'a volume of Comte', although she denies any adherence to Positivism (GG, *IC* I 61). The heroine of *Demos*, however, finds 'work in the cause of humanity other than that which goes on so clamorously in lecture-halls and at street corners' (GG, *D* 470), seeing more hope for moral improvement in art than in politics or religion.

The heroes of Gissing's later novels tend to be 'ashamed of the connection with street-corner rationalism' (GG, *BE* 132). Walter Egremont expresses distaste for 'vulgar propagators of what is called freethought' (GG, *T* 14), such as the obnoxious Bunce, who forces his children to recite 'a secularist's creed' every night (24) and protests noisily against Egremont's attempts at religious reconstruction, which have clear affinities with the Religion of Humanity. Egremont's philosophy, however, proves to be 'a sham, a spinning of cobwebs for idle hours', powerless to protect him against his passion for Thyrza (253). Working-men such as Luke Ackroyd reject his attempt to make them 'priggish and effeminate' in the face of 'the hard facts of life' (410) and he himself adopts a more robust faith embodying a zest for life derived from Whitman, whose powerful soul 'may stand for Humanity itself' in contrast with 'the contemptibleness of average humanity' (421–4).

In *The Nether World* Michael Snowdon encourages his granddaughter to read the Bible 'as a source of moral instruction' of 'a purely human significance'. 'Sensitive to every prompting of humanity', she prefers meditation upon 'those beings amid whom she had lived her life' to any form of theistic prayer (GG, *NW* 151–2). The lessons of compassion and of service which she learns from his 'religious teaching' lead her 'to exercise all human and self-forgetful virtues' and to consecrate herself 'to a life of beneficence' (227). The kind of 'altruism' she is supposed to acquire from Miss Lant, however, smacks of the zeal which comes from perverted 'natural satisfactions' in spite of its 'purely human' sanction (229). Her grandfather too becomes fanatical in his attempt to make her 'a sort of social saint' (236), undergoing the 'dehumanisation' which always threatens to overtake 'idealists of his type' (255). The 'burden of duty' which she is called upon to bear and the ideas she is made to contemplate prove beyond her scope (312). She catches 'a gleam of hope in renunciation itself' while Sidney Kirkwood is still with her (318) and treasures her grandfather's memory. 'In her', she resolves, 'his spirit must survive, his benevolence still be operative', in a form of subjective immortality (348). The novel ends with the vestiges of a faith in humanity. Jane and Sidney face sorrow and probable defeat even in their 'humble aims' but their lives remain 'a protest against those brute forces of society which fill with wreck the abysses of the nether world' (391–2).

The impoverished novelist in *New Grub Street*, Edwin Reardon, has been called 'an up-to-date positivist of the eighties' (Bergonzi 1968: 17). He retains an 'obstinate idealism', impractical and ineffectual, which his friends ridicule and rebuke (GG, *NGS* 477). He cultivates 'altruism', which he defines as a 'rarefied form of happiness' requiring 'twice as much faith' as the Athanasian Creed (378), and is seen to have 'worshipped' his unworthy wife (532). Godwin Peake comes even closer to Comtism. The lectures at Whitelaw College disappoint him because they fall short of 'the bold annunciation of newly discovered law, the science which had completely broken with tradition' (GG, *BE* 53). He writes 'several papers of sociological tenor' to ' "advanced" reviews' (142), limiting his knowledge to 'the mere relations of phenomena' as opposed to any 'Absolute faith' (185). He confesses to the French-reading Sidwell Warricombe, who is interested in 'systems of philosophy which professed to establish a moral code, independent of supernatural faith' (244), that he too, in his 'stage of optimism', had harboured hopes for 'the conversion of the educated to a purely human religion' (292). He tells a friend of hers to be 'more positive' but not to 'become a Positivist' (350). He retains his contempt for all forms of neo-Christianity, the 'pious jugglery' that attempts to reconcile science and religion (127), writing, like Harrison, an outspoken critique of 'The New Sophistry' (153) and attacking the 'vague humanitarian impulse' behind Mr Chilvers' lecture on

'Altruism' (289), ostensibly from the point of view of an orthodox Christian but actually from a more rigorously sceptical position.

The relationship between Rhoda Nunn and Everard Barfoot in *The Odd Women* has been labelled 'an ideological struggle between Comte and Schopenhauer' (Goode 1978: 155). Rhoda, however, displays little sympathy with Positivism. She mocks the belief in 'the essential human spirit' of religion expressed by Mary Barfoot, who accuses her later of being cold and 'inhuman' to weaker women (GG, *OW* 77, 195). She ends the novel by preaching the need to live in hope and think of others (451–2) but there is nothing to link her more specifically with Comte. Her work for the emancipation of women is directly opposed to Positivist principles. The French social theories propounded by Dyce Lashmar in *Our Friend the Charlatan* derive from Jean Izoulet rather than Comte, while Huxley's more pessimistic view of evolution finds expression in Lord Dymchurch (Korg 1963: 236–8). None of Gissing's characters after *Workers in the Dawn* can properly be called Positivist even if some of them retain a faith in humanity and the cultivation of altruism.

Gissing's novels, however, do portray a struggle between humanity and animality, altruism and egoism, which owes something to the Religion of Humanity. The difference between the real and the ideal, evident in his first novel, returns at the very beginning of his second. The second chapter of *The Unclassed*, entitled 'Mother and Child', violently subverts the Positivist picture of the family. The mother drinks and walks the streets while the child nearly murders a classmate. When Lotty Starr visits her father with Ida in her arms, the very symbol of Humanity, she is turned away. She has a primitive 'maternal instinct' to keep her child but Ida's passionate devotion to her mother only illustrates the little regard nature has for 'social codes' (GG, *U* 23–5). The hero of the novel has even less regard for conventional morality. His early idealisation of the virtuous Maud Enderby as a 'being from a higher world' who occupies for a time 'the sanctuary of his imagination' (80–1) soon gives way to the more 'passionate imaginings' aroused by Ida's beauty (107). He remains for a long time unattracted by the prospect of a conventional marriage with Ida, who is associated with his 'least noble instincts', in contrast with his 'good angel', Maud (224), but Ida does in the end win both his respect and his hand.

Nowhere is the battle between humanity and animality more fiercely fought than in *The Nether World*. The quality of humanity, that compassionate concern for others which Comte saw as raising men above animals, is only noted at the beginning of the novel for its absence (GG, *NW* 1, 5). Gissing lingers with fascinated repulsion over the 'animal' nature of the masses and ponders over the changes required to 'humanise the multitude' (109). The slums of Shooter's Gardens teem with the 'hapless spawn of diseased humanity' born only 'to embitter and brutalise yet further the lot of those who unwillingly gave them life' (130). Clem Peckover is constantly called 'brutal' and even Sidney Kirkwood is subject to 'brutal' and 'animal instincts' (92, 118). Clara Hewett's arguments with her father about leaving home bring out 'all the selfish forces of her nature' (28) while her quarrel with Sidney Kirkwood, which pierces his 'core of love and pity', only exasperates her 'egotism' (93–5). She soon becomes 'abandoned to a fierce egoism' in which all 'noble feeling was extinct' (203). Even her last desperate bid for his hand is described as an act of 'supreme egoism' (294), which remains her main contribution to their marriage. The moral framework here is Comte's but it has been coloured with a pessimism peculiarly Gissing's.

Gissing's low view of mankind emerges all too clearly in *The Private Papers of Henry Ryecroft*, whose combination of 'despairing agnosticism' and 'tentative positivism' can be taken for his own (Korg 1963: 243–4). Ryecroft, who sees man as anti-social, 'by nature self-assertive, commonly aggressive' and always hostile to anything unusual (GG, *HR* 92), turns his back on the 'well-millinered and tailored herd' (114) to live in splendid isolation in the country, where he finds the life of the birds 'far more reasonable, and infinitely more beautiful, that that of the masses of mankind' (221). 'History is a nightmare of horrors', he announces, holding out just as little hope for the future, in which science will not be the saviour but 'the remorseless enemy of mankind' (265–8). The ideals he retains are those of the Religion of Humanity very much watered down. He looks to bloodless solutions to future international quarrels, although tempted to indifference by warmongering newspaper articles (95–7). He deplores the esoteric spiritualist cults he observes springing up in reaction to 'scientific positivism' and 'agnosticism', which were 'far too reasonable to endure' (174–5). But he derives some comfort from contemplating the possible, if unlikely, dawning of 'the age of true positivism', a 'rationalist millennium' to be fostered by 'the habits of thought favoured by physical science' (181–2) and the book ends on a relatively optimistic note. For although Ryecroft himself remains frightened of the world he retains great admiration for those 'bright souls' who form 'a great brotherhood, without distinction of race or faith' in the service of humanity. They 'constitute the race of man, rightly designated, and their faith is one, the cult of reason and of justice' (289). Ryecroft's tentative affirmations are all that remain of the Positivist faith Gissing had proclaimed with such confidence at the dawn of his career. As with Hardy, however, Comte seems to have provided many of the modes of thought within which his mind worked.

Propaganda and satire

The Religion of Humanity, like any other subject of widespread interest, was reflected in a broad range of Victorian literature, the source of propaganda and the target of satire. One of the stages through which the villain passes in William Conybeare's novel of 1856, *Perversion; or, The Causes and Consequences of Infidelity*, Positivism comes between Unitarianism and Mormonism on a downward-sliding path of sin and unbelief. The latitudinarian hero of Charles Davies' 1875 *Broad Church* also attends Chapel Street for a while, pilfering Positivist ideas for his sermons. Much study of Mill and other Positivist texts takes place in Ada Bayly's *Donovan* of 1882 and Olive Schreiner's *story of a South African Farm* the following year, while a South Kensington flat provides the setting for a discussion of the Religion of Humanity by a 'Comtist Lover' and his fiancée, who finds the Positivist faith far too bleak, too reminiscent of George Eliot's grave (E. R. Chapman 1886: 96).

Perhaps the most didactic of all Positivist novels was written by Fanny Byse, the English wife of a Swiss pastor, who used to worship at Chapel Street on her visits to London and published under the pseudonym of Mrs Worthey. Hero and heroine of *The New Continent*, which appeared in 1890, come independently to a faith in the Religion of Humanity. Arthur de Varenne, a protestant pastor, meets a practising Positivist in the Luxembourg Gardens and hears of Comte's life and thought over a meal and a bottle of Beaujolais at almost exactly the same time as Laura Bell meets a college friend in Westminster Abbey and is recommended to Dr Travers, 'the priest of Humanity' who has 'given up all worldly prospects for his religion' and is clearly modelled on Congreve. He is 'tall, stately, and cordial, immediately putting her at ease when she visits him and imparting 'The blessing of Humanity' with fatherly affection (Worthey 1890: 265–9). There is even an extended description of a Positivist service. When Arthur returns to London from Paris, Laura explains for his benefit how the 'objective God . . . has become subjective' in Humanity (298) before the two converts to Positivism visit Dr Travers together to receive his blessing and advice for a future in which they plan to study Comte, serve Humanity, and never remarry.

Three missionaries are subjected to Positivist propaganda in *Agnostic Island* created by F. J. Gould in 1891 in response to W. H. Mallock's satirical portrait of *The New Paul and Virginia, or Positivism on an Island* in which the hero, shipwrecked on an island with the beautiful Virginia St John, tries to convert her to his own half-baked devotion to Humanity. He is just about to initiate her into the joys of crooning to the moon when they are rescued. An appendix of quotations from Harrison, Huxley, Tyndall and Harriet Martineau identifies Mallock's target beyond all doubt. Harrison has also been seen as one of the many figures satirised in Mallock's *The New Republic* (Lucas 1966: 99) while Mrs Humphry Ward seems to have been the model for Mrs Morham, with her 'positivist religious service', one of the exotic substitutes found necessary to replace the supernatural, in *The Individualist* (R. L. Wolff 1977: 501–2).

Mrs Humphry Ward herself never espoused the Religion of Humanity. She encountered Comtism in Oxford in the 1860s, probably at Mrs Pattison's salon, but her husband reports her shuddering at Comte's name in 1871 (Peterson 1976: 82–3). In London in the 1880s she befriended a number of Positivists, including the Harrisons, who persuaded her to join the anti-suffragettes. Her description of Harrison as an 'old friend' (H. Ward 1918: 347) suggests that he was not the model for the barrister, James Wardlaw, a 'devoted and orthodox Comtist', in *Robert Elsmere*. Mrs Wardlaw's dutiful tending of their children entirely by herself, 'as a Positivist mother is bound to do', arouses a slightly satirical pity in the narrator. As she wheels her pram 'through the dreary streets of a dreary region' of London it is difficult to accept her as 'their Providence, their deity, the representative to them of all tenderness and all purity'. But her charitable work among the sick and poor make 'her dowdy little figure and her face' genuine 'symbols of a divine and sacred helpfulness in the eyes of hundreds of starving men and women'. There may be 'a certain narrowness in their devotion' but there can be no doubting 'that potent spirit of social help which in our generation Comtism has done so much to develop' (H. Ward 1888: 470). Wardlaw's lack of tact, developed by his 'many crude Jacobinisms' and his 'solitary eccentric life', emerges at dinner with the Elsmeres, when he assumes, 'as every good Comtist does, that the husband is the wife's pope' and describes in great detail the ceremony of baptism performed for their child by 'an eminent French Comtist' (510). He is deeply offended by the 'strongly religious bent' of Elsmere's 'New Brotherhood of Christ', which goes too far beyond the verifiable for his own less mystical taste (576).

Robert Elsmere's own religious development involves a specific rejection of Positivism. His High-Church college friend and correspondent, Armitstead, argues for all or nothing: 'If it were not for the Gospels and the Church I should be a Positivist tomorrow.' Elsmere, however, feels a desperate need for a religion 'capable . . . of welding societies and keeping man's brutish elements in check' and cannot 'believe that Positivism or "evolutionary morality" will ever satisfy the race' (409–10). Yet the vaguely theistic and idealistic faith with which he ends, retaining though it does a belief in Jesus as an ideal human being, incorporates some elements of the Religion of Humanity. He plunges energetically into historical scholarship 'to realise for himself and others the solidarity and continuity of mankind's long struggle from the beginning until now' (198). He also insists upon the 'unvarying and rational order of the world' (494). The aim of his new religion, like that of Comte's, is to establish 'a new social bond' (572). There were, apparently, even more references to Comte in the original manuscript of the novel (Peterson 1976: 147).

Harrison found *Robert Elsmere* 'very thin' and advised Mrs Humphry Ward not to reply to Gladstone's lengthy review since her own position would alter within a year (FH to Mrs Betham-Edwards, 16/12/14, BC). He was wrong. *The History of David Grieve* portrays a similar development away from the extremes of fundamentalist Christian belief through encounters with Secularists at Holyoake's Hall of Science in Manchester to a liberal or modernist form of Christianity. Grieve travels to Paris, where he is impressed by 'the great Positivist', Littré, but comes to reject both Positivism and Secularism:

If the race should ever take the counsel of the Secularists, or of that larger Positivist thought, of which English Secularism is the popular reflection, the human intellect would be a poorer instrument with a narrower swing. So much was plain to him. For nothing can be more certain than that some of the finest powers and noblest works of the human mind have been developed by the struggle to know what the Secularist declares is neither knowable nor worth knowing. (H. Ward 1892: 426–7)

He eventually achieves 'a conception of Christianity far more positive, fruitful, and human' which he would 'fain believe . . . the Christianity of the future' (453).

This is the ideal consistently sought by Mrs Humphry Ward both in her writing and in her work at the Passmore Edwards Settlement, where she was happy to introduce Modernists such as Sabatier (*Times* (26/2/08) 7). The Positivists, of course, continued to attack her variety of neo-Christianity as inconsistent and dishonest. Bridges protested against the 'insincere use of smooth words' in her famous plea for 'A Church Without a Creed'. There was no possibility of compromise, he argued, between a theological and a scientific understanding of the historical development of Christianity. You could not 'strip Jesus of his miraculous legend' and 'continue to regard him as the central figure of the world's history' (*PR* VII (1899) 192–5). When Harrison raised similar objections to the Modernism of *Richard Meynell* in 1912, Mrs Ward insisted that 'Christianity *works*' in practice and could be made of even greater 'social value . . . if we could clear away some of its absurdities'. She no longer expected an 'old church' to agree to a 'new creed' but hoped it might accept 'a new symbolism' open to 'many forms of interpretation' (HP 1/113, ff.28–9). Her autobiography looks forward to a similar development of Christianity along modernist lines (H. Ward 1918: 367), a development to which Positivism had contributed but which it could not supersede.

Typical of many eminent Victorian men of letters in his reluctance 'to call himself a Positivist, while being one in very fact', according to Philip Thomas, was George Meredith (*PR* XXVI (1918) 270). A friend of Morison, Harrison, Morley and Leslie Stephen, he suggested to Maxse in the mid-sixties that they hammer out the subject of 'Comte's philosophy' in private over a suitable text such as Lewes's *History of Philosophy* (GM 1970: I 347). His friendship with 'St Bernard', his private name for Morison, dated from the early 1860s, when they went yachting, duck-shooting and dining together. He used to pull Morison's leg about the Positivist pilgrimages. 'I suppose you plead for Guido Fawkes publicly somewhere on the 5th November', he wrote in 1883 (II 719). But his epitaph to 'J. C. M.' (GM 1912: II 253) and his rage at the funeral, in which Morison was buried with full Christian honours (McCabe 1932: 54–5, 105), suggest a sympathy with his views. He assured Ethel Harrison that her husband was 'one of the men I hold to be giving us hope of our present day' (GM 1970: III 1537) but was less complimentary about his 'effusive' style to John Morley (1665), whose own battle for 'poor humankind' he celebrated in another sonnet (GM 1912: I 205). He could also be scathing about the pious Positivist gatherings at the Priory, where 'the Bishops' sat about the feet of George Eliot (GM 1970: III 1460).

There are two sides also to Meredith's portrayal of Positivism in his novels. *The Ordeal of Richard Feverel* represents a damning attack on all narrow-minded pseudo-scientific systems. Sir Austin, the 'Scientific Humanist' whose mind is 'bent on the future of our species' (GM 1961: 14) and who looks forward to the time when 'science shall have produced an *intellectual aristocracy*' (323), destroys those he loves best by adhering strictly to his 'scientific' system of education. His unremitting pursuit of 'the System' turns the best of intentions into misanthropy: 'He had experimented on humanity' in the form of his son, who has then to shoulder 'all humanity's failings' (297). Among the aphorisms collected in his anthology is a definition of 'the coward' as '*He who sneers at the failings of Humanity*' (448), but the more cynical Adrian, who accepts 'humanity as it had been, and was' (15), turns out to have greater insight. The novel ends with a parody of Positivist devotion as the impulsive Richard, restored too late to his beloved Lucy, 'held her to him, and thought of a holier picture: of mother and child; of the sweet wonders of life she had made real to him' (458). He is left after her death with nothing but the memory of his own folly, 'striving to image her on his brain' (465).

The characters with Positivist tendencies in Meredith's later novels receive more charitable treatment. *Beauchamp's Career*, he feared, would be thought dull by those unable to enter 'his idea of the advancement of Humanity' (GM 1970: I 485), which finds expression in strong sympathy, shared with 'other positivist Radicals of the day', with the Paris Communards (I. Fletcher 1971: 189). But the primary Positivist to be found in Meredith is Vernon Whitfield, the altruist whose grumpiness and addiction to walking combine with his faith in Humanity to suggest Leslie Stephen as a model. Whitfield defends Comte's calendar and its celebration of 'the benefactors of humanity'

against Willoughby's objection to the 'pretension in all that, irrecon-
cilable with English sound sense' and against Dr Middleton's muttering about 'new-fangled notions' (GM 1968: 135–6). He submits to
being labelled as one of the 'admirers' of humanity (196). Treating the
world with 'common sense' as neither good nor evil but to be accepted
and served (110), he wins Clara's love because 'He lives for others'
(430). He refuses to take part in the 'mechanical service' of family
prayers (310) but earns Willoughby's scorn for his 'nincompoopish
idealizations' of women (355). Having meditated for hours upon
Clara's virtues, he is eventually rewarded for his devotion by winning
her love. Meredith's understanding of egoism has been shown to be
bound up with Comtean cerebral theory (I. Fletcher 1971: 205–14).
Willoughby is certainly full of the basic egoistic instincts. His 'military
letter I' (GM 1968: 50) delights in hunting both animals and women.
His desire for Clara is clearly of the 'animal' nature which finds expression in the 'primitive egoism' of jealousy (284). But he is a 'social
Egoist', a 'civilized Egoist', whose raw instincts have been partially
tamed by those intermediate instincts in the Comtean scale, pride and
vanity, which are partly personal and partly social (467). Many of
Meredith's insights into the subtleties of Willoughby's self-obsession
owe nothing to Comte. The book is by no means 'a Positivist
manifesto' but it is 'saturated', like Meredith himself, 'with the Comtist ambience' (I. Fletcher 1971: 208).

Meredith's general adherence to a faith in altruism and social
morality emerges in his poetry, especially the *Ballads and Poetry of
Tragic Life* and 'The Woods of Westermain', which breathe a spirit of
Comtean fetichism (Wimsatt 1969: 230). The wisdom of 'Earth's
Secret' is to be gained by combining a love of nature with

> hearing history speak, of what men were
> And have become. (GM 1912: I 188)

Other poems also celebrate 'Progress' and 'The World's Advance'
(196–7). *An Essay on Comedy* has been seen to offer

a substitute for traditional Christianity resembling that of Comte; for there is
an affinity between the cult of 'Earth' in the novelist and poet, and 'the Grand
Fétiche' (that is, the Earth) in the French philosopher – something short of
the 'Grand Être,' or universal object of worship (that is, Humanity). Further-
more, the 'Comic Spirit' of Meredith's essay is an efflux or emanation of
human society, and is regarded as the presiding or tutelary genius of human
civilization. (GM 1978: 10–11)

Such a comparison should not be stretched too far. There is a basic incompatibility between Comte, with his total lack of the comic spirit, and Meredith, with his hatred of system, which inhibits identification of Meredith as a Positivist in anything but the broadest sense.

Henry James, who also encountered a number of the London Comtists, also expressed a distaste for the cataloguing quality of 'the French mind', which 'likes to squeeze things into a formula, that mutilates them'. The 'great enterprises' of Balzac and Comte were to James 'characteristic of the French passion for completeness, for symmetry, for making a system as neat as an epigram' (HJ 1878: 102–3). James himself, in T. S. Eliot's phrase, 'had a mind so fine that no idea could violate it' (Hocks 1974: 71). He 'always liked' Morison, however, and visited him during his final illness (HJ, *Letters* III 214). He met both Beesly and Harrison as early as 1869, finding the latter 'very good company' in spite of his radical views and dandy appearance (II 158). Austin Harrison recalled him sauntering along Oxford Street, complaining about the desire to interfere and 'save others' and calling Positivism a 'moral socialism inspired by a modern Caligula'. Comte, James declared, 'knew nothing about women and thought of them like a Catholic priest'. Life was 'far more interesting than its regularisation', which he proceeded to demonstrate by going to a dance rather than 'talk the thing out' (A. Harrison 1926: 185–6). James's letters to the Harrisons in the final years of his life are full of praise and encouragement, claiming to have 'felt with you, rallied to you and applauded you' in all 'your gallantry of public service and heroism' (HJ to FH, 3/7/15, HRC). Harrison was less polite, calling 'dear old Henry the most over-rated man in England or in America' and complaining to Hardy of 'the unmeaning jabber of that unfortunate fossil' (FH to TH, 21/3/14, DCM). Morley held a similarly low opinion of James as a trivial chronicler of the life of the idle rich (Edel 1972: 558–60).

James in turn seems to have regretted the Positivism in George Eliot, which he saw as artificial, a product of the 'high-minded circle' into which she had fallen, and rejoiced at her renunciation of the principle of eternal widowhood, writing after her marriage to Cross that she 'had begun a new (personal) life: a more healthy, objective one than she had ever known before' (Edel 1962: 372). An obsessive concern with subjective immortality is depicted in his short story, 'The Altar of the Dead', in which George Stranson develops an elaborate cult of the dead from his original habit of celebrating the date of his fiancée's death. Kneeling before the candles on his side-altar, he feels he has 'saved' the souls of his departed friends, not theologically but 'for actuality, for continuity, for the certainty of human remembrance' (HJ, *CT* IX 267). At the centre of the blaze of light which greets him on his final visit to the altar she appears as a symbol of 'human beauty and human charity', persuading him to include among the remembered dead even his treacherous friend, Sir Acton Hague (270).

'The Madonna of the Future' depicts an equally obsessive concern with the symbol of Humanity. The crazed painter who pounces upon the narrator and marches him to Raphael's 'Madonna in the Chair' insists that 'in meditation we may still woo the ideal' (HJ, *CT* III 21). The real, however, in James's work, tends to override the ideal. Among his heroines, Isabel Archer refuses to play the role of 'guardian angel' (HJ 1966: 479). Basil Rathbone, who 'had read Comte', detects 'the religion of humanity' behind Olive Chancellor's cold passion for personal duty and social reform (HJ 1921: I 22). She certainly believes in 'the amelioration of humanity' (II 107) and makes up for the paucity of furniture in her holiday cottage with 'all George Eliot's writings, and two photographs of the Sistine Madonna' (167). Her beliefs, however, are suggested rather than made explicit. James is more concerned to explore the psychological motivation of his characters than their philosophical commitment.

Virginia Woolf's bitter resentment of her father's attempt to impose the Religion of Humanity upon his children has already been discussed (see p. 144). Her most unpleasant characters, such as Mr Tansley, spend their time 'preaching brotherly love' in vast halls while failing to practise it at home (VW 1977: 181), in marked contrast to the adorable Mrs Ramsay, who feels bound to the rest of her family as 'all one stream' to be continued after her death (105) and turns 'infallibly . . . to the human race' in her many acts of kindness to the poor and sick (181). Rudyard Kipling held Positivist preaching in similar disdain. An unsigned article, 'On Certain Uncut Pages', rejoices in the unreadability of Harrison's prose, ensuring as it does the failure of his religion (A. Wilson 1977: 8). 'The Conversion of Aurelian McGoggin' relates the sad fate of a brilliant young Comtist in the Indian Civil Service who bores all his colleagues by preaching the Religion of Humanity until he is literally struck dumb by aphasia. The problem with Comte and Spencer, Kipling insists, is that 'they deal with people's insides from the point of view of men who have no stomachs'. Their creeds are products of city life, where 'man grows to think that there is no one higher than himself' which bears little relation to the object of his religion (Kipling 1949: 107–13).

H. G. Wells was often claimed by the Positivists as one of their number. In an abrasive lecture to the Sociological Society in 1906, however, Wells objected to Comte's extension of 'cock-sure science' from astronomy and physics to everything else, dismissing both him and Spencer as 'pseudo-scientific interlopers' who were incapable of adopting the more imaginative and literary approach sociology demanded: 'We cannot put Humanity into a museum, or dry it for examination' (Wells 1914: 192–206). In 1903 he had called himself 'a Positivist without knowing it' in the sense that Huxley and the study of anatomy had limited his understanding of the subjective elements in life (Wells 1967: 376). Worried about the esoteric nature of his readers, however, especially the subscribers to the *Positivist Review* who exaggerated those elements in his work which fitted their system (Parrinder 1972: 2), he went out of his way to separate himself from them. There is a facetious reference to Frederic Harrison 'adjusting all our tiny efforts to the scale of the divine Comte' (Wells 1903: 371) in *Mankind in the Making* and at least one reviewer saw something of Harrison in the unsympathetic Caterham apoplectically refusing to allow 'Humanity' to be changed in *The Food of the Gods* (Wells 1904: 295; *BP* 8/11/07). Harrison thought Wells at this time 'a very ignorant and bumptious young man' (Bod.L. d 256, f.98) but grew to admire his later efforts at world history. Wells had studied Comte but retained 'a real personal dislike, a genuine reluctance to concede him any sort of leadership' or even the 'priority he had in sketching the modern outlook'. The intellectual leaders of mankind, he felt, should light the fire of knowledge and vanish, not choke the fire with their ashes (Wells 1934: II 658).

Positivism seems to have cut little ice with Victorian poets, though it confirmed Clough in his rejection of theology as well as bringing him Arnold's scorn (Biswas 1972: 139). Robert Buchanan confessed to Harrison never to have been 'able to share your beautiful faith in the progress of Humanity' (HP 1/25, f.2) but dedicated his lengthy poem, *Drama of Kings*, to Comte. This includes an 'Ode to the Spirit of Auguste Comte', who is addressed as the 'greatest and last' of a procession of 'the great friends of Man' beginning with Voltaire. Having walked 'the sad road/ Of all who seek for God', he is seen to have been 'blinded' by 'looking at light so long' but is finally forgiven for failing to find God because he loved and benefited mankind (Buchanan 1874: 277–8). Mark Call was profoundly attracted to Comte's 'magnificent survey of the present and past life of humanity' (Call 1875: 33–8) and contributed both moral and financial support to Positivism, reviewing the *Catechism* with generosity and translating the *Discourse* himself.

The Religion of Humanity inevitably attracted the attention of writers of comic verse such as Mortimer Collins, who included 'The Positivists' among his collection of *British Birds* after the manner of Aristophanes:

> Wise are their teachers beyond all comparison,
> Comte, Huxley, Tyndall, Mill, Morley, and Harrison;
>> Who will adventure to enter the lists
>> With such a squadron of Positivists?

Collins, for all his irony, captures some of the fear with which they were regarded but his inclusion of Huxley and Tyndall and his suggestion in the following stanzas that the Positivists were opposed to marriage and in favour of evolution indicates the very hazy notion he seems to have had of the movement whose religion he mocks in the final stanza:

> If you are pious (mild form of insanity),
> Bow down and worship the mass of humanity.
>> Other religions are buried in mists;
>> We're our own Gods, say the Positivists.(W. D. Adams 91)

Robert Bulwer Lytton teased Morley for his treasonous association

> With the *Fortnightly* chiefs of the Radical garrison,
> Implacable Beesly and high-minded Harrison,

whom he told that he cared 'not a d–n' for 'posthumous vicarious vitality' (B. Balfour 1906: I 325, II 99). Browning actually tried to help the persecuted Congreve but Tennyson had little sympathy. 'Well if I were a Comtist', he told Harrison at the Metaphysical Society, 'No God – no soul – no future – *no right and wrong*!! I should not care to live' (HP 1/75, f.19). The Positivists may have been miserable but no-one else accused them of immorality.

Positivism enters few plays. Oscar Wilde referred to the 'Comtian

Law of the three stages of thought' in his 1879 essay on 'The Rise of Historical Criticism' (Wilde 1913: 47) but a later dismissal of 'that sordid necessity of living for others which . . . presses so hardly upon almost everything' seems more in character (Wilde 1950: 227). Bernard Shaw was exceptional among the Fabians in not being impressed by Comte. A scribbled note in his hand on the manuscript of Pease's *History of the Fabian Society* criticises the Religion of Humanity on the grounds that its 'theology and religion, offered as new, were really both obsolete; and that the Utopia, unlike most Utopias, was so unattractive that one shuddered at its practicability' (R. Harrison 1965: 339). Comte's belief in an 'intelligently worked Capitalist system' was all right in theory but 'our millionaires and statesmen are manifestly no more "captains of industry" or scientific politicians than our bookmakers are mathematicians' (Shaw 1934: 102). Napoleon, in *The Man of Destiny*, cloaks his ambition under acceptable Comtean phrases, winning battles 'for humanity' and preaching the need to 'think of others, and work for others' (Shaw 1946: 182–3). Mrs Clandon also arouses suspicion by claiming a devotion to 'the Cause of Humanity' in *You Never Can Tell* (276). Incidental references to Comte can be found in other plays, for instance in Granville-Barker (G-B 1909: 250–1); the movement was too pervasive to be ignored. But the central artistic medium for the discussion and dissemination of the Religion of Humanity was undoubtedly the novel.

6

THE FINAL YEARS: DECLINE
AND FALL

Positivist reviewers: Swinny, Marvin, Thomas and Gould

Positivism entered the twentieth century in a peculiar position. As a set of ideas it had already permeated society through the controversies and the literature just considered but as an organised movement it was in disunity and disarray. Quarrels over the succession to Chapel Street in 1901 led to the effective separation of Newcastle and Liverpool, along with the provincial pockets of Positivism they had established, from the two London centres, who reunited, mainly in order to pool their meagre resources, in 1916. The *Positivist Review* struggled on until 1925, repeating Comte's basic ideas to an ever-diminishing readership, and Chapel Street closed altogether in 1934. But all was not gloom and despair. The final generation of Positivists, many of whom were teachers by profession, saw their role as educators of society in general. S. H. Swinny, F. S. Marvin, Philip Thomas and F. J. Gould, the leading lights of the Positivist Society in the twentieth century, sought to extend their influence beyond the movement itself to the outside world. Despondent though they were at the decline in their numbers, they took heart at the spread of their ideas.

Alfred Haggard's nomination as successor to Henry Crompton at Chapel Street, in spite of the manoeuvres of Malcolm Quin and Walter Westbrook, pious Positivists who saw themselves as spiritual heirs to Congreve, was welcomed by Frederic Harrison as ushering in a new period of peaceful co-operation between the Positivists in London. An Indian magistrate who had become a Positivist after the schism, Haggard held no personal animosity towards the Newton Hall triumvirate. Formal reunion remained impossible because of the strong influence still wielded by Mrs Congreve but when ill health forced him to retire in 1904 Haggard issued a circular expressing his own desire that all opposition and rivalry should cease. There were seldom more than six or seven in the congregation at Chapel Street at this time, while Newton Hall itself had to be abandoned because there were insufficient funds to renew the lease when it expired in 1902. Subsequent meetings of the London Positivist Society took place in rooms first at Clifford's Inn and then Lincoln's Inn with places like Essex Hall hired for lectures. A special meeting of subscribers in May 1904 heard just how precarious their financial position was. Income had fallen below expenditure before the turn of the century and, since most subscribers were in their seventies, could only be expected to decline. The *Positivist Review* alone lost forty pounds a year, nearly half of their annual budget (LPS 1/4). The obvious solution was re-union with Chapel Street but negotiations to achieve this, renewed after a joint service to celebrate the fiftieth anniversary of Comte's death, foundered on the continuing distrust of veterans of the schism. When it finally took place a number of pamphlets were published still protesting about the absurdities of Congreve's liturgy (McGee 1931: 216–17). The new title, however, 'Church of Humanity: London Positivist Society' and the division of direction between Philip Thomas as Church Leader and S. H. Swinny as President reflected the prevailing spirit of compromise and reconciliation.

Most of the administrative problems of Positivism devolved upon Shapland Hugh Swinny, an Irishman with a Cambridge education who eked out a meagre existence as a private tutor. He succeeded Beesly as President of the London Positivist Society in 1901 and as editor of the *Positivist Review* in 1903, taking over from Harrison as President of the English Positivist Committee in 1904. Always keen to defend Comte at meetings of the Sociological Society, the 'Friar of Sociology', as Branford called him (*Soc.R* XV (1923) 275), never ceased to expound his ideas in the *Positivist Review*. Nine full-length articles in the first volume under his editorship, along with a number of notes and reviews, rose to sixteen in the second and twenty-two in the third, staying at this sort of level until his death in 1923. Attacks on British imperialism throughout the world, especially in Ireland and in India, combined with an attempt to relate all developments in modern thought to Comte. The discoveries of Darwin, Le Play and Mendel, he boasted, had all found their way into his pages (*PR* XXVI (1918) 214). Swinny sometimes grew despondent, muttering of resignation in May 1911 and actually carrying out the threat six years later, under pressure from opponents of reunion with Chapel Street, only to be coaxed back into office. His death in 1923 certainly hastened the end of Positivism as an organised movement, for there was no-one as committed as he to continuing the Comtean tradition.

The best qualified of the regular reviewers upon whom Swinny was able to call was Francis Sidney Marvin. Educated with his lifelong friend Gilbert Murray at Merchant Taylors and then at St John's College, Oxford, where he followed a double first in classics with a degree in history after six months, Marvin was too busy as a School Board Inspector to take up a permanent position in the Positivist Society. Harrison, who warned him in 1889 that lecturing at Newton Hall might damage his 'prospects of advancement by the Education Department' (Bod.L. d 248, f.103), seems to have pulled enough strings to enable him to obtain promotion in 1892. Harrison pinned his hopes on Marvin as 'the only man under thirty connected with our group who has the best philosophical and historical training that the old school affords' along with the requisite 'energy and skill and self-devotion'. But he was worried that the younger man might not fully appreciate the need to preserve the distinctive qualities of Positivism, which was in danger of becoming only 'one of the many mutual improvement institutes' to be found in late-Victorian London (e 105, ff.64, 91–2). Bridges urged him to fill the gaps in his scientific education by systematic study over a period of twenty years (e 106, ff.66–8). Brilliant though he is reported to have been, 'master of half a dozen modern languages' in addition to history and the classics (d 252, f.96), Marvin found it difficult to meet all their hopes.

The broad-mindedness which worried the older Positivists surfaced in some of Marvin's contributions to the *Positivist Review*. An article on 'Neo-Christianism' in 1894 welcomed such liberal developments in Christian theology as the notion of progressive revelation (*PR* II (1894) 167–70) while another explored additional links between Positivism and theology (V (1897) 5–8). He extended a pious hand of welcome into the 'Kingdom of Man' to the Catholic Modernists, Sabatier and Loisy (XXVIII (1920) 205–6) while Baron von Hügel was among the contributors to a series of Summer Schools he arranged from 1915 on a variety of vaguely positivist themes. The papers, by committed Positivists such as Swinny, Gould and the chemist, Cecil Desch, along with a range of sympathetic liberal thinkers including Gilbert Murray, A. N. Whitehead and Julian Huxley, were edited by Marvin for the 'Unity Series'. His own contributions were heavily punctuated, needless to say, with references to Comte. Marvin also encouraged the Positivists to co-operate with Ethicists, Rationalists and Socialists rather then compete with them. His own publications were of a very general nature, surveys of history such as *The Living Past*, some of whose chapter titles reveal its Comtean pattern, tracing a development from 'The Childhood of the Race' through 'The Middle Ages' to 'The Rise of Modern Science'. The success of this volume, which went through four editions from 1913 to 1920, encouraged Marvin to write on *The Century of Hope*, looking at the nineteenth century 'from the same point of view from which *The Living Past* treated Western progress as a whole' (Marvin 1919: iii).

Marvin continued to produce general surveys of history through the 1920s and 30s as well as a full-length study of *Comte* and a book called *The New Vision of Man*, full of belief in humanity as 'the culmination of all living forms' (Marvin 1938: 9). He was a frequent contributor to the *Hibbert Journal*, where his references to Comte were not always wholly complimentary. His belief in the rapid triumph of Positivism, for example, is taken as an illustration of the 'curiously old-fashioned air' worn by mid-nineteenth-century prophecy (*HJ* XXVII (1928–9) 249), one of the 'egregious mistakes' to which scientists were prone (XXXI (1932–3) 73). There are indications too of a compromise with liberal Christianity. Comte's 'Grand Être' is likened to the 'Supreme Spiritual Reality' that other people call 'God' (XXVIII (1929–30) 173). It was not, however, 'the creator of the universe' (XXXVII (1938–9) 188). Comte may have been overoptimistic, Marvin admitted, he may have included an 'undue preponderance of Frenchmen' in his calendar, but any religious revival, though it might not be called Positivism, would incorporate many of his ideas (474–5). Marvin died in 1943, a disappointed man, shocked by the horrors of the Second World War, denied the academic recognition for which his correspondence with Gilbert Murray shows that he was always hoping (MP 160) and worn out by the continual travel required by his job.

Philip Thomas is generally known only as the father of the poet Edward Thomas. A civil servant from Tredegar whose religious development traced a familiar path from Nonconformity through Unitarianism to Ethicism and the Religion of Humanity, Philip Thomas found in Comte the synthesis of all that he had come to believe. Lecturing on Positivism to the School of Ethics in 1908, he explained that Humanity offered a more concrete focus of faith than the Moral Ideal and a clearer source of authority (*PR* XVI (1908) 87–8, 256–8). He was asked to lecture at Chapel Street the following year and to become leader in place of Henry Dussause in 1910. A series of pamphlets published in that year celebrates his new-found faith, asserting the sanctity of marriage, the dignity of women and the historical importance of Chapel Street. A discourse on *Auguste Comte and Richard Congreve* ended with the confident prediction that

before the end of the present century the world will come to the conclusion that the greatest and most enduring religious work done in England in the nineteenth century was the establishment of Positivism and the founding of this first Church of Humanity by Richard Congreve. (Thomas 1910b: 14)

A selection of his addresses, published under the title *A Religion of This World*, expresses similar confidence in the Religion of Humanity as superior to all other forms of free-thought. The Ethicists in particular were warned not to allow jealousy of a great man and fear of a definite system to blind them to the merits of personal inspiration and specifically-focussed faith (Thomas 1913: 41–6).

Thomas's appeal as a Positivist leader in a period of decline lay in his ability to detect Positivism everywhere and in everything. He discovered 'Positivism in Goethe', which was not altogether surprising since he took Lewes's biography as his primary text (*PR* XVI (1908) 134–7), in Shelley, prevented only by the intolerance of early nineteenth-century England from establishing the Religion of Humanity before Comte (XIX (1911) 14–18), in Wells and Meredith, as we have seen, and, perhaps the most unlikely place of all, in Chesterton, who was 'really a Positivist' while 'honestly believing himself a Catholic' (XXV (1917) 15–19). Thomas managed to convince himself that it only required some of those crypto-Positivists to acknowledge their allegiance for their movement to regain the prominence it once held. His claim that Loisy was really voicing 'the principles and aspirations of Positivism' and could therefore be called 'Humanity's New Apostle', 'finding his way . . . to a wider Catholicism, a truly universal religion' (XXIV (1916) 269–72; XXVI (1918) 49–54), brought an indignant denial from the Catholic Modernist himself. Thomas explained that there was no charge of plagiarism but of shared beliefs. Positivism too desired 'to see man's life inspired by a human religion, guided by a philosophy founded on science, and directed to the service of mankind' (XXVI 117). Given such a broad definition of the faith which Thomas continued to preach until his death in 1921 it is hardly surprising that he found it so pervasive.

Frederick James Gould followed a similar path from evangelical Anglican faith through a period of vague theism to Secularism before finding in Positivism the creed which came closest to his independent views. *The Life-Story of a Humanist* traces the different answers he found to meet the basic need first felt at his conversion in 1871, to be 'a living unit of a larger whole, which in 1871 I called God, and in 1923 Humanity' (F. J. Gould 1923: 22). Struggling from 1879 to 1896 as a London School Board Teacher first in Bethnal Green and then in Limehouse, Gould came into contact with a wide range of non-believers. He heard Bradlaugh and Foote at the Hall of Science and went on to write for the *National Reformer* and the *Secular Review*. He met Charles Watts in 1882 and became a close friend, writing for his *Literary Guide* and helping him to found the Rationalist Press Association. Many of Gould's books were published by Watts. He also assisted Stanton Coit in setting up the East London Ethical Society and the *Ethical World*. But it was Auguste Comte, whose message he first heard preached by Frederic Harrison in 1881, who most 'governed (this does not mean tyrannized over!) his mind (51). He 'never lost touch' with Newton Hall and when appointed Secretary and Organizer to the Leicester Secular Society in 1899 he made no secret of his 'deep respect for the teachings of the "Religion of Humanity" ' (79).

The Leicester Secular Society had a long history of association with Positivism. First set in motion by a Positivist bookseller, George Findley, the meetings were enlivened by readings at the suggestion of Malcolm Quin and then by hymns after they moved in 1881 to a magnificent new hall with seating for some five hundred people. Gould, who had complained in the *Secular Review* about the negative attitudes of members more intent on mocking Christianity than 'improving the world and increasing the moral happiness of mankind' (Royle 1980: 117), turned more and more to the Religion of Humanity for the positive teaching he required. He embarked on a close study of all Comte's works in 1902, 'reshaping his views to my own Twentieth Century outlook' but retaining the 'essentials of the moral reorganization of society' marked out by the founder of Positivism, about whom he wrote in the *Agnostic Annual* in 1904 (F. J. Gould 1923: 90). *The*

Religion that Fulfils, a pamphlet he wrote for the Rationalist Press Association the following year, was, as its subtitle acknowledges, 'A Simple Account of Positivism', while his 1908 *Catechism of Religion and the Social Life* was a personal 'statement of the Religion of Humanity' (F. J. Gould 1908: 7). All this was too much for the Leicester Secularists, who objected to their hall being turned into 'a Positivist Society and Labour Church'. Gould resigned in April 1908 and tried for two years to establish a genuine Leicester Positivist Society in a 'transfigured shop' before returning to London in 1910 as a demonstrator for the Moral Education League (F. J. Gould 1923: 108–12), work which involved five years of world travel until once more the funds ran out.

Marvin was so impressed by Gould's enthusiasm and energy that he persuaded the Positivists in 1916 to pay for his services as an organiser and preacher. He had been a frequent and lively contributor to the *Positivist Review* since 1905, on educational issues in particular, proffering an ingenious reading of the gospels as an allegory of 'the tragedy of the proletariat', and seeing the 'documents known as Pauline' as an anticipation of the main strands of Positivism (*PR* XVII (1909) 174–8). His many books of moral education, retelling biblical, eastern and classical legends for the benefit of children, were sometimes openly Positivist, as in *History the Teacher*, with its subtitle, 'Education Inspired by Humanity's Story', and its definition of history as the story of 'human love, human order . . . and human progress' (F. J. Gould 1921: 3). He produced a clear exposition of the Religion of Humanity in 1916 and an informative and unsentimental life of Comte four years later. He took over the editorship of the *Positivist Review* in 1924, changing its name to *Humanity* and arguing in its final number, in December 1925, before it too expired for lack of funds, that Positivism should adapt itself to modern needs (*PR* XXXIII (1925) 162).

Gould was easily the most energetic of the final generation of Positivists. He even wrote a masque entitled 'Life's Quest', performed in the Temple of Humanity in Liverpool in 1925, at the end of which, in spite of the machinations of Famine, War, Disease and other evil characters,

> Youthful Life,
> Guided by Wisdom and inspired by Love,
> Goes forth unconquered and unconquerable. (177)

His understanding of Positivism was a broad one, leading him to caution colleagues against a rigid or 'too purist rendering' of Comte's ideas (Bod.L. c 266, f.47), to complain that 'Positivism, on its social side, has always been too bourgeois' and to speculate freely about Comte's sexual psychology (Gould to Hillemand, 25/12/85, MAC). He resigned from the English Positivist Committee in 1926, but continued to believe in a modified Religion of Humanity, as expounded in 1931:

I think the *Philosophie Positive* is the mind of the Human Race; and the real *Politique* is the daily organisation of the Human Race:–Comte's work being of great value in interpretation of this mind and work. That is why I am NEVER low-spirited, – as so many Positivists are. I NEVER weep over the slowness of mankind to reach the Final Religion. I have more respect for one poor proletarian mother, struggling with poverty, than for a congregation of Positivist philosophers in a comfortable library.

(Gould to Henry Edger, 21/6/31, MAC)

The Life-Story of a Humanist ends with a similar vision of a future religion infinitely superior to the declining 'old theology' (F. J. Gould 1923: 170).

In Thomas and Gould even more than in Marvin and Swinny can be seen a gradual broadening of Positivism, particularly in its attitude towards Modernism and towards other brands of unbelief. The old guard were constantly warning their younger colleagues against co-operation with the many neo-Christian missions springing up in London. Harrison, for example, complained to Marvin in 1890 that 'in order to get any interest from young Oxford and Cambridge you must be utterly vague and think "there may be a sort of something after all", and live four miles east of Charing Cross' (Bod.L. d 249, f.112v). Bridges told him flatly not to teach at Toynbee Hall but to direct all his energies to 'objects directly concerned with Positivism' (e 105, f.31). The papal encyclical of 1907, *Pascendi Gregis*, with its list of condemned modernist propositions, brought new impetus into the discussion. Harrison renewed the attack with two articles in the *Positivist Review*: 'The New Theology', full of 'gush and prevarication' about Jesus and 'unctuous balderdash' about 'the immanence of God in man' (*PR* XV (1907) 102–4), and the signs of liberalisation evident in 'Decadent Theology' should not blind Positivists to the need to abandon discredited creeds and rituals (121–4). Others took a similar line: Pius X had revealed the 'great gulf fixed between faith and reason' (254), declared Paul Descours, a civil servant born in York of Franco-Belgian descent who became Secretary of the London Positivist Society and wrote sympathetic reviews of Loisy. It was good for Catholics to think that their Church was being 'lightened of some of her dogmas', he wrote of *Choses passées*, but 'ultimately the old religion must give place to the new one' (XXII (1914) 82–4). Swinny also welcomed the encyclical as forcing people to 'draw to their proper side in the great contest' between faith and reason (XVI (1908) 33). There was no future in old churches with new views; what was needed was a new church (XXI (1913) 180). Gradually but perceptibly, however, the Positivists relaxed their hostility towards liberal and sympathetic Christians.

A similar development took place in relations between Positivists and other humanist groups. Harrison, about to lecture to the Ethical Society in 1893, announced confidently, 'These Ethicists are simply Positivists *minus* the definite dogmas and formulae of Comte' and therefore 'fertile soil' for potential converts (Bod.L. e 108, f.126). When his wife visited the West London Ethical Society two years later she is supposed to have asked, 'Is it not rather vague?', only to receive the reply, 'Ah! but we like it vague' (Sulman to Gouge, 13/1/95, MAC). Marvin, while welcoming the growth of Ethicism in the *Positivist Review* in 1898, took Coit to task for attacking the Positivist worship of Humanity and reverence for Comte. Positivism, he claimed, remained 'the natural and inevitable development of the Ethical Movement' (*PR* VI (1898) 187–91). But there was now increasing co-operation between the two groups. At a meeting in Newton Hall at the end of 1900 Harrison formulated four main grounds of agreement while Coit acknowledged that their differences were far less than those which separated the various Christian churches (X (1901) 29–30). There was a joint conference in 1902, a shared series of lectures in Essex Hall in 1905 and the Ethicists gave South Place Chapel to the Positivists for a series of well-attended Sunday afternoons in the first three months of 1906. Philip Thomas lectured on Positivism to the Ethical Society in 1908 and on Ethicism to the Positivist Society the following year. But there was still the occasional row, as when Harrison objected to Coit's 'silly sneers' at Humanity as an object of worship (XIV (1906) 191), and the Positivists rejected Coit's offer of a 'permanent federation' in 1911 (LPS 1/5, 29/11/11). A similar friendly but distanced relationship was maintained with the Rationalist

Press Association through men like Gould and Desch, who spoke at their annual dinner in 1908. When Gilbert Murray addressed them in 1914, however, Swinny felt uneasy about printing his speech in the *Positivist Review* before it appeared in the *Literary Guide* in case it aroused 'the suspicion of friends who are rivals in business' (Bod.L. d 262, f.137v).

Positivism, however, was rapidly going out of business. The annual general meeting of the London Positivist Society in April 1925, faced with the need to drop the *Review* and to abandon all organised meetings for the summer, could only deplore the general lack of interest in religion and philosophy (LPS 1/7). Seven years later, Desch reported, when a new lease was required on Chapel Street, 'it was unanimously decided to bring the organisation to a close'. The gradual dwindling of their numbers, the result of a failure to replace the old guard with new recruits, was attributed by some to too much ritual and by others to too little. 'The real fact is that the movement is dead because the few surviving members have been content to preach Comtism, ignoring all that has happened since 1857' (Bod.L. c 268, f.51). A series of Comte Memorial Lectures was delivered at the Ethical Church, Bayswater, from 1935 to 1940 and the remaining funds of the London Positivist Society were used to establish a further series at the London School of Economics from 1953. Positivism as an organised movement had become a lost cause but not before its spirit, in the words of Gilbert Murray, had 'got abroad and permeated other bodies' (Bod.L. c 268, f.95).

Provincial piety: Newcastle and Liverpool

Two bodies which continued to practise Positivist piety well into the twentieth century were the provincial Churches of Humanity in Newcastle and Liverpool, both of which attempted to develop the Religion of Humanity beyond the limits of its founder before expiring of public apathy and neglect. Their history remains worth telling, in spite of the inevitability of this outcome, because it sheds additional light upon the general decline of Positivism. The leaders of these churches, full of energy and enthusiasm though they were, fell some way short of the intellectual and imaginative stature of the generations which had first discussed Comte's ideas. But they were men and women with powerful religious needs which orthodox Christianity failed to meet. Positivism, in this final phase, came to be not so much a substitute for Christianity as a liberal interpretation of it. Many traditional Christian symbols, at least, found their way into the exotic liturgy which evolved in these two churches.

The Church of Humanity in Newcastle upon Tyne was the work of Malcolm Quin, an active member of the Leicester Secular Society until his move to Newcastle in 1878. He began a lengthy correspondence with Congreve the following September, joining the Positivist Society in January 1880 once he had been assured that Comte was not 'held to have given Positivism its final and infallible constitution'. For no system, he believed, could meet men's needs unless 'subjected to the enlarging and perfecting power of many minds' (BL 45229, ff.176–7). He held some informal meetings in a variety of gardens, lumber rooms and hired halls before opening the 'Positivist Room', complete with busts of the saints and a copy of the Sistine Madonna, in January 1883. His ambitions were higher than this, and he introduced music, singing and 'devotional readings' in order to emphasise 'the essentially religious character of Positivism' but he succumbed for the moment to Congreve's reserve in 'calling a room a room' (Quin 1924: 107–10).

Having received the Sacrament of Destination to the Priesthood in 1885, Quin erected an iron church, bought with all its furnishings from the Church of England, on a site in St Mary's Place. A trilingual notice,

> Aedes Humanitatis
> Church of Humanity
> Chiesa dell'Umanità

'stared the good people of Newcastle in the face' for some twenty years without inspiring 'the slightest curiosity' except, by Quin's own admission, in a few cranks (141). But now that he had a Church, Quin was free to develop a liturgy, replacing Congreve's dry 'Ordinary Morning Service' with his own 'Office of Public Worship' which contained additional invocations by the priest to Humanity, responses from the people, 'A Hymn in Praise of Humanity', a litany, benediction and the 'Credo Positivisto' in the universal language, Italian. He also added a Festival of Machines to those already celebrated by the Positivists in London.

Quin's most striking innovations, however, after abandoning journalism in 1895 to devote himself to the priesthood, involved visual symbols. In order to give the altar 'a definitely Positivist character' while making it 'in appearance, more Catholic' he suspended a red lamp over six lighted candles beneath the Sistine Madonna, representing Comte's hierarchy of the sciences with morals in the ascendancy. One of the side-altars was devoted to Comte, the other to his three angels. A tablet containing the Ten Commandments in Hebrew, a small crucifix and a statuette of the Virgin were added to the statutory busts of the major Positivist saints. At the west end of the church, facing the high altar, was a painting of Humanity by the Liverpool Positivist, Jane Style (see p. 257), and Quin himself wore vestments combining the Positivist colours, red for active love and the present, white for purity and the past, and green for immortality and the future. It was, as he admitted, 'an orgy of ritual, or symbolism' (153–5).

Quin had composed 'hymns of ethical platitude' in Leicester in the seventies, later recalling that in those days 'people who believed in nothing else believed in hymns' (52). He now compiled a collection of his own *Hymns of Worship*, full of complex rhetorical techniques and echoes of earlier religious poets, in particular Herbert, Newman and Clough (T. R. Wright 1983: 15). Their tone is often melancholy, a section entitled 'Hymns of the Soul's Conflicts' positively bulging with doubt and despair, struggle and strife. The same seriousness permeates his 'Annual Addresses', for example in his insistence in 1895,

We are not Positivists if the sense of human suffering, of human failure, of human ignorance, of human weakness – of the passions that degrade men, of the hatred that divides them, of the war of nations and classes, of the waste and chaos of our social life – does not eat into us and fill us with an almost intolerable impatience and sorrow.   (Quin, *AA* 1896: 9)

He was forever issuing tracts and pamphlets on contemporary political issues, campaigning vigorously for an end to the Boer War and to all self-interested intervention by Britain in the Middle and Far East. He does not seem to have expected to change people's minds, only to fulfil the duty of preaching Positivist values to an unsympathetic world. Repeated failure and constant neglect led to the occasional letter of loneliness and despair. But he was naturally ebullient and the activities of the Newcastle Positivists included picnics and play-readings as well as hymns and tracts.

The other Positivists regarded Quin with a certain suspicion and reserve. Congreve, though flattered by a steady stream of sycophantic letters from this dangerously energetic disciple, felt he was 'far too sanguine' about the financial problems of establishing a church (Bod.L. e 68, f.17) and disapproved altogether of his receiving pay for a full-time priesthood. Quin 'rather feeds on words', he explained to a colleague (BL 45231, f.41v) and refused to nominate him as successor. The old guard at Newton Hall were openly hostile and contemptuous, Beesly warning Hillemand of the 'narrow sectarian' attitudes of this self-appointed 'missionary apostle' (8/2/01, MAC), while Quin was equally abrasive about the 'philistinism' of Newton Hall and its 'untrustworthy interpreters' of Comte (Quin to Grant, 2/1, 13/2/94, BLUL). The trouble with Beesly, the 'political pugilist', and Harrison, the 'vivacious littérateur', he complained, was that they were insufficiently religious; they would not 'go on their knees' (8/1/01).

This was a complaint Quin came increasingly to make of Comte himself, whose complete neglect of Christ was the most important example of the 'revolutionary spirit' he had imbibed in his youth (Quin, *AC* 1906: 14). Religious Positivists, Quin claimed, should always revere 'the Crucified Man-God and His Mother' if only as the symbols to whom 'the heart of devout men and tender women have turned in their distress'. The word 'Christ', he told a congregation in Liverpool in 1906, the year in which he introduced the Festival of the Nativity, 'is the supreme, classic word of religion' (Quin, *AC* 1908: 26–7). The following year saw him urging Positivists to develop Comte's ideas into a fuller understanding of Catholicism and by 1909 he admitted quite openly that the Religion of Humanity was inadequate to men's needs: 'the common instinct which has rejected it has been sound' (Quin, *AC* 1909: 22). Renaming the building 'St Paul's Catholic Church', he added Holman Hunt's 'Light of the World' to the Sistine Madonna and replaced the small crucifix with a much larger one. He procured the 'requisite vessels' and vestments to begin saying Mass and Benediction (Quin 1924: 196), combining Christian symbols with Positivist sentiments. 'The Canon of the Mass' in his new 'Offices of Public Worship' referred to 'Jesus Christ, thy Son, our Lord, Supreme Vicar and Voice of Humanity' and to 'Mary, Mother of our Lord and God Jesus Christ and supreme exemplar and type of all Holy Women' (Quin 1909a: 12).

Quin felt obliged, understandably, to explain what he was doing.

He published a pamphlet entitled *Notes on a Progressive Catholicism*, which described how his search for 'a reasonable faith' had led him to a belief in Humanity which in turn had brought him to Catholicism as 'the mind and life of Jesus Christ working in the mind and life of mankind' (Quin 1909b: 13, 18). *Aids to Worship*, subtitled 'An Essay towards the Positive Preservation and Development of Catholicism', claimed it could also have been called 'an essay in the religious inter- pretation of Auguste Comte'. For Quin insisted that he was merely completing the work begun by Comte, whose significance lay not in his attempt to found a new religion but in his interpretation of the old. He was 'the supreme "modernist" ', co-ordinating the discoveries of science with the truths of Catholicism (Quin 1909c: 49).

Much of Quin's argument at this stage centred on the nature of religious language, which he regarded as closer to poetry than to metaphysics. History too was less important than the imagination. Just as Christ, a representation of the highest human ideals at the time the 'gospel poems' were written, required reinterpretation in the light of the highest ideals of later ages, so the 'place of Mary in our religious consciousness' was 'not determined by . . . the New Testament, but by the religious needs and affirmations of man in the Catholic World' (100–1). The difference between traditional and progressive Cath- olicism lay in the acknowledgement of the 'figurative and symbolic' nature of its language (106–7). All this was too much for Quin's former supporters, whose desertion forced him to abandon his church in 1910. He continued, however, to expound his new brand of Pos- itivism in *Catholicism and the Modern Mind*, which contained 'A Prefatory Letter to His Holiness Pope Pius X' arguing that Cath- olicism was 'the positive presentation and realization of Christ in the life of mankind' (Quin 1912: xiv). The book itself analysed in turn the demands upon the Church being made by progress, liberty, moder- nisation and science, explaining once more the role of symbolism in religious language. Modern Catholicism, he insisted, was by no means bound by the intentions of its creed-makers, whose symbols had outgrown their original meaning.

Quin published two more books of Positivist propaganda, *The Pro- blem of Human Peace* (1916), which reiterated his belief in the need for an international spiritual power to control warlike nations, and *The Politics of the Proletariat* (1919), which advertised itself as 'A Con- tribution to the Science of Citizenship based chiefly on the Sociology of Auguste Comte'. A series of articles in the final volume of the *Positivist Review* traced 'The Development of Positivism' from Comte's original 'religious reconstruction', which was 'imperfect and incomplete' (*PR* XXXIII (1925) 92) to later elucidations of his basic truths. Comte, he confessed in 1933, was 'still for me the prince of modern thinkers' even though his ideas required further development and interpretation (Quin to A-P. Edger, 14/1/33, MAC). He kept himself busy in his long retirement until his death in 1946, giving frequent talks to a wide variety of societies, working and reworking a range of different manuscripts on Positivism and Catholicism which were forever being given new titles and never being published, writing articles for journals such as the *Free Catholic*, and visiting a number of churches, mostly Catholic, always bringing to their services 'a Positivist mind' (Quin 1924: 214). In 1935 he circulated a letter to an Anglican clergyman under the title, *Science and Religious Unity*, in which he claimed that after twenty-five years of attendance at Mass he felt the time was ripe for a renewal of Comte's Religious League, with all sympathetic minds uniting to preach 'a Scientific Catholicism', maintaining 'organic continuity' with the Church of history but 'understanding its so-called "supernaturalism" as a Poem of Man shaped by men of spiritual and metaphysical imagination' (BPH 118/40).

Among the progressive theologians Quin named as sympathetic to the Religion of Humanity were the Catholic Modernists, George Tyrrell and Friedrich von Hügel, who wrote him long letters acknowledging the similarity of their respective positions. 'We are both governed by the same idea of the value and significance of religion and of the principles of its interpretation', admitted Tyrrell, 'making for the same Catholicism from opposite approaches'. Both Positivism and liberal Catholicism, he feared, were 'too philosophical to be ever a power with average humanity'. But while he would not want to impose 'meat for the strong' on them, he objected to the tendency of the Church to 'diet the strong on what is milk for babes'. The answer, according to Tyrrell, was not for the schismatic separation of small groups such as the Positivists but the gradual leavening of the 'savourless mass' by all progressive thinkers (Petre 1912: II 410–12). Von Hügel was more critical of two aspects of Positivist thought, its identification of morality and religion, which gave it a 'curiously heavy, opaque doctrinaire "feel" and tone', and its sympathy for the 'centralising, absolutising of authority'. He too deplored the creation of separate bodies, preferring to reform the Church from within (Hügel 1927: 173–5).

No-one could claim that Quin's attempt to establish a separate Church of Humanity had succeeded. But as he argued in his amusing and ironic *Memoirs of a Positivist,* 'a given "failure" may have a deeper interest and significance than a given "success" ' (Quin 1924: 10). For all his energy and enthusiasm, Quin failed to persuade the people of Newcastle upon Tyne that they did in fact need a new Church with a new creed. He had no option, therefore, but to take up the modernist position, attempting to modify the existing Church in accordance with principles which remained fundamentally in tune with those of Comte.

A number of small Positivist churches sprang up in the north east in the 1890s, at Sunderland, Batley and Hartlepool, with Quin as their travelling minister and Congreve as their financial support. Congreve used also to visit the small communities centred upon George Findley in Leicester and John Oliver in Birmingham in the 1880s, a decade which saw the foundation of the Manchester Positivist Society, affiliated to Newton Hall. But by far the most successful attempt to establish a Church of Humanity outside London was in Liverpool, where the Positivists were sufficiently numerous and wealthy to maintain their own Temple of Humanity until after the Second World War. The first Positivist meetings in Liverpool took place in 1879 when a number of committed Comtists invited Congreve to conduct a full-scale service the following March, which in turn led to a series of regular services at the Temperance Hotel run by the veteran Chartist, Edmund Jones. A converted stable in Falkland Street became the Church of Humanity, officially opened on the first day of 1883.

The first leader of the Church of Humanity in Liverpool was an Irish surgeon called Thomas Carson whose emotional nature and Catholic upbringing emerged in a particularly pious brand of Positivism. He first wrote to Congreve in 1878 to confess the immense comfort he derived from the study of the Positive Philosophy, 'a perpetual novel' which he could open at any page, 'in the highest sense a poem' idealising human life (BL 45227, f.188v). Congreve remained unimpressed by Carson's gushing letters but the Liverpool Positivists held their 'Apostle of Humanity' in great reverence, calmly accepting his introduction in 1884 of a form of Comtean eucharist, a 'mode of consecrating his memory' by following his practice of chew-

10   The Temple of Humanity, Liverpool, LPS 5/4

ing a piece of bread after each meal while meditating upon those in
need (BPH 118/5). The following year he introduced a new Festival
of the Virgin-Mother while in 1886 he published *Some Sentiments of
our South American Brethren*, a collection of the most extravagant out-
pourings designed 'to offer English brethren the opportunity of making some spiritual acquaintance' with more overtly religious Positivists
(Carson 1886: 1). Some of Carson's own sentiments, later collected
under the title *The Message of Humanity*, insist upon the need for more
'direct worship of Humanity' (Carson 1908: 8), attacking rationalism,
the 'craving to account for everything' (22), and urging his Liverpool
colleagues to create their own liturgy rather than rely upon the 'rags
and tatters of the old dead forms of art' (72). Overcome in 1887 by a
debilitating nervous disease which confirmed Congreve's suspicions
of insanity, Carson died in 1890.

Carson's successor was Albert Crompton, who had come to Liverpool to work for Holt's shipping line, of which he was to become a
director, in 1872, the year he joined the Positivist Society. The product of a very different background, Harrow, Trinity College Cambridge and the Bar, he was equally pious and emotional in his faith,
particularly after the death of his wife in 1885, which plunged him into
perpetual widowhood: 'Each morning he knelt with his children at
her altar, each night he communed with her upon the events of the

11   Jane Style's painting of 'Humanity', MAC

day' (S. Style 1908: 22). He translated Comte's daily prayers, instituted weekly study of the *Catechism* and preached 'sermons full of practical piety – like those of a devout curé' (Sulman to Gouge, 13/1/95, MAC).

After Crompton's death in 1908, Sydney Style, a solicitor who had moved to Liverpool in 1875 and helped to found their church, continued the tradition of liturgical experiment, composing a prose-poem upon all three deities of the Subjective Synthesis, 'Space, The Earth, Humanity', a number of prayers, copied and illustrated by his wife in their private devotional manual, and reams of handwritten sermons urging the cultivation of Positivist habits of prayer and meditation. Jane May Style was largely responsible for the decoration of the church with symbolic arrangements of flowers to match her symbolic painting of Humanity, a mother blessing her different-coloured children while priests of various religious traditions worship on either side. She also wrote a number of Positivist hymns and two books on Comte, *The Voice of the Nineteenth Century*, to which the twentieth should have listened and thereby averted the First World War, and a sentimental biography, *Auguste Comte: Thinker and Lover*. With her 'flowing red hair and determined face', her radical short skirts and shocking paintings of the Liverpool poor, she was, for one of her col-

257

leagues at least, 'the most remarkable woman that English Positivism has possessed' (Baier 1938: 7–11).

The most remarkable feature of Liverpool Positivism, however, was its development of the liturgy, especially after the opening of their impressive new Temple of Humanity in Upper Parliament Street in December 1913. The result of a generous donation by Crompton's daughter, who was mysteriously murdered in its basement on the eve of the inauguration, the Temple, with its 'symbolic pictures', and 'the statue of Humanity radiant in its pillared shrine', struck many with admiration and awe (Baier 1930: 19). Quin was less impressed by this 'Greek building', its simple relief of Mother and Child on the outer wall facing the street, its bare plain walls 'with meagre half-moon windows, high up and affording inadequate light' (QD, 22/2/30). But with the large Crompton Hall in the basement beneath, which housed social events ranging from plays and masques to talks and dances, it was clearly an improvement on his iron church. Under Sydney Style the congregation rose to about a hundred (BPH 118/16) while for his memorial service there were about two hundred mourners. 'Religiously', recorded Quin, 'the Service was unimpressive', leaving an effect of 'coldness', with 'hardly anything that could be called a prayer' (QD, 23/2/30). But his liturgical standards, it should be remembered, were high in every sense.

The service sheets that survive show that the Liverpool liturgy was not that cold. There was a tendency to talk of 'the appointed person' rather than the priest and to instruct visitors to 'keep silence' and prepare 'for a serious all round consideration of the human problem' (CL B2255, H91). But there was also a tradition of devotion to the Virgin-Mother extending from Carson's introduction of the festival in 1885 to an elaborate celebration of the same festival in 1909. The rubric for this service explains,

Mary the Virgin-Mother of Jesus Christ was the creation of our Virgin-Mother Humanity living in the hearts of the women of Europe, of the Saints of the Catholic Church, of the Knights of Chivalry, and of the poets, painters and musicians of the Middle Ages, for the guidance of Her children at a time when she was as yet unable fully to reveal Her own glory.

Further elaboration on Humanity and 'the loving kindness which is the centre of our being' leads on to a series of biblical readings involving Mary, interwoven with the Magnificat sung by women and the

Nunc Dimittis sung by men together with quotations from Wordsworth, Sir Walter Scott, Byron, Crashaw and Petrarch. After all this comes a sustained meditation on Mary, 'who has lived in the Heaven of the Human imagination' for centuries, 'in company with God the Father, the idealization of Power' and the other members of the Trinity. The congregation is then exhorted to 'more determined efforts to live with the unseen, with our own saints and angels, with the saints, sages and heroes of all time' before the service ends with a prayer, a hymn and an organ voluntary (Fraser 986 (42)).

The Liverpool Positivists clearly enjoyed singing hymns, many of which were modelled on obvious Christian originals. Number six in a collection entitled *Hymns and Anthems for Use in the Church of Humanity* of 1901 begins,

> Great Humanity, we raise
> Hearts and voices in thy praise,

and number seventeen,

> Now come with joyful heart
> To sing aloud in chorus
> The tale of all that Love
> Hath won and suffered for us.

'Lead Kindly Light' is included unaltered from Newman's original while Herbert's famous hymn suffers only a change of sex:

> Queen of glory, queen of peace,
> I will love thee.

A section of hymns for use at particular Positivist festivals is followed by various 'Chants or Anthems', including an 'Ave Clotilde' in Italian and English and an aria from Bellini's *I Puritani* which was apparently 'sung by Auguste Comte as a portion of his private devotions' (CL B2255, H99). The Liverpool liturgy was not, like Congreve's, a parody of the Book of Common Prayer, being more Catholic in every sense. But drawing as heavily as it did from other traditions it could not help sounding second-hand.

The congregation at Liverpool began to decline even under the Styles. An average attendance of about thirty in the 1920s went below twenty in the thirties and reached single figures during the Second World War. Otto Baier, who entered Britain from Germany in 1900, was interned during the First World War and succeeded Sydney Style as leader in 1929, struggled like Quin to establish a Religious League with Unitarians, Quakers, Swedenborgians, Theosophists and even Buddhists. Also like Quin, he attempted to introduce a more positive Positivist attitude to Jesus as 'the creation of the ages', embodying man's highest aspirations. A sermon on 'The Place of Jesus in the History of Humanity' criticised Comte's omission of Christ from his calendar, for the figure of Jesus, a product of man's religious imagination, had been of great importance in human history (BPH 118/18, 15/7/34). But it was Humanity and not Christ who should be at the centre of their worship (5/12/37). Like Quin, Baier believed that Comte instituted rather than constituted the Religion of Humanity, which needed to be developed by succeeding generations (14/11/37). Unlike Quin, he rejected the notion of joining the Catholic Church, whose treatment of Modernism he held to have quenched all hope of reform (118/41).

The Church of Humanity continued to function both socially and liturgically through the Second World War and beyond, and a play about Prometheus, symbolising both the value of fire and the nobility of suffering Humanity, was performed there as late as January 1947. But the building was closed and sold later in the year. Clair Baier, Otto's son, who ran a small Positivist group in Birmingham from 1938 to 1940, recognised that the movement that had been broken by the First World War was killed off by the Second. Its language seemed outdated and its services unnecessary. His father died disappointed and dejected in 1949, by which time what was built as the Temple of Humanity had become the Third Church of Christ Scientist while the statue of Humanity gathered dust in the Liverpool Maternity Hospital.

Professed sympathisers: Geddes and the sociologists

Among the many academics born and bred in the nineteenth century but flourishing in the twentieth who found in Comte an admirable if outdated attempt to synthesise human knowledge and turn it to some social purpose and who therefore kept in touch with the Positivist Society while making it clear that they did not accept the entire Comtean system, the most famous, the most influential, the most energetic and the most extraordinary was Sir Patrick Geddes. First attracted to Positivism in 1874 at the age of twenty by the attacks of his professor, T. H. Huxley, Geddes soon became a regular visitor to Chapel Street, where he enjoyed 'the bright week-night meetings of the Positivist Society' in spite of the 'touch of pontificalism' he detected in Congreve. He confessed in an article in the *Positivist Review* which was incorporated in the introduction to Bridges' biography, that he found him the 'most congenial' and most scientific, the others being too 'essentially Oxonian and humanistic' to take much interest in science (*PR* XXXIII (1925) 107–14; Liveing 1926: 1–4). The fundamental doctrines of the Positivist faith which he learnt from them, however, were to remain with him throughout his astonishing career as biologist, sociologist, town-planner and self-appointed missionary to the human race.

The Positivists, Geddes admitted, could only be disappointed at his 'too rare and limited participation in their work and teaching' but he had 'constantly been applying' their principles (Liveing 1926: 13–14). In Edinburgh at the Outlook Tower, as Professor of Botany at University College Dundee, in Bombay as Professor of Sociology and Civics, and finally at the Scots College in Montpellier, which he called the 'strategic centre of the world and city of Comte' (NLS 19270, f.156), he can be seen to have wrestled with the Religion of Humanity, producing reams of notes, diagrams, charts and 'thinking machines', his celebrated method of chewing over ideas. Some of his enthusiasm was shared by fellow-sociologists such as Branford, Hobhouse and Mumford, Fabians such as Sidney and Beatrice Webb, liberals such as Gilbert Murray and a number of other academics, more or less sympathetic to the Positivist cause while uncommitted to its details, who can be taken as characteristic of a generation for which the organised Religion of Humanity ceased to be a serious option even though many of its fundamental concepts had become widely accepted. The Positivist Societies had dwindled, Geddes admitted, but 'the man in the street' was becoming 'far more of a positivist than he knows' (Liveing 1926: 9).

Geddes, as he confessed to Laffitte in 1881 (6/12/81, MAC), remained an incomplete Positivist, too interested in other thinkers such as Huxley, Spencer, Ruskin and Le Play, to commit himself to a narrow Comtism. That his enthusiasm for the Religion of Humanity continued through the 1880s, however, is indicated by his attempts to convert his friends to the faith (Kitchen 1975: 79–80). Anna Morton, whom he married in 1886, dutifully read the chapter on women in the *General View* and defended 'our religion' against the combined attacks of clergy and family, worshipping at Chapel Street when she visited

London in the 1890s (NLS 19253, ff.6, 37, 42). Geddes seems to have brought up his son, Alastair, to worship both her and 'St Clotilde' (106244, f.82). He subscribed to Paris, Chapel Street and Newton Hall in the 1880s, being elected a member of the London Positivist Society in April 1883. Under continual pressure from Congreve, who came to stay with him the following March, he contemplated establishing an official Positivist centre in Edinburgh. Instead, he adopted a broader, looser mode of operation, disappointing Congreve by dissipating his energies so widely. The annual summer school he began in Edinburgh in 1887, which Branford claimed 'might almost be called a Positivist School' (*PR* I (1893) 218), developed in 1892 into the Outlook Tower, whose many activities he later described as an indirect form of Positivist propaganda (Branford to Paul Edger, 22/1/29, MAC). He continued to visit and address the Positivist Society until the end of his life, speaking at Chapel Street as late as July 1931. Men like Ingram urged him to align himself unequivocally with them (GS 3: 12/5, ff.1–2) but as he explained in a long letter to Swinny which was published in the *Positivist Review* as 'A Current Criticism of the Positivist School', they had become too traditional and conservative, displaying 'a real dislike of scientific research'. Their only hope was for working scientists such as Desch to revive and restate Comte's synthesis (*PR* XXIX (1921) 145–7). An even longer letter of 1922, asking Swinny what had been written on that 'master-key for Sociology', the law of the three states, beyond 'mere repetitions and popularisations', placed himself on the side of 'the more complete Positivists' who had passed with Comte away from his 'youthful and Revolutionary severity' to 'the fuller doctrine and teaching' of his later years (NLS 10516, ff.203–13).

Geddes was seen, not only by himself but by some of the more liberal Comtists, as a potential leader of a revived and revised Positivism. He suggested in 1927 that they should establish a permanent institute in Montpellier, which could also be the centre for an international conference of Comte's followers. He assured Gould, who had been a fervent admirer of his from 1880, contributing to the Outlook Tower and looking to him for leadership, that he had never been 'quite satisfied' by the Positivists' 'too simple following of the teaching of their master, himself too incomplete' (10517, f.107). He also urged upon Paul Edger the need to accept new ideas and escape from the Comtist closed circle (22/1 and 12/2/29, MAC). He merited an entry into *The*

Positivist Year Book in 1929 as having 'developed Positivist ideas in new directions' (*PYB* 1929: 93) and his death in 1932 was regarded by Desch as 'a great blow', depriving the Positivists of the one man with the intellect and the energy to bring them up to date (Bod.L. c 268, f.51v).

Geddes' attempt to drag Positivism into the twentieth century is recorded in his voluminous papers, which include charts of thinkers, outlines of western thought from Aristotle to Comte (GS 21: 3/15, f.6) and of sociology from Vico to Comte (NLS 10622, f.174). There are variations on the Comtean hierarchy of the sciences, including one of his first thinking machines, which traces a diagonal ascent from mathematics and logic to physics and chemistry to biology and finally sociology, with interconnections between these and a number of related sciences (Kitchen 1975: 63). There are curves of human progress from barbarian beginnings through slavedom, serfdom and wagedom to the progressive liberation provided by membership of the guild, the city and finally Humanity (NLS 19998, f.13). Geddes reworked the law of the three states into a myriad of different shapes, preserving the Comtean basis of a development from the theological through the metaphysical to the positive, from the military through the political to the industrial. But Comte, as a mathematician, had taken too little account of biological discoveries, new ideas on evolution and psychology, which Geddes represented by three additional stages, the Biotechnic, the Geotechnic and the Ethopolitic, which promised to bring about a future Peacedom to replace the old Wardom (Boardman 1978: 478–80). Geddes seems never to have tired of inventing variations on this particular Comtean theme.

Another central aspect of Positivist thought which Geddes mulled over in diagrammatic form was the function of the four social types, chiefs and people, who comprised the temporal power, and intellectuals and emotionals, who made up the spiritual power. It was among the people, Geddes noted, that Positivism had failed (GS 14: 6/26, f.6). A set of notes on the 'Spiritual and Temporal Power', from September 1888, points to the gap between science and the 'Existing Church', the leap required to create the 'Church of the Future'. His own notion of the 'Strategy of the Spiritual Power' was more flexible and informal than that of the orthodox Positivists. Reformers like Christ, 'whom Comte wrongly excludes', brought about a change through 'undogmatic influence', being necessarily in advance of the existing powers, by whom they were 'martyred today – and worshipped tomorrow'. The true Church was always 'militant in fact' and triumphant only 'in ideal'. Success was poisonous, for there could be no permanent hierarchy, 'no Pontificate and Priesthood of Humanity – but only a society of friends'. The spiritual power was therefore 'constantly nascent', emerging through a cycle in which the 'Philistines' were always challenged and finally converted by a new spiritual leader, becoming 'Children of Light' in a new synthesis which then became fixed in forms which themselves became outdated: the 'Children of Light thus slowly become the New Philistines'. For 'no synthesis can be final' and it was the error of the Church, the Positivists and the Socialists alike to think that it could (11: 1/12).

Geddes certainly took the liturgy and sacraments of the Religion of Humanity seriously enough to make several sketches for a Temple of Humanity, complete with busts, library and cult of the dead (1/1). Another set of notes brings out the 'profound difference in moral temper' between the impersonal Spencerian belief in the Unknowable, characterised by 'a shopkeeper who says the person before left some excellent fittings' but 'poor sanitary arrangements', and the warmer Positivist faith in Humanity, characterised by an old officer telling regimental stories to his successors 'while even wife and daughter listen with a thrill'. Among the features to which Geddes attributes this greater warmth of feeling are the sense of continuity and solidarity with Humanity evident in the Positivists' gratitude to the past, worship of the dead, preservation of family ties, and reverence for women (3/20). Further 'Notes on Ethics' include a number of sketches representing Positivist teaching on order and progress, thought, feeling and action, family, country and humanity, priesthood and cult, altruism and egoism, and the social and the personal (4/9). These notes, fragmentary though they are, indicate the extent to which Geddes' ideas were a reworking of Comte. For 'the eclipse of Positivism by newer and nearer luminaries of science', whether in evolution or psychology, he wrote under the title 'Renaissance of Positivism', was 'not permanent' (1/2).

Notes that survive of Geddes' lectures reveal a similarly critical enthusiasm for Comte, whose educational principles, he claimed, were 'tacitly becoming the method of our schools and universities' (NLS 10615, f.15). The Positivist Calendar, he continued later in the

same series of lectures, was 'much derided' by individuals who refused
to recognise themselves as parts of 'a larger whole' but it represented the
'largest synthesis of the historic past which has yet been attempted'.
This 'vast and glorious construction of Comte' contained some of the
limitations of its creator, who had 'somewhat iron hands and clutches
the human soul in the grasp of its dead ancestors, absolutely repelling
people from the great gifts he has to offer them' (ff.145–7). A lecture
on Comte in a sociology course of 1891 which began by discussing his
life in order to 'disengage . . . those of his doctrines that are valid'
went on to complain of the long neglect and unreasoning hostility to
which his 'anti-theological attitude' and 'attempts at reconstruction'
gave rise and to stress his 'many-sidedness; artistic and poetic, lover
and hierophant, but also a mathematician', a scientist and an historian
(GS 3: 1/1). Two lectures of 1902 on 'Comte's Law of the Three
States' made a similar complaint about the neglect into which he had
fallen (NLS 10616, ff.69–88). It was quite unfair, Geddes insisted at
the Edinburgh Ethical Society in 1905, to dismiss Comte as 'pre-
evolutionary'; he was rather 'the very foremost of evolutionaries . . . in
his vision and hope of the species, in his demands upon it and upon us
as its individuals' (GS 11: 4/9). Geddes gave a lecture on the 'Spiritual
Peerage' in 1909, recommending that presidents of learned societies,
such as Frederic Harrison, should be made life peers (NLS 19270,
ff.30–2); another on 'Comteanism' in Bombay in the 1920s, attacking
the Positivists for sticking too much to the 'Book' rather than developing their master's ideas through further research (19271, ff.177–9);
and three more in 1927, insisting upon Comte's importance in spite of
the failure of his followers (10616, f.89ff).

The completion and reinterpretation of Comte's preliminary synthesis, for which Geddes called in some additional notes on 'Positivism' (GS 3: 4/14), was a task beyond the powers of any individual.
His own energies were dispersed in an amazing variety of activities
from town planning to the production of pageants and masques,
dramatic illustrations of human progress. 'The Masque of Learning',
originally devised as a celebration of fifty years of University Hall,
Edinburgh, in 1912, was transferred to London the following year.
After a prologue in which a professor explains the contents of a
schoolboy's bag, the history of mankind unfolds from a primitive
family gathered round the first Promethean fire through various
phases of ancient, medieval and modern civilisation until the final

enthronement of Alma Mater, the goddess of the city, during which Prometheus passes on the torch of learning to the hands of Hope. The London cast numbered about five hundred, including a group from the Positivist Society, with Geddes, who played the part of Galileo, moving among them during rehearsal like a sheepdog (Defries 1927: 45–7). Henry Ellis complained that Comte, who was its inspiration, received only one mention (GS 9: 1131) but Geddes, who addressed the Positivists on the subject at Essex Hall, made no secret of 'how closely the scheme follows Comte's theory of the intellectual development of medieval and modern civilisation, as explained in the New Calendar of Great Men' (*PR* XXI (1913) 69). An extended version of the masque published in Bombay in 1923 included an open acknowledgement of the deep 'indebtedness to the founder of sociology' evident here and in 'the writer's sociological teaching during many years past' (Geddes 1923: ii–iii).

Geddes' work as a sociologist can certainly be seen as an elucidation and development of Comte in the light of Darwin and Le Play. These three thinkers, he argued in 1910, should be the major influence on the future development of the Sociological Society, especially

Comte, with his concrete historical knowledge, and his interpretations of this heritage as phases of a great evolution, a great transition from the old order before the political and industrial revolution, towards a nobler and more concrete utopia than that revolution has ever seen.   (Kitchen 1975: 236)

He may have lacked that essential 'first-hand observation of the city and community', Geddes admitted to the society in 1904 (*Soc.R* I (1904) 59) but the distinction between the temporal and spiritual powers, he reminded them the following year, was of crucial importance (II (1905) 279). Faced in 1912 with a world on the brink of disaster, Geddes and Branford drew strongly upon Comtean concepts for their programme of Renewal, Re-education and Reconstruction. Their manifesto, 'What to Do', stressed the need to develop a spiritual power independent of the state through a stronger sense of 'the history and culture of mankind at large' (Kitchen 1975: 331–3). An article by Geddes on 'Wardom and Peacedom' in 1915 called for a Comtean analysis of the causes of war in terms of the four categories which comprised the spiritual and temporal powers (*Soc.R* VIII (1915) 15–25). In *The Coming Polity*, the first of a series called *The Making of the Future*, Geddes and Branford complained bitterly of the neglect of Comte even in Paris, describing the *Système* as 'a matchless monument of social idealism . . . an immense cairn of stones, sometimes rough-hewn, from which future generations will continue to quarry building materials' (Geddes and Branford 1917: 52–3). *Our Social Inheritance*, while paying tribute to the 'long and gallant efforts of the small English Positivist Society and its *Review* of that name', claimed that 'Comte's fertile impulse has ranged far beyond his immediate followers' (Geddes and Branford 1919: 338–40). Geddes continued to apply the law of the three states to the social and political problems of Britain as late as 1929 (*Soc.R* XXI (1929) 89–124).

Geddes' correspondence with Branford indicates the extent to which he saw their work as a fulfilment and development of the Religion of Humanity. He defended Comte against the attacks of psychologists and political economists in 1911 (NLS 10556, f.237) and saw the failure of sociology in general to have more influence as bound up with the virtual 'eclipse of Comte's teaching', once more blaming the Positivists for being 'too simply expository and discipular' and for failing to develop the 'gigantic aim and opus of the master' whose works should not only be re-read but revised (10557, ff.156–61). 'Mis-readers' of Comte as an 'iconoclast of religion', he commented on Branford's *Science and Sanctity* the following year, ignored his 'characteristic saying . . . that "man is ever growing more religious" ' (10560, f.74). 'May we not with advantage turn back to Comte even more definitely than we are doing in our series?' he asked in 1929, fleshing out the over-mathematical and physical law of the three states with biological, psychological, evolutionary and idealistic developments through which Comte himself had passed in his later years: 'We thus escape the bitterness of the young Comte's rationalistic negations' and 'defend the Religion of Humanity also' (10559, f.14).

Branford was equally enthusiastic about Comte, the 'fertilising and formative power' of whose central hypotheses of human development and spiritual organisation he acknowledged at the Sociological Society in 1904, even if they were more a matter for 'laborious investigation' rather than 'dogmatic utterance' (*Soc.P* I (1905) 25–42). *Science and Sanctity* criticises Comte for drawing too much from outdated books instead of inductive research of the kind conducted by the complementary tradition of Le Play (Branford 1923: 90–3). But it ends with a restatement of the Comtean aim, a synthesis of the 'extant body of verified knowledge' with the religious and 'humanist tradition' maintained by an 'apostolic succession of saintly and heroic types', and the integration of the individual with his family, neighbourhood, city, region, nation and civilisation, all of which comprised, in the final words of the book, the 'Great Organ of Humanity' (239–53). *Living Religions*, subtitled 'A Plea for the Larger Modernism', also celebrates 'the march of humanity' to be displayed in historic pageants, calling for 'a renovated spiritual power', a new synthesis of facts and ideals, 'a New Mysticism that is both naturalist and humanist' (Branford 1924: xi, 245–84). Some of the language has changed but the message is basically the same.

Branford was certainly seen as sympathetic enough for the Positivists to invite him to address them in 1919 and 1920. A number of articles in the *Sociological Review* in the last two years of his life developed his attitude towards Comte and religion still further. 'Liturgies are not made, or remade, in a day', he argued; they are natural, organic growths, 'the flowering and fruiting of humanity' (*Soc.R* XX (1928) 1–2). The Blessed Virgin Mary remained a 'source of inspiration', for example, because she continued to act as a 'model of Motherhood' and source of hope (125). Comte's 'magistral labours' and 'constructive genius' were valuable because they contributed to an understanding of such natural processes (122, 331). His synthesis may have been 'premature' but it had been 'inadequately quarried by the body of sociologists' (XXII (1930) 201), apart from Geddes, of course, who was not only a 'continuator' of the Comte–Le Play tradition but also a 're-initiator', interpreting and developing their ideas (195).

Another sociologist sympathetic to the Religion of Humanity was Lewis Mumford, who had been a pupil of Geddes, but his many volumes on the past, present and future condition of mankind breathe a spirit of humanitarian concern too general to be labelled Positivist. Leonard Hobhouse, Professor of Sociology at London University, spoke at the commemoration of Comte in Essex Hall in 1907 and aligned himself with Geddes and Branford in defence of the founder of sociology during the heated discussion of the subject at the Sociological Society that year (*PR* XV (1907) 262, 282). His enthusiastic account of 'The Law of the Three States' in the first volume of the *Sociological Review* claimed that the 'general notions' on which it rested had 'passed into ordinary thought and common language' (*Soc.R* I (1908) 262). The *Sociological Review*, in fact, could be seen as an alternative *Positivist Review*, more liberal in its interpretation of the master but working on similar lines towards similar ends. Many of the Positivists were regular contributors, especially Swinny, whose 'hand was in every number' until his death in 1923 (XV (1923) 274). There were, of course, sociologists such as Graham Wallas, who disliked Comte's large monistic theories. But the tone of critical sympathy which is perhaps most characteristic of the journal was encapsulated in an article on 'The Present Position of Positivism' by James Oliphant in 1909, which argued that Positivism had so successfully permeated the prevailing currents of thought as to make its continuation as a 'distinctive faith' and 'separatist organisation' redundant (II (1909) 179–80). All the pioneers of British sociology have been called Positivist in the general sense that it was largely in reaction to Comte that they developed their own conceptions of the subject (Abrams 1968: 57).

A general but pervasive Comtean influence has also been detected among the various socialist groups which emerged towards the end of the nineteenth century. Charles Booth learnt much about Comte from his relatives, the Cromptons (PR XXVII (1919) 63–7). Belfort Bax attended the Positivist Society in the 1870s before distancing himself in the following decade from its 'moralisation of capital' and 'travesty of Christian rites' (R. Harrison 1965: 335). Many of the Fabians also attended either Chapel Street or Newton Hall in their youth and retained Comte's belief in science and dislike of classical economics long after they had abandoned his politics and religion. Sydney Olivier, tutor to Henry Crompton's son, continued to complain about ignorant critics of Comte from the 1880s to the 1940s (Olivier 1948: 55, 180). Sidney Webb spoke so favourably to the Fabian Society on 'The Economics of a Positivist Community' in January 1886 that he was forced to deny that he belonged to one (McBriar 1962: 14). But for the Fabians Positivism proved only a transitional stage between liberalism and socialism. They adopted some of Comte's ideas, especially the notion of altruistic service of the state, and also the Positivist tactic of laying their political eggs in other people's nests, working, that is, through existing organisations to achieve the reforms they desired (MacKenzie: 1977: 60–2).

Beatrice Webb, who attributed her interest in the Religion of Humanity partly to her reading of George Eliot, Lewes and Mill and partly to her friendship with Frederic Harrison, ordered all the works of Comte from the London Library and discussed them with her sister on the Westmorland Moors. Margaret thought the Positivists too servile but Beatrice, with her evangelical temperament, scientific interests and social ardour, found them more sympathetic (B. Webb 1926: 142–50). She copied passages from the *Catechism* into her diary and told her father how 'immensely interested' she was in the Positive philosophy (MacKenzie 1978: I 28). But her doubts about the Religion of Humanity were confirmed by a sermon of Harrison's in 1889:

> The whole address seemed to me *forced* – a valiant effort to make a religion out of nothing, a pitiful attempt by poor Humanity to turn its head round to worship its tail. Practically we are all Positivists; we all make the service of Man the leading doctrine of our lives. But in order to serve Humanity we need the support and encouragement of a superhuman force above us to which we are perpetually striving. (MacKenzie 1982: I 276)

She allowed Sidney Webb, however, to worship her and to take her for his Clotilde (MacKenzie 1978: I 155, 244). They may even have modelled their role as enlightened leaders of opinion upon Comte's priesthood (II ix). Disillusioned with the politics of gradualism they were later to find in Soviet Communism, with its articulate ideology, its sense of purpose and its clear 'code of conduct', genuine affinities with 'the religion of humanity' (III 406).

A number of other academics maintained some kind of contact with the Positivists. Percy Harding, a Professor of Mathematics at University College London, became a Positivist after five years' study of the system and used occasionally to lecture at Newton Hall, as did C. H. Herford, Professor of English Literature at Manchester University. He became President of the Manchester Positivist Society and continued to lecture on Positivist topics both in London and in Liverpool into the 1920s. His contributions to the *Positivist Review*, whose editorship he declined in 1923, tended to underplay its difference from contemporary culture in general. Malcolm Quin continued to urge both Herford and A. J. Grant, Professor of History at Leeds University, to involve themselves more closely in the movement. Grant's *Outlines of European History* was welcomed by Marvin as offering 'abundant evidence' of Comte's influence (*PR* XV (1907) 108–12) but the historian himself grew increasingly out of sympathy with Positivism as a sectarian organisation rather than a set of ideas.

Perhaps the best known of the professed sympathisers with

Positivism was Gilbert Murray, who was introduced to Comte by his schoolfriend, Marvin, and taken to worship at Chapel Street by his aunt Fanny. 'I never became a Positivist', he recalled, but found in Comte's system a liberation from superstition and a justification for morality (Murray 1960: 83). He was a member of the Comte Society founded by Marvin at Oxford, whose members did not have to be Positivists but students of Comte. When Marvin sent the young Professor of Greek at Glasgow a copy of the *Positivist Review*, however, Murray assured him that there was little 'chance of my becoming a professed Positivist'. He appreciated Marvin's own essay on the dead, however, seeing 'the value of having such subjects religiously and frankly treated by thinkers who are free from superstition', and promised to take the review on a regular basis (Bod.L. e 110, f.56). Beesly urged him in 1900 to make the 'occasional contribution' himself, even offering to append a note to the effect that such participation did not entail acceptance of all their doctrines (MP 7, ff.94–5). But Murray needed no such note since his infrequent contributions tended not to mention Comte and even praised *The Living Past* for successfully masking its author's Comtist convictions (*PR* xx (1913) 199). Marvin, on the contrary, exaggerated Murray's debt to Comte, describing him as 'a passionate friend of Humanity' (xxvi (1918) 133–7). Murray played along with this, promising, for example, to impart 'some good Positivism' into his Gifford lectures on 'Natural Religion' in 1909–10 (Bod.L. d 259, f.84). But his debt to Comte emerges only in general principles.

The Positivists, of course, tried to pin Murray down, Swinny praised his lecture on 'Stoicism' at South Place in 1915, apart from the 'little dash of vague Theism at the very end' (e 263, f.39), while Henry Ellis craved 'a rather more distinct statement as to what his own actual belief is' (*PR* xxiii (1915) 161). Harrison disputed his claim at the Classical Association in 1918 that to read ancient poetry was in itself religion (MP 37, f.116). But Murray's lecture on 'What is Permanent in Positivism' at the Ethical Church in Bayswater in 1939 made his position quite clear. He began by paying tribute to Comte as 'a very great figure in the history of thought' whose 'main doctrines' had achieved 'general acceptance' and concluded,

I cannot but feel, as did Mill, Morley, George Eliot, Spencer, as well as Bridges, Beesly, and Harrison, first, that his system forms a wonderful achievement of sincere and constructive thinking, and, secondly, that the thing he is trying to say, if only he could succeed in saying it, is not only sublime but true. (Murray 1940: 153–4, 189)

He continued to reserve a greater place for man's sense of mystery than Comte had allowed but also to take an interest in such events as the first International Congress on Humanism and Culture in Amsterdam in 1952, of which he was a vice-president. In men like Murray the main aims of the Religion of Humanity, even though they required reformulation, can be seen to have survived the death of Positivism as an organised movement.

7

THE DEATH OF POSITIVISM:
POST-MORTEM

In one sense, then, Positivism did not die but experienced a form of subjective immortality or assimilation. Its ideas lived on in the minds of others – readers of George Eliot, for example – often without their knowing it. The last number of the *Philosophie positive* argued that it had achieved its purpose by bringing Comte's ideas firmly into the mainstream of modern thought (*PP* XXXI (1883) 458). This, the last ploy left to a dying movement, was used by the Secularists as well. The last issue of the *National Reformer* disputed the notion that ideas could 'get in the air' except by someone 'putting them there' (Royle 1980: 330). This book should have given some indication of how such a process takes place, not only through conscious propaganda, controversy and critical discussion but also through unconscious literary dissemination. Lévy-Bruhl insisted by the end of the century that the positive spirit was as pervasive as the air (*RDM* (15/1/98) 398). These claims have been echoed by more recent sympathisers, one of whom went so far as to credit Comte with providing 'the ground of morality of the majority of people in the mid-twentieth century' (R. Fletcher 1971: I 183). Even those unsympathetic to his ideas have been tempted to focus their attack on scientism, historicism and collectivism in general upon the 'system of thought which . . . the whole world has taken over from Comte' (Hayek 1952: 140). The widespread impact of Positivism on Britain which has been the subject of this book gives some substance to these claims, exaggerated though they may be.

Any modern discussion of the possibility of establishing a non-metaphysical humanist religion, for instance, has to take into account what the editor of the *Humanist* called 'Comte's brave attempt to found a Religion of Humanity and its unfortunate failure' (*Humanist* (1961) 323). The controversy which ensued over Julian Huxley's attempt to resurrect the notion of *Religion Without Revelation* split into the same camps as those earlier arguments involving his grandfather, who was quoted by some of the hard-liners opposed to all forms of sentimental optimism ((1962) 57–8). 'No Ritual, Please' was the caption for one letter, 'No Humanist Pope' another (124). More recent humanists have been more aware of the difficulties and dangers of founding a new religion. The humanist, Ronald Hepburn admits, 'lacks an adequate and appropriate object of reverence and awe'. A concept such as Humanity runs the risk of simplifying or personifying the evolutionary process, forgetting about its wastefulness and its dead ends. Humanist liturgy too is difficult to create because religious language is 'embarrassingly over-rich in metaphysical meanings and associations'. In spite of these difficulties he hopes for the survival of 'ways of seeing humanity, transfigurations of the supposedly familiar world, which . . . can haunt and trouble and goad the imagination' (Blackham 1963: 29–54). Comte's claims have been significantly reduced and his holistic tendencies averted but the temperamental needs which his system was designed to meet linger on.

There was, however, something very Victorian about the Religion of Humanity, its attitudes to morality, freedom and mystery in particular, which contributed to the suddenness of its decline. Human nature itself seems to have changed, whether or not it was in December 1910, as Virginia Woolf claimed. Her father was 'the most typical of Victorians' in his respect for Comte as well as his worship of women and rigid moral code, from all of which she was eager to escape (VW 1978: 125). Austin Harrison showed a similar distaste for his father's puritanical ethics, finding a key to Positivism's failure in its frigid attitude to sex (A. Harrison 1926: 209). Even Freud talked in terms of the development of altruistic love from instincts which were initially egoistic but his complaints about the 'ideal' of the family demanded by society were directed against an earlier generation of which Comte was representative (Freud 1973: I 240–2). Some would place the change in attitudes earlier, at 1890, up to which point everything was 'subordinated to morality' (Cockshut 1964: 181). What is indisputable is that such a change occurred.

It was not just in sexual morality that later generations demanded more freedom. All religious institutions seem to have declined from the 1880s, even Secularism, which reached its peak with the defeat of the Affirmation Bill but then quickly fell away. The Religion of Humanity can be seen to have suffered from a general decline in all forms of church attendance (Chadwick 1975: 91–2). Those who continued to worship, however, wanted something more exciting than what was on offer at Chapel Street and Newton Hall, whose want of ecstasy 'chilled the women' (A. Harrison 1926: 167). A sense of mystery, of areas of experience beyond the explanations of scientific rationalism, finding expression in such disparate areas as the Russian novel, impressionist painting, late Wagner and Nietzsche, rebelled against the limitations which Positivism imposed (Chadwick 1975: 239–49). One of the reasons why the *Morning Post* felt Positivism had been rejected was its failure to 'stir the emotions' (*MP* 5/12/07). Again, however, this does not seem to have been true of an earlier generation of more earnest Victorians.

Perhaps the biggest problem that Positivism failed to solve was that of death and the demand for personal immortality. The vogue for claiming death-bed conversions of prominent Positivists from Bridges to Gissing continued with von Hügel, who began his *Essays and Addresses* with the dramatic story of such a volte-face by an anonymous 'Positivist of European renown' faced with his own imminent extinction (Hügel 1921: 3–4). Canon Henry Lewis found a similar inadequacy on the part of many Victorian agnostics to cope with this final fact of human experience (Lewis 1913: 383–404). It is a problem that modern humanists have to face and against which they need to posit the eternal value of human experience (Blackham 1963: 105–27). Comte's own solution, as Balfour pointed out and as George Eliot discovered, left a great deal to be desired. Positivism was never a very hopeful creed and many of its followers seem to have suffered from severe depression. This has no bearing on its truth, of course, but may help to explain its decline.

A number of other reasons have been posited for the rapid demise of the Religion of Humanity, that it was too French, too Roman Catholic and, most importantly, too difficult. It was, according to the *Saturday Review*, too esoteric and too high-minded. For ordinary people in the twentieth century are 'less disposed than ever for the worship of humanity' now that they know themselves to be descended from monkeys (*SR* CIV (30/11/07) 672). Austin Harrison felt that there were 'too many long words to get keen about' (A. Harrison 1926: 166). It was certainly difficult to become a Positivist, requiring years of patient and laborious study. Comtism could therefore be seen as elitist, although it went out of its way to give a free education to working people. It did not help, of course, that the science it offered was often out of date. Such has been the speed of scientific advance that no synthesis of human knowledge could have lasted very long. A modern equivalent of the *Cours* is inconceivable; no single mind could comprehend let alone compile it.

Positivism has also been seen as synthetic in the worst sense, bringing together too many ideas too quickly to form an artificial system lacking the resonance of religions which have grown up historically, evolving a tradition over centuries. W. E. Orchard claimed it was the only religion apart from Christianity which was 'worth a moment's consideration', only it remained too abstract, lacking the focus for faith provided by the Incarnation (Orchard 1918: 17–23). Raymond Aron, who also thought the Religion of Humanity 'not so absurd as is generally believed', argued that 'history failed Auguste Comte' by disproving his belief that war was a thing of the past. The Great War disillusioned his disciples and left his optimism about human nature open to ridicule (Aron 1965b: I 104, 73–4). The Religion of Humanity, as we have seen, came in for more than its fair share of abuse, not just because of its mistaken prophecies and idiosyncratic details but because of its apparent arrogance in attempting to replace existing religions.

But someone had to have that arrogance and that courage if the many suggestions for the reconstruction of society on the basis of scientific knowledge and humanist values were to be made specific. The most positive contribution Comte made to this debate was to provide a complete coherent system for others to discuss. It is the function of such systems for others 'to sharpen their teeth on them' (Simon 1963: 271). Philosophers such as Mill and Lewes, theologians such as Caird and Westcott, the many historians, scientists, critics and men of letters who have been the subject of this book, and, most important of all, novelists such as George Eliot, Thomas Hardy and George Gissing, all contributed to this critical process. Because of them the impact of Comtean Positivism on Victorian Britain can be said to have been considerable.

No-one in his right mind, of course, would want to resurrect Comte's religion. No-one in his right mind, as we have seen, invented it. Yet the story of its unfolding, reception, rejection and transformation has not, I hope, been without interest. As is so often the case, to be wrong (and to the extent that Comte failed in his major aim, which was to meet men's religious needs, he was clearly mistaken) is not to be fruitless. Comte and his disciples illustrate what might be called a religious dead end; that way, the reconstruction of an institutional religion on 'scientific' grounds, seems to offer little but loneliness, frustration and despair. For a religion based above all upon utility that is particularly disastrous. Men and women who continue to feel the need for religion, remaining impatient with the slowness with which the Christian churches have adapted to the philosophical, critical and scientific advances of the last two centuries and yet dissatisfied by a life entirely secular, devoid of ultimate significance, must seek elsewhere for fulfilment. Perhaps the future, as many critics of Comte and even some of his followers came to believe, does lie with a reformed and more self-critical Christianity, incorporating within itself, as it always has, the best of all other philosophies. Religion, Comte showed, does not have to be wedded to metaphysics. Worship can be aware of the 'subjective' nature of its object, the extent to which it is a construct of human perception and therefore, necessarily, of human imagination. These are lessons humanity can learn from Comte's religion. Whether it will is another story which has yet to be told.

BIBLIOGRAPHY

Note: Place of publication is London unless otherwise stated

Abbott, Evelyn and Campbell, Lewis, eds. (1897). *Life and Letters of Benjamin Jowett*, 2 vols.

——— (1899). *Letters of Benjamin Jowett*

Abrams, Philip (1968). *The Origins of British Sociology: 1834–1914*

Acton, H. B. (1951). 'Comte's Positivism and the Science of Society', *Philosophy* XXVI 291–310

——— (1962) [1955]. *The Illusion of the Epoch: Marxism – Leninism as a Philosophical Creed*

——— (1974). *The Idea of a Spiritual Power*

Adam, Ian, ed. (1975). *This Particular Web: Essays on 'Middlemarch'*, Toronto

Adams, W. Davenport, ed. (nd). *Comic Poets of the Nineteenth Century*

Adams, W. E. (1903). *Memories of a Social Atom*, 2 vols.

Alexander, Edward (1965). *Matthew Arnold and John Stuart Mill*

Allott, Miriam (1961). 'George Eliot in the 1860's', *VS* V 93–108

Altholz, Josef L. (1962). *The Liberal Catholic Movement in England: 'The Rambler' and its Contributors, 1848–1864*

——— (1977). 'Periodical Origins and Implications of 'Essays and Reviews'', *VPN* X 40–54

Altholz, Josef L. and McElreth, Damian, eds. (1971–5). *The Correspondence of Lord Acton and Richard Simpson*, 3 vols., Cambridge

Altick, Richard D. (1973). *Victorian People and Ideas*

Ames, Percy W. (1895). 'Positivism in Literature', *Transactions of the Royal Society of Literature of the U.K.* XV 79–121

Andreski, Stanislav (1974). 'Auguste Comte's Place in the History of Sociology', *The Human World* XIV 5–14

——— (1974). *The Essential Comte*

Annan, Noel (1949). 'The Strands of Unbelief', *Grisewood* (1949) 150–6

——— (1951). *Leslie Stephen*

——— (1959). *The Curious Strength of Positivism in English Political Thought*, Oxford

——— (1960). 'Kipling's Place in the History of Ideas', *VS* III 323–48

——— (1984). *Leslie Stephen: The Godless Victorian*

Aquarone, Stanislas (1958). *The Life and Works of Emile Littré, 1801–1881*, Leyden

Bibliography

Arbousse-Bastide, P. (1957). *La Doctrine d'education dans la philosophie d'Auguste Comte*, 2 vols., Paris

(1968). *Auguste Comte*, Paris

Arnaud, Pierre (1965). *Politique d'Auguste Comte*, Paris

(1969). *Sociologie d'Auguste Comte*, Paris

(1973). *Le 'Nouveau Dieu'*, Paris

Arnold, Matthew (*CPW*). *The Complete Prose Works of Matthew Arnold*, ed. R. H. Super, 11 vols., 1965–77, Ann Arbor

Aron, Raymond (1958). *War and Industrial Society*, trans. Mary Bottomore

(1965a). *Auguste Comte et Alexis de Tocqueville: Juges d'Angleterre*, Oxford

(1965b, 1968). *Main Currents in Sociological Thought*, trans. Richard Howard and Helen Weaver, 2 vols.

Ashton, Rosemary D. (1979). 'The Intellectual "Medium" of "Middlemarch" ', *RES* XXX 154–68

(1980). *The German Idea: Four English Writers and the Reception of German Thought*, Cambridge

Aubyn, Giles St (1958). *A Victorian Eminence: The Life and Works of Henry Thomas Buckle*

August, Eugene (1975). *John Stuart Mill: A Mind at Large*

Ayer, A. J. (1964). *Man as a Subject for Science*

Baier, Otto (1928). *God in the Modern World. An Affirmation*, Liverpool

(1930). *An Address in Memory of the Life and Work of Sydney Style, Apostle of Humanity*, Liverpool

(1938). *An Address in Memory of the Life and Work of Jane May Style*, Liverpool

Bain, Alexander (1882). *John Stuart Mill*

(1904). *Autobiography*

Baker, William (1973). 'The Kabbalah, Mordecai and George Eliot's Religion of Humanity', *YES* III 216–21

(1975). *George Eliot and Judaism*, Salzburg

(1976–85). *Some George Eliot Notebooks: An Edition of the Carl H. Pforzheimer Library's George Eliot Holograph Notebooks, MSS 707–11*, 4 vols., Salzburg

Balfour, A. J. (1895). *The Foundations of Belief*

(1915). *Theism and Humanism*

Balfour, Betty, ed. (1906). *Personal and Literary Letters of Robert First Earl of Lytton*, 2 vols.

Barnes, H. E. B., ed. (1948). *An Introduction to the History of Sociology*

Barton, F. B. (1867). *An Outline of the Positive Religion of Humanity*

Baumer, Franklin L. (1960). *Religion and the Rise of Scepticism*, New York

(1977). *Modern European Thought: Continuity and Change in Ideas, 1600–1950*

Beaty, Jerome (1957). 'George Eliot's Notebook for an Unwritten Novel', *Princeton University Library Chronicle* XVIII 174–82

(1960). *'Middlemarch' from Notebook to Novel: A Study of George Eliot's Creative Method*, Urbana

Bibliography

Beer, Gillian (1983). *Darwin's Plots: Evolutionary Narrative in Darwin, George Eliot and Nineteenth-Century Fiction*
Beesly, Edmund Spencer (1869). *The Social Future of the Working Class*
(1870). *Letters to the Working Classes*
(1881). *Some Public Aspects of Positivism*
(1886). *Home Rule*
(1888a). *Positivism Before the Church Congress*
(1888b). *Comte as a Moral Type*
(1888c). *The Life and Death of William Frey*
Beesly, Edmund Spencer, ed. (1866). *International Policy: Essays on the Foreign Relations of England*
Benn, A. W. (1912). *History of Modern Philosophy*
Bennett, Joan (1948). *George Eliot: Her Mind and Her Art*, Cambridge
Bergonzi, Bernard (1968). 'Introduction' to George Gissing's *New Grub Street*, [1891] Harmondsworth
Berlin, Isaiah (1967) [1953]. *The Hedgehog and the Fox: An Essay on Tolstoy's View of History*
(1954). *Historical Inevitability*
Betham-Edwards, Matilda (1898). *Reminiscences*
(1919). *Mid-Victorian Memories*
Bettany, F. G. (1926). *Stewart Headlam: A Biography*
Bevington, M. M. (1966). *The Saturday Review, 1858–1868*, New York
Bibby, Cyril (1959). *T. H. Huxley: Scientist, Humanist and Educator*
Billingham, James H. (1960). 'The Intelligentsia and the Religion of Humanity', *AHR* LXV 807–21
Biswas, Robindra Kumar (1972). *Arthur Hugh Clough*, Oxford
Björk, Lennart, ed. (1974). *The Literary Notes of Thomas Hardy*, 2 vols., Goteborg
Blackham, H. J. (1976) [1968]. *Humanism*, Guildford
Blackham, H. J., ed. (1963). *Objections to Humanism*
Boardman, Philip (1978). *The Worlds of Patrick Geddes*
Bockett, F. W. (1886). *The Workman's Life: What it is, and What it might be*
Bonaparte, Felicia (1975). *Will and Destiny: Morality and Tragedy in George Eliot's Novels*, New York
(1979). *The Triptych and the Cross: The Central Myths of George Eliot's Imagination*, New York
Bonner, Hypatia Bradlaugh (1894). *Charles Bradlaugh: A Record of His Life and Work*, 2 vols.
Bosanquet, Theodora (1927). *Harriet Martineau: An Essay in Comprehension*
Bourlhonne, P. (1933). *George Eliot: Essai de biographie intellectuelle et morale, 1819–1854*, Paris
Bowen, Desmond (1968). *The Idea of the Victorian Church: A Study of the Church of England, 1833–1889*, Montreal
Bowra, Cecil Maurice (1966). *Memories 1898–1939*

Bibliography

Branford, Victor (1923). *Science and Sanctity*

    (1924). *Living Religions*

Bray, Charles (1863). *The Philosophy of Necessity*, 2 vols., 2nd edn

Bridges, John Henry (1865). *The Unity of Comte's Life and Doctrine*

    (1882). *Five Discourses on Positive Religion*

    (1883). *Comte: The Successor of Aristotle and St Paul*

    (1885). *Positivism and the Bible*

    (1907a). *Essays and Addresses*

    (1907b). *Illustrations of Positivism*

Bridges, M. A., ed. (1908). *Recollections of John Henry Bridges*

Briggs, Asa and Saville, John, eds. (1967). *Essays in Labour History*

Brodrick, George Charles (1900). *Memories and Impressions, 1831–1900*

Brose, Olive (1960). 'F. D. Maurice and the Victorian Crisis of Belief', *VS* III 227–48

Brown, Alan Willard (1947). *The Metaphysical Society: Victorian Minds in Crisis, 1869–1880*, New York

Brown, E. K. (1935). *Studies in the Text of Matthew Arnold's Prose Works*, Paris

Buchanan, Robert (1874). *Poetical Works*, 3 vols.

Buckle, Henry Thomas (1857, 1861). *History of Civilization in England*, 2 vols.

    (1872). *Miscellaneous and Posthumous Works*, ed. Helen Taylor, 3 vols.

Budd, Susan (1977). *Varieties of Unbelief: Atheists and Agnostics in English Society, 1850–1960*

Bullen, J. B. (1975). 'George Eliot's "Romola" as a Positivist Allegory', *RES* XXVI 425–35

Burrow, J. W. (1963). 'Evolution and Anthropology in the 1860's: The Anthropological Society of London, 1863–71', *VS* VII 137–54

    (1966). *Evolution and Society: A Study in Victorian Social Theory*, Cambridge

Bury, J. B. (1921). *The Idea of Progress*

Caird, Edward (1885). *The Social Philosophy and Religion of Comte*, Glasgow

    (1892). *Essays on Literature and Philosophy*, 2 vols., Glasgow

    (1893). *The Evolution of Religion*, 2 vols., Glasgow

Call, W. M. W. (1875). *Reverberations*

Cannon, Walter F. (1964). 'The Normative Role of Science in Early Victorian Thought', *JHI* XXV 487–502

Carr, Robert (1962). 'The Religious Thought of John Stuart Mill: A Study in Reluctant Scepticism', *JHI* XXIII 475–95

Carroll, David (1971). *George Eliot: The Critical Heritage*

Carson, Thomas (1894). *Some Selected Thoughts from his Letters and Other Writings*, Liverpool

    (1908). *The Message of Humanity*, Liverpool

Carson, Thomas, ed. (1886). *Some Sentiments of our South American Brethren*, Liverpool

Carver, Marcella M. (1976). *A Positivist Life: A Personal Memoir of My Father, William Knight (1845–1901)*

Bibliography

Cazamian, M. L. (1923). *Le Roman et les idées en Angleterre: L'Influence de la Science (1860–1890)*, Strasbourg

Chadwick, Owen (1966, 1970). *The Victorian Church*, 2 vols.

(1975). *The Secularization of the European Mind in the Nineteenth Century,* Cambridge

Chapman, Elizabeth Rachel (1886). *A Comtist Lover and Other Stories*

Chapman, Raymond (1968). *The Victorian Debate: English Literature and Society, 1832–1901*

Charlton, D. G. (1959). *Positivist Thought in France during the Second Empire, 1852–1870,* Oxford

(1962). 'New Creeds for Old in Nineteenth-Century France', *Canadian Journal of Theology* VIII 258–69

(1963). *Secular Religions in France, 1815–1870*

Clagett, Marshall, ed. (1959). *Critical Problems in the History of Science,* Madison

Clark, G. Kitson (1973). *Churchmen and the Condition of England, 1832–1885*

Clarke, M. L. (1962). *George Grote: A Biography*

Clive, John (1958). 'More or Less Eminent Victorians: Some Trends in Victorian Biography', *VS* II 5–28

Clodd, Edward (1916). *Memories*

Cockshut, A. O. J. (1959). *Anglican Attitudes: A Study of Victorian Religious Controversies*

(1964). *The Unbelievers: English Agnostic Thought, 1840–1900*

Cohen, Victor (1959). 'Auguste Comte', *CR* CVC 360–3

Cole, G. D. H. (1953). *A History of Socialist Thought*, 2 vols.

Collingwood, R. G. (1946). *The Idea of History,* Oxford

Collins, K. K. (1978). 'G. H. Lewes Revised: George Eliot and the Moral Sense', *VS* XXI 463–92

Comte, Auguste *(Appeal)*. *Appeal to Conservatives,* trans. R. Donkin and R. Congreve, 1889 [Paris, 1855]

(Cat). *The Catechism of Positive Religion,* trans. Richard Congreve, 1858 [Paris, 1852]

(CG). *Correspondance générale et confessions,* ed. Paulo E. de Berrêdo Carneiro, 4 vols., 1973–81, Paris

(CI). *Correspondance inédite d'Auguste Comte,* 4 vols., Paris, 1901–4

(Circ). *The Eight Circulars of Auguste Comte,* trans S. Lobb and others, 1882

(Con). *Confessions and Testament of Auguste Comte and His Correspondence with Clotilde de Vaux,* trans. A. Crompton, Liverpool, 1910 [Paris, 1884]

(Cours). *Cours de philosophie positive,* 6 vols., Paris, 1830–42

(Crisis). *The Crisis of Industrial Civilization,* ed. Ronald Fletcher, 1974

(Disc). *A Discourse on the Positive Spirit,* trans. E. S. Beesly, 1903 [Paris, 1844]

(Essays). *Early Essays on Social Philosophy,* trans. Henry Dix Hutton, 1877

(LC). *Lettres d'Auguste Comte à Richard Congreve,* 1889

Bibliography

(*LD*). *Lettres d'Auguste Comte à divers*, 3 vols., Paris, 1902–5

(*LE*). *Lettres d'Auguste Comte à Henry Edger et à John Metcalf*, Paris, 1889

(*Letters*). *Passages from the Letters of Auguste Comte*, trans. John K. Ingram, 1901

(*LH*). *Lettres d'Auguste Comte à Henry Dix Hutton*, Dublin, 1890

(*LPA*). *Lettres d'Auguste Comte à des positivistes anglais*, 1889

(*LV*). *Lettres d'Auguste Comte à Valat*, Paris, 1870

(*Phil*). *The Positive Philosophy of Auguste Comte*, freely translated and condensed by Harriet Martineau, 2 vols., 1853. Subsequent editions 1877 and 1896

(*Pol*). *System of Positive Polity*, trans. J. H. Bridges and others, 4 vols., 1875–7 [Paris, 1851–4]

(*Subj*). *Subjective Synthesis*, trans. R. Congreve, 1891 [Paris, 1856]

Congreve, Richard (*Essays*). *Essays Political, Social and Religious*, 3 vols., 1874, 1892, 1900

(1898). *The Religion of Humanity*

(1900). *Historical Lectures*

Conway, Moncure Daniel (1904). *Autobiography*, 2 vols.

Cooke, G. W. (1883). *George Eliot: A Critical Study of Her Life, Writings and Philosophy*

Copleston, Frederick (1966, 1975). *A History of Philosophy*, vols. VIII and IX

Coser, Lewis A. (1971). *Masters of Sociological Thought: Ideas in Historical and Social Context*, New York

Cotton, H. J. S. (1885–8). *Annual Addresses*, Calcutta

Couch, J. P. (1967). *George Eliot in France: A French Appraisal of George Eliot's Writings*, Chapel Hill

Coustillas, Pierre (1968). 'The Stormy Publication of Gissing's "Veranilda" ', *Bulletin of the New York Public Library* LXXII 588–610

Coustillas, Pierre and Partridge, Colin (1972). *Gissing: The Critical Heritage*

Cowling, Maurice (1963). *Mill and Liberalism*, Cambridge

Cox, C. B. (1963). *The Free Spirit: A Study of Liberal Humanism in the Novels of George Eliot, Henry James, E. M. Forster, Virginia Woolf, Angus Wilson*

Cox, R. G. (1970). *Thomas Hardy: The Critical Heritage*, New York

Crompton, Albert (1890). *An Address in Memory of the Life and Work of Thomas Carson*, Liverpool

Crompton, Albert, ed. (nd). *Auguste Comte and Clotilde de Vaux*, Liverpool

Crompton, Henry (1893). *The Religion of Humanity*

(1899). *The Funeral Sermon in Commemoration of Richard Congreve*

(1900a). *Annual Address*

(1900b). *The Virgin-Mother: The Positivist Ideal of Humanity*

(1901). *Thomas Sulman: A Memorial Sermon*

Darwin, Charles (1958) [1882]. *The Autobiography of Charles Darwin*

Darwin, Francis, ed. (1887). *Life and Letters of Charles Darwin*, 3 vols.

(1903). *More Letters of Charles Darwin*, 2 vols.

Bibliography

Davies, Charles Maurice (1873). *Unorthodox London*
(1874). *Heterodox London*, 2 vols.

Deegan, Thomas F. (1970). 'George Eliot's Historical Thought and Her Novels of the Religious Imagination', Northwestern University Ph.D.

Defries, Amelia (1927). *The Interpreter Geddes*

Delaura, David J. (1967). 'The Ache of Modernism in Hardy's Later Novels', *ELH* XXXIV 380–99

Delaura, David J., ed. (1973). *Victorian Prose: A Guide to Research*, New York

Dodd, V. A. (1975). 'Some Religious and Philosophical Influences upon the Nature of George Eliot's Imagination, with particular reference to Thomas Carlyle and John Stuart Mill', Oxford B. Litt.

Donnelly, Mabel Collins (1954). *George Gissing: Grave Comedian*, Cambridge, Mass.

Drummond, Henry (1899). *The Ascent of Man*

Duff, Mountstuart E. Grant (1897–1901). *Notes from a Diary*, 8 vols.

Duncan, David, ed. (1908). *Life and Letters of Herbert Spencer*

Dunkley, C., ed. (1888). *Official Report of the Church Congress*

Dussauze, Henry (1910). *The Gospel of Maternal Love*, Newcastle

Earnshaw, L. S. (1964). *A Short History of British Psychology*

Eastin, Linda S. (1969). 'George Eliot's Clergymen: The Priesthood of Humanity', Exeter University M.A.

Edel, Leon (1962). *Henry James: The Conquest of London, 1870–1883*
(1972). *Henry James: The Master, 1901–1916*

Eisen, Sydney (1957). 'Frederic Harrison: The Life and Thought of an English Positivist', Johns Hopkins University Ph.D.
(1964). 'Huxley and the Positivists', *VS* VII 337–58
(1967a). 'Frederic Harrison and the Religion of Humanity', *SAQ* LXVI 574–90
(1967b). 'Herbert Spencer and the Spectre of Comte', *JBS* VII 48–67
(1968). 'Frederic Harrison and Herbert Spencer: Embattled Unbelievers', *VS* XII 33–56

Eliot, George (*Essays*). *Essays of George Eliot*, ed. Thomas Pinney, 1963
(*GEL*). *George Eliot Letters*, ed. G. S. Haight, 9 vols., New Haven, 1954 and 1978
(*Life*). *Life of George Eliot*, ed. J. W. Cross, 3 vols, Edinburgh, 1885
(1878–85). *Works of GE*, Cabinet Edition, 24 vols., Edinburgh. Titles are abbreviated as follows: *AB Adam Bede, DD Daniel Deronda, FH Felix Holt, LJ The Legend of Jubal and Other Poems, MF The Mill on the Floss, MM Middlemarch, R Romola, SCL Scenes of Clerical Life, SG The Spanish Gypsy, SM Silas Marner, TS Impressions of Theophrastus Such*

Elliott-Binns, L. E. (1946) [1936]. *Religion in the Victorian Era*
(1952). *The Development of English Theology in the Later Nineteenth Century*
(1956). *English Thought, 1860–1900: The Theological Aspect*

Ellis, A.J. (1880). *Auguste Comte's Religion of Humanity*
(1894). *Discourses Delivered at South Place Chapel*

Bibliography

Ellis, Henry (1884). *The Commemoration of the Dead*

   (1887). *What Positivism Means: A Brief Summary of its Doctrines and Aims*

Emery, Léon (1957). 'De Comte à Marx', *Le Contrat sociale* I 142–8

Evans, Lawrence (1970). *Letters of Walter Pater*, Oxford

Everett, E. M. (1971) [1939]. *The Party of Humanity*, New York

Faber, Geoffrey (1957). *Jowett, a Portrait with a Background*

Fasnacht, G. E. (1952). *Acton's Political Philosophy: An Analysis*

Feltes, N. N. (1968). 'Phrenology: From Lewes to George Eliot', *SLI* I 13–22

Feuerbach, Ludwig (1957) [1854]. *The Essence of Christianity*, trans. George Eliot

Figgis, J. N. and Laurence, R. V., eds. (1917). *Selections from the Correspondence of the First Lord Acton*

Fleay, F. G. (1883). *Three Lectures on Education*

Fletcher, Ian, ed. (1971). *Meredith Now: Some Critical Essays*

Fletcher, Ronald (1966). *Auguste Comte and the Making of Sociology*

   (1971). *The Making of Sociology: A Study of Sociological Theory*, 2 vols.

Flint, Robert (1874). *The Philosophy of History in Europe*

Foote, G. W. (1879). *Secularism: The True Philosophy of Life*

Forbes, Geraldine Hancock (1975). *Positivism in Bengal*, Calcutta

Francis, C. J. (1960). 'Gissing and Schopenhauer', *NCF* XV 53–63

Freud, Sigmund (1973–). *Pelican Freud Library*, ed. Angela Richards, 15 vols.

Frey, William (1888a). *Farewell Address to the London Positivists*

   (1888b). *On Religion*

Geddes, Patrick (1923). *Dramatisations of History*, Bombay

   (1949) [1915]. *Cities in Evolution*

Geddes, Patrick and Branford, Victor (1917). *The Coming Polity: A Study in Reconstruction*

   (1919). *Our Social Inheritance*

Geddes, Patrick and Slater, Gilbert (1917). *Ideas at War*

Geddes, Patrick and Thomson, J. Arthur (1914). *Sex*

Ginsberg, Morris (1947). *Essays in Sociology and Social Philosophy*, 3 vols.

   (1956). *Reason and Experience in Ethics*

Gissing, George (*BE*). *Born in Exile*, Nelson's Library, nd [1892]

   (*CB*). *George Gissing's Commonplace Book*, ed. Jacob Korg, New York, 1962

   (*D*). *Demos*, Brighton, 1972 [1886]

   (*Diary*). *London and the Life of Literature in Late Victorian England: The Diary of George Gissing, Novelist*, ed. Pierre Coustillas, Brighton, 1978

   (*Essays*). *Essays and Fiction*, ed. Pierre Coustillas, 1970

   (*HR*). *The Private Papers of Henry Ryecroft*, 1914 [1903]

   (*IC*). *Isabel Clarendon*, Brighton, 1969 [1886]

   (*LB*). *Letters of George Gissing to Eduard Bertz, 1887–1903*, ed. Arthur C. Young, 1961

   (*LC*). *Letters of George Gissing to Edward Clodd*, ed. Pierre Coustillas, 1973

   (*LMF*). *Letters of George Gissing to Members of his Family*, ed. Algernon and Ellen Gissing, 1931 [1927]

Bibliography

(*NGS*). *New Grub Street*, Harmondsworth, 1968 [1891]

(*NW*). *The Nether World*, London, 1973 [1889]

(*OW*). *The Odd Women*, Nelson's Library, nd [1893]

(*T*). *Thyrza: A Tale*, 1927 [1887]

(*U*). *The Unclassed*, 1930 [1884]

(*WD*). *Workers in the Dawn*, 3 vols., 1976 [1880]

Gittings, Robert (1978) [1975]. *Young Thomas Hardy*

(1980) [1978]. *The Older Hardy*

Giustino, David de (1975). *The Conquest of Mind: Phrenology and Victorian Thought*

Goode, John (1978). *George Gissing: Ideology and Fiction*

Gore, Charles, ed. (1890). *Lux Mundi*

Gouhier, Henri (1931). *La Vie d'Auguste Comte*, Paris

(1933–40). *La Jeunesse d'Auguste Comte et la formation du Positivisme*, 3 vols., Paris

Gould, F. J. (1905). *The Religion that Fulfils*

(1908). *A Catechism of Religion and the Social Life*

(1916). *The Religion of Humanity*

(1920). *Auguste Comte*

(1921). *History the Teacher*

(1923). *The Life-Story of a Humanist*

Gould, S. J. (1971). *The Rational Society*

Granville-Barker, Harley (1909). *Three Plays*

Gray, Alexander (1946). *The Socialist Tradition: Moses to Lenin*

Grisewood, Harold, ed. (1949). *Ideas and Beliefs of the Victorians*

Gross, John (1969). *The Rise and Fall of the Man of Letters: Aspects of English Literary Life Since 1800*

Grote, George (1862) [1846–56]. *History of Greece*, 8 vols.

Grote, Mrs (1873). *The Personal Life of George Grote*

Gruber, R. P. (1893). *Le Positivisme depuis Comte à nos jours*, Paris

Gwynn, Stephen and Tuckwell, Gertrude M. (1917). *Life of the Rt. Hon. Sir Charles Dilke*, 2 vols.

Haggard, Alfred H. (1901–3). *Annual Addresses*

Haight, G. S. (1940) *George Eliot and John Chapman*, New Haven

(1968). *George Eliot: A Biography*

Hainds, J. R. (1946). 'John Stuart Mill and the Saint Simonians', *JHI* VII 103–12

Halperin, John (1982). *George Gissing: A Life in Books*, Oxford

Hamer, D. A. (1968). *John Morley: Liberal Intellectual in Politics*, Oxford

Hamerton, Philip Gilbert (1897). *An Autobiography, 1834–1858, and a Memoir by his Wife, 1858–1894*

Hanson, Lawrence and Elizabeth (1952). *Marian Evans and George Eliot*, Oxford

Hardy, Barbara (1959). *The Novels of George Eliot*

Hardy, Barbara, ed. (1967). *'Middlemarch': Critical Approaches to the Novel*

286

Bibliography

Hardy, Thomas (*CL*). *Collected Letters*, ed. Richard Little Purdy and Michael Millgate, 3 vols., 1978–84, Oxford

(*CP*). *Collected Poems*, 4th edn, 1930

(*Life* I). *The Early Life of Thomas Hardy, 1840–1891*, by Florence Emily Hardy, 1928

(*Life* II). *The Later Years of Thomas Hardy, 1892–1928*, by Florence Emily Hardy, 1930

(1974–5). New Wessex Edition of the novels, paperback version. Titles of novels are abbreviated as follows: *L A Laodicean, DR Desperate Remedies, FMC Far From the Madding Crowd, HE The Hand of Ethelberta, Jude Jude the Obscure, MC The Mayor of Casterbridge, PBE A Pair of Blue Eyes, RN The Return of the Native, Tess Tess of the d'Urbervilles, TM The Trumpet-Major, TT Two on a Tower, UGT Under the Greenwood Tree, W The Woodlanders, WB The Well-Beloved*

(1977) [1903]. *The Dynasts*

Harrison, Austin (1906). 'George Gissing', *NC* LX 453–63

(1926). *Frederic Harrison: Thoughts and Memories*

Harrison, Ethel, ed. (1890). *The Service of Man*

(1908). *The Service of Man*, 2nd edn

Harrison, Frederic (1879). *Science and Humanity*

(1880). *The Present and the Future*

(1884). *In Memoriam Mr Alfred Cutler*

(1887). *New Year's Address*

(1888a). *New Year's Address*

(1888b). *In Memoriam James Cotter Morison*

(1889). *A New Era*

(1890). *The Memory of the Dead*

(1891). *The Presentation of Infants*

(1895). *George Eliot's Place in Literature*

(1899). *Tennyson, Ruskin, Mill and Other Literary Estimates*

(1902). *John Ruskin*

(1906). *Memories and Thoughts*

(1907a). *The Creed of a Layman*

(1907b). *The Philosophy of Common Sense*

(1908). *National and Social Problems*

(1911). *Autobiographic Memoirs*, 2 vols.

(1913). *The Positive Evolution of Religion*

(1917). *Memoir and Essays of Ethelbertha Harrison*, Bath

(1921). *Novissima Verba*

(1975) [1875]. *Order and Progress*, ed. Martha S. Vogeler

Harrison, Frederic, ed. (1892). *The New Calendar of Great Men*

Harrison, Royden (1959). 'E. S. Beesly and Karl Marx', *International Review of Social History* IV 22–58 and 208–38

(1965). *Before the Socialists: Studies in Labour and Politics, 1861–1881*

Harvey, W. J. (1961). *The Art of George Eliot*

Bibliography

Harvie, Christopher (1976). *The Lights of Liberalism: University Liberals and the Challenge of Democracy*

Havard, William C. (1959). *Henry Sidgwick and Later Utilitarian Political Philosophy*, Gainesville, Florida

Hayek, F. A. (1951). *John Stuart Mill and Harriet Taylor: Their Correspondence and Subsequent Marriage*

(1952). *The Counter-Revolution of Science*, Glencoe, Illinois

Hennell, Sara S. (1860). *Thoughts in Aid of Faith*

(1865–87). *Present Religion*, 2 vols.

Herford, C. H. (1913). *The Living Dead*, Liverpool

(1931). *Philip Henry Wicksteed: His Life and Work*

Higginson, Charles Gaskell (1885). *The Sciences: What They Are and How They Grow*

(1887). *Auguste Comte: An Address on His Life and Work*

(1889–92). *Annual Circulars*, Manchester

Himmelfarb, Gertrude (1968) [1952]. *Victorian Minds*

(1974). *On Liberty and Liberalism: The Case of John Stuart Mill*, New York

Hirshberg, Edgar W. (1970). *George Henry Lewes*, New York

Hirst, F. W. (1927). *Early Life and Letters of John Morley*, 2 vols.

Hobson, J. A. and Ginsberg, Morris (1931). *L. T. Hobhouse: His Life and Work*

Hocks, Richard A. (1974). *Henry James and Pragmatist Thought*, Chapel Hill

Holloway, John (1965) [1953]. *The Victorian Sage*, New York

Holthoon, F. L. van (1971). *The Road to Utopia: A Study of John Stuart Mill's Social Thought*, Assen

Holyoake, Austin and Watts, Charles, eds. (nd). *The Secularists' Manual of Songs and Ceremonies*

Holyoake, George Jacob (1893). *Sixty Years of an Agitator's Life*, 2 vols.

(1905). *Bygones Worth Remembering*, 2 vols.

Hort, Arthur Fenton (1896). *Life and Letters of Fenton John Anthony Hort*, 2 vols.

Houghton, Walter (1969). *The Victorian Frame of Mind*, New Haven

House, Humphrey (1955). *All in Due Time*

Hudson, Stewart (1970). 'George Henry Lewes's Evolutionism in the Fiction of George Eliot', University of Southern California Ph.D.

Hügel, Friedrich von (1921). *Essays and Addresses on the Philosophy of Religion*

(1927). *Selected Letters, 1896–1924*

Hutton, H. D. (1855). *Modern Warfare: Its Positive Theory and True Policy*

(1870). *Europe's Need and England's Duty*

(1880). *Humanity: The True Object of Worship, Faith and Service*, Dublin

(1891). *Comte, the Man and Founder: Personal Recollections*

(1901). *The Positivist Propaganda: Its Difficulties and Dangers; Its Resources*

(1906). *Comte's Life and Work*

Hutton, R. H. (1887). *Essays on Some of the Modern Guides of English Thought in Matters of Faith*

288

Bibliography

Huxley, Leonard (1900). *Life and Letters of T. H. Huxley,* 2 vols.

Huxley, T. H. (1894–5). *Collected Essays,* 9 vols.

Hyde, H. Montgomery, ed. (1947). *A Victorian Historian: Private Letters of W. E. H. Lecky,* 1859–1878

Hyman, Virginia R. (1975). *Ethical Perspectives in the Novels of Thomas Hardy*

Hyndman, Henry M. (1911). *The Record of an Adventurous Life*

Hynes, Samuel (1968). *The Edwardian Turn of Mind*

Inglis, K. S. (1963). *Churches and the Working Classes in Victorian England*

Ingram, J. K. (1878). 'The Need for Sociology', *Presidential Address to the British Academy,* Section F, in Abrams (1968) 177–95

  (1880). *Work and the Workman*

  (1897). *Auguste Comte and One of His Critics,* Dublin

  (1900). *Outlines of the History of Religion*

  (1901). *Human Nature and Morals According to Auguste Comte*

  (1904). *Practical Morals: A Treatise on Universal Education*

  (1905). *The Final Transition: A Sociological Study*

Irvine, William (1955). *Apes, Angels, and Victorians: A Joint Biography of Darwin and Huxley*

Jackson, A. W. (1900). *James Martineau: A Biography and Study*

Jackson, William (1871). *Positivism*

James, D. G. (1970). *Henry Sidgwick: Science and Faith in Victorian England*

James, Henry (*CT*). *Complete Tales,* ed. Leon Edel, 12 vols., 1962–4

  (*Letters*). *Henry James Letters,* ed. Leon Edel, 3 vols., Cambridge, Mass., 1974–80

  (1878). *French Poets and Novelists*

  (1921) [1886]. *The Bostonians*

  (1966) [1881]. *The Portrait of a Lady*

Jex-Blake, T. W. (1907). 'Rugby Memories of Three Eminent Rugbeians', *N Rev.* IL 232–6

Jones, Enid Huws (1973). *Mrs Humphry Ward,* New York

Jones, Henry and Muirhead, John Henry (1921). *The Life and Philosophy of Edward Caird,* Glasgow

Kaines, Joseph (1880). *Seven Lectures on the Doctrine of Positivism*

  (1883). *Our Daily Faults and Findings*

  (1884). *The Beauty of Holiness*

Kaminsky, Alice R. (1955). 'George Eliot, George Henry Lewes, and the Novel', *PMLA* LXX 997–1013

  (1968). *George Henry Lewes as Literary Critic,* Syracuse, New York

Kent, Christopher (1978). *Brains and Numbers: Elitism, Comtism, and Democracy in Mid-Victorian England,* Toronto

Kent, William (1932). *London for Heretics*

Kingsley, Charles (1860). *The Limits of Exact Science as Applied to History*

  (1879). *Charles Kingsley: His Letters and Memories of His Life,* edited by his wife, 2 vols.

Kipling, Rudyard (1949) [1890]. *Plain Tales from the Hills*

Bibliography

Kitchel, A. T. (1933). *George Lewes and George Eliot: A Review of Records,* New York

(1950). 'Quarry for "Middlemarch" ', *NCF* IV, supplement

Kitchen, Paddy (1975). *A Most Unsettling Person: An Introduction to the Ideas and Life of Patrick Geddes*

Knoepflmacher, U. C. (1965). *Religious Humanism and the Victorian Novel,* Princeton

(1968). *George Eliot's Early Novels,* Berkeley

Kofman, Sarah (1978). *Aberrations. La devenir-femme d'Auguste Comte,* Paris

Kolakowski, Leszek (1972) [1968]. *Positivist Philosophy from Hume to the Vienna Circle*

Korg, Jacob (1963). *George Gissing: A Critical Biography,* Seattle

Kramer, Dale, ed. (1979). *Critical Approaches to the Fiction of Thomas Hardy*

Kremer-Marietti, Angèle (1981). *Entre le signe et l'histoire. L'Anthropologie d'Auguste Comte,* Paris

Laffitte, Pierre (*CA*). *Circulaires annuelles de Pierre Laffitte et Charles Jeannolle, 1864–1913,* Paris

(1908). *The Positive Science of Morals,* trans. J. Carey Hall

Laird, J. T. (1975). *The Shaping of 'Tess of the D'Urbervilles',* Oxford

Lawrence, D. H. (1978) [1936]. *Phoenix, The Posthumous Papers, 1936,* ed. Edward D. McDonald

Lecky, W. E. H. (1865). *History of the Rise and Influence of the Spirit of Rationalism in Europe,* 2 vols.

(1869). *History of European Morals,* 2 vols.

(1896). *Democracy and Liberty,* 2 vols.

(1909). *A Memoir of the Rt. Hon. William Edward Hartpole Lecky,* by his wife

Lenzer, Gertrude, ed. (1975). *Auguste Comte and Positivism,* New York

Letwin, Shirley Robin (1965). *The Pursuit of Certainty*

Levine, George (1962). 'Determinism and Responsibility in the Works of George Eliot', *PMLA* LXXVII 268–79

(1965). 'Intelligence as Deception: "The Mill on the Floss" ', *PMLA* LXXX 402–9

Lévy-Bruhl, L. (1900). *The Philosophy of Auguste Comte*

Lévy-Bruhl, L., ed. (1899). *Lettres inédites de John Stuart Mill à Auguste Comte,* Paris

Lewes, George Henry (*PLM*). *Problems of Life and Mind,* 5 vols., 1874–9

(1845–6). *A Biographical History of Philosophy,* 4 vols.

(1853). *Comte's Philosophy of the Sciences*

(1857). *A Biographical History of Philosophy,* 2nd edn

(1867). *The History of Philosophy from Thales to Comte,* 2 vols.

(1871). *The History of Philosophy from Thales to Comte,* 4th edn

Lewis, Henry (1913). *Modern Rationalism as Seen at Work in its Biographies*

Lindsay, Jack (1956). *George Meredith*

Littré, E. (1863). *Auguste Comte et la philosophie positive,* Paris

Bibliography

Liveing, Susan (1926). *A Nineteenth-Century Teacher: John Henry Bridges*

Lock, W. (1881). *Some Religious Aspects of Positivism*, Oxford

Locker-Lampson, Frederic (1896). *My Confidences*

Lowry, H. F., ed. (1932). *The Letters of Matthew Arnold to Arthur Hugh Clough*

Lowry, H. F., Young, K., and Dunn, W. H., eds. (1952). *The Notebooks of Matthew Arnold*

Lubac, Henri de (1945). *Le Drame de l'humanisme athée*, Paris

Lucas, John (1966). 'Tilting at the Moderns: W. H. Mallock's Criticism of the Positive Spirit', *RMS* x 88–143

Lushington, Vernon (1883a). *Mozart: A Commemorative Address*

(1883b). *The Day of All the Dead*

(1885a). *Shakespeare: An Address*

(1885b). *Positivist Hymns*

(1886). *The Worship of Humanity*

Lynd, Helen Merrell (1945). *England in the Eighteen-Eighties: Towards a Social Basis for Freedom*

MacKenzie, Norman, ed. (1978). *Letters of Sidney and Beatrice Webb*, 3 vols., Cambridge

MacKenzie, Norman and Jeanne (1977). *The First Fabians*

MacKenzie, Norman and Jeanne, eds. (1982–4). *Diary of Beatrice Webb*, 4 vols.

Mackintosh, H. R. (1937). *Types of Modern Theology*

Macrae, Donald G. (1973). *Ages and Stages*

Mairet, Philip (1957). *Pioneer of Sociology: The Life and Work of Patrick Geddes*

Maitland, F. W. (1906). *Life and Letters of Leslie Stephen*

Mallock, W. H. (1877). *The New Republic*

(1879). *Is Life Worth Living?*

(1903). *Religion as a Credible Doctrine*

(1905). *The Reconstruction of Belief*

(1970) [1878]. *The New Paul and Virginia, or Positivism on an Island*, ed. John D. Margolis, Lincoln, Nebraska

Mallone, Sydney Herbert (1902). *Leaders of Religious Thought in the Nineteenth Century*

Mandelbaum, Maurice (1971). *History, Man and Reason: A Study in Nineteenth-Century Thought*

Manuel, F. E. (1951). *The Age of Reason*, Ithaca, New York

(1956). *The New World of Henri Saint-Simon*, Cambridge, Mass.

(1962). *The Prophets of Paris*, Cambridge, Mass.

Margolis, John D. (1967). 'W. H. Mallock's *The New Republic*: A Study in Late Victorian Satire', *ELT* x 10–25

Martin, A. Patchett (1893). *Life and Letters of the Rt. Hon. Robert Lowe*

Martineau, Harriet (1877). *Autobiography*, 3 vols.

Martineau, James (1885). *Types of Ethical Theory*, 2 vols.

291

(1889) [1888]. *A Study of Religion*, 2 vols.

(1891) [1890]. *The Seat of Authority in Religion*

Marvin, F. S. (1913). *The Living Past*, Oxford

(1919). *The Century of Hope*, Oxford

(1938). *The New Vision of Man*

Mason, Michael York (1971a). ' "Middlemarch" and Science: Problems of Life and Mind', *RES* XXII 151–69

(1971b). ' "Middlemarch" and History', *NCF* XXV 417–31

Masterman, N. C. (1963). *John Malcolm Ludlow: The Builder of Christian Socialism*, Cambridge

Maurice, F. D. (1873) [1872]. *Moral and Metaphysical Philosophy*, 2 vols.

(1893) [1869]. *Social Morality*

Maurice, Frederick (1884). *Life and Letters of Frederick Denison Maurice*, 2 vols.

Mazlish, Bruce (1975). *James and John Stuart Mill*, New York

McBriar, A. M. (1962). *Fabian Socialism and English Politics, 1884–1918*, Cambridge

McCabe, Joseph (1908). *Life and Letters of George Jacob Holyoake*, 2 vols.

(1932). *Edward Clodd: A Memoir*

McCarthy, Justin (1899). *Reminiscences*, 2 vols.

McClaren, Angus (1974). 'Phrenology: Medium and Message', *JMH* XLVI 86–97

McCosh, James (1871). *Christianity and Positivism*

McGee, J. E. (1931). *A Crusade for Humanity: The History of Organized Positivism in England*

McLaverty, James (1981). 'Comtean Fetishism in "Silas Marner" ', *NCF* XXXVI 318–36

McLeod, Hugh (1974). *Class and Religion in the Late Victorian City*

(1978). 'Recent Studies in Victorian Religious History', *VS* XXI 245–55

Mead, George H. (1936). *Movements of Thought in the Nineteenth Century*

Meredith, George (1912). *Poems*, 2 vols.

(1961) [1859]. *The Ordeal of Richard Feverel*, New York

(1968) [1879]. *The Egoist*, Harmondsworth

(1970). *Letters of George Meredith*, ed. C. L. Cline, 3 vols., Oxford

(1978) [1897] *An Essay on Comedy*, ed. Lane Cooper, New York

Merz, John (1914). *A History of European Thought*, vol. IV

Metcalf, Priscilla (1980). *James Knowles: Victorian Editor and Architect*

Metz, Rudolf (1938). *A Hundred Years of British Philosophy*

Mill, John Stuart (*CW*). *The Collected Works of John Stuart Mill*, ed. Francis E. Mineka, 20 vols., Toronto, 1963–

(1843). *A System of Logic*, 2 vols.

(1859). *On Liberty*

(1861). *Considerations on Representative Government*

(1863). *Utilitarianism*

(1865). *Auguste Comte and Positivism*

Bibliography

(1869). *The Subjection of Women*

(1873). *Autobiography*

(1874). *Three Essays on Religion*

(1910). *The Letters of John Stuart Mill*, ed. H. S. R. Elliot, 2 vols.

(1942). *The Spirit of the Age*, ed. F. A. Hayek, Chicago

Millgate, Michael (1982). *Thomas Hardy: A Biography*, Oxford

Monsman, Gerald C. (1970). 'Old Morality at Oxford', *SP* LXVII 359–89

(1971). 'Pater's Aesthetic Hero', *UTQ* XL 136–51

Moore, John (1939). *Life and Letters of Edward Thomas*

Morison, James Cotter (nd). *On the Relation of Positivism to Art*

(1888). *The Service of Man*

Morley, John (1867). *Edmund Burke*

(1874). *On Compromise*

(1878). *Diderot and the Encyclopaedists*, 2 vols.

(1908a). *Miscellanies*, Fourth Series

(1908b). *Life of William Ewart Gladstone*

(1921a) [1917]. *Recollections*, 2 vols.

(1921b). *Critical Miscellanies*

(1923a) [1872]. *Voltaire*

(1923b) [1873]. *Rousseau and His Era*, 2 vols.

Morris, William (1973) [1962]. *Selected Writings and Designs*, ed. Asa Briggs

Mueller, Iris Wessel (1956). *John Stuart Mill and French Thought*, Urbana, Illinois

Muggeridge, Kitty and Adam, Ruth (1967). *Beatrice Webb: A Life, 1858–1943*

Mulhauser, F. L., ed. (1957). *The Correspondence of Arthur Hugh Clough*, 2 vols., Oxford

Murphy, Howard (1955). 'The Ethical Revolt against Christian Orthodoxy in Early Victorian England', *AHR* LX 800–17

Murphy, James Maurice (1968). 'Positivism in England: The Reception of Comte's Doctrines, 1840–1870', Columbia University Ph.D.

Murray, Gilbert (1940). *Stoic, Christian and Humanist*

(1960). *An Unfinished Autobiography*

Myers, F. W. H. (1883). *Essays Modern*

Myers, William (1966). 'Politics and Personality in "Felix Holt" ', *RMS* X 5–33

(1984). *The Teaching of George Eliot*, Leicester

Naamani, I. T. (1967). 'The Theism of Lord Balfour', *History Today* XVII 660–6

Nethercot, Arthur H. (1960). *The First Five Lives of Annie Besant*, Chicago

Newman, John Henry (*Letters*). *Letters and Diaries of John Henry Newman*, ed. C. S. Dessain and others, 31 vols., 1961–

Newton, K. M. (1981). *George Eliot: Romantic Humanist*

Norton, Sara and Howe, M. A. DeWolfe, eds. (1913). *Letters of Charles Eliot Norton*, 2 vols.

Olivier, Margaret, ed. (1948). *Sydney Olivier: Letters and Selected Writings*

Bibliography

Olson, Richard (1975). *Scottish Philosophy and British Physics: A Study in the Foundations of the Victorian Scientific Style*, Princeton

Orchard, W. E. (1918). *The True Patriotism and Other Sermons*

Orel, Harold, ed. (1967). *Thomas Hardy's Personal Writings*

Osborne, C. E. (1929). *Christian Ideas in Political History*

Packe, Michael St John (1954). *The Life of John Stuart Mill*

Page, Norman, ed. (1980). *Thomas Hardy: The Writer and His Background*

Pankhurst, Richard (1957). *The Saint-Simonians: Mill and Carlyle*, Norwich

Paris, B. J. (1962). 'George Eliot's Religion of Humanity', *ELH* XXIX 418–43

   (1965). *Experiments in Life: George Eliot's Quest for Values*, Detroit

   (1969). 'A Confusion of Many Standards: Conflicting Value Systems in "Tess of the d'Urbervilles" ', *NCF* XXIV 57–79

Parrinder, Patrick, ed. (1972). *H. G. Wells: The Critical Heritage*

Passmore, John (1957). *A Hundred Years of Philosophy*

   (1970). *The Perfectibility of Man*

Pater, Walter (1901) [1873]. *The Renaissance*

   (1910) [1885]. *Marius the Epicurean*, 2 vols.

   (1973). *Essays on Literature and Art*, ed. Jennifer Uglow

Paterson, John (1959). ' "The Return of the Native" as Antichristian Document', *NCF* XIV 111–27

   (1960). *The Making of "The Return of the Native"*, Berkeley

Pattison, Mark (1885). *Memoirs*

   (1889). *Essays*, 2 vols., Oxford

Paul, Charles Kegan (1899). *Memories*

Paul, Herbert, ed. (1904). *Letters of Lord Acton to Mary, daughter of the Rt. Hon. W. E. Gladstone*

Paulin, Tom (1975). *Thomas Hardy: The Poetry of Perception*

Pease, Edward R. (1963) [1916]. *The History of the Fabian Society*

Peckham, Morse (1970). *Victorian Revolutionaries: Speculations on Some Heroes of a Culture Crisis*, New York

Percival, P. (1892). *The Position of Positivism*

Peterson, William S. (1976). *Victorian Heretic: Mrs Humphry Ward's 'Robert Elsmere'*, Leicester

Petre, M. D., ed. (1912). *Autobiography and Life of George Tyrrell*, 2 vols.

Pinion, F. B. (1976). *A Commentary on the Poems of Thomas Hardy*

Pinney, Thomas (1966a). 'More Leaves from George Eliot's Notebook', *HLQ* XXIX 353–76

   (1966b). 'The Authority of the Past in George Eliot's Novels', *NCF* XXI 131–47

Pollard, Sidney (1968). *The Idea of Progress*

Pollock, Frederick (1933). *For My Grandson: Remembrances of an Ancient Victorian*

Poole, Adrian (1975). *Gissing in Context*

Prasad, Thakur Guru (1968). *Comtism in the Novels of George Eliot*, Lucknow

Pratt, John C. and Neufeldt, Victor A., eds. (1979). *George Eliot's "Mid-*

dlemarch" Notebooks: A Transcription, Berkeley, Los Angeles

Presswood, W. L. (1935). 'The Influence of Auguste Comte and the Rise of Positivism in England up to the Formation of the English Positivist Society in 1867', Sheffield University Ph.D.

Quick, Jonathan R. (1968). 'A Critical Edition of George Eliot's "Silas Marner" ', Yale University Ph.D.

Quin, Malcolm (*AA*). *Annual Addresses*, 1887–98, Newcastle

(*AC*). *Annual Circulars*, 1899–1910, Newcastle

(*PT*). *Political Tracts*, 1898–1906, Newcastle

(1899). *Richard Congreve: A Commemorative Address*, Newcastle

(1900). *Some Principles of Positivist Education*, Newcastle

(1901). *The Rule of Auguste Comte*, Newcastle

(1902). *The Angels of the Founder*, Newcastle

(1903). *On the Positivist Idea of the Church*, Newcastle

(1904). *The Way of the Positivist Life*, Newcastle

(1909a). *Offices of Public Worship*, Newcastle

(1909b). *Notes on a Progressive Catholicism*, Newcastle

(1909c). *Aids to Worship*, Newcastle

(1912). *Catholicism and the Modern Mind*, Newcastle

(1916). *The Problem of Human Peace*, Newcastle

(1919). *The Politics of the Proletariat*, Newcastle

(1924). *Memoirs of a Positivist*

Ratcliffe, S. K. (1955). *The Story of South Place*

Reade, Winwood (1948) [1872]. *The Martyrdom of Man*

Reardon, Bernard M. G. (1966). *Religious Thought in the Nineteenth Century*, Cambridge

(1971). *From Coleridge to Gore: A Century of Religious Thought in Britain*

Robbins, William (1959). *The Ethical Idealism of Matthew Arnold*

Roberts, Morley (1958). *The Private Life of Henry Maitland*

Roberts, Neil (1975). *George Eliot: Her Beliefs and Her Art*

Robertson, J. M. (1891). *Modern Humanists*

(1895). *Buckle and His Critics*

(1927). *Modern Humanists Reconsidered*

(1929). *A History of Freethought in the Nineteenth Century*

Robinson, Carole (1962). ' "Romola": A Reading of the Novel', *VS* VI 29–42

(1964). 'The Severe Angel: A Study of "Daniel Deronda" ', *ELH* XXXI 278–300

Robson, John M. (1968). *The Improvement of Mankind*

Roll-Hansen, Diderik (1957). *The Academy, 1869–1879: Victorian Intellectuals in Revolt*, Copenhagen

Rose, William, ed. (1931). *An Outline of Modern Knowledge*

Rothblatt, Sheldon (1968). *The Revolution of the Dons: Cambridge and Society in Victorian England*

Royle, Edward (1971). *Radical Politics, 1790–1900: Religion and Unbelief*

Bibliography

(1974). *Victorian Infidels: The Origins of the British Secularist Movement, 1791–1866*, Manchester

(1980). *Radicals, Secularists and Republicans: Popular Freethought in Britain, 1866–1915*, Manchester

Ruse, Michael (1975). 'The Relationship between Science and Religion in Britain, 1830–1870', *CH* LXIV 505–22

Ruskin, John (*Works*). *The Works of John Ruskin*, ed. E. T. Cook and Alexander Wedderburn, 39 vols., 1903–12

Russell, Bertrand and Patricia, eds. (1937). *The Amberley Papers: The Letters and Diaries of Lord and Lady Amberley*, 2 vols.

Russell, George W. E., ed. (1895). *Letters of Matthew Arnold, 1848–88*, 2 vols.

Rutland, William (1962) [1938]. *Thomas Hardy: A Study of His Writings and Their Background*, New York

Ryle, Gilbert (1962). *A Rational Animal*

Saint-Simon, Henri de (1834). *New Christianity*, trans. J. E. Smith

Salter, C. H. (1981). *Good Little Thomas Hardy*

Sarton, George (1952). 'Auguste Comte, Historian of Science', *Osiris* X 328–57

Saville, John, ed. (1970). *A Selection of the Social and Political Pamphlets of Annie Besant*, New York

Schneewind, J. B. (1977). *Sidgwick's Ethics and Victorian Moral Philosophy*, Oxford

Schneewind, J. B., ed. (1969). *Mill: A Collection of Critical Essays*

Schoff, Wilfred H. (1896). *A Neglected Chapter in the Life of Comte*, Philadelphia

Schorer, Mark (1949). 'Fiction and the "Matrix of Analogy" ', *KR* XI 539–60

Schuettinger, Robert L. (1976). *Lord Acton, Historian of Liberty*, La Salle, Illinois

Scott, James F. (1972). 'George Eliot, Positivism, and the Social Vision of "Middlemarch" ', *VS* XVI 59–76

Scott, J. W. Robertson (1950). *The Story of the 'Pall Mall Gazette'*

Seeley, J. R. (1866). *Ecce Homo*

(1870). *Lectures and Essays*

(1891) [1882]. *Natural Religion*

Seeley, J. R. and others (1900). *Ethics and Religion*

Seiler, R. M., ed. (1980). *Walter Pater: The Critical Heritage*

Semmel, Bernard (1976). 'H. T. Buckle: the Liberal Faith and the Science of History', *BJS* XXVII 370–86

Shaw, Bernard (1934). *Prefaces*

(1946). *Plays Pleasant*

Sherman, G. W. (1953). 'Thomas Hardy and Professor Edward Beesly', *NQ* CXCVIII 167–8

(1976). *The Pessimism of Thomas Hardy*

Shuttleworth, Sally (1984). *George Eliot and Nineteenth-Century Science*, Cambridge

Bibliography

Sidgwick, Arthur and Eleanor (1906). *Henry Sidgwick: A Memoir*

Sidgwick, Henry (1885). *The Scope and Method of Economic Science*
(1902). *Philosophy: Its Scope and Relations*

Simon, W. M. (1963). *European Positivism in the Nineteenth Century*, New York
(1964). 'Auguste Comte's English Disciples', *VS* VIII 161–72
(1965). 'Comte's Orthodox Disciples: The Rise and Fall of a Cenacle', *FHS*
I 42–62

Smith, Goldwin (*Sel*). *A Selection from Goldwin Smith's Correspondence*, ed.
Arnold Haultain, nd
(1865). *Lectures on the Study of History*, 2nd edn
(1897). *Guesses at the Riddle of Existence*
(1906). *In Quest of Light*

Smith, Warren Sylvester (1967). *The London Heretics*

Sokoloff, Boris (1975) [1961]. *The 'Mad' Philosopher: Auguste Comte*,
Connecticut

Spencer, Herbert (1901). *Essays: Scientific, Political, and Speculative*, 3 vols.
(1904). *An Autobiography*, 2 vols.

Stang, Richard (1959). *The Theory of the Novel in England, 1850–1870*

Stebbing, William, ed. (1900). *Charles Henry Pearson*

Stephen, James FitzJames (1967) [1873]. *Liberty, Equality, Fraternity*, ed. R.
J. White, Cambridge

Stephen, Leslie (1865). *Sketches from Cambridge*
(1877). *Essays on Freethinking and Plainspeaking*
(1882). *The Science of Ethics*
(1895). *The Life of Sir James FitzJames Stephen*
(1896). *Social Rights and Duties*, 2 vols.
(1900). *The English Utilitarians*, 3 vols.
(1902). *George Eliot*
(1924). *Some Early Impressions*
(1931) [1893]. *An Agnostic's Apology*
(1956). *Men, Books and Mountains*, introd. S. O. A. Ullmann
(1977). *Sir Leslie Stephen's Mausoleum Book*, introd. Alan Bell

Stern, B. J. (1936). 'A Note on Comte', *Science and Society* I 114–19

Stillinger, Jack (1961). *The Early Draft of John Stuart Mill's Autobiography*,
Urbana

Storr, Vernon (1913). *The Development of English Theology in the Nineteenth
Century, 1800–1860*

Strauss, David Friedrich (1973) [1846]. *The Life of Jesus Critically Examined*, trans. George Eliot

Style, Jane M. (1920). *The Voice of the Nineteenth Century: A Woman's Echo*
(1928). *Auguste Comte: Thinker and Lover*

Style, Sydney (1908). *An Address in Memory of the Life and Work of Albert
Crompton*, Liverpool
(1911). *An Address in Memory of the Life and Work of Hubert Congreve*,
Liverpool

Sulman, Thomas (1899). *Funeral Service of Dr Richard Congreve*

Sumner, Rosemary (1981). *Thomas Hardy: Psychological Novelist*

Svaglic, Martin (1954). 'Religion in the Novels of George Eliot', *Journal of English and Germanic Philology* LIII 145–59

Symondson, Anthony, ed. (1970). *The Victorian Crisis of Faith*

Taine, H. A. (1864). *Le Positivisme anglais*, Paris

Taylor, Richard H., ed. (1978). *The Personal Notebooks of Thomas Hardy*

Thomas, Philip (1910a). *Auguste Comte on Marriage and Divorce*
  (1910b). *Auguste Comte and Richard Congreve*
  (1910c). *Our Church and Faith of Humanity*
  (1913). *A Religion of This World*

Thompson, Fred C. (1959). 'The Genesis of "Felix Holt" ', *PMLA* LXXIV 576–84

Thompson, Kenneth (1976). *Auguste Comte: The Foundation of Sociology*

Tjoa, Hock Guan (1977). *George Henry Lewes: A Victorian Mind*, Cambridge, Mass.

Torlesse, Frances H. (1912). *Some Account of John Henry Bridges and His Family*
  (1914). *Bygone Days*

Trevelyan, Janet Penrose (1923). *Life of Mrs Humphry Ward*

Tribe, David (1967). *A Hundred Years of Freethought*

Trudgill, Eric (1975). *Madonnas and Magdalens: A Study of Victorian Sexual Attitudes*, Leicester

Tucker, Albert V. (1962). 'W. H. Mallock and Late Victorian Conservatism', *UTQ* XXXI 223–41

Tulloch, John (1971) [1885]. *Movements of Religious Thought in Britain during the Nineteenth Century*, Leicester

Turner, Frank Miller (1974). *Between Science and Religion: The Reaction to Scientific Naturalism in Late Victorian England*

Vaughan, C. E. (1925). *Studies in the History of Political Philosophy*, 2 vols., Manchester

Vidler, Alec (1972). *The Church in an Age of Revolution*

Vidler, Alex R. (1966). *F. D. Maurice and Company*

Vogeler, Martha S. (1962). 'Matthew Arnold and Frederic Harrison: The Prophet of Culture and the Prophet of Positivism', *SEL* II 441–62
  (1975). 'Frederic Harrison and John Ruskin: the Limits of Positivist Biography', *TQ* XVIII 91–8
  (1976). 'Comte and Mill: The Early Publishing History of Their Correspondence', *MNL* XI (2) 17–22
  (1979a). 'More Light on "Essays and Reviews": The Role of Frederic Harrison', *VPN* XII 105–116
  (1979b). 'Frederic Harrison: The Positivist as Urbanist', *Victorian Writers and the City*, ed. Jean-Paul Hulin and Pierre Coustillas, Lille
  (1980). 'George Eliot and the Positivists', *NCF* XXXV 406–31
  (1982). 'The Choir Invisible: The Poetics of Humanist Piety', *George Eliot:*

Bibliography

A Centenary Tribute, ed. Gordon S. Haight and Rosemary T. VanArsdel (1984). *Frederic Harrison: The Vocations of a Positivist*, Oxford

Wallace, Elisabeth (1957). *Goldwin Smith: Victorian Liberal*, Toronto

Ward, Anthony (1966). *Walter Pater: The Idea in Nature*

Ward, Mrs Humphry (1888). *Robert Elsmere*

(1892). *The History of David Grieve*

(1918). *A Writer's Recollections*

Ward, W. R. (1965). *Victorian Oxford*

Warren, Howard (1921). *A History of Association Psychology*, New York

Weatherby, H. L. (1967). 'Jude the Victorian', *SHR* I 158–69

(1970). 'Atheological Symbolism in Modern Fiction: An Interpretation of Hardy's "Tess of the D'Urbervilles" ', *SHR* IV 81–91

Webb, Beatrice (1926). *My Apprenticeship*

Webb, Clement C. J. (1933). *A Study of Religious Thought in England From 1850*, Oxford

Webb, Sidney and Webb, Beatrice (1894). *The History of Trade Unionism*

Wells, H. G. (1903). *Mankind in the Making*

(1904). *The Food of the Gods*

(1908). *First and Last Things*

(1914). *An Englishman Looks at the World*

(1920). *The Outline of History*

(1922). *A Short History of the World*

(1934). *An Experiment in Autobiography*, 2 vols.

(1967) [1905]. *A Modern Utopia*, Lincoln, Nebraska

West, Francis (1984). *Gilbert Murray: A Life*

Westcott, Arthur (1903). *Life and Letters of Brooke Foss Westcott*, 2 vols.

Westcott, Brooke Foss (1886) [1883]. *The Epistles of St John*

(1900). *Social Aspects of Christianity*

Wheatley, Vera (1957). *The Life and Work of Harriet Martineau*

Whitehead, A. N. (1933). *Adventures of Ideas*, Cambridge

Whittaker, Thomas (1908). *Comte and Mill*

Wilde, Oscar (1913) [1908]. *Essays and Lectures*

(1950). *Essays*

Willey, Basil (1956). *More Nineteenth-Century Studies: A Group of Honest Doubters*

(1973) [1949]. *Nineteenth-Century Studies*

Williams, Blanche (1936). *George Eliot*, New York

Williams, David (1983). *Mr George Eliot: A Biography of George Henry Lewes*

Williams, Ioan, ed. (1971). *Meredith: The Critical Heritage*

Wilson, David Alec (1927). *Carlyle at His Zenith*

Wilson, David B. (1977). 'Victorian Science and Religion', *HS* XV 52–67

Wilson, Angus (1977). *The Strange Ride of Rudyard Kipling: His Life and Works*

Wiltshire, David (1978). *The Social and Political Thought of Herbert Spencer*, Oxford

Bibliography

Wimsatt, W. K. (1969). *The Idea of Comedy*, Englewood Cliffs, New Jersey

Wolff, Michael (1958). 'Marian Evans to George Eliot', Princeton University Ph.D.

Wolff, Robert Lee (1977). *Gains and Losses: Novels of Faith and Doubt in Victorian England*

Woolf, Virginia (*Diary*). *The Diary of Virginia Woolf*, ed. Anne Oliver Bell and Andrew McNeillie, 5 vols., 1978–81

    (*Letters*). *The Letters of Virginia Woolf*, ed. Nigel Nicholson and Joanne Trautmann, 6 vols., 1975–81

    (1977) [1927]. *To the Lighthouse*

    (1978). *Moments of Being*, ed. Jeanne Schulkind

Wormell, Deborah (1980). *Sir John Seeley and the Uses of History*

Worthey, Mrs (1890). *The New Continent*

Wright, T. R. (1981). 'George Eliot and Positivism: A Reassessment', *MLR* LXXVI 257–72

    (1982). 'From Bumps to Morals: The Phrenological Background to George Eliot's Moral Framework', *RES* XXXIII 34–46

    (1983). 'Positively Catholic: Malcolm Quin's Church of Humanity in Newcastle upon Tyne', *DUJ* LXXV 11–20

Wright, Walter (1967). *The Shaping of 'The Dynasts'*, Lincoln, Nebraska

Young, R. M. (1970). *Mind, Brain and Adaptation in the Nineteenth Century*, Oxford

INDEX

Index

302

Index

Index

Index

Index

Sociological Society, 168, 237, 241, 266, 267, 268
South Place Chapel (later South Place Ethical Society), 118, 156–7, 248, 271
Spectator, 127, 202
Spencer, Herbert: attacks Comte, 3, 163–8; and George Eliot, 164, 173; Geddes on, 261, 264; *see also* Harrison, Frederic; Lewes
Spenser, Edmund, 37
Spinoza, Baruch, 173
Spurzheim, Johann Christoph, 30
Standard, 167
Stanley, Kate, 78
Stead, W. T., 130
Stebbing, William, 128
Stephen, James, 160
Stephen, Sir James FitzJames, 106, 126, 145–6, 147, 176
Stephen, Sir Leslie, 1, 2, 142–5, 156, 204, 207, 232, 233
Sterne, Laurence, 110
Strauss, David Friedrich, 173
Style, Jane May, 251, 257–8
Style, Sydney, 83–4, 120, 257–8
subjective immortality: Comte on, 21; George Eliot on, 178, 183, 199; Hardy on, 215; James on, 235–6; Pater on, 135, 136; Leslie Stephen on, 144
Sulman, Thomas, 89, 96, 97, 177
Swinny, Shapland Hugh: and Geddes, 262, 268; and Marvin, 271; at Newton Hall, 122, 240, 241–2; in *Positivist Review*, 241, 247, 248

Taylor, Harriet (later Harriet Mill), 42, 45, 49
Temple, Frederick, 104
Temple of Humanity, Liverpool, 246, 255, 258–60; photograph, 256
Tennyson, Alfred Lord, 238
Thomas, Philip, 232, 240, 241, 243–4
Thompson, William (Archbishop of York 1862–90), 153, 169
Times, 66–7, 76, 113, 127–8, 167, 168
Tompkins, Henry, 123
Toynbee Hall, 247
Trade Union Act, 105, 119
Trollope, Anthony, 101

Truelove Edward, 123
Turgot, Anne-Robert Jacques, Baron, 8
Tylor, Sir Edward Burnet, 163
Tyndall, John, 163, 230
Tyrrell, George, 254

Unitarianism, 155–6, 229, 243

Valat, Paul, 188
Vaux, Clotilde de, 6, 67, 99, 138, 148, 149, 259; and Comte, 13–15; hullabaloo over, 107, 126, 127; and worship, 35–6
Vestnik Evropy, 219
Vico, Giambattista, 263
Voltaire, Francois Marie Arouet de, 137, 138, 204, 237

Wagner, Richard, 275
Wallas, Graham, 269
Ward, Mrs Humphry, 3, 230–2; *Robert Elsmere*, 136, 230–1
Ward, W. G., 61
Ward, Wilfrid, 130, 155
Watts, Charles, 245
Webb, Beatrice, 261, 269–70
Webb, Sidney, 261, 269, 270
Wells, H. G., 3, 233, 237, 244
Westbrook, Walter, 240
Westcott, Brooke Foss, 3, 129, 152–3, 276
Westminster Gazette, 112
Westminster Review, 45, 46, 61, 63–5, 112, 125, 128, 159, 174, 199
Whewell, William, 67, 164
Whitehead, A. N., 242
Whitman, Walt, 96, 225
Wicksteed, Philip, 156
Wilde, Oscar, 238–9
Williamson, Alexander, 70, 172
Williams, Rowland, 104
Winstanley, James, 71, 77, 150, 174
Woolf, Virginia, 144, 236, 274
Wordsworth, William, 135, 156
Working Men's College, 103, 119, 133, 161

York, Archbishop of, *see* Thompson, William
Young, Edward, 174

Zola, Émile, 110